Your Universal Soul Abundance

The Ouroboros is an ancient symbol depicting a serpent or dragon eating its own tail. The name originates from within Greek language; (oura) meaning "tail" and (boros) meaning "eating", thus "he who eats the tail". The Ouroboros represents the perpetual cyclic renewal of life and infinity, the concept of eternity and the eternal return, and represents the cycle of life, death and rebirth, leading to immortality, as in the Phoenix. It can also represent the idea of primordial unity related to something existing in or persisting before any beginning with such force or qualities it cannot be extinguished. Time, life, continuity, completion, the repetition of history, the self-sufficiency of nature and the rebirth of earth[1]

An Imprint of YUSA LTD

www.YUSALIFE.com

Connect@YUSAbundance.com

609 Quayside Tower 252-260 Broad Street, Second Floor, Birmingham, United Kingdom, B1 2HF

The YUSA GUIDE TO BALANCE, MIND, BODY, AND SPIRIT

Disclaimer: This book is sold with the understanding that the Author is not engaged in rendering psychological, medical or other professional services. The information presented was obtained through personal experience and extensive research, and any other content or referenced links are for informational purposes only. The content is not intended to be a substitute for professional medical advice, diagnosis or treatment. Always seek the advice of your physician or other qualified health-care provider with any questions you may have regarding a medical condition.

Cover Art and Illustration provided by Tom Crow Design and Illustration.

Published In England

ISBN - 978-0-9930859-1-8

Acknowledgements

I take this opportunity to express my profound gratitude and deep regards to my great Shaman friends and guides Ronin & Monique for their exemplary guidance, healing works, monitoring and constant encouragement throughout the course of this thesis. The knowledge, support and guidance given by them time to time shall carry me a long way in the journey of life on which YUSA is about to embark.

I also take this opportunity to express a deep sense of gratitude to Dhammika Panagamuwa, for his cordial support, valuable input of belief and guidance, which helped me in completing this task through various stages and help pick up the pieces throughout some of the most intense and painful times.

Looking back in hindsight, I hold gratitude to the universe and my higher self for guiding me into and through some of the heavy losses which were experienced in the Foreign exchange market that ultimately served as powerful practices for material detachment, consciousness expansion and personal growth which ultimately delivered the inspiration towards the creation of YUSA in order to assist others with their life lessons.

I am particularly grateful for the assistance given by my mother Julie alongside the whole of my friends and family who stuck with me along the journey and who over-stood the importance of the extensive long nights at the computer and the journey of a dream chaser. I am grateful for their cooperation during the period of my assignment,

I would also like to include a huge thanks to Tom Crowe for the ongoing YUSA graphic design work and a massive well done to all of the teachers out there spreading the upmost truth and positivity into the world without fear of judgement by others.

Lastly, I am obliged to thank my business partner Aman over at AstroFxc for the valuable dedication and persistence provided by him in his respective field in order to achieve the success and the service to others which we embrace to this day after the multiple past failures and business incarnations.

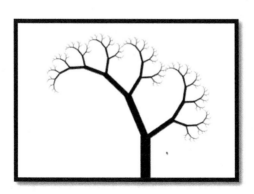

Introduction to the YUSA guide

Even though there is an abundance of wonderful opportunities in the world, there are many distractions which can steer you away from the path of personal growth, whether it be due to poor nutrition, lack of sleep, stress, money problems, health issues or simply an overactive mind. A lack of self- love and nourishment can wreak havoc on your external reality.

Sadly, overall, the world's commercial interests have seduced many into believing that happiness is dependent on externals. The externals show up naturally in response to your inner state of being, not the other way around. That's why acquisition itself is empty and never satisfies. Externals can only be enjoyed from an inner state of contentment, never in reverse. Uncover your heart, and you will discover your treasure. Externals are only the bow and pretty wrapping paper around the present.

This book introduces a range of topics and information the reader that will help him or her achieve proficient states of self-betterment such as deprogramming the mind from the saturation of external conditioning, detoxing the body from the atrocity synthetic substances (found in the 'standard diet') and reconnecting with the heart, spirit and divine essence. The mind, body and spirit are the three essential foundations a human being must bring into a state of equanimity to activate the full creator potential many have lying dormant inside.

Believe it or not, every human being is an extension of the divine and has a substantial amount of power available upon choice. When this inner power aligns with pure intention, an array of external life conditions can be modified and created. These conditions can be modified with what you think (mainly with what is programmed into the subconscious mind), what you feel (the emotional frequencies given from the heart space) and with what you speak (as words are very much alive and the universe is a construct of vibratory elements).

It will come to light that a large majority have lost touch with the only thing that is real in the world, their true selves and nature. Many are causing inner conflict by consuming processed and dead alongside the embracement of unhealthy thoughts and emotions, in turn, giving away most of their power to outside sources. This consequently drains a large percentage of one's physical, emotional and mental energy, making it difficult to hold a solid vibration and foundation for personal growth. Many are literally committing spiritual suicide.

The information and practices presented in the YUSA handbook of balance, when put to use, can improve one's overall health, well-being and self-gratification. Do not merely believe anything in this booklet: take the information and dissect it, research it and, most importantly, put it to practical use. Approach this book with an open mind.

For some people, this information will have deep resonance. Some may disregard it totally, and others may pick it up at a later date. As Bruce Lee said, 'Take what is useful and discard the rest'. We are now in the age of information where truths are slowly reaching levels of awareness as many are now choosing to awaken spiritually at the level of self.

Many on the planet are coming to the realisation that there must be something more to this dream world, where the average person struggles to make ends meet, corporations use the masses as free-range slaves and the minority of parasitic, so-called 'elite's' harness and dictate the energies of the masses.

YUSA over-stand it is now time for all beings to be released from suffering. We have constructed this content the best we could to deliver the key foundations and resources for growth and personal progression. Life is to be enjoyed, to have fun whilst keeping everything in moderation. All souls are equal, experiencing temporary embodiment. The YUSA community is free from the limitations of gender, race or religion inspiring others and gaining freedom from the materialism trap. Enjoy.

Chapter 1. The Mind

Chapter 2. The Spirit

Chapter 3. The Body

References

Chapter 1, The Mind.

Many hold the belief that the mind is somewhat part of the brain or connected to another physical part of the human body. This is incorrect as the human brain is very physical and can be realised within the range of the five main senses. It is physical object that the eyes can see and the hand can hold.

The mind on the other hand is not physical. It cannot be seen with the eyes, measured with instruments or repaired in surgery. This entails that the brain is not the mind, but simply a part of the physical body. There is nothing within the body that can be identified as being the mind because your body and mind are different. For example, sometimes, when your body is relaxed and immobile, the mind can be very busy, darting from one thought to another.

If the mind is neither the brain nor any other part of the body, then what is it? It is a formless continuum that functions to perceive and understand objects. Because the mind is formless or non-physical by nature, it is not obstructed by physical objects, an advanced aspect of your true being.

It is very important to be able to distinguish the disturbed states of mind from peaceful states. Only an unbalanced state of mind can disturb your inner peace. Thoughts based on anger, jealousy and desirous attachment can be labelled 'delusions', the principal underlying cause for much of humanity's suffering.

You may think that your suffering is caused by other people, poor material conditions or society, but in reality, it derives from your own deluded states of mind. The essence of most spiritual practices is to reduce and eventually eradicate your delusions and replace them with permanent inner peace. This is a large aspect of human life.

An essential understanding in which you need to align with is that liberation from suffering cannot be found outside of mind and your own heart. Permanent liberation can only be realised by purifying the mind. Therefore, if you want to become free from problems and attain lasting peace and happiness, then you need to increase your knowledge and understanding of how the mind operates.

Scientific research suggests that humans are only using about 8% to 12% of their brain power; the same goes for the capacity of the mind. When we are consciously awake, we are utilising 10% of the mind. The other 90% is the subconscious mind, which is programmable similar to a computer. Many have been programmed by outside sources in ways only the subconscious intelligence can define and store, mainly from symbolic advertisements, radio, TV, society's expectations and so on. This conditioning can build up layers of an illusory personality, causing somebody to never be themselves from heart, a catalyst for suffering and unhappiness.

This section delves deeper into different aspects of the mind. How to reprogram the mind with what you want to attract and achieve in your life, daily goal achievement and meditation practices to help still thoughts, manifest harmony, abundance and experience an increased sense of joy and overall happiness.

You may have heard the term 'thoughts are things', as there are many published self-help books available centred on the subject of thought power. Remember, you are a creator being in the creator universe. Anything is possible with the right knowledge, dedication and self-belief.

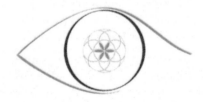

Metaphysical perspective of the mind & thoughts

You may ask, what is meant by 'metaphysical'? Metaphysics is the study of the non-physical, spiritual/unseen realm, the formless realm that examines the nature of reality, including the relationship between mind and matter, substance and attribute, fact and value. The study and origin of metaphysics (if there is one), would tie in with the fundamental structure, nature and dynamics of the universe.

The thousands of thoughts a human being emits on a constant basis are all charged with a vibratory frequency that goes unrecognised to the five senses, etheric and energetic in nature. You cannot visually see these vibrational force with your physical eyes. This is also evident with the dynamics of light, heat, electricity, magnetism and waves of sound. With modern day technical advancements, a range of frequencies have been discovered that where beyond measure beforehand.

Knowing that this energetic signal exists and that you have constant control over it can be life changing. If you can start to apply the concept of thought vibration in a positive and constructive manner, it can be directed toward your advantage in everyday life.

Have you ever noticed that, when your thought patterns are scattered, fearful and doubtful in nature that more circumstances arise in your reality of the same nature, therefore creating more distress? Well this can be changed. The moment you change your attitude and energetic vibration, the universe responds instantaneously. There is no lag time in the etheric fields, as time and space is a linear concept within third-dimensional reality, also known as the realm of duality.

This dimension of duality consists of balanced factors such as; Love/fear, peace/war, rich/poor, you/them, life /death, up/down etc. with all aspects having their polar opposite or dual point. The lower dimensional realities of the Universe are created, controlled and maintained by mind. Your mind is a microcosm of the Universal 'macrocosm' Mind. The word 'Maya' represents the lower four dimensions of reality – the worlds of duality, created and maintained through personal and collective belief systems, known as the collective consciousness.

Absolutely everything you see, touch and feel is *energy*. All matter is a construct of atoms, positively and negatively charged particles that are bound together by an electromagnetic static charge. This static charge is what keeps the particles constantly orbiting the nucleus. The majority of atomic makeup is the formless light spacing between the nucleus and orbiting particles. Everything you perceive to be solid in reality, at the deepest level, is actually formless.

The point expressed here is that everything perceived by the naked eye is a construct of moving energetic particles. However solid and lifeless they may appear, the atoms that make up solid matter are actually in constant motion, energetic and vibrational forces. It might look like certain things are doing nothing but on the atomic level they are quite busy.

The human mind processes around 50,000 thoughts (on average) every single day (roughly one thought every 2.2 seconds). For many, a large majority of these thoughts are wild and order less, scattered etheric vibrations which communicate an array of mixed signals into the universal field. At first, when trying to change the vibrational patterns of your brain and mind, it can be quite difficult but with the help of brainwave entrainment, subconscious programming and meditation, it then becomes a possible achievement for anybody within a short space of time.

Brainwave frequencies are in constant fluctuation, even whilst sleeping, causing conflict in the realm of mind and thought. It is wise to attain such frequencies within a balanced state for optimised creation and mental balance. There are many outside sources that can drive your brainwaves out of balance, examples being; television advertisements, mainstream music and radio, externals which are engineered with specific frequencies that communicate to the unconscious mind and plant seeds: seeds that grow into cravings, wants and needs that are illusory and out of your control.

With distorted brainwave activity follows negative mind chatter and unsupportive thoughts. These thought forms tend to creep into your mind, distract and ultimately convince you that where you now in your life is comfortable and you're not able to achieve much more. To flip this mental process around, you must stop allowing your brain to run on 'auto pilot' and respond to everything around you with pre-programmed subconscious reactions. When a thought arises, do not be a slave to it, own the thought, and be the awareness behind it. Making this shift is a huge step toward the mastery of the mental realm.

When you observe specific patterns of thought, check to see if they are non-supportive ways of thinking. Are your thoughts spiralling energy into circumstances that you have no control over? Or are they a construct of fear-based, illusory stories that most of the time never come true?

If you are directing most of your powerful thought energy on false stories and circumstances that do not serve your future best interests, then something needs to change to support the happiness you deserve as a creator being.

The observation and awareness of thought is one of the most beneficial and crucial steps towards the transformation of your vibrational pattern. On the deepest levels, the majority of human suffering, greed, unhappiness and judgement of others are mostly mind-made constructs in which people choose to believe. What can be a positive thought for one person can be extremely negative for another, but only when one places judgement upon a thought and circumstance contrary to his or her programmed belief system does it then trigger feelings of emotional sadness and depression.

'The mark of an educated mind is to be able to entertain a thought without accepting it' ~ Aristotle

We later expand on exactly how you can make this knowledge work for you in order to achieve your goals and desires in life. We also explore specific dynamics behind various practical techniques and information that can be directed towards achieving mental stillness, a mind that works in favour of the bearer.

Raising your energetic vibration and gaining mastery over your own thought processes is a lifelong learning curve. Many call the power of thought creation the Law of Attraction. When your mind becomes unclogged of 10,000 thought forms, all that power is now at your disposal for the utilisation of manifestation.

Human life is governed by two minds, the subconscious and the conscious mind. Ninety percent of your reality is governed by the subconscious, whilst the remaining 10% is governed by the conscious mind. The subconscious is the mental structure which is constantly in action, even whilst in stages of sleep way beyond the level of conscious awareness.

The subconscious mind is the highest projection of yourself, an aspect of the spirit/soul body and is responsible for most, if not all, the dreams you experience. Human experience is centred on conscious evolution whilst being bounded by the alchemy of time. Consciousness is the realisation of who/what you are beyond the limitations of form and mind.

Mental unrest in itself does not tend to eradicate upon the attainment of desirable objects. Although achievement is certainly pleasant, it is mental tranquillity which holds greater value and is what intensifies feelings of joy, that which must be sought first for genuine internal fulfilment.

You may be so defensive because you mistake your identity to be a certain pattern of thought but you must realise that you are far more than what is perceived by the mind. You are the infinite awareness behind all thought forms, something much greater which holds infinite intelligence.

The Universal Law of Attraction

The most efficient way to over-stand the Law of Attraction is to first return to the realisation that you are an important part of the vibrational Universe. Information travels through waves of light, and formless light energy is the foundational structure of atomic form. The world is not an inanimate collection of stones and timber. It is a living entity, constructed by the heartbeats of humanity. Whether we are speaking about humans, cars, money or houses, it is all energy, consisting of electrons, protons and neutrons: positive and negative.

The Law of Attraction is one of the most fundamental of all universal laws. Outpacing the laws of gravity and the law of velocity, it is well beyond the measurements of science. The Law of Attraction is who you are[2].

The way in which your brain emits a range of frequencies is very similar to a radio being 'tuned' into a desired station. For instance, if you're tuned into one frequency, you cannot hear what is being broadcasted on another as they operate on different wavelengths. Only by focusing your mind to one frequency are you able to align with a broadcasted desire. Over-standing that the brain transmits and receives vibrational energy (and can do so on a wide range of vibrational frequencies) is fundamental for many aspects of personal growth.

Although the energy of though sustain powerful vibrations, the emotional frequencies derived from the heart space are another, but much more potent in nature. Think of it this way; your focused thoughts derived from the mind's eye acts as the steering wheel to your goals whilst the hearts emotional stream and burning desire acts as the gas pedal to your dreams. This is the process of creation; you really have to *feel* like you would when you have your desire right in the *present moment* (the now). Think and act like you have it, then it's a done deal. No creation happens outside of self. There is no lack or limitation, only error in thought.

To simplify this law, the experiences (within your sphere of reality) are the circumstances that match the vibrational frequency and intention of your thoughts and heart felt emotions. This is very similar to the law of karma. What goes around comes around, so to speak. You are transmitting frequencies 24 hours a day, 7 days a week, and the universe is responding in accordance.

As your brain transmits vibrational frequencies, it affects physical matter as the deepest levels of all matter are bound by light. Light travels at 186,000 miles a second, and to do so, it must flow through constant ether. Everything in the Universe moves, vibrates and expands. Nothing ever remains stagnant.

There are four levels of thought consciousness

1. **Unconscious Unconsciousness** - At this stage, you are not even aware that you are unconscious. You attract negative things into your life at a rapid pace, like a negative ball of energy rolling downhill. Nothing is ever your fault, and you are always looking for someone to blame. (Most people never make it out of level one and are condemned to suffer in this self-imposed hell of an inner world).

2. **Conscious Unconsciousness** - Here you are aware of your negative thinking and the consequences it may bring. You might see your negative pattern and have become aware of what it is that you are attracting. You may not like what you are attracting, but you have taken responsibility for it.

3. **Conscious Consciousness** - You deliberately decide to focus pure and positive thought about something and remove all resistance to its arrival. Your creation might be something as simple as visualising a parking space opening up for you at the supermarket. You deliberately intended it, allowed it to come to you and acknowledged it when it arrives. In due course, it arrives.

4. **Unconscious Consciousness** - When you get to this point, you do not have to work so hard to create things in your life. You are a believer in how the 'mind game' works, and you spend conscious time each day making your mind important. New creations come to you easily and quickly; everything you do is unconsciously competent! You have built a positive ball of energy that continues to roll forward in your favour. People label you the 'lucky one'.

A large majority are stuck in stage one. They hold the belief that they do not have the power to make major changes in their own lives and for that reason could not possibly be creating their own reality optimally. What they don't realise is that their thoughts and feelings simply send out the initial signals into the Universal field. These specific energies are then amplified by the cosmos and returned in order to create unique life experiences ultimately rearranging one's personal circumstances.

If only people knew that they have the energetic power to ask the Universe to change their reality, they would over-stand that they are not weak and helpless victims of circumstances and nothing less than empowered Children of Light exercising their birth right as co-creator beings.

Every soul is empowered to ask the Universe because the Universe is also a construct of light. When you send a signal out in the Universe, you are sending a signal into the essence of your own being. The Universe recognises you as a Child of Light, one with itself in essence therefore obliged to obey the specific request. Manifesting your own reality is fundamentally you and the Universe as one, progressing together as a whole. This is the real secret of your own higher nature and your inner power.

'We are all connected to each other biologically, to the earth chemically and to the rest of the universe atomically[3]'. ~ Dr. Neil deGrasse Tyson

The Judgment of Mental Activity & Forms of Thought

When you judge your mental activity, it places you within the vibration of judgement. Every time a thought comes into your head that doesn't suit your likings, you may often label it as negative whilst other times even try to push it away or suppress it. Doing so may make you only experience more turmoil and confusion; it will create a split inside your brain/mind as there will be two voices informing views of the opposite nature.

The neutralisation of so called 'negative' thought forms is essential in order to stretch beyond the realm of mental duality. Thoughts then just become thoughts with no emotional bearing attached to them. The second you judge a thought, it completely takes you over, along with the emotions associated with it. Once you judge a thought, you then believe everything that it tells you and it may even start to negatively impact your self-worth. If you want to stop judging others, you must stop judging yourself. To stop judging yourself, you first need to stop believing absolutely everything the mind brings forth.

There is a big difference between witnessing thoughts and suppressing them. A common misconception is that witnessing your thoughts means you don't have to deal with them but this is not entirely true. The witness state allows you to examine and observe thoughts for what they truly are, free from emotional attachment. The ultimate observation from a non-biased perspective.

Once you get to the root of a specific thought (which is usually a negative core belief you have about yourself) you can begin to identify and locate where this thought pattern and belief originated. You can now start to work with it and eventually experience it pass in a detached manner of awareness.

All beliefs can be changed. You differentiate between beliefs all the time. Beliefs are what structure the neural net in your brain. This collaboration of ideas, beliefs and experiences are what shape your personality, structure and ego. Once you judge or energise a thought by identifying with it or believing what it is communicating, it is easy to get lost in the maze of objectification, therefore providing you with a limited perception of your reality in that specific moment. To overcome this, you first need to adopt a belief that tells you beliefs can be changed. In doing so, you will be able to change the core beliefs that can be held responsible for the construction and foundations of the ego.

Many people believe the majority of thoughts that arise from the mind. This is insanity. The mind has now completely taken over, and it's evident on a mass collective level. As mentioned, humans have about 50,000 thoughts per day. Do you really think every one of them holds truth? Most of them are simply irrelevant. They are but an essence of the past living inside of you. Memories that team up with delusions created by excessive overthinking often thrusts you into a web of seemingly never-ending misery. This is a complete misuse of imagination. Worrying or imagining future scenarios that most of the time never happen creates an anxiety gap within the mind.

The art of detachment is key. Detachment from your thoughts gives you an upper hand in not only discerning what is true for you from what isn't but also towards living a more simple and balanced life. When a 'negative' thought presents itself that you know deep down is not true for you, observe it without emotions; be the witness of the thought. Root out the core belief from which this thought pattern materialised and again simply let it pass like a cloud in the sky. Remember not to suppress the thought as doing so will only manifest more feelings of pain inside you, and it will keep returning until the lesson is acknowledged and understood.

The mind is a very complicated and advanced tool. Hopefully, the information presented within this section can aid towards the over-standing of the ins and outs of how you can work towards perceiving such things in a more positive light. Judgement and self-hate all arise from this complete identification with the lower mind. The game is over; take back your free will. Stop hating yourself, practice self-love and become who you truly prefer to be. Remember you can change beliefs any time you want. Start to shape your reality from the *present*, because in reality, it is all that exists.

Manifestation of your thoughts from the etheric to the physical

The universe is mind. Mind is creation. Thoughts hold electromagnetic energies, and the hearts emotional value is raw subatomic power. Absolutely everything whether matter or consciousness is connected through a vast nervous system, a frequency pattern which is a product of a higher vibratory realm.

Within the construct of your body's nervous system, neurons and synapses deliver rapid electrical impulses between your five main senses and the brain, engineered in order for you to feel and be aware of pain and so forth. Similarly, your thoughts and emotions are delivered as electrical impulses into the core of the creator/universal field and are returned. It is said humans were created in the image of 'god', you could apply this to the metaphysical image of what you truly are, the construct and makeup of your luminous energy body. We explore this topic further in the spirit chapter.

Seventy percent of the universe is thought to consist of dark energy and matter, again formless in nature. The whole spectrum of light is birthed from darkness. Darkness or the colour visually known as 'black' cannot be formed from a lighter vibrational spectrum without returning upon itself. This concept suggests that all of creation manifests from darkness.

How does this piece of information provide any benefit for you as a co-creator being? Well, when you close your eyes, there is a void. Metaphorically, it is a void of pure darkness. This is the dimension of the mind and third eye that looks inwardly. The third eye is located in the centre of the brain; physically, it takes a form similar to a small raisin, the seat of the soul. In actuality, it is your *first eye,* the All-Seeing Eye.

Positive change comes from the process of applying the four Universal Laws of Creation. Below are the four main steps of manifestation using the mind:

1.) Attraction - Creating strong desire to see a particular thing manifest. First, you have to have a burst of inspiration, a new *idea* or **Thought = Mental Plane (steering wheel of focus).**

2.) Intention - Regular (daily) focus upon the desired outcome, invested with the emotion you will feel at the time it manifests. Then you *'feel'* the goose bumps, *gratitude* and *emotions* attached to this **Inspiration = Spiritual Plane (plane of emotional energy and burning desire)**

3.) Allowance – Forget the how and leave the orchestration of events to the universe.

Then you take action on your goals, meaning your emotions have now become active or *'in motion',* thus *energy in motion* and as you *move* or *are in motion,* you create *force.* As movement occurs, it causes *unseen atomic particles* to *electrically 'attract'* to your *holographic image* or *images,* coming from the *black space* of your Mind (darkness). **Magnetic Attraction** and **FORCE = Plane of Force (law of attraction).**

4.) Balance – Pursuing your peace, passions and joy in the midst of manifestation creation. You then begin to experience the specific manifestation in the three Solid visible realities as *persons* you might meet to assist you into bring this *idea into solid reality*, *places* that you might go to *bring* this *IDEA* into *Solid Reality,* or things you might need to acquire to bring this Thought, IDEA, or Inspiration into Solid Reality.

Central to this creative process is the core belief and faith in what you desire is really going to come forth and take place. When that core belief is strong enough to become faith, the whole process steps up a gear. Through a faith-filled link with the Universe, you transcend time and create in a more effective manner.

Faith holds great importance as it is the most intense and focused energetic form in which a core belief can be moulded. When you hold the vibration of complete faith, aligning it with your energy, higher self and physical body, your whole being is then functioning in a state of equanimity and oneness. Oneness is the nature of the Real. Through the ability to function in this manner, you start to resonate in harmony with the Universal Web, engaging in direct and instant creation. You now have the power to change all circumstances that are present within your sphere of reality.

We expand on visualisation methods further on the meditation page. Also, in the spirit section, we delve deeper into the workings of creation from the heart space, harnessing and aligning with the vast, spacious energy that is present at the centre of your being.

Polarity of the brain

As mentioned previously, every aspect of the third dimensional state of reality is based on duality. Every action, (big or small) triggers an equal and opposite reaction; as above, so below, so to speak. As the human brain is separated into two hemispheres, it is therefore limited by the law of polarity (according to the theory of left-brain or right-brain dominance).

A person who is 'left-brained' is often said to be more logical, analytical and objective, while a person who is 'right-brained' is said to be more intuitive, thoughtful and subjective. Theoretically, the left brain's main job is to place everything in this reality into a timeline, creating an illusion that we as creator beings are finite in nature, separate from the universe and each other.

The right hemisphere understands that you as an energetic being is nothing less than infinite, connected within unity to one another and to the universal creator. There is no judgement of good and bad, everything is simply an experience. But, since the Fall of Man (when humanity's consciousness moved from the heart to the brain), humanity has mainly been opposing the dark side of virtually everything. With this being said, the creation of a large majority of experiences from the brain (which is a polarised tool) is a major catalyst to one's imbalanced way of living.

Mankind is now offered the opportunity to embrace an individual inner awakening and it is the left hemisphere of your brain that is being adapted towards greater awareness. This involves a rewiring process that is aimed at establishing new synaptic pathways between the two sides, which will promote a new relationship with linear space and time. As the left and right brain start to merge, consciousness can step back into the heart space (a higher dimensional state of being), promoting the end of duality and the return to Unity consciousness.

Anything polarised encourages actions with opposite reactions and the same principle is apparent when you create from the brain and mind. Anything you pull toward yourself that you focus on as being positive, anything that you manifest and label a 'good' experience, will also, somewhere in your sphere of reality, attract something negative to counteract and enforce laws of balance. So remember, the bigger thoughts you emit into the universe, the bigger the opposition that will come to test the worthiness of your desires!

This opposite reaction of polarity/balance cannot be overseen until you work on the midbrain in order to encourage an electromagnetic, harmonious field which will in turn balance the two hemispheres of the brain. This activation bypasses the neo-cortex. The neo-cortex lives in the midst of past events and deals with memory (mainly traumatic) and an imbalance can make it difficult for you to be fully grounded in the present moment. When you focus on past experiences and visualise them out of your memory bank, then you are recreating the same past circumstances that will be manifested into your reality once again, making it difficult for you to focus and manifest positive change in life.

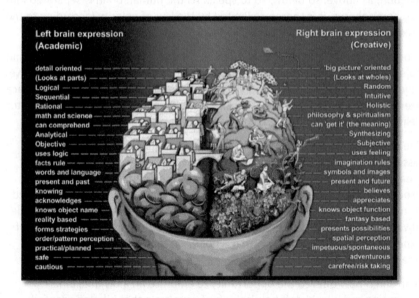

Left brain expression (Academic)	Right brain expression (Creative)
detail oriented	'big picture' oriented
(Looks at parts)	(Looks at wholes)
Logical	Random
Sequential	Intuitive
Rational	Holistic
math and science	philosophy & spiritualism
can comprehend	can 'get it' (the meaning)
Analytical	Synthesizing
Objective	Subjective
uses logic	uses feeling
facts rule	imagination rules
words and language	symbols and images
present and past	present and future
knowing	believes
acknowledges	appreciates
knows object name	knows object function
reality based	fantasy based
forms strategies	presents possibilities
order/pattern perception	spatial perception
practical/planned	impetuous/spontaneous
safe	adventurous
cautious	carefree/risk taking

The academic and creative examples between left and right brain expressions.

The concept of midbrain activation

The midbrain, also known as the mesencephalon (Greek), is a small region of the brain that serves as a relay centre for your visual, auditory and motor system coordination. Midbrain activation is known to be the worker of miracles, anchoring you more deeply into the present moment, bringing electromagnetic balance to the hypothalamus and pineal gland which in turn expand the gateway for the passing of higher information.

The interbrain has to be awakened by stimulating a specific hormonal discharge. In the human body, it is the pituitary gland that regulates the hormone secretions and this is the function which has to be awakened. For this, it is necessary to activate the neighbouring pineal body. The pineal body secretes two hormones: melatonin and serotonin. The secretion of melatonin increases in the hours of night (peaks at 3am) and decreases during sunlight hours.

It seems that the ancestral lineage of ancient Kemetians were very aware of this knowledge and carved the symbolic images in stone.

As you can see in the above image, the two beings display a cobra/serpent extended from the mid-forehead region. This is a symbolic representation of midbrain and third-eye activation. The serpent energy is also known as the extension of Kundalini. Tantric scriptures suggest that Kundalini energy arises from the root chakra (base of the spine) and meets at the crown (Shiva meets

Shakti). This is what many yogis and meditators refer to as 'enlightenment', complete balance of the chakras and luminous energy body.

It seems that Khemetian ancestors were very connected to higher knowledge. Real history has been hidden and rewritten, mainly to suppress and hide the amount of power humans hold, with the aim of preventing humanity realising self-knowledge and attain wisdom. As mentioned previous, humanity fell from these enlightened states (the last golden age 26,000 years ago), In the times of ancient khemet, Atlantis and Lumeria were when human beings experienced upmost connection with self, the source and open to E.T.-type information.

Main benefits of midbrain activation:

(Sourced from Dr. Baskaran Pillai[4])

Success without sweat

- Zero conceptual complications - simplicity in success
- Right time, right place and right person: when midbrain is active, it will put you within the right place at the right time with the right person and right resources.
- Healing the body naturally
- Road to Heavenly experiences
- Youthfulness forever, because then you will understand time. The DNA is processed in a different way, and aging is arrested.
- Omniscience, omnipotence, omnipresence. The neo-cortex will never understand these concepts. The orientation for these come from the mid-brain; it adheres to different orientations.
- Super thoughts come from the mid-brain. The poverty brain can be activated to have prosperity thoughts; you need to have super thoughts.

Above are just a fraction of the benefits which can be achieved through midbrain activation. Working with the midbrain alongside other information in this booklet can bring extremely fast, positive results into your life. The most efficient way to activate the midbrain is through listening to the binaural frequency meditation of 850 Hz to 936 Hz. This can be found on the YUSA YouTube channel. You can also learn more from Dr. Pillai about this special miracle activation: www.pillaicenter.com.

When listening to the frequency audio, try to maintain concentration for at least 30 minutes, (preferably the full hour) five times a week, leaving two days for brainwave recovery. Meditation is an important tool for self-development and mastery over your own mind.

The physical flesh is bioelectric. The energy field or body it radiates is bio-magnetic. Mental clarity assures no static exists between these two. This clarity transcends both negative and positive emotions. This is the key that opens the lock of luck, and no one can have any measure of real success without this understanding.

An enemy of the midbrain is alcohol.

Ever wonder why alcohol is so highly advertised, even though the dangers, medical statistics and crime rates are higher than any other classified substance? It is almost like the powers that be want to see the majority of the population destroy themselves and ultimately lose all balance of true being.

Alcohol completely reverses the midbrain balance, not to mention the acids that have a harmful effect on the pineal gland and melatonin secretion. With the midbrain frequencies distorted upon intoxication, the bodies toroidal magnetic energy field (also known as the auric field) tends to lose conductivity. Your aura then loses strength, and gaps are prone to arise.

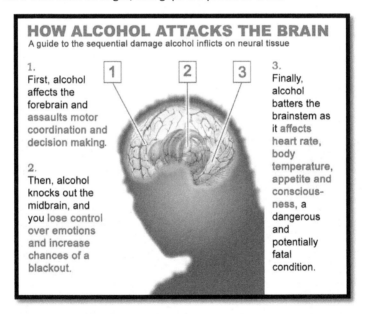

HOW ALCOHOL ATTACKS THE BRAIN
A guide to the sequential damage alcohol inflicts on neural tissue

1.
First, alcohol affects the forebrain and assaults motor coordination and decision making.

2.
Then, alcohol knocks out the midbrain, and you lose control over emotions and increase chances of a blackout.

3.
Finally, alcohol batters the brainstem as it affects heart rate, body temperature, appetite and conscious-ness, a dangerous and potentially fatal condition.

Alcohol, the enemy of the midbrain. Causes distortion in the midbrain, slowing down and impairing auditory, visual and motor system coordination[5].

The information presented within this section thus far has been focused on the achievement of highly positive, powerful streams of thought; not allowing thoughts to dictate your emotions; creating with the mind and so forth. As mentioned briefly, a still mind is needed for optimal results as thoughts are charged with electromagnetic creative energy.

You must focus deeply and be very sure of the intentions, desires, thoughts and visualisations you wish to emit into the universe. We are going to expand on the practice of meditation that, when used daily, over a period of time can deliver a healing stillness to your mind and body.

Western ideologies regard meditation as a form of 'hippie practice' but this is indeed false. Meditation and bathing in complete stillness is a natural state, the state of the soul. The awareness of meditation is growing and is an increasingly popular practice, used all across the world for reasons that are unique to each person who does so. The definition of meditation is 'any form or family of practices in which practitioners train their minds or self-induce a mode of consciousness to realise some benefit'. Simply put, those who mediate know that the answers to all their questions and problems are found within themselves, nowhere else.

It does not stop there; the results of meditation are key factors for health optimisation, balancing of the mind, body and soul. With the aid of technological advancements and the use of binaural beat audio frequencies, there are now meditation practices that only require half an hour's relaxation time per day and can be practiced almost anywhere.

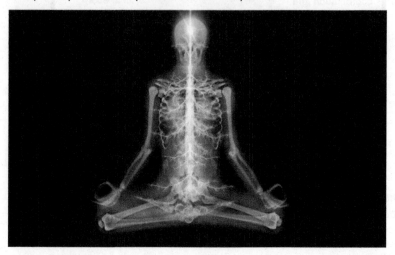

Regular meditation practice will deliver stillness of mind, tackle anxiety and promote a sense of wellbeing

The primary aim for anybody who mediates is to train the busy mind in becoming quiet whilst releasing the psyche from the stress, anxiety or depression that is amalgamated from physical reality. Once the meditative state is embraced and scattered thought energy starts to clear, the cosmic forces can then flow in through the crown of your head and saturate your etheric body in a loving, healing manner.

Upon realising and utilising the limitless power of your mind, you can attract what you desire in life and contribute to the reversal of physical DIS-EASE. Those who meditate to bring peace and serenity into their lives rapidly benefit from a deep feeling of being at one with their inner selves. This begins the process of healing and improving mental and physical health. Regardless of the reason for practicing it, new and ancient meditation techniques alike will set in motion the most important journey and discovery of life.

There are various forms of meditation practised around the world, including Transcendental Meditation, Vipassana Meditation, Zen Meditation, Taoist Meditation, Mindfulness meditation and Buddhist Meditation. They all have the same fundamental principle, the principle of reflection and deliberation to achieve a state of awareness on one's own emotions, health alongside other external situations which can be pondered upon. Through this deliberation, the practitioner can discover new perceptions, answers and self- mastery /enlightenment.

'Underlying intelligence is always there. As long as we relate with our underlying primordial intelligence and as long as we push ourselves a little, by jumping into the middle of situations, then intelligence arises automatically. When you're in the middle of a situation, you automatically pick up on what is needed. It's not a question of how to do it — you just do it. And you find yourself doing it perfectly, even surprising yourself.' ~ **Chögyam Trungpa**[6]

Studies relating to the impacts of meditation on the brain

Meditation has been shown to impact psychological well-being by reducing stress, depression, anxiety, blood pressure and addictions (re-configuration of neurological pathways). It also boosts the immune system whilst improving memory. But did you know that meditation can change brain structure in powerful and positive ways? Science has always believed that the brain essentially stops changing after adulthood.

You have the capacity to heal the emotional dysfunctionality of your own brain. When you increase your awareness with mindfulness, you can transform your brain, create new circuits and change the way neurons communicate with each other. Whenever you engage in a behaviour repeatedly, this can lead to physical changes in your brain. Following are studies that help reveal meditation's effect on the brain:

- Yale and Harvard universities have demonstrated that regular meditators not only increased function in their frontal lobes but also literally increased the lobe's size and volume[7].

- A study conducted by Sara Lazar showed that an eight-week mindfulness meditation program can lead to structural brain changes, including increased grey-matter density in the hippocampus (known to be important for learning and memory) and in structures associated with self-awareness, compassion and introspection[8].

-A 2005 study on American men and women who meditated a mere *40 minutes* a day showed that they had thicker cortical walls than non-meditators. What this meant is that their brains were aging at a slower rate. Cortical thickness is also associated with decision-making, attention and memory.

Pain matrix

In one study that was conducted by Dr. Hedy Kober from Kober and Associates[9], the subjects were given a painful stimulus, an uncomfortably hot sensation on their arms. They were first given the hot sensation without any instruction. Then it was repeated with the instruction to practice mindfulness in the form of asking themselves, 'Is this a tolerable pain? Can I handle it?'

After using the mindfulness technique, the researchers found that not only did the study's participants report about a 27% lower pain sensation, but they were also able to measure 45% less activity in the brain's neuropathic pain matrix. They concluded that mindfulness can improve both the perception of pain and the actual neural response to pain. The number of hours in a meditative state was correlated directly with the subject's pain threshold.

Amygdala

The Amygdala is involved in the way we experience lower vibrational emotions like stress and can be negatively influenced by the release of excess cortisol. Those who practice meditation show decreased activity in this area during stressful moments and also a reduction of density over time. That suggests meditation can alter acute stress responses and play a role in shaping the structure of the brain.

In one study, cigarette smokers were divided into two groups. One group attended eight mindfulness meditations sessions, and the other was assigned to a popular smoking cessation course. While both parties smoked less, the group that practiced regular meditation showed less stress response in the Amygdala when they were asked to recall painful memories during MRI neuroimaging. This demonstrates that the practice of thought control can have a long-term impact and actually reshape one's perceptions, habits and unconscious fear-based belief systems.

Prefrontal cortex

The prefrontal cortex begins to thin with age, therefore contributing to cognitive function decline in later years. Meditation practitioners encourage a reversal in this pattern, inversing the correlation between prefrontal cortex thickness and meditation practice alongside the reversal of neural degeneration.

This area of the brain is also responsible for the mental conflict when one's belief systems are contradicted with new information, a concept developed by psychologist Leon Festinger[10] in the late 1950s. He showed that, when a person is confronted with challenging, new information, they are likely to reject it to preserve their current understanding of the world. This is known as cognitive dissonance and is responsible for the change in one's attitude. Meditation supports the expansion of a person's cognitive dissonance, helping to expand one's view of themselves and the world around them.

Heart space

Meditation can aid in protecting one against heart disease. One study of 40 adults found that eight-week meditation training reduced concentrations of the marker C-reactive protein, (which is associated with the development of heart disease). Meditation also forms a reconnection with the sacred heart space as you unwind from the mental realm, ultimately taking you back home into timeless, still presence.

It's fascinating to be aware of the positive effects of meditation. Just being 'aware' can lead to changes in the physical structure of the brain, a phenomenon known as 'neuro-plasticity'. The kind of life you lead is solely within your own control, and everybody has a conscious choice and capacity to control their destiny. Simply meditating for 30 minutes every day can change your brain, your heart and your life.

reathing meditation

ion will deliver an increase of oxygen, alkalisation and energy into
~~the bod~~ ellular structure (heart, lungs and digestive systems).
Strengthening these systems support the health of the other parts of the body
and therefore assist with healing numerous other aspects of your being
including mental and physical. By simply focusing your attention at the level of
the body diverts energy towards it! You can use this meditation to enjoy a
sense of well-being and enliven your physical, mental and emotional structure.

- **Sit comfortably, and close your eyes.** Take a few moments to 'simply
  be'. Notice whatever is being experienced in the moment — sounds,
  physical sensations, thoughts, feelings — without trying to do
  anything about it. Continue like this for a while, allowing yourself to
  settle.

- Now **bring your attention to your breathing**. Simply notice the breath
  as it moves in and out as the body inhales and exhales. Notice how the
  breath moves in and out automatically, effortlessly. Don't try to
  manipulate it in any way. Notice all the details of the experience of
  breathing — the feeling of the air moving in and out of the nose and
  the way the body moves as you breathe.

- **Important-** Breathe in deeply from the belly, then ribs, then
  collarbone area. Diaphragmatic breathing is the giver of life. Learn to
  utilise the full volume of the lungs.

- The mind will wander away from the breath — that's fine, it doesn't
  matter. This is a part of the meditation! When you notice that you are
  no longer observing the breath, easily bring your attention back to it.
  **Make each inhalation last for four seconds, holding for a further four
  seconds and then exhaling for another four out of your nose.** Let all
  of your experiences — thoughts, emotions, bodily sensations — come
  and go in the background of your awareness of your breathing. Notice
  how all of these experiences come automatically and effortlessly, just
  like the rhythm of the breath.

- After a few minutes of four-second inhalation, holding and exhalation,
  start to go deeper. **Now inhale through the nose for seven seconds,**
  hold the breath for a **further seven seconds and finally exhale for
  seven seconds** — this time, **out through the mouth.** After a few more
  minutes, return to the comfortable, relaxed breathing that suits you.

- After about **ten to fifteen minutes of focused breathing,** the incessant stream of thoughts should have eased somewhat. If you are meditating without music, bring your attention beyond any sounds you may hear, and focus on the deep silence and the empty, spacious void of darkness. Within the darkness, visualise a pure white light. Go further into the light, bathe in it, feel the stream of positivity and warmth firing in your chest/heart area. This is your soul light. Visit this space as much as you can for fulfilling healing.

- In time, you can become aware of the tendencies of your mind. You will see how it resists certain experiences and tries to hold onto others. The natural settling of the mind allows you to notice these underlying tendencies and creates the possibility of letting them go. If you experience a resistance to what is occurring, an attempt to change what is happening or the tendency to hold onto experiences of the past, work toward letting them go. You can do this by breathing into the past, experiencing and thanking the universe for the growth you achieved. It is now time for it to leave.

Alpha wave creative meditation practice

Whether you are a beginner or advanced meditator, with the assistance of brainwave entrainment technology you can gently lower your brainwaves to a focused alpha level whilst remaining in complete thought awareness. In this altered state of consciousness, you will gain access to your subconscious mind, intuition and other great powers hidden within.

- Start by sitting upright, back straight and listening to the recommended alpha frequency audio which can be found on the YUSA YouTube channel (remember to use headphones). Again, like the first meditation exercise, start to get comfortable with breathing and the vibrations of the audio. **Practice inhaling, holding the breath, then exhaling for four seconds, moving on to seven seconds after some time.**

- After 15 to 25 minutes of stillness, you will be in the alpha state of mind. You will start to feel very relaxed, and your eyes will be heavy. Now, **tilt your head upward about 20 degrees. Project a mental screen outward, roughly two metres in front of you at this angle.** Now, once comfortable at this angle, you can start to project images, scenarios and events that you want to create onto this mental screen. Breathe in deeply through the nose whilst making vivid mental pictures of your scenario in the mid-brow forehead region (third eye). Repeat this for a short while.

This is the process of creative visualisation. **It is important that you project your scenarios and images in high definition and colour**. It is even more important you project scenarios with the **belief they have already happened!** Feel the burning desire in your heart-space and intense gratitude for receiving your desires at such speed! You can practice this for as long as you would like.

Remember to skip two days per week for brainwave recovery and stabilisation. The more you start to detoxify your pineal gland, the more it starts to visualise colour images on the mental screen. The mind is the watchman of the heart, it is what directs your focus in a laser beam fashion. The heart is the great gas pedal of empowerment, you must learn to balance both in order to achieve your dreams, goals and desires.

Believe. Act as if *it has already happened*. Live like you already have it. It's coming; it's a done deal.

After approximately 25 minutes of alpha activation, the gap between the conscious and subconscious mind is bridged. When powerful thoughts are matched with high energy, positive feelings and creative visualisations, the subconscious starts to store these images and thoughts, encouraging positive reprogramming with what you want to create in your life. Your hopes now fly like arrows in the air, seeking a target that only a focussed mind can see!

However, alpha meditation itself only one aspect of recovering from a specific health condition. Simply visualising good health and healing is not enough. For a healthy body, you need balance: a high energy, highly mineralised diet, exercise, fulfilling sleep and so forth. Visualisation can play a big role in moving the body toward health, partly by helping you 'tune in' to the expressions and language it produces.

Reprogramming usually takes about 30 days of consistent practice and perseverance. Later in this section, we delve deeper into the workings of the subconscious mind, exploring two other powerful methods of reprogramming that complement alpha brainwave entrainment. Vision equals discipline, equals success, equals reflection, equals self-knowledge therefore equalling a sense of presence.

'Alpha waves in the human brain are at a frequency between 8 and 12 hertz. The wave frequency of the human cavity resonates between 8 and 12 hertz. All biological systems operate in the same frequency range. The electrical resonance of the earth is also between 8 and 12 hertz. Our entire biological system – the brain and the earth itself – work on the same frequencies. If we can control that resonate system electronically, we can directly control the entire mental system of humankind.' ~ **Nikola Tesla**

The Five Brainwave States

As mentioned previously, your brain ranges through a variety of frequency patterns during your day-to-day life. Below are the five main brainwave states that are responsible for altered states of consciousness. Each brainwave state occurs in a specific frequency range that can be scientifically measured in cycles per second (Hz).

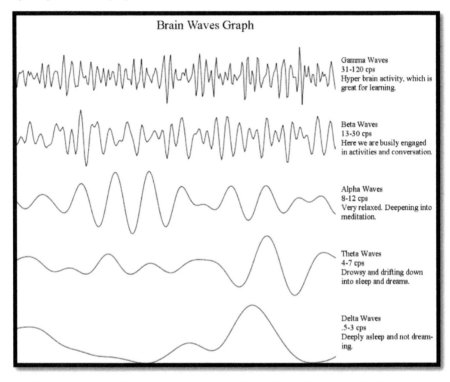

Brain Waves Graph

Gamma Waves
31-120 cps
Hyper brain activity, which is great for learning.

Beta Waves
13-30 cps
Here we are busily engaged in activities and conversation.

Alpha Waves
8-12 cps
Very relaxed. Deepening into meditation.

Theta Waves
4-7 cps
Drowsy and drifting down into sleep and dreams.

Delta Waves
.5-3 cps
Deeply asleep and not dreaming.

The image above is a simple representation of how the various brainwave states would display in oscillated form.

Gamma Waves

'God and Man Manifesting All'

The Gamma state is mostly active when one is processing and concentrating on new information. These waves are considered to be sensory-binding, ones that enable you to link and process information from all the different parts of the brain. The Gamma wave is associated with having high levels of intelligence, intellectual capabilities, self-control, feelings of natural happiness, great memory and an increased perception of reality.

People who lack Gamma brainwaves tend to experience difficulties with learning and mental processing. If you currently have difficulty remembering things such as names, dates, events, plans etc., you would benefit from increasing your Gamma brainwave range.

An increase in one's Gamma brainwave activity has been known to boost the perception of reality through the five senses. Gamma is responsible for making smells become more potent and increasing your visual acuity whilst sharpening your hearing and taste senses.

People with high amounts of Gamma brainwaves tend to include quick learners and highly motivated, ambitious individuals alongside those who hold a lot of mental focus. If you have above-average intelligence or are among a group of top athletic performers, chances are good that you already know what Gamma brainwaves feel like.

Beta Waves

'Busily Engaged in Thought Analysis'

These brainwaves are characterised by logical, analytical and intellectual thinking, verbal communication and acute awareness of one's surroundings. People who think logically tend to have a lot of Beta brainwave activity, and these brainwaves have been known to increase as you get older. In the majority of healthy adults, Beta waves seem to be the dominant rhythm.

Beta waves have also been associated with an increased ability to focus on your external reality. When you are in a Beta state, you are far from relaxed. You may have a lot of energy in the form of nervousness, excitement or anxiety, and you are able to think quickly and rapidly with the ability to come up with logical solutions to problems.

The Beta waves state is ideal for solving maths problems, conducting research, reading books and writing articles. Beta brain waves can greatly improve your writing and literary ability and can contribute to an increase in one's I.Q.

Alpha Waves

'Almost Lulled; Present, Happy, Aware'

Alpha brainwaves most commonly occur when one is calm and relaxed, yet mentally alert. These brainwaves are also present during meditation, energy healing and daydreaming. When you take the time to breathe deeply, meditate or even close your eyes, there will be an increase in the amount of alpha brainwave activity within your brain. Classical music and natural sounds are also great for promoting an alpha state of mind.

Adjusting the brain into an alpha state, you can dramatically improve the quality of your life alongside improving your ability to learn. An alpha state will significantly reduce your stress and anxiety levels as well as bring you to a state of peak performance and mental processing. Alpha states are also known to enhance your immune system whilst allowing you to think divergently, encouraging your ideas and physical manifestations to become more creatively active.

Theta Waves

'Threshold Consciousness'

Threshold consciousness is that blissful state between being asleep and being consciously awake where anything and everything is now possible. Theta brainwaves are characterised by one being deeply relaxed and inwardly focused.

This brainwave state is also associated with the assimilation of new information with a high retention rate. Theta waves are connected with states of enhanced creativity, deeper relaxation, day-dreaming, sleep-dreaming, heightened motivation to achieve goals, new behaviour patterns and an insight into oneself.

You can harness your inner creativity and experience what many famous artists, musicians and authors experience with Theta brainwaves. Theta brainwaves are activated when you have an instinctual-intuitive sensation in the pit of your stomach. Out-of-body experiences and lucid dreaming are also a result of theta threshold consciousness.

Delta Waves

'Deeply Entering Low Task Activity'

These brainwaves are associated with being extremely relaxed and are characterised by deep, dreamless sleep. Though this brainwave state is typically dominant whist in the deep stage of sleep, you can also train yourself in learning to increase the delta activity whilst being consciously awake. People with high amounts of Delta waves have also been found to have an increased sense of empathy and compassion.

An increase in Delta brainwaves coincides with an increase in the body's natural ability to release anti-ageing/growth hormones, balance melatonin (vital for balanced sleep patterns), resolve mental tensions and repair muscles after exercise.

It has been known that Delta brainwaves can drastically reduce and balance the levels of cortisol (stress hormone) in your body. Typically, Delta brainwave activity is observed while a person is experiencing deep sleep. However babies, infants, monks and advanced meditators have been scientifically proven to have a higher amount of Delta brainwave activity.

So forth

When you consciously guide yourself into the **Alpha** and **Theta** levels of mind through centring techniques, it is possible **to reprogram your mind like a computer.** Why is this important? Well, imagine being able to rewire your own limiting belief systems without spending thousands on a professional hypnotherapist.

What if you could **more easily overcome bad habits** such as smoking or snacking? What if you could raise your IQ, cultivate a positive wealth mind-set or **awaken your mind's natural healing capacities?** Simply by working with and embracing brainwave entrainment, visualisation and your own mind the results that can be brought forward are highly encouraging. More benefits include: **stress relief, enhanced creativity and intuition** alongside **accelerated physical and emotional healing**.

With the knowledge each brainwave state, you can begin to experiment with the range of frequencies to identify which one is most beneficial for your current life circumstance. It is advised you explore the audio tracks on the YUSA YouTube channel. There are many to choose from; simply start listening for 30 minutes until your attention span increases. Practice five times a week, again allowing two days for rest.

Note: Many illnesses and mental imbalances (especially depression) with which people are diagnosed in our modern age can stem from a distortion and imbalances of their brainwave frequencies. Medication, advanced diets and living an overall cleaner lifestyle may help but could only result in minor improvements without the use of brainwave entrainment and meditation.

Metaphysics of The Pineal Gland/Third eye

In retrospect, the third eye is actually your first eye. It is formed in the womb well before your physical eyeballs and is the melanin construct which is commonly known as the 'seat of the soul'.

The pineal gland is very misunderstood by Western medicine and scholars. It was not until 1958 that more information was made available to a larger audience. The information pertaining to the pineal gland was kept hidden, (mainly by secret societies) for many years prior. The subject of the pineal gland was first studied by the occultists. They were able to connect with the universe, higher energies and extra-terrestrial influences to gather this information. They had their greater connection to the higher spiritual realm, enabling them to gain access to more in-depth knowledge.

The word 'occult' comes from the Latin word *occultus*, which means *hidden*: secret or mysterious. - Of, relating to, or dealing with supernatural influences, agencies or phenomena; - Beyond the realm of human comprehension, inscrutable; - Available only to the initiate, secret.

Once the information was studied by the occultist, it was then formatted in writing, interpreted and then passed to the scholars. In the East, the pineal gland has always been given recognition. Ancient Kemetians/Egyptians showed symbology of the pineal gland and Kundalini carved in the walls of the great pyramids and surrounding areas whilst Hindus symbolise it with the red dot on the forehead. You may be familiar with the eye of Horus/the All-Seeing Eye.

Remarkable similarities exist between the Kemetian symbolism and the anatomical structure of the pineal gland and midbrain region of the human brain

The Westerners are the new people on the planet. Only now are they beginning to understand and accept this ancient knowledge of self. The pineal gland takes form similar to a pinecone, and in many people it is the size of a grain of rice. The pineal gland is actually the remnant of a higher gland called the Barathary gland. At one point, the two were connected. Located in the throat, the Barathary gland was responsible for ensuring the spiritual connection between human consciousness and fourth-dimensional energies. It was responsible for supporting higher senses of telepathy, clairvoyance, intuition and psychometry.

The pineal gland is also connected to the body's endocrine system. This system is like an information gateway that uses different chemical messengers called hormones to control bodily functions and feelings of intuition. The third eye is responsible for the secretion of melatonin and serotonin into the endocrine system. When it is light and solar energy is present, serotonin is secreted into the bloodstream, and when it is dark and lunar energy is present, then melatonin is secreted. The quality of the secretion is based on the amount of light information present in the environment.

Serotonin is responsible for the feelings and sensations of being awake and energised, while melatonin is the opposite, as it prepares the body for the stages of sleep. Feeling low on energy and suffering from insomnia can be closely related to an imbalance in one of these chemicals. When you detoxify (physically and energetically) and choose to work towards enhancing the functioning of the pineal gland, higher intelligence is gradually accessible (mainly in meditational states). Modern science views the hormonal messengers as chemicals on a physical level only. However these chemicals are full of light codes and information that go far beyond comprehension of the human mind.

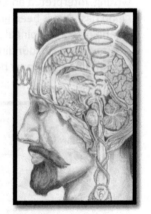

Image to the right displays the Pineal gland and its energetic connection with the higher chakra counterparts.

The higher chakra energy system's relation to the third eye.

Alongside the physical dimensions and understandings of the pineal gland, there are also non-physical aspects to the third eye. Every human has a third eye/Ajna chakra located on the central forehead, whilst the crown chakra is located at the top of your head. The third-eye chakra relates to intellectual commands, perception, knowledge and authority.

The crown chakra element is a representation of the cosmic and divine energy flow, often experienced as an inner light that emanates from the deepest part of one's being. The crown chakra also represents multidimensional consciousness. Your reality is no longer limited as your consciousness extends beyond the ego and a greater sense of self is realised.

To enable the flow of higher information into your conscious energy field, these higher energy centres must be free from blockages (emotional or mental). Blockages only serve to disrupt the passing of information and delivery of hormonal messengers. When you feel things and get emotional, that's information. There is a reason why emotions are arising. You must listen to that which is a part of your intuition. A large part of this is fear. If you fear something, then you should study that fear and develop a greater understanding to conquer it in order to serve your evolution.

All of your spirit guides, angels and higher beings in which you are in constant connection with communicate through the pineal gland. Information is processed through emotional messages that need to be acknowledged to interpret guidance regarding daily life and situations. As detailed earlier, the brain is just a processor, it is not where the mind is located. Information and light codes are sent from the universal mind and picked up by the third-eye transmission device.

We also mentioned that information travels through light at the subatomic level, a main factor in regards to human evolution which encourages the construction of, and how your DNA is upgraded, unlocked and expanded. Ultimately working to enhance ones state of consciousness and a contributing factor for personal growth.

A final point worth noting in regards to the pineal gland is its relation with DMT. Dimethyltryptamine is widely known as the 'spirit molecule'. Its presence is widespread throughout the plant kingdom and present (in trace amounts) within mammals, including humans, where it functions as a trace amine neurotransmitter. DMT is present in all living beings, and it is secreted at different times from the pineal gland, mainly during the dreamscape and Theta sleep cycles.

When present in the dreamscape, the pineal is actually secreting DMT. It is responsible for your imagination crossing the formless borders into other realms. The same goes for when you practice out-of-body travel/astral projection. DMT is secreted right before death, assisting the transition of the soul.

Meditation practices alongside the consumption of natural alkaline foods has been known to stimulate the natural production of DMT. You can learn more about DMT from the book and documentary called *DMT: The Spirit Molecule* by Dr. Rick Strassman[11].

Detoxification of the pineal gland

The Pineal gland is heavily calcified in many by the time they are 17 years old, mainly due to the consumption of contaminated, genetically modified foods, harmful processed sugars, alcohol, acidic thought processes and fluoridated water. It appears as a mass of calcium during an MRI scan. Calcification is the build-up of calcium phosphate crystals in various parts of the body, an absolute enemy to consciousness.

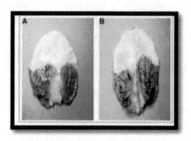

Above is a representation of a calcified Pineal gland

Avoid all things fluoride, such as: tap water, (including cooking with tap water and showering without a filter), fluoridated toothpaste, inorganic fruits and vegetables, red meat and any other artificial foods or drinks. It can be difficult to maintain a strict supply of purely organic fruit and vegetables in your diet, but it is important to start from where you are and begin to make changes where they become possible.

Pineal gland detoxifiers and stimulants: Wheatgrass, Chlorella, Spirulina, blue-green algae, Iodine, Zeolite, ginseng, borax, Bentonite clay, chlorophyll-dense foods and blue skate liver oil (derived from fish). *More information in chapter 3.*

Natural foods: Raw cacao, goji berries, cilantro, watermelon, bananas, honey, coconut oil, hemp seeds, seaweed and noni juice. *Stop eating white sugar completely. Juice fasting and urine therapy are most effective.* The body chapter delves deeper into detoxification and foods, heavy-metal detox and colon detox. Ayahuasca and Ibogaine also awaken the pineal. *More information in chapter 2.*

Essentials oils can be used to help stimulate the pineal gland and facilitate states of spiritual awareness, meditation and astral projection. Particularly effective oils include: lavender, sandalwood, frankincense, parsley, davana, pine and pink lotus.

Raw apple cider vinegar: (Contains malic acid. Make sure it's raw, as that is very important. Braggs is the best brand.) You can fill a glass bottle with ionised alkaline water, eight tablespoons of Bragg's Apple Cider Vinegar and 2 tablespoons of raw, local honey.

Sungazing: Gazing at the sun during the first 15 minutes of sunrise and last 15 minutes of sunset will do wonders for your pineal gland. More information in chapter 3

Regular meditation and chanting: Chanting causes the tetrahedron-shaped nose bone to resonate which encourages pineal gland stimulation, ultimately enhancing the secreted amounts of beneficial hormones. These beneficial hormones (such as HGH) work toward keeping the appearance youthful. The sound 'OM' resonates with the fourth chakra, known as the heart centre, the seat of unconditional love. The sound 'AIM' resonates with the crown chakra. Chanting OM and AIM opens you up to Universal and cosmic awareness. You can chant anywhere from five minutes to however long you desire. *More information in chapter 2.*

Crystals that benefit the pineal gland include: Amethyst (wand), laser quartz (wand), moonstone, Pietersite, purple sapphire, purple violet tourmaline, rhodonite, rose aura and sodalite. Any indigo, violet or dark purple gemstone or crystal can also be used to stimulate the pineal gland and open, balance and align the sixth and seventh Chakras. Placing crystals directly onto the third eye or brow chakra for 15 to 30 minutes a day can greatly accelerate the opening, balancing and alignment of the nonphysical aspects of the glands.

The best exercise for pineal gland and health stimulation is to use an amethyst obelisk crystal or wand and point it at the third eye. (The point of the wand should touch your skin.) Then look up directly at the sun with your eyes closed. The sun's rays penetrate through the base part of the obelisk wand and beam directly into the pineal gland, Do this every day ideally or whenever possible for about 5 to 10 minutes.

Note: Many people become fixated on the opening the third eye as a shortcut to spiritual awakening. They may hope for a vision or to meet a spiritual being with all the answers to their questions. It is, however, deeper than this. As mentioned earlier, all energy centres need to be in balance. Many people who provide information on opening the third eye often forget to add the importance of an open and aware heart space.

Without an open and activated heart, you could have visions, messages and visitations from higher dimensional beings but be unable to tell truth from trickery. The heart only deals with truth on a very deep, intuitive level and is what connects you to everything else in the universe. Without the inner knowing of the heart, a person can easily be deceived.

The mind can really mess with you! Awakening should be a gradual, natural process throughout one's life. It is not about phenomena; extra-sensory perceptions and 'powers' are side effects, not the goal. Most often, people should be focused on the heart. We expand on the heart in chapter 2.

Conscious breathing & CHI/QI life-force energy

Correct forms of breathing is something that many underestimate. The breath is sacred and many yogis, sages and spiritual gurus refer to the breath as being the underlying life force, the ether/prana/spirit or CHI energy. Breathing is what keeps you connected to source and ensures constant energetic flow throughout your higher etheric body.

People do not know how or remember to breathe in the correct manner. Breathing is usually involuntary: your breath is literally breathing you. The average person completes a cycle of breath approximately 18 times per minute. That's 1,080 times an hour and 25,920 times a day - and you don't even think about it.

Many people breathe too shallowly, tend only to take sips of a breath and hold it when feeling stressed or anxious. Both these can have a ripple effect through the system and cause a disruption in natural biorhythms. One bad habit, such as shallow breathing, triggers another. Many of the things you do day to day may actually be tiring you out, rather than building you up!

It can be said that way too much physical and mental stress is created in daily life alongside working out. The goal is to work out smarter, not harder so practicing abdominal breathing holds great importance mainly because the lowest area of the lungs is richest for oxygen. For this reason, you should also work to strengthen your core muscles around your abdomen and lower back.

Breathing properly through the nose and from the abdomen assists in keeping the mind clear, enabling you to think about who you are, what you're doing and why. When you breathe in the correct manner, you'll experience improved digestion, your overall balance will be improved, and you will develop the optimal posture.

Benefits of deep belly/diaphragmatic breathing

- Cancer struggles to thrive when cells are bathed in high levels of oxygen.
- Shortness of breath and heart disease are directly linked - the heart goes into spasms when it is deprived of oxygen.
- There is a positive correlation between poor breathing and high blood pressure.
- Most emotional issues, including breathing-related anxiety and depression, result from the nervous system being out of balance. Conscious breathing balances the electrical impulses of the nervous system.
- Oxygen burns fat and calories; optimal breathing helps promote weight loss.
- Breathing well is the key to sleeping well and waking up feeling rested.
- Breath is life. Virtually every health condition and human activity is improved with optimal breathing as CHI energy is circulated more readily.
- Breathing incorrectly can make you more susceptible to lower back pain.

Your five senses are an extension of your nervous system. It is important to keep them within an abundance of life-force energy. Many people focus on rebuilding strength and muscles but discard this underlying foundation, the nervous system. When you focus on building the nervous system, everything else follows, promoting the regeneration of mind, body and spirit. Simply breathing in the correct manner can, in turn, shift the atomic structure of your bodily functions, supporting optimal well-being and a strong immune system.

Stress wears out the body while intensity grows the body. *The only difference between stress and intensity is breathing!* It is breathing through your *nose* vs *breathing* through your mouth. Diaphragmatic breathing starts in the stomach, rises up into the ribs and ends further up in the clavicle, filling up the full volume of the lungs. This is opposed to shallow breathing, which hardly fills a third of the lung space.

When you breathe properly throughout the day, the alveoli pockets in the lungs can absorb more oxygen to pass onto the brain, muscles, organs etc. So what does this result in? Enhanced *LIFE force* energy. The lungs occupy a square area that is the equivalent of a tennis court. When shallow breathing becomes habit, the lower half of the lungs gradually loses efficiency.

You can actually have a ten times more intense workout when exercising when you breathe in and out of the nose. The brain, the heart and the lungs all function on individual sine waves. These sine waves can be measured with a scientific oscillator. For optimal intensity and nervous system growth, these need to be balanced and in synchronisation!

When you breathe in through the nose, there is a spiralling vortex of energy flowing up the left and right nostrils. At the epicentre of the vortex, in between the eyes, there is an induction, and an electrical charge is produced. This is the building process of CHI or QI energy, the unseen force. Remember the nervous system influences the health of your whole physiology. Therefore, practise breathing in and out through the nose when exercising. Do not stress the body unnecessarily; go slower, Lift weights slower, and breathe deeply from the abdomen. Work smarter, not harder, and results will follow.

CHI building exercises can be practised by anybody, of any age, in order to increase longevity and life force. For this particular exercise you will need a bicycle and some cold-pressed organic coconut oil. Find a peaceful, level and preferably a natural route so you can stay seated.

Take a tablespoon of coconut oil, place it in your mouth, and keep swishing it side to side until it becomes fully liquid. This will form a seal so no air can pass through the closed mouth. Start riding the bicycle along flat ground, staying seated. Keep your back straight, chest out and arms relaxed. Breathe deeply in and out through the nose. Do not spit the coconut oil out until the ride is over; drop into a lower gear if needed. The first time will be the hardest as the brain, heart and lung sine waves will be off balance. Ride for about 20 minutes a day a few times a week if possible, or every day, if you are experiencing health issues. A tool to aid in lung capacity and lung regeneration can be found at **www.powerlung.com.**

What is CHI/QI life force energy?

In order to live, humans extract prana from the environment; prana exists within all living elements. The Chinese word for 'prana' is Chi or Qi; the closest English translation for this substance is 'life force energy'. If you don't intake sufficient amounts of pranic energy, the body can begin to degenerate prematurely. Very simply put, to reach your highest potential, you need to ingest only the purest elements: pure food, pure water and pure air.

Einstein proved energy, whether derived from a plug socket or a nuclear reactor, is interchangeable with matter, and matter is measurable. Your vibrational essence, prana, is also measurable. In effect, human beings are highly sensitive to energy mechanisms, you extract it, store it and you use it up. Your deepest self exists on an atomic/subatomic level.

For example, monks who practice Tibetan martial arts, over time, learn to cultivate and store the CHI energy in their solar plexus chakra. They can transmute this energy into fighting force and protection. Many ancient meditation techniques hold credit for the techniques that assist one into harnessing the CHI energy from the natural environment.

Raw foods contain high amounts of prana; hence, this is why eating raw foods is a great way to obtain substantial quantities of it alongside it being the number 1 key to longevity. Why raw foods? Because they contain active enzymes and are highly alkaline in nature. If, like many in modern society, you can't be 100% raw, you can still consume a mostly alkaline diet. *More information in chapter 3.*

Negative thoughts, fearful emotions & their impact on your health & body

Your mind and body are linked in ways that can only be felt, not seen. The physical body reflects emotional and psychological states. It is only when you ignore the body that illness is then able to interfere with your natural defence systems.

Thoughts have the power to impact cellular arrangements and program water (bodily fluids). Water holds unique consciousness and is affected by energy and vibration, including words. Harbouring a positive intention creates clear beauty. Infuse the waters of your body with positive affirmations as they can be a powerful transformative tool for your consciousness and characteristics.

Remember, do not underestimate the power of your own thoughts!

Think of a time when your heart was racing with anticipation, fear or fright. The mix of feelings in your stomach are the results of the thoughts and emotions which transfer into to the physical body and the delivery of chemical messenger hormones.

Fear is a powerful form of thought. It affects nerve centres, therefore affecting the circulation of blood. This, in turn, paralyses the muscular system. Fear thus affects the entire being, body, brain, nervous and mental systems.

Your body movement is reflective of your inner world. You need to learn how to live inside your body, for example, feel your feet when they strike the ground and know which way to turn your foot to align your body and be pain free. This practice allows you to become more conscious of the workings of the inner body whilst instinctively bringing more awareness to your life. It is great for enhancing the mind and body connection. A clearer mind helps you expend less energy on bodily functions and direct it toward a life you love.

Below are examples of areas of physical pain and probable causes:

- **Neck pains**: Being stubborn and refusing to see other sides of an argument, mainly because of ego and inflexibility.
- **Shoulder strains**: Represents your inability to carry all past experiences in the present moment joyously, without making life a burden by your attitude.
- **Spine pain:** The spine is the overall support of life. **Upper:** Reflects lack of emotional support, feeling unloved, holding back love for others, a closed heart and unresolved emotional issues. **Middle:** Dealing with guilt, holding onto past events or trauma. **Lower:** Fear or lack of money, fear of abundance and operating from the lower chakras.
- **Elbows**: Reflects a changing direction in life and having to accept new experiences.
- **Hips:** Psychologically related to the fear of going forward in major decisions or having nothing to move forward into, anxious thoughts and a fear of what lies ahead in the future.
- **Knees**: Stubborn pride and ego, inability to bend to others' perspectives.
- **Arthritis:** Emotionally and psychologically linked to feeling unloved, receiving criticism from others and a deep resentment toward others.
- **Inflammation:** linked to fearful emotions, seeing red and inflamed, out-of-control thinking processes.
- **Joint pain**: Random joint pains can arise to the surface when your life changes direction and you struggle or have uncomfortable feelings about these changes.
- **Loss of balance:** You are not centred and grounded in life. Brainwaves may be out of synchronicity.
- **Weakness and stiffness:** Related to rigid, stiff thinking, close minded with a much-needed mental rest.
- **Sprains:** Holding resistance and not wanting to move down a certain path in your life, often holding onto anger relating to non-acceptance of a past experience.

Your thoughts and feelings are interlinked with various areas of the body and are the foundations for specific illnesses that manifest from energy blockages. When you fall sick, the body is communicating that your way of thinking (unconscious) is out of sync with what is beneficial to your being. Your body is asking you to live in harmony, at peace with yourself and your surroundings.

Stress causes acid. Emotion causes acid. If you are stressed or emotional a lot of the time, you will need a mountain of therapies and some time in retreat to recover. And the recovery will be short, if you go back to being emotional and stressed. It's all in your head, but acid is all in your body. It builds up in knees, spine, muscles, wrinkles, lungs, kidneys, feet and hands.

In nature, anything that is not fulfilling its purpose gets recycled. Simple. A tree stops producing oxygen, and when it's functioning is inefficient, nature takes it, recycles its minerals and grows a new tree which is smarter, smaller and more efficient. This is evolution! But blocked evolution is a counterpart of acid overload. Acidic people are achieving everything on the ego plane, but zero in the true measure of nature's law. Acidity is what is produced as discomfort in the body when you have negative lower vibratory thoughts and emotions. Conversely, positive and higher vibratory emotions restore alkalinity, soul balance and healing to the physical body.

Self-esteem is the search to value who you are based on how you feel about yourself. If someone makes you feel good about yourself, then your self-esteem goes up, and you say you like them. The better they make you feel, the more you love them. There are many ways to build self-esteem: greed, possession, blame, victim, power, self-importance, righteousness, hate, anger, resentment. These lower vibratory emotions encourage acidity cause acidity, so this is why, in spiritual terms at least, self-worth is heralded over self-esteem!

So, the desire for high self-esteem makes people addicted to feeling good, to phenomena such as; peace, being liked, approved of, admired, applauded, wanted, desired, pursued and pleasured; succeeding; money; drugs; lovers and self. But the question is; which one is real?

Here are a few tips for maintaining emotional balance:

1. Maintain good physical health as the greatest wealth is health.

2. Learn to release anger and let go of grudges. 'For every minute you are angry, you lose sixty seconds of happiness'.

3. Raise your awareness and look for the hidden message or lesson in negative or difficult situations.

4. Keep your brain active; don't let complacency or boredom set in.

5. Stimulate your senses: enjoy beautiful art, listen to music that lifts your spirits or try a new gourmet dish.

6. Have fun, and don't take yourself too seriously. Balance in life is important for maintaining emotional health.

7. Maintain supportive and good relationships with friends and family.

8. Share. Donate your old clothes, furniture or items you don't use anymore to your local Goodwill

9. Relax. Take some yoga classes, learn to meditate or incorporate a relaxation technique into your routine.

10. Learn to have gratitude for exactly where you are. Remember, there is always somebody experiencing worse!

Programming the body's cellular structure with thought vibrations and emotions

As you are aware, thoughts and emotions hold vibratory frequencies and unique power. As the very basis of atomic structure is light and information travels in light photons, it entails that the atomic structure of the physical body is a receiver of these vibrations and can be programmed on a deep, microscopic cellular level.

In September 1939, the international musical pitch of 432 Hz (which also happens to be in sync with the natural tuning of the universe) was changed to 440 Hz with the persuasion of Nazi propaganda minister Joseph Goebbels. Prior to the change, musicians worldwide had carried out a widespread rejection of this tuning. So why was the pitch changed? Without delving too far into the conspiracy side of things, during the time between world wars I and II, scientists were researching music frequencies wanting to establish the range of frequencies that best induced fear and aggression.

It is said that the 432 Hz tuning tone vibrates with the universe's golden mean, PHI, and unifies the properties of light, time, space, matter, gravity and magnetism with biology, the DNA code and consciousness. When atoms and DNA structures begin to resonate in harmony with the spiralling pattern of nature, your sense of connection with the whole is magnified.

Vibrations impact solid matter. The human body is composed of 78% water content. Water is highly intelligent and can form structures around frequencies, both positive and negative. Through the 1990s, frequency expert Dr Masaru Emoto[12] performed a series of experiments observing the physical effect of words, prayers, music and environment on the crystalline structure of water. Emoto hired photographers to take pictures of water after being exposed to the different variables. The water was subsequently frozen to form crystalline structures.

Below are examples of the differences in the frozen structure of the water. Water has a consciousness; it is truly beautiful. This is just one example. You can research more on this topic yourself. Search for 'Dr Masaru Emoto' online, or purchase his book *The Hidden Messages in Water.* You can also research Cymatics, the study of visible sound and vibration for a deeper understanding.

The above diagram is a representation of the various frozen water images after being exposed to certain phrases and sound waves. Sourced from Dr. Masaru Emoto's book: The hidden messages in water.

The Subconscious Mind

We mentioned the subconscious mind briefly in this section previous. The subconscious is the second, hidden mind which exists deep within. We also mentioned that the conscious, awake mind is just a small fraction, accounting only for around 10% of your overall mental potential. The subconscious mind accounts for the other 90%.

The subconscious mind is the doorway to infinite intelligence and is estimated to be 30,000 times more powerful than the conscious, awake mind. It is said, 'As a man thinketh in his subconscious mind, he shall be'. This part of the mind is built on the Law of Belief, but more so, it responds to the mental picture or thought that has been repetitively practised and played out. The Buddhist, the Muslim, and the Christian all may get answers to their prayers, not because of their particular creed, religion, ceremony or offering, but solely because of their *belief* or *mental acceptance* upon which they pray.

Whatever you think, feel and match with emotions, desire and genuinely believe, will be programmed into your being at the subconscious level. You may not know about this great programmable aspect of yourself and leave it a victim for external forces to program for you! Below is a representation of the conscious and unconscious mind, the latter of which is very deep.

Representation of the subconscious mind. The largest part goes unseen.

If you feel as if you are always hitting barriers in life and are having a hard time in achieving success, there is a good chance there are some beliefs and programs deeply rooted in your subconscious that may no longer serve your best interests. The first step is to practise and form a bond with this part of yourself, turning it into a partner for success so circumstances and events can be attracted into your sphere of reality for the greater good! You now over-stand that thoughts and emotions attract circumstances and events of a similar vibration. Likewise, the subconscious stores your strongest thoughts and belief systems and they remain deep rooted, like a magnet, constantly attracting circumstances of the similar vibration into your life. Simple, right?

Any affirmations, thoughts, sounds and beliefs repeated again and again will form an energetic imprint in this area of the mind. The subconscious cannot distinguish whether they are totally real or just a figment of imagination. What you put there, it will store. You *will* attract external circumstances and conditions on a similar vibration to what resides there. As mentioned earlier in this section, visualisation meditation techniques hold great power for their ability to imprint and reprogram this part of the mind and bring great changes into one's life.

Neuroscientists like to say, 'Neurons that fire together, wire together,' meaning that, when you think and do things in a repeated fashion, the neural pathways in your brain take a new form and get deeper over time. Wherever you direct your attention will define you on a neurological level, meaning whatever you think about, practise and believe, you become on a neurological level.

Thoughts are spiritual seeds that, when planted in the subconscious mind, have the tendency to sprout and grow!

Thoughts are seeds. When these thought seeds are watered with emotion, visualisation and repetition, they grow into trees: some beautiful, some not. Think of the subconscious as a large area of fertile soil that accepts any seed that is planted, good or bad, whilst the conscious mind acts as the gardener, the one that filters the seeds and chooses which ones to plant or program. Schools do not teach this knowledge and information, so many are unaware and lay victim to outside programming and control. You have probably allowed thousands upon thousands of seeds to be planted subliminally in your mind, completely unaware.

Overall, the subconscious mind does not censor, judge or discriminate any thoughts and beliefs with which you choose to program. Prosperity, abundance, money, wealth and good health can be manifested just as easily as ill health, misfortune tragedy and any other poverty circumstances. It will not label positive and negative thought processes like the conscious mind does. It is a strictly programmable device and stores information until it is overwritten, exactly like a USB data stick you may use to store files, music and so forth.

PTSD, anxiety and stress disorders can be linked to past experiences and traumas buried deep within the subconscious mind. You can probably think back to a traumatic circumstance in your life and as you visualise the scene and think about it, you may feel past emotion arise again. The specific scenario was deeply programmed into the subconscious with a strong emotion. If you do not deal with past issues, face them and accept them so they lovingly move on, then they may continue to arise in the present as similar circumstances and events.

After reading this section, you may have a greater understanding of energetic principles, vibration and how it is present within everything you do in day-to-day life. We are fortunate that, in our modern age, advancements are being made to understand the mechanics behind this physical reality and the universe. Years ago, it would have seemed farfetched and unbelievable that humans actually create their own reality in the very moment and can actively utilise this knowledge in order to empower goals and live the life of their dreams.

Reprogramming the subconscious mind

Old data and unwanted memory can still be stored within the subconscious mind. Externals such as television, mainstream media, radio and advertisements are society's biggest enemy and hold most of the blame for social conditioning. Corporations and advertisements use subliminal messages in their advertisements, the conscious mind may not pick up on this, but the subconscious is highly intelligent and can decipher frequencies, tones, repetition and symbols in a way you cannot comprehend. The reason being is so that you buy into their message or product without even thinking consciously why you are doing so.

It takes around 28 days, or four to five weeks, of daily reprogramming to undo, erase and reformat some of the old content. We already mentioned that the alpha visualisation meditation bridges the gap between the subconscious and conscious mind, allowing thought seeds, visuals and desired emotions to be planted efficiently. It is recommended that you follow our Alpha meditation once or twice a day. Use the power of visualisation, deep breathing and strong, positive emotions to start to overwrite old and useless mental data. Stop watching TV altogether. Try to listen to more natural relaxation music and some classical as these sound waves promote healthy Alpha brainwave activity. At the end of the mind section in this booklet are some good methods of reprogramming. Remember the 3 D's: Detach, Detox and Deprogram!

Five steps of reprogramming
1. Identify the beliefs that support your intention.
2. Embrace your positive emotions.
3. Visualise goals (past tense) in the Alpha meditation state.
4. Take actions that support your intention.
5. Repeat, repeat, repeat.

Many positive thinkers know that thinking good thoughts and reciting affirmations for hours on end doesn't always bring about the results that feel-good books promise. This is because positive thoughts come stem from the conscious mind, while contradictory negative thoughts are usually programmed within the more powerful subconscious mind alongside many other factors you will be aware of upon the completion of this book!

A major problem for many people is that they are only aware of their conscious beliefs and behaviours, not of subconscious beliefs and behaviours. Most people don't even acknowledge that their subconscious mind is at play or even exists. The fact is that the subconscious mind is a much more powerful than the conscious mind and humans on the whole operate 95% to 99% of their lives from subconscious programs.

Your subconscious beliefs are working either for you or against you. The truth is that you are not consciously controlling your life, as your subconscious mind supersedes all conscious control. So when you are trying to heal from a conscious level, when maybe citing affirmations and telling yourself you're healthy, there could potentially be an invisible, subconscious program that's sabotaging your progress.

'Whatever we plant in our subconscious mind and nourish with repetition and emotion will one day become a reality." ~ **Personal development pioneer Earl Nightingale**[13]

The Moment of Creation, Presence

Space and time is a linear concept within third-density reality. Linear time is a concept where time is seen sequentially, as a series of events that are leading toward something: beginning and end. The mind identifies very much with time, always wanting something that isn't necessarily there, whether it be for comfort or material gain. It is a lifelong learning curve to gain mastery over your thoughts and 'step out of the mind', so to speak.

The mind and ego are a major distraction for many people. The constant wanting and the illusion of needing more can easily distract your awareness from the present moment. A compulsion to live almost exclusively from memory and anticipation. Identification with the mind and your thoughts is an indication that you are trapped within the boundaries and limitations of time.

The only moment where life can and always will be found is right now. Escapism from the now is quite common and many are always wanting to be elsewhere whilst holding up resistance to what is. The mind may agree and say 'of course, everything is now' but may fail to understand the deeper levels of presence as it is something which needs to be 'felt'.

A mental unwillingness to honour the present moment may in fact lead to discomfort and an endless preoccupation with the illusion of past and future. The more focus you divert to the essence of time, past and future, the more the beauty of now is neglected. The mind may trick you into believing that something, somewhere in the future holds salvation but this is ultimately illusory as you create the 'future' with what you think and feel in the present!

Whatever passes by, happens or changes the underlying factor of now remains consistent, it is the only ever constant factor in your life meaning that upon the surface, the present moment may seem only one of many moments. Beyond third-density reality, in higher densities/dimensions, there is no time, meaning the universal energy field is operating in the moment: no past, no future, just the eternal, divine moment. Also known as the heart space.

'If you are depressed you are living in the past. If you are anxious you are living in the future. If you are at peace you are living in the present'. ~ **Lai Tzu**[14]

When you think or speak in terms of 'I wish for, I want or I need something', you are sending out vibrational frequencies in the form of thought and emotion that express your 'lack of' whatever is desired. This is why it's important for you get into the habit of really feeling and acting as if you already have your desire. Speak and think of it in the past tense. Creation happens now, not in the future. You are a creator being, a vital part of the creator universe. This factor is often overlooked by many who speak about the Law of Attraction.

It is almost impossible to truly feel comfortable upon the resistance of present circumstances and the moment of now. As there is never anyway in which you can escape the now, why not welcome it and become friendly with it? If not then unease will always be present at the deepest part of your being. Think of the workings in nature; everything flows in synchronicity. The flow of a stream is permanent and most often in one direction. The energetic flow of the universe and the events that arise in your sphere of reality all flow in one direction almost making it insane for one to fight against.

If you stop for a second and think on a deeper level, the past can only be remembered *now,* whilst any event that you may remember took place in the *now,* and you are remembering it now. The future, when it arrives is also the *now.* So with this being said, the division of life into the past, future and present is completely mind-made and again illusory.

Many always seem to seek external comforts and illusory needs. They identify with the belief that, when they attain these outside, temporary satisfactions, they can be 'happy'. This could not be any further from the truth. Happiness and inner peace must be attained *now,* or you move throughout life bouncing from one external to another, only feeling bursts of temporary gratification, not the everlasting flow of joy and surrender that lies deep at the core. This ultimately leads to suffering.

Many people often treat the moment of now as an obstacle in their life, an absolute inconvenience which always needs to be overcome whilst they search for future moments that the mind may think holds greater importance. This leads us onto the question of; what is more important? The *doing* of a certain task, or the *results* you will achieve from the doing? Remember, the future never arrives, except as the present. This attitude will slow down your ability to reach success in life; these mental thought forms only encourage a dysfunctional way of living.

Life is now. Now is the only place that life can be found. It is extremely hard and almost impossible for you to *realise* deep inner stillness when identified with a mind that is living in the past or wanting to be somewhere else in the future. Not to mention the undercurrent of constant unease and tension. You cannot truly appreciate the beauty of life and nature alongside the beauty of your own existence when living in an illusory mind-made reality.

'The trouble is, you think you have time'. ~ Buddha

You can have your consciousness consumed by the mind and irrational streams of thought or choose to direct it toward the centre of your being, the heart and inner body. The mind's mental chatter burns up Qi life force energy effortlessly. You lie in bed, you worry; you travel to work, you worry: all going around in circles. If you could exit the mental realm even for a few minutes to find stillness, it would be a great start toward building a reconnection to 'what is'. The mind can then be utilised in a highly constructive manner.

You may be thinking, 'If I am not my mind and should stop identification with my thoughts, then what am I'? The answer to this is simple for one who has wisdom and has attained inner stillness. The mind is a separate, dimensional aspect of the true self. The true self is located deep within the heart space. This space of your eternal being resides in a higher vibrational plane where time is absent.

Take moments throughout the day to breathe deep into the heart area, feel the inner warmth, practice meditation, and build a feeling for the inner body. When stepping into the now, you step out of the content of the mind. The incessant stream of thinking slows down, gaps arise in between thoughts, and they no longer absorb all of your attention. You begin to realise how much vaster and deeper you really are. *We delve deeper into the heart space in chapter 2.*

Clarity and simplicity can become the foundations for daily living when you completely divert your attention to the present moment. You may experience an alertness as you step out of the dream of thought, *past* and *future*. The room for problem making no longer exists as you now remember that life is sacred. Harnessing the now is the only thing that can take you beyond the limited confinements of the mind, being the only point of axis into the formless, eternal and timeless realm of *being*.

The present moment is the primary factor in the universe. You need to divert all attention and feelings towards this sacred space. Once you are fully grounded in the now, then you can deal with your secondary life circumstances with great ease. When you have made friends with, acknowledged and started to honour the present moment, your life will unfold with serenity. You now flow in the direction of the universe. The richness of life is found in a day well lived. This day is like no other, for it is now that all your passion, all your intensity and all your joy can be expressed. Celebrate your life, and decorate it with love! Don't be shy, for this is the day you've waited for!

'Peace is not something that happens by accident. Peace is like silence; it is always there. The lack of harmony in our lives is like noise superimposed on the silence. The issue is not how to create peace, but how to live in a way that eliminates the noise'. ~ Gabriel Cousens, MD[15]

Resisting a present situation in your life

The most simple but radical spiritual practice is to accept whatever arises in the *now,* within and without. Do not label or place judgement on an event. Judgement is a thought form, again illusory. Accept all 'good' and 'bad' circumstances as neutral. Take the middle path, and let external events simply *flow to you* and *through you*. Everything is an experience. You must practice the art of acceptance for a truly peaceful and happy life. The middle path of acceptance is the core foundational practice in Zen Buddhism.

The now is deeper than what happens in it; it is the space in which it happens. Everything that may rise in your sphere of reality, in the form of circumstances and events, are merely content, life's experiences. It is said that life is 10% of what happens to you and 90% of how you respond.

The body reacts to every thought as if it is truly real. When you are operating within the illusion of fear, the mind sends your body chemical messengers in the form of fight or flight. The body is then constantly constricted to 'o no! Dreadful things are happening right now'. Powerful vibrations of fear and dread are sent into the universal field, ultimately forming a barrier of resistance. When you transmit fearful vibrations that stem from your mind's illusory thought forms, you create signals that will attract more of the same vibration into your reality: hence, the Law of Attraction.

'Surrender to what is. Let go of what was. Have faith in what will be'. ~ **Sonia Ricotti**[16]*- bestselling author of Unsinkable*

Resistance is the ultimate form of blocking the universal flow. Many experience traumas or events that the mind identifies as a 'bad' situation. The emotions of anger and fear then step in uncontrollably. Cortisol stress hormones and adrenaline flood the physical body, irrational shaking arises, acid production is increased, and the crystalline structure within the water content of your body becomes negatively programmed. Scattered thinking becomes the result. All of these fear factors distort your biological resonance in a radical manner, automatically dragging you out of harmonious balance with 'what is'. Once your energy field becomes disrupted, energy doesn't flow freely anymore.

Negative subconscious programming can accumulate very easily when you hold resistance to what is. As mentioned previously, a powerful form of thought coupled with strong emotions and visuals are the foundations of seed planting within the subconscious mind. When you resist a trauma and construct illusory barriers, it is almost guaranteed to get lodged in the subconscious field, encouraging high chances of an external replay in the form of negative circumstances and events.

So many things in life would be far more beautiful if you were no longer imposing interpretations on them. Step out of the vibration of judgement. Practise going into the body and out of the mind, simply being the awareness behind the judgement and thoughts. Once you become tuned into the awareness, it becomes apparent that the mind is not who you are. You then tap into the hidden stillness, peace, intuition and creativity of your true self. Too many people are hooked on stimulation, mental stimulation, as they cannot feel the aliveness that is realised inside the body on a much deeper and natural level. It can be said that the beggar has been sitting on a box of gold but has never looked inside!

Many find it hard to get from A to B in life as a result of the dreadful mental torture they endure. The mind just won't stop chattering. They then go to alcohol. After one drink, they feel a bit better. With another one, the mind starts to slow down; another, they feel a sense of relaxation, temporary freedom from the mind. Then another and another and another. The mind stops completely, but the drinker is heading toward unconsciousness.

Start to use your problematic events that may arise in life as tests for acceptance and personal growth. Think about it, humans are constantly trying to solve a problem somewhere in their lives. It **is** possible to drop your problems. Hold back from the moaning and labelling. You must realise that the many thoughts you may have about anything or anybody is just one of many, many possible perspectives on this person, this situation, this place. So remain from identifying your entire self or others with such labels.

When a negative situation arises, observe it, and remain as the awareness witnessing it. Practice deep belly breathing when you feel agitation arising, then place your attention on the inner body. Focus on the heart space, and repeat in your head: 'I am present. I am remaining present in this situation'. Most importantly, let the event come *to you, through you* and *out of you* without forming a subconscious imprint. After practising this for some time, life becomes quite simple. You no longer get intertwined in the complications of the mind, and problems start to fade away effortlessly.

'Nothing in the world can bother you as much as your own mind, I tell you. In fact, others seem to be bothering you, but it's not others. It's your own mind'.
~ Sri Sri Ravi Shankar[17]

Modern physicists confirm that there are no isolated events in the universe. Underneath the surface appearance, all things including matter and energy are interconnected, linked within the totality of the cosmos. When you say yes to 'what is', you snap into the alignment, power and intelligence of life itself. It is impossible to become a pillar of positive change in the world until you over-stand this underlying factor.

The truth is, the ever present moment is not even well defined as a matter of neurology, as the inputs to the brain relay at different moments and that consciousness is built upon different layers of inputs, again, where the timings have to be different. Your conscious awareness of the present moment in some relevant sense is already a memory, but as a matter of conscious experience, the reality of your life is always now and never not now.

This is a liberating truth for the assistance of mental mastery. There is probably nothing more important to over-stand in regards to your mind than this basic factor if you want to be happy in this world. The past is a memory. It is nothing more than a thought arising in the present. The future is merely anticipated, just another thought arising now. What we truly have is this moment ... and this ... and this. The horror is that you may never have had success in realising the present moment on a deeper level, so much beauty has already been overlooked. Many are continually hoping to become happy in the future but remember, the 'future' is created from what happens now!

Overcoming Life's Problems & Surrender

Life's problems show themselves in various shapes and sizes. It's the negative attitude and perception towards the so-called 'problem' that encourages suffering, mainly mental. It is the quality of your consciousness within the present moment that determines your future experience. You are on this planet to experience certain event, to learn new skills and interact with other people, ultimately for the growth and evolution of your soul.

Ultimately, the hidden reason for a problematic event in life is for the attainment of wisdom and teachings which will favour personal growth, serving a universal purpose for the attainment of your higher self. If you surrender to a problem, accept it for what it is on the deepest level, learn from it and move on, the unfoldment of satisfaction may arise within your being.

When a problem arises, do not judge it or become identified with it. Whether it be a physical illness, a car breakdown, relationship problems, a loss of money or a phone dropped in the toilet, do your best not to let it increase your heart rate. Breathe deeply into the problem, and let go of all attachment. At the end of the day, you do not take anything with you beyond the physical, apart from experience. Attachment to things leads to suffering. You feel empty inside, now that the item to which you were attached has left you. You must push beyond these limitations in order to strive towards pure excellence.

If somebody has caused you grief or hurt you in some way, again you must remember that everyone is doing their best in accordance to their level of consciousness. When you hold anger or hate toward somebody else for a past mistake, it is just like grasping a piece of hot coal, only *you* feel the burn. Holding emotions of hate and jealousy promote negative energetic imprints within your heart space and subconscious mind.

These imprints only impose a burden upon your own life. The more you entertain the cycle of placing judgement on others alongside the expression of jealousy or hate, the deeper these vibrational energies get lodged into the depths of your being. This makes it harder for you to let go and release these false illusions, not to mention that the frequencies associated with these deeply lodged energetic vibrations attract more circumstances in your life that you will again envy and place judgement upon.

If you become sick or seriously ill at some point in your life, it may be the surface appearance of a hidden message and something beautiful. Many highly respected teachers in the health and well-being community had epic life transformations when they fell very ill and almost died. When they were ill, they made the conscious decision to become well again, not just moderately well so they could function again, but they embraced a journey down a whole new avenue of life where they gained wisdom and experience that they now share with other people. If it wasn't for their 'traumatic' event, they would not be able to help others in preventing such disasters on a large scale. They now hold a high sense of gratitude for the lesson and are living fulfilled lives.

The universe provides circumstances of suffering when you need it most. These transform you into a better person if you drop your ego and stubbornness. For some people, it takes more pain and speed bumps for them to realise the underlying lessons. This is mainly due to the size of one's ego and the mind-made false sense of 'self'. Writing out circumstances and events helps a great deal. Dissect them, and look for what they are trying to teach you.

When a problem arises in the now, it is extremely important that you don't fall into the vibration of *victim*. Feeling sorry for yourself is an act of weakness, a sorry vibration that again only attracts more victim-like circumstances. You should be getting this by now, right?

The hell realms do indeed exist, deep within your mind. Most are unaware they are even operating from the realm of 'hell'. These are mental prisons where lust, jealousy, anger, fear and other demons have control over the way you're manifesting your reality. These are all lower forms of thought and emotions that are related to the lower self.

The universal creator always wants what is best for your soul evolution. Remember what we said in the manifestation section: before light, there was darkness. Same goes for life's difficulties. You must endure the temporary pain of the darkest situations for you to fully respect and appreciate the lightest times that are yet to come. It is highly important in every bad situation that you re-affirm to yourself that something beautiful and great will come out of the situation. Keep the heart alive, and hold a solid vibration of faith. Accept everything for what it is, and push forward.

All in all, problems are a test of inner strength. When you emit big thoughts and ideas into the universe, you will be tested for your worthiness. The more you push the boundaries of limitation and step out of your comfort zone the stronger the impacts of cause and effect. You must keep your inner sun fruitful! Your inner sun is located in the solar plexus area, divert your attention and focus to this space as much as you can so it can expand, shine bright and deflect low vibratory emotions. The universe holds great promise for the strong-hearted, and there is *always* light at the end of the tunnel. Just embrace the moment.

'I wish I could show you, when you are lonely or in darkness, the astonishing light of your own being'. ~ **Hafiz**

Where there is no identification, there is no attachment. Nobody can live in enthusiasm all of the time. Make sure your goals do not all include having this or that, $10 million in the bank or an enlarged image of yourself. This isn't to say that dreams of acquiring wealth are unworthy, but on a deeper level, it is this underlying attachment that will make you suffer once you hit a speed bump and the images in your head become much more distant.

It is wise you ensure your goals are not too big to start with. This is not to say that having a big dream or goal is out or order but it may be more suitable that you make steps in which you can cross off the list in order to sense fulfilment upon completion. Plan your goals in terms of small, medium and long term. Maybe even envision yourself inspiring many others with your work and enhancing another person's life circumstances. Start to feel how helping others will also enrich your own life.

Feel yourself being an opening into which energy flows, from the un-manifested source of all life through you for the benefit of all. All of this implies that your goal or vision is already a constructed reality within you, both on the level of mind and of feeling. The enthusiasm is the underlying force that transfers the mental blueprint from the mental realm into the physical dimension. There is no wanting here. You cannot manifest what you 'want', as mentioned previously. The vibration of wanting expresses 'lack of' to the universe. You can only manifest what you already have.

Upon exerting extra physical and mental efforts into work you may achieve what you want but high levels of stress could be the counterpart. As humanity on the whole moves into new levels of consciousness, extra stress is no longer needed. Many people do feel strongly towards creating, inventing building etc. but if these specific acts are carried out in an unconscious manner then the flow of creative energy is greatly reduced.

Acceptance means that, for now, this is the situation. This moment requires you to do, so you must do it willingly. For example, you may not feel happy about getting up early 7 days a week to start work, never mind be passionate about it, but you can find inner peace by accepting it as a period that will serve the greater good. Performing an action in the state of acceptance means you are fully at peace whilst you do it. That peace is a subtle energetic vibration that then flows into what you do. It is highly active and creative, bringing something entirely new into this world.

With great PAIN comes great CHANGE. If you're not ready to CHANGE, then you're not in enough PAIN.

Surrendering to a specific life event or circumstance is a main way for the energies of higher consciousness can enter the world. Your very own state of consciousness is the most important thing in this world so if you cannot bring joy into whatever it is you may be doing, it is wise that you stop.

The emotion of enjoyment can be cultivated from the inner peace which can be realised through surrendering to what *is*. Quality of life can easily be increased when you realise that 'wanting' is a delusion of the egoic self.

Expansion and positive change on the outer level is much more likely to come into your life by embracing what you have now rather than waiting for some change so you can start enjoying what you do. The mind will say 'maybe tomorrow you can start enjoying', but tomorrow never comes. Realising this allows you to come to grips with 'you' as the witness of events. Not realising this has you fighting with what is and suffering. It is just a simple shift of perspective that frees you from such heaviness and pain. Don't be surprised to find that if you change your perspective, your world changes also!

Suffering is also felt once an external object is taken away, the mental construct of ownership contribute towards a fictional story. Just the words 'I own' can distract one into a delusional sphere of identification with such object but on the whole has nothing to do with who you really are!

For a large majority of people who form their identity around certain materials, illnesses and thought forms, it only becomes clear that they are not part of such illusion and external source once they are on their deathbed. Leaving the whole construct of ownership and mental content absolutely meaningless.

For those who have endured many of life's problematic transformations, could say they have a deeper connection to self. Change did not occur when things were added externally in their life and became bigger, no. The deep inner growth happened when things were taken away and content was removed, there was a higher divine plan that served the best possible outcome for evolution. The point here is that suffering is your best teacher. It knows what is best for you.

When change comes, embrace it, be thankful for it, and ride all events and circumstances with great joy. When you can surrender and allow problems to flow out your life as fast as they came in, then life turns into something wonderful. You are now connected with the infinite consciousness that resides in all things. You can now express deep gratitude. Remember, the problem is not the problem: it is your attitude about the problem! Joy does not come from what you do; it flows into *what* you do, ultimately flowing into this world *through you only,* nowhere else.

'Life has many ways of testing a person's will, whether by having nothing happen at all, or by having everything happen at once'. ~ Paul Coelho[18]

The mind, Ego & the False Identification of 'Self'

The ego is impatient because it knows it's time is limited but spirit is patient because it knows it is eternal. Each day, direct your attention to whether you are choosing to live in fear or love, feeding your demons or your angels. The essence of fear can keep you disconnected from the loving presence within as light cannot shine through a cloudy heart of hate. Causing fear is a tactic of the ego. You can make the decision to be free from fear and doubt and return to the love that lies at the core of your being.

Humans have been conditioned to label events and circumstances as good, bad, pleasant or painful, whereas they are simply nothing more than elements of vibration. If you observe one of these vibratory elements by itself, you won't know its location on the scale. That is to say, you only know red is red by contrast. You do not know a certain sound is loud unless you are aware of softer sounds. Saying this, we can relate it to the ego, as it is only a mere construct. The ego may tend to put a lot of value on these certain vibrations.

The ego is a mind-made construct of self, not the real self. You may be in a situation where other people are present in conversation, and it becomes apparent you may be more knowledgeable regarding a certain subject than the others. For a brief moment, the satisfaction that arises is of the ego and is derived from feeling a stronger sense of self relative to the other people. You now feel superior in that moment because you know 'more'. Many people are addicted to slandering others for this reason. They are disconnected to the real self and live for short bursts of satisfaction so they can feel a heightened sense of themselves.

In addition, slandering carries an element of malicious intent, automatically placing you within the vibration of judgement. If somebody else knows more, and has more than yourself, then the ego feels threatened as it feels it has 'less'. The ego may then try to prove its worthiness by diminishing or criticising the other's character, knowledge or ability. The egoic sense of oneself often strengthens whenever you apply a negative judgement upon another person.

Now, instead of slandering or even competing with the other person, the ego may start to enhance its association with another person if he or she is 'important' in the eyes of others. Maybe something in which you can relate to on a personal level, commonly known as 'name dropping'.

Name dropping is when you or somebody you may know mentions other people, such as a person with a 'higher' ranking in society or somebody with a large amount of material wealth etc. The main reason for the mentioning of such people is for the speaker to feel a sense of superiority, feel special in the eyes of other people and overall gain a stronger sense of self.

'If you don't get what you want, you suffer. If you get what you don't want, you suffer. Even when you get exactly what you want, you still suffer because you can't hold on to it forever. Your mind is your predicament. It wants to be free of change. Free of pain, free of the obligations of life and death. But change is a law, and no amount of pretending will alter that reality'. ~ Dan Millman[19].

In the modern world of stardom and fame, when a certain celebrity for example is worldwide known, they can end up being drawn into a certain collective image or identity. Not one they have created themselves but one which the public and mainly the media have constructed for them. For many who gain recognition in the world it can be easy to get swallowed by the material aspects of success therefore entertaining many false layers that one may fall into the trap of. It can be said that the more you identify with the false mental constructs, the more alienated you become to 'normal' people and your true, deeper self.

Those who greatly identify themselves with egoistic structures and external comforts have a hard time in developing and holding onto genuine relationships with others. It is a constant battle to remain humble when achieving success or recognition for something you have achieved. From personal experience, YUSA found that when you fall into the trap of expressing too much ego, the universe will send a circumstance that will crush your ego and bring you back home to the core. In a genuine relationship, there should be a genuine and outward flow of humble attention toward the other, where wanting is not present.

In terms of work, success is actively achieved upon the unconscious 'no ego' intent. Successful people tend to act directly from the moment, fully embraced in what they do. Again, from the work experience YUSA has attained, you can be technically good at what you do, but with unbalanced psychological deliverance and workings from the ego, work can be totally destroyed!

Outside circumstances, difficulties and personal issues may serve as major distractions in the field of ones work. Especially in the corporate environment, where it can become rather competitive if somebody else is absorbing most of the attention and the end goal becomes a figment of profit and power. Upon such a situation, the one who feels victimised by another may experience a downfall as their ideology behind working becomes competitive and ultimately becomes a means to an end.

YUSA again have first-hand experience in regards to a range of great difficulties which had manifested in the field of work when things did not go in accordance to the mental construct envisioned. It was an extremely hard task to surrender and become one with such problems and losses to say the least. Sometimes the 'poor me' attitude took over, sabotaging the moment therefore encouraging deep feelings of resentment. Looking back in hindsight, such material losses and painful times were merely stepping stones to success and personal growth, a catalyst towards the deliverance of knowledge and wisdom which are presented in this very guidebook!

Overall, the ego can serve as a major distraction when trying to fully embrace the present moment. The constant wanting and false sense of satisfaction is always directing you toward a future moment, an illusion. If the ego was truly who you were, then it would seem crazy to deny it. What remains is a light of consciousness in which experiences, perceptions, thoughts and feelings come and go. This is the deeper, true feel of being: the infinite creator consciousness that lies within, separate from the realm of mind.

Now, let's see if you can relate to such important aspects: can you sense the underlying aspect of yourself, the beingness that is present in the background of your life at all times? Can you sense the 'I AM' that you are, the everlasting presence that holds no label and is free from the mental judgement associated with a thought form?

Your essential identity is consciousness itself, try your best to remain conscious of this underlying aspect whilst trying not to lose yourself in the midst of mental activity. You do not want to completely eradicate the ego, as it holds value to your sense of character. Just keep it under control and realise what lies beneath!

Your heart energy centre is your key to your connection to the symphony of the universe and the 'I AM presence'. Open your door.

Television & Its Impact on the Mind

The function of thought is not totally confined to the brain. It is the totality of the human participating towards the mental thinking process. Feeling is a combination of thought processes by the cells of the body utilising the pathways of the nervous system as you use telephone lines. But just as you receive TV and cellular phone messages without the benefit of wires, the body also has similar and far more refined capabilities. What is known as intuition is an illustration of this more refined ability. It is a knowingness that takes place at a cellular and hormonal level and registers in the awareness at varying degrees of understanding, depending on the belief system of the individual.

The brain is designed to participate in a multitude of processes. It houses the most vulnerable and finely tuned of your endocrine glands. The precious secretions of the pituitary and pineal gland are the drivers of the human body/mind awareness.

The brain is the switching station for the receiving and transmitting of the thinking processes. The combined thought process of the body wholeness is gathered and focused through the brain mechanism that it may be exchanged between humans. However, it must pass through the belief system stored within the finer energies surrounding the body and hold the belief patterns of not only the individual's experiences, but also the norms of the experience and belief patterns surrounding the various levels of of the entire planet.

You are now aware of how sensitive and sacred your very own brain and energy mechanisms are. For the highest quality life experience, it is wise to keep these mechanisms as pure as possible, programming only the reality and experience *you* want to embrace instead of having it infiltrated by outside sources, which are only in the best interest of others.

In the Western world, 95% of the population watch television at least two hours per day. It is the favourite 'activity' for many people. By the time the average American has reached the age of 60, he or she has watched around 10 years of television. In many other countries, the figures are similar.

Most people who watch television find it to be a relaxing hobby, but if you observe the activity more closely, you will find that the more the TV screen remains the focus of your attention, the more your thought activity becomes suspended and infiltrated. For long periods, your consciousness can easily become numb from watching various shows, encouraging little to no thought processing whatsoever, ultimately serving as an escape mechanism from realty.

Imagine what impact this has on your life. Television encourages a state of hypnosis upon watching it for around 12 to 15 minutes. Why is this? It is because the TV's output is working at the frequency of Alpha, around 8 to 12 cycles per second. Advertisements and programs are intentionally set in accordance with the time it takes for your brain to enter this meditative state. As mentioned previously, the Alpha state of mind is the one that bridges the conscious and subconscious mind.

Without the watcher even being aware that this connection is forming on the level of mind, shortly after becoming victim to the advertisements, your subconscious is now being bombarded with illusions that also give rise to inner emotions matched with visualisations. This is how the creation seeds are planted, as we mentioned earlier in this section. The shows that are on the television are even named 'programs', but many people will strive to defend their TV-watching habits because it is no more than an addiction and comfort mechanism.

Imagine the benefits you could receive in life if you used the time you watched television to work and reprogram yourself toward enhancing your own reality. The conditioning that TV encourages, can construct false personality layers, programming you to believe that something is deadly true, idolising others whilst being open to fear-based stories. These layers contribute to the construction of the ego, directing you toward wanting more and more content because you have been unconsciously programmed to buy into corporations. To realise the true self, you have to de-program and remove the layers on top of your mind and heart. Television is just a distraction and does not serve your best interests in terms of growth.

Many people are addicted to watching television and playing videogames due to the temporary feeling of comfort and escapism from the here and now: They no longer remember their problems and become temporarily free from themselves. Does TV create inner space and ground you to the present moment? The answer is no.

Although your thoughts may seem still and not a lot of thought is being generated when you're sitting in front of the television, they are highly engaged in the activity of the television show, linking up with the TV version of the collective mind and thinking *its* thoughts. Your mind is inactive only in the sense that it is not producing thoughts. It is, however, absorbing the continuous stream of thoughts and images that come through the box with lights.

The TV induces a passive, high trance state of heightened susceptibility, again similar to hypnosis. This is why it is associated with the manipulation of public opinion. Politicians, special interest groups and advertisers know this and will pay millions of dollars to catch you in this receptive state of unawareness. They want their thoughts to become your thoughts, most often with success!

Television does however have a strong addictive quality similar to drugs and alcohol, but just as these other substances do, will only contribute to the loss of consciousness and temporary relief from the torture of one's mind. On the contrary, if television was actually thought-provoking, it would stimulate your mind into thinking for itself again.

The box with lights has manipulated a large proportion of minds on the planet. There are however some programs that have been extremely helpful to many people and may have changed their lives for the better, assisting in the opening of their hearts and aiding in consciousness expansion.

Most of the content on television, however, is controlled by those who are totally controlled by the ego. The hidden agenda of the television then takes control of you by putting you to sleep. If you watch TV, it is wise to study commercials, types of music and what types of messages and emotions it is endorsing. Be careful when listening to news. News stations are highly controlled and deliver propaganda and fear stories. Remember that your subconscious mind and biorhythms of the physical body cannot tell the difference between a real or false story. It will store and recreate it in areas of your life.

The TV makes you numb. Turn it off. You will live better and you will begin to observe reality for what it really is.

Dream Building & Daily Affirmation Techniques

Everybody has a dream: some big, some small. Many just want to experience a smoother external reality and be free from stress, worry and so forth. Whatever it may be you desire in life, short or long term, it must be envisioned within your sphere of reality as much as possible. The frequency vibrations of any objects, symbols, sounds and even people can be absorbed into your energetic field and leave imprints.

First, it is wise to de-clutter your life and surroundings, removing anything that no longer serves your best interests. Stop paying attention to illusory outside sources, as you are literally paying them with your attention and energy!

Focus all of your energy not on fighting the old, but on building the new. Stop wasting time looking back, and start looking forward. Take your attention away from thought forms identified with future moments. This only holds you back further.

You now know how to reprogram your subconscious mind with visualisation, repetition and strong emotion. Below are a few techniques that will assist your daily dream building and reprogramming. Utilise these techniques in your daily life, and start to live your dream like it's already a reality right now! This is creation in motion. Feel the deep gratitude, and be truly thankful for what you are about to receive.

YUSA Dream board construction

You may have come across the workings of a dream board previously if you have studied the Law of Attraction elsewhere. The name speaks for itself. The intention of creating a dream board is so that you can have all your visualisations in one place, hung up on the wall, so your subconscious mind can absorb the images and construct a program which is stimulated every time it is envisioned.

We mentioned earlier in this section that creation manifests itself from darkness. To take advantage of this factor, it is recommended you get yourself a blackboard or chalkboard. You can find these here **www.chalkboardsuk.co.uk.** A2 size is best.

Now that you have your board, you need to take some time out and really decide what your short- medium and long-term goals are in life. If you want a new car, then find the image of the exact car you want. If you want to lead a healthier lifestyle, then find an image of the food you want to eat. If you want to find a new job, then find an image of your ideal job. It is also good to include images in relation to sacred geometry on your board as they are high in vibrational energy. We delve deep into sacred geometry in the spirit chapter.

Once you have all of your images printed out in *high-quality colour,* which is important, write on the back of them what they represent. In doing this, you are programming your subconscious with a statement so every time you look at the images in the future, it constructs a repetitive imprint.

Once all your images are done, take a felt pen, preferably gold, and write affirmations on the back of the board. Example: 'Every image and desire I place on this board will manifest into my reality. I am living the life of my dreams, and I attract great circumstances with grace and ease. I am thankful for all of my dreams that have been delivered to me at the speed of light' and so on: whatever makes you feel good!

Now it is time to stick all of your images onto the blackboard. When you do this, ensure you feel good and positive. Simply dot the edges of each image with superglue, and construct it in a neat manner. You can always add new images in the future when new desires and plans need attention. Last, hang this board in your bedroom if you can so it is the first thing you see once you wake up in the morning.

Take at least a few minutes throughout the day focusing on the dream board. Breathe deep, and feel inside the satisfaction and gratitude of having each of your desires. A few minutes of doing this each day is equivalent to a few days of manual work. Again, we are working smarter, not harder. This is creation in motion. Once you extract your desires and plans from your head, it leaves space for other things, taking away some static build-up and encouraging mental clarity.

Affirmations by Deepak Chopra[20]

Positive affirmations are a powerful way to embed empowering thought seeds into your mind. Repetition of these affirmations when holding the vibration of faith can deliver positive change into one's life. For maximum effect, repeat these three times in the morning, looking into your eyes in the mirror, holding true expectation.

'**I will** put the Law of Pure Potentiality into effect by making a commitment to take the following steps':

(1) **I will** get in touch with the field of pure potentiality by taking time each day to be silent, to just be. **I will** also sit alone in silent meditation at least twice a day for approximately thirty minutes in the morning and thirty minutes in the evening.

(2) **I will** take time each day to commune with nature and to silently witness the intelligence within every living thing. **I will** sit silently and watch a sunset, or listen to the sound of the ocean or a stream, or simply smell the scent of a flower. In the ecstasy of my own silence, and by communing with nature, **I will** enjoy the life throb of ages, the field of pure potentiality and unbounded creativity.

(3) **I will** practice non-judgment. **I will** begin my day with the statement, 'Today**, I shall** judge nothing that occurs', and throughout the day **I will** remind myself not to judge.'

(4) **I will** practice Acceptance. Today **I will** accept people, situations, circumstances, and events as they occur. **I will** know that this moment is as it should be, because the whole universe is as it should be. **I will** not struggle against the whole universe by struggling against this moment. My acceptance is total and complete. I accept things as they are this moment, not as I wish they were.

(5) **Having accepted** things as they are, **I will** take Responsibility for my situation and for all those events I see as problems. **I know** that taking responsibility means not blaming anyone or anything for my situation (and this includes myself). **I also know** that every problem is an opportunity in disguise, and this alertness to opportunities allows me to take this moment and transform it into a greater benefit.

(6) **Today** my awareness **will** remain established in Defencelessness. **I will** relinquish the need to defend my point of view. I will feel no need to convince or persuade others to accept my point of view. **I will** remain open to all points of view and not be rigidly attached to any one of them.

A powerful affirmation for when you feel stuck is: **Whatever I need is already here, and it is all for my highest good.** Jot this down and post it conspicuously throughout your home, on the dashboard of your car, at your office, on your microwave oven and even in front of your toilets! Remind yourself: **I live in a friendly universe that will support anything or desire that is aligned with the universal Source of all.**

I attract whatever I desire into my life. I desire love. I desire peace. I desire health. I desire happiness. I desire prosperity.

YUSA Daily unfoldment planning

Some write autobiographies; others write diaries. The problem with this is that it is all past tense and encourages mental thought forms that revisit what has already been and gone. If you are serious about achieving what you want in life, then you must take some time out and make daily planning your ritual.

This method is very simple. You need a black ballpoint pen and a small A5 notepad. In the mornings, take just five minutes to write out some desires and goals for the day in past tense. **Example:** *'Today is the best day of my life. This is the day that I have awaited. I am thankful for all the positive people that engaged with me today and the wonderful positive circumstances that came directly to me. I am driving the car of my dreams, and I excel greatly in my field of work. In my sphere of reality, I attract large sums of money easily, and the joy of my internal wealth flows greatly into the external. Today is truly beautiful, and I had a positive impact on other people's lives'.*

That is just an example. Again, ensure when writing you are feeling super positive and giving out high vibratory emotions. Most importantly, when creating your day, ensure you write with your *left hand*. Writing with your left hand will stimulate and activate the right hemisphere of the brain, in turn opening you up to a flow of creativity that gets absorbed into the subconscious mind.

Write out one A5 sheet every morning, and hold true faith that your day is brilliant. There is only this day, no other. Make sure you keep each piece of paper, and read it back to yourself with enthusiasm. To take this ritual to the next level, at the start of every month, collect all of the pages you wrote out in the previous month (should be around 30 pages if you do this properly), and burn them outside at night when the new moon is present. By doing this, you are now sending the written vibrations into another energetic structure: *energy cannot be destroyed, only transformed.* Your plans and affirmations are now in the higher ethers. The new moon symbolises the seed planting stage, whilst new moon represents harvesting time. You can find the dates of each monthly new moon here: **www.moonconnection.com.**

Audio entrainment jogging

Audio entrainment is a powerful way to aid reprogramming, especially when the audio is built on specific frequencies and tones that the subconscious recognises but your conscious mind fails to pick up. This is the simplest method; allow about 15 minutes jogging time, preferably once a day.

The best audios are classical music, natural sounds and Chinese flute music. You can also use 'I AM' affirmation audios. YUSA have a variety on the YouTube channel for you to experiment with. Natural sound waves enhance balance and a harmonious frequency into the neurons of your brain. It rewires the brain if you will, more so when the oxygen and blood levels have been increased. This is why this method is ten times more efficient whilst running. When jogging with the 'I AM' affirmations, start to repeat the I AMs in your mind and feel the underlying sense of power they deliver.

Attracting money

Money is a burden for many, many people. On the deepest level, humans seem to repel money from their reality solely because of their negative belief system surrounding it. As you know, you cannot attract anything into your life if you are focused on the 'lack of' it. You can probably think back to a time when you were completely broke. All that was going around in your mind and out of your mouth was 'I need money', 'I want money', 'I have no money' etc. Remember, when you say or think in desperate terms, you are only expressing your 'lack of' to the universe. You are the creator; the universe is the responder.

A good trick is to keep a bundle of notes in your pocket when going about daily activities, a bunch of £5 notes, for example. The reason for the £5 notes is that it feels like you really have a large wad of cash when you stuff it all in your pocket. Keep it in a top shirt pocket close to your heart. As you walk around and feel it in your pocket, keep repeating positive money affirmations in your head such as: 'I AM richly rewarded with money. Money flows to me easily. I always have money'. When you go to spend the cash from your top pocket, you will not feel as bad, as to the mind, multiple £5 notes seem a much smaller amount in comparison to £10s, £20s etc.

Another factor you may not be aware of that is largely responsible for you not being able to attract money are the feelings and thoughts you produce when you spend it or give it out. Many do not like to spend money, and when they do they produce a negative emotion in the heart. This only embeds energetic vibrations into your being, which in turn bring about circumstances where your money runs from you. To turn this around, you must hold gratitude for what you are about to receive in exchange for the money. Repeat positive thoughts in your head such as 'I am thankful for this money, and I am helping others to improve their lives by giving it away'. Do not feel bad about it. Be thankful that you have it in the first place, and hold the feeling and thought that plenty more is coming your way as you give it out. Giving is receiving in universal law. Do not put up resistance.

Think of yourself as a container for wealth. If your container is small and your money is big, what's going to happen? You will lose it. Your container will overflow, and the excess money will spill out all over the place. You simply cannot have more money than the container. Therefore, you must grow to be a big container so you cannot only hold more wealth but also attract more wealth. The universe harbours a vacuum, and if you have a very large money container, it will rush in to fill the space.

'Everything is energy and that is all there is to it. Match your frequency to the vibration of the reality you want and you cannot help but get that reality. It can be no other way. This is not philosophy, this is physics'. ~ **Albert Einstein.**

YUSA Creation optimisation

So, you hold knowledge regarding your formless energetic structure, emotions and thoughts all work in unison and can attract circumstances and events into your reality similar to the law of gravity. Creation optimisation is about giving you some hints and tips that will raise your energetic vibration. When you work on raising your overall energetic frequency, you then harness greater energy and power to direct toward manifestation and healing.

Below are the main steps to take when wanting to enhance your creator potential and energetic vibration:

- Meditation practices to still useless thoughts and bring forth enhanced mental clarity.
- Subconscious re-programming that favour your desires.
- Stepping away from judgemental patterns of thought.
- Breathing deeply, eradicating fear and being grounded to the present moment
- Acceptance, surrender and looking for the best in life's problems.
- Reconnecting to the heart space and practicing stillness.
- Working on any energetic blockages in your chakra energy system.
- Realising the bigger picture of the soul's journey and reasons for pain and suffering.
- Body detoxification, eradicating toxins and deeply rooted heavy metals.
- Physical CHI building exercise.
- Fasting for super health and spiritual awareness.
- A natural diet full of living enzymes and superfoods.
- Reconnecting with nature on the whole.

All of the above topics are expressed in detail throughout this book. The main aim is to take segments of information from each section to suit your needs, then start to make the changes desired to bring balance into your life.

Brain regeneration

How do you regenerate your brain, eliminate depression and improve your outlook to increase your happiness level? Easy! Sunlight on your skin and in your eyes, as much fresh, unpolluted air as possible. Get outside to play, and breathe deep! Essential fats like flax, hemp and coconut protect your brain and the myelin sheath on your nerves.

The brain is more than 60% fat. Long-term low-fat diets are dangerous! Be smart. Glucose from fruits and vegetables are the number-one source of energy for the brain. Fresh fruit and vegetable juices are rocket fuel for the body and mind. Avoid negative people. Love those who hate you. Develop a love relationship with yourself. Take yourself out on a date. Be your own best friend. Relinquish the need to criticise yourself or anybody else. It will kill you slowly. Get more than enough sleep. Wake up slowly every chance you get. Your brain loves sleep. Listen to classical music to build healthy neurons and inspire creativity.

Meditation balances the left and right hemispheres of the brain. Cuddle with your partner, friend or pet to increase oxytocin and release feel-good chemicals. Read spiritual books to give you hope and inspiration. Surrender attachments. The joy of life is inside of you. (The kingdom of heaven is within you.) It does not depend on external conditions.

One of the most important decisions you'll ever make is choosing the kind of universe you exist in: is it helpful and supportive or hostile and unsupportive? Your answer to this question will make all the difference in terms of how you live your life and what kind of Divine assistance you attract.

Remember that you experience exactly what you feel and think about, whether you want it or not. So if you believe that this is an unfriendly universe, you'll attract examples to support this specific point of view. You'll anticipate people attempting to cheat, judge, take advantage of and otherwise harm you. You'll blame the antagonistic, inhospitable cosmos for not cooperating with you in the fulfilment of your desires. You'll point the finger at belligerent people and bad luck for the kind of world we all live in.

YUSA implore you to see the universe as a warm and supportive one because you'll attract sufficient evidence to support this view. When you anticipate that the universe is friendly, you see friendly people. You look for circumstances to work in your favour. You anticipate good fortune flowing into your life.

'Our greatest ally and enemy is our own minds. Do not underestimate its ability to create, convolute, mutate, evolve, integrate, break down, segmentise and more at the same time' ~ Shamala Tan[21], Holistic health coach

Ten tips for prosperity by Peter Ragner[22], The longevity sage

Tip #1 'Let your close association be only with thankful, appreciative people, who know how to say, thank you' and ask nothing in return'.

Tip #2 'Never listen to the whiner or complainer, if you do, you may just begin to feel the world is unjust and unfair. The complainers throw hot coals into your eyes and blind you to the beauty and richness that is yours. Avoid complainers like the plague'.

Tip #3 'Associate only with people who follow through and those whose word is their honour. People who do not do what they say are dishonest. Dishonesty breeds poverty on all levels of being'.

Tip #4 'End each day by writing all the blessings you have incurred that day; all the reasons to say, thank you. You will sleep sweetly and richly. Your night will be a continuous affirmation of prosperity'.

Tip #5 'Make beauty a god and worship it in everything you see, feel, and experience. Then your life will be beautiful, peaceful, and rich. Remember, ugliness becomes beauty when you see the reason for contrast. The star shines more brightly because the night is dark'.

Tip #6 'Do not envy others. For to do so is only to affirms your own lack. If you envy others, you are only saying, poor me. So be it ... you have two wishes left'!

Tip #7 'Rejoice and celebrate in others' success. For some this may be difficult, and yet, this is another overlooked universal law. You will never be successful until you first love success in others'.

Tip #8 'Let your self-talk be free of condemnation. Learn from your mistakes and forget them. That's why pencils have erasers on them. If you focus on your mistakes, remember, you get what you set'!

Tip #9 'Value time, spend it wisely. Don't allow others to steal it with trivia. Many people have lots of time, while other people have lots of money. The prosperous person has both'.

Tip # 10 'You must be rich inside first, if outer richness is to have any meaning. You will only become rich outside by enriching the lives of others. You will only become rich inside when you can understand what real value is all about. Never confuse glass with diamonds ... a few diamonds go a long way'!

Before You Judge Others or Claim Any Absolute Truth, Remember That:

You can see less than 1% of the electromagnetic spectrum and hear less than 1% of the acoustic spectrum. As you read this, you are travelling 220 kilometres per second across the galaxy. Ninety percent of the cells in your body carry their own microbial DNA and are not 'you'. The atoms in your body are 99.99999999999999% empty space. None of those are the ones you were born with, but all originated in the belly of a star. Human beings have 46 chromosomes, two less than the common potato. The existence of a rainbow depends on the conical photoreceptors in your eyes: to animals without cones, the rainbow does not exist. So you don't look at the rainbow; you create it. This is pretty amazing, especially considering that all the colours you see represent less than 1% of the electromagnetic spectrum.

Chapter 2, Spirit.

The spirit is not a topic that is largely discussed in the Western world. If you ask yourself 'What is spirit', you are basically asking who you really are beyond the limitations of form and body. When your awareness allows you to come to the deep realisation that your very own natural state is in the form of spirit—that is, formless—you can still be deluded by the mind and the ego's sense of self.

You must master your mind, ego and emotional body so that you can realise to a greater extent that your spirit is not something outside of you; rather, it has major involvement in everything you feel, think and do. Once you overcome the continuous cascade of thoughts, emotions and sensations reconnecting with the heart space then life unfolds in a unique and magical way.

Society's conditioning is directed towards distracting and disconnecting your conscious awareness from your PURE AWARENESS, causing the majority of humanity to become lost and to forget the roots and soul purpose for their current incarnation.

Within every single person lies a powerful light that is awake and encoded in the fibres of human existence. Divine ecstasy is the totality of this marvellous creation experienced in the hearts of humanity. The majority of the population has lost touch with its divine essence, steering many away from the activation of unconditional love needed in order for the current system to be modified. A system where unity is the necessary foundation for the planet's survival.

Within this planet's third-density physical reality, exists linear time, duality and separations that offer each soul unique opportunities for evolutionary development. This development involves incarnating into a density in which time and space appear real. When you enter the lower third-dimensional world, the conscious memory of many previous experiences is temporarily lost, alongside your spiritual blueprint and approved earthly contract for this incarnation.

All souls inhabiting temporary human body vehicles are believed to have originated from ALL THAT IS—light source, energy and universal creators. Each energetic spiritual body holds a unique evolutionary purpose; your purpose for being on earth is known by your higher self. All material form has a limited lifespan. Your true energetic soul self, however, is highly intelligent and immortal. Energy can only be transferred, never destroyed.

In addition to taking care of your physical body, you also have a responsibility to focus your priorities on your energetic body. Your luminous energy field and chakra system are closely related to the physical body, organs and your emotional wellbeing. To maintain a healthy body, it is highly important to ensure that your energetic makeup is functioning optimally and is balanced for maximum energetic flow. Blockages in these systems are amongst the main factors contributing to disease and depression.

When a person can halt the incessant stream of thoughts and 'get out' of the mind, he or she can then truly start to feel the inner body and stillness that lies much deeper within. When a person can truly embrace and live fully in the present moment and operate from the heart space, he or she is met with a formless, timeless presence that holds vastness. A deeper dimension which uncovers the language of the universe. Allowing this to flow can bring miracles into your life.

In this chapter, YUSA delves deeper into the numerous aspects of the heart, energy field, Kundalini, sacred geometry, DNA and more, and is ultimately written to give you a deeper understanding of the true self and assist you towards remembering what is real. This chapter expands on healing modalities that develop different aspects of your being so that you can utilise the information and align yourself with the greater good for personal and spiritual development.

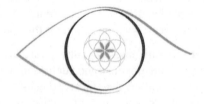

The Infinite Heart

Spirituality is not a belief system or ideology; it entails surrendering one's ego to the infinite wisdom and knowledge that is the universe. Humanity as a whole is still in the learning process of reconnecting with and living back within the heart space. It has been around 13,000 years since the human race 'left the heart' and went to the brain.

This is described as 'the fall' in biblical texts (Joshua 14 v. 2). Such a long time has passed that many do not even know that there is another way to exist. Living in this space is literally a moving of spiritual awareness from the mind, into the heart. It is not something that you think about, such as 'OK, I am in my heart', as this is merely your imagination. When you truly shift your awareness deep into the heart and begin to operate out of compassion, it changes your life forever and, in turn, slowly changes the world.

Upon shifting your awareness into the heart space, the true way of life and the deep nature of existence will unfold and become recognisable again. Almost all life in existence resides in the heart, not the mind, and most of the universe is in love with itself, as one spirit moves through everything. When you make the shift from the mind to the heart, you come to the realisation that you are a great deal more than you thought you were. The realisation of the true potential of life arises in your reality which is beyond measure.

The initial steps in being able to solve **all** the planetary problems in the world today are quite simple. You do not have to try to protect yourself by digging a hole in the ground and filling it with guns. It is a very specific thing, which many ancient civilisations spoke about. Tuning into a vibration—a very specific frequency that needs to be activated within your own heart.

You simply need to *be* in the heart, not the polarity of the mind and to feel the connection with the heart of the earth! When you connect with the heart of the earth/Gaia, you then understand that it is a living being, the mother of humanity. The final step is then to connect to the heart of the sun, which is the bringer of life and information (light codes). This is the construct of the Trinity—child, mother and father— the three points of connection, wholeness and complete balance.

Upon embracing this connection, a very specific vibrational frequency is created within the sacred space of your heart. When you hold this vibration and connection to mother and father, you can never be harmed; you will always be protected and connected. An energetic shift then takes place in your heart's electrical field as this finely tuned frequency is brought to life. This frequency is extremely high, and it stands strong with the emotion of unconditional love.

This is a state of fearlessness—of being in love with life, the earth, the sun and yourself. You then realise your connection to all life everywhere. Reality is a function of human consciousness, and it appears to be holographic in nature. Your heart and emotions play the largest role in the creation of your reality.

For humans to transcend properly into the heart, all of the lower vibratory energies and emotions of a lower nature which are stored must be dealt with and willingly accepted so that they can be eradicated in a loving manner. Love cannot shine through a cloudy heart filled with hate.

On the planet, there is war, pain, disease, starvation and suffering. There is, in fact, something much greater going on—a bigger picture. It is something that is exciting and extraordinary beyond humanity's current understanding. There is in fact a great deal of hope as everything that is going on in the world today has a much higher spiritual purpose, one which is beautiful, far reaching into the realms of higher consciousness.

It can take a while to comprehend, but each and every individual on the planet is actually far more than just a simple 'person' so to speak. You have in your heart something that is beyond the measure of what anybody knows in the world; it is not something that just simply beats. One who is connected to the universe in this manner holds more power than a million who are not, everything in which the soul yearns for resides on the opposite side of fear.

If you feel yourself being gripped by the illusory limitations of fear, greed, jealousy, hate, anger, etc., just open yourself up to life on the whole alongside what it is you deeply desire. Remember that you are on the right track and certain setbacks are needed for the purpose of growth. Be mindful of dissociating from these feelings just as much as over-identifying with them. Neither of them is the truth of you, but healing your perception of them is necessary.

Practice the arts of diaphragmatic belly breathing in order to release any blockages which remain stagnant within in your energy field. Keep moving and keep going. Act from, and remember that you are, pure love. There is no hurry in love, only truth, and the truth will set you free from any illusion that binds you into limitation.

'At any moment you have a choice, that either leads you closer to spirit or further away from it' ~ **Thich Naht Hahn**

The hearts brain & consciousness

Many believe that conscious awareness originates within the brain alone. Recent scientific research suggests that consciousness actually emerges from the brain and body acting together. A growing amount of evidence suggests that the heart plays a particularly significant role in this process, again, far more than a simple pump as the heart is now recognised by scientists as a highly complex system with its own functional 'brain', so to speak. The brain in the heart is so small that it is composed of around 40,000 cells only.

There is a new discipline of neuroradiology emerging in the field of science and technology. The research conducted proves that the heart is actually a highly sophisticated sensory organ and that, just like the brain, it is a processing agent for high-level information.

The complex nervous system found in the hearts physical structure supports its ability to learn, remember and make functional decisions as an entity which is independent to the cerebral cortex of the brain. Numerous experiments and bodies of research have demonstrated that signals sent from the heart and its nervous system have an immense influence on the higher, more refined brain centres that are responsible for emotions, cognition and perception.

The heart communicates information with the brain and body via a complex system of electromagnetic field interactions; this is separate to the physical neural connection, indicating there is more than one information gateway transmittance from this centre of intelligence. The heart is actually the organ that generates the most powerful and extensive rhythmic electromagnetic field in the human body. Scientists have compared the electric heart field against that of the brain and concluded that the heart field has greater amplitude—of around 60 times— and it permeates every cell in the body.

The heart's magnetic component, however, is a massive 5000 times stronger than the brain's magnetic field and is picked up by sensitive magnetometers several feet away. This ever-present field has a huge impact on specific processes throughout the physical body, the brain being one of them as it works to stay in synchronisation with the heart's frequencies in order for it to stay in balance.

Your respiratory rhythms, blood pressure and sustained flow of emotion also synchronise with the heart's electromagnetic rhythm. Whether it be high vibratory emotions such love, gratitude and excitement or lower vibratory emotions such as fear, hate and anger, will in fact impact your energy field at the deepest level. Whichever vibration is sustained for the most consistent period of time within the subtle energy field of the heart, will determine the quality of your life experience on the whole.

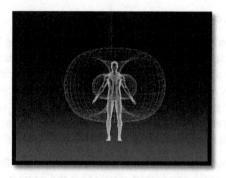

Diagrammatic representation of the toroidal heart energy field

The heart and emotional balance

You are now aware that your heart is a complex, highly intuitive part of your being. You know that it is the centre for creation, beyond the mental, producing a high magnetic field of energy. Emotions and breath work can be a very dominant aspect to the biorhythms of the heart, brain and body.

Emotional streams have a very sensitive impact towards the heart's energetic vibratory frequencies. Your emotional state is communicated throughout your body in alignment with the heart's electromagnetic field. As you may know, your heart rate fluctuates upon feeling a range of emotions, significantly changing the rhythmic beating patterns. The emotions that reside in the lower state of vibration such as anger, frustration, jealousy and envy are associated with an erratic, disordered and incoherent rhythmic pattern, ultimately releasing distorted vibratory frequencies along the universal field.

It has been mentioned that the heart's magnetic field is 5000 times stronger than that of the brain, serving as a very interesting indication towards the sheer power of emotions in comparison to thoughts! The realm of the mind and the realm of the heart are very different indeed. The brain and mind deal with time and duality/polarity but the heart however is completely variant; it deals towards the infinite and universal source energy, connecting you to stillness and the timeless presence of all life. You are nothing less than an extension of the divine.

The energetic, electrical field of the heart merges with your feelings and emotions on a subatomic level. Therefore communicating hyper dimensionally through the interconnecting universal web of synapses and neurons which connect us all as one. Whichever vibrational frequency you choose to embrace in the present moment, will be matched instantaneously and rebounded back into your sphere of reality in the form of circumstances and events that make you feel the same way.

This is the deepest aspect of the law of attraction and how the law operates when creating from the heart space; you receive only what you give out so it is very important that you control lower-vibratory emotions and start to take full control of your hearts intelligence!

Negative emotions wreak havoc towards the heart's electromagnetic field, providing little benefit to the brain, body, or health in general. The brain and body are constantly working towards balancing the sine waves in relation to the heart, as it is the source of all creation. How can you expect to have mental clarity, healthy blood pressure and a strong nervous system when the foundation of balance is completely distorted? The heart is greatly overlooked by many, it needs the due care and attention **you** deserve.

On the contrary, higher vibrational emotions towards the more positive end of the scale such as love, appreciation and gratitude are closely associated to a smoother, ordered and highly structural pattern in the hearts rhythmic activity. In turn, these changes encourage more of a harmonious energetic imprint that is released into the ethers by your heart and returned back into your sphere of reality in the form of positive circumstances and events. Positive heart rhythms exhibit an organised sine wave-like pattern, and the heart's electromagnetic field becomes correspondingly more organised. With new technological advancements the heart's field can now be measured with a technique known as **spectral analysis**.

Breathing and the heart

Breathing is very important for balancing the heart's biorhythms. Deep breathing encourages an expansion in the diameter of the heart's toroidal field, creating a larger energetic flow surrounding the physical body. Many seem to have a very weak energetic structure radiating from the heart; this can be largely due to shallow breathing alone, using only one third of the lungs' surface area, neglecting the region of the diaphragm.

Deep and diaphragmatic breathing through the nose encourages the production of Chi/Qi energy. In chapter 1 we touched on the electrical discharge which takes place as the two vortexes as ether/air are inhaled. This Chi/Qi energy is directed towards powering the conductivity of the heart's electromagnetic field and increasing your energy levels. Anytime you feel frustrated or detect any low-vibrational emotions, take a few minutes to do some deep belly breathing; this practice is known as **golden bridge breathing**.

Your every breath has an outward and an inward spiral, expiration and inspiration. The flow of the breath follows the same pattern of the evolutionary spiral which is a universal basic, the *uni*-verse, the **one** turn. It is also said that each of us has breathed in and out the same atoms as everyone else in existence.

When your heart and breath are in synchrony, (when your breath moves in, your heart rate goes up, and when your breath moves out, your heart rate goes down), you get greater heart rate variability (HRV), which is known to be a correlate and/or cause of better health, longevity, positive emotions, greater cognitive function, improved immune function, increased intuition (direct knowledge) and protection against negativity.

The heart's magnetic field between you and others

Communication in the social world is known to involve verbal language, facial expressions, bodily movements and other physical gestures. There is now evidence that the hearts electromagnetic/energetic communication system plays a huge role that is subtle yet highly influential. This system operates on a level just below your conscious awareness; the magnetic factor is responsible for attractions and repulsions between individuals, thus having the most impact on your friend circles and relationship choices.

Moreover, it appears that the heart's field plays an important role in communicating physiological, psychological and social information between individuals. *Representation of the toroidal field to the right.*

Institute of HeartMath experiments

'Experiments conducted at the Institute of HeartMath have found remarkable evidence that the heart's electromagnetic field can transmit information between people. We have been able to measure an exchange of heart energy between individuals up to 5 feet apart. We have also found that one person's brain waves can actually synchronize to another person's heart. Furthermore, when an individual is generating a coherent heart rhythm, synchronization between that person's brain waves and another person's heartbeat is more likely to occur. These findings have intriguing implications, suggesting that individuals in a psycho-physiologically coherent state become more aware of the information encoded in the heart fields of those around them.

The results of these experiments have led us to infer that the nervous system acts as an 'antenna', which is tuned to and responds to the electromagnetic fields produced by the hearts of other individuals. We believe this capacity for exchange of energetic information is an innate ability that heightens awareness and mediates important aspects of true empathy and sensitivity to others Furthermore, we have observed that this energetic communication ability can be intentionally enhanced, producing a much deeper level of nonverbal communication, understanding, and connection between people. There is also intriguing evidence that heart field interactions can occur between people and animals.'

'Our energetic fields respond to trauma and healing energies. They also react to emotions and love. When two people interrelate, their energy fields experience distortions and merge. We can even swap energy with people hundreds of miles away.' ~ Mohsen Paul Sarfarazi, PhD[23]

Intuition of the heart

The hearts intelligence can perceive information before your brain. Research suggests that the heart field operates in alignment with an energetic information field way out of the bounds of space and time, giving it capabilities that are involved with intuitive perception.

'Using a rigorous experimental design, we found compelling evidence that both the heart and brain receive and respond to information about a future event before the event actually happens. Even more surprising was our finding that the heart appears to receive this 'intuitive' information before the brain. This suggests that the heart's field may be linked to a more subtle energetic field that contains information on objects and events remote in space or ahead in time. Called by Karl Pribram and others the 'spectral domain', this is a fundamental order of potential energy that enfolds space and time, and is thought to be the basis for our consciousness of the whole.' ~ HeartMath research.

This research suggests that the heart is the main gateway or connection to the unseen realm, the realm of infinite intelligence and stillness. The heart is located at the centre of the body; it is the pivot point, the star gate that needs to be unlocked for the evolution of expression, emotion, consciousness and connection to all that is. Start to **feel more** and **think less**!

'In the heart of man the whole universe is reflected; and as the whole universe is reflected in it, man may be called the heart of the universe.' ~ Hazrat Inayat Khan[24]

Making the shift to the hearts universal presence

We covered some basic information surrounding the heart to give you an idea of its other properties besides beating, whilst mentioning that returning to the heart and rising from the low-vibrational limitations is humanity's next step in evolution.

Shifting from the headspace to the heart space is easier said than done. The main distraction that makes it hard to shift is the incessant thought patterns in one's mind. Worries, challenges, fears and external distractions are constantly in motion for many people, literally sucking life force from the mind, encouraging the need for mental simulation so they can hold on a little longer.

All of the distraction-thought forms must be put to rest in your mind in order to tap into the unlimited potential of the heart. You must gain discipline and mastery over the mind so it can rest. Stop labelling, stop making unnecessary judgements and reduce all negative/fearful thought forms that encourage distortions throughout the heart's electromagnetic field. The mind's limiting language is largely based on 'should' and 'have to' thoughts.

Limiting options will always be primary for as long as your sphere of reality is dominated by the mind. Operating from the mind alone encourages the return of memories, programs, beliefs and assumptions largely based from previous experiences. However, when you're awareness is saturated within the heart space, you have made a huge leap towards stillness, the stillness of thought; now the biorhythms of the brain and heart are compatible, giving you extreme clarity of mind and alertness. You are now grounded into the now, where creation takes place, outside the illusory time construct of the mind.

When you are consciously in the heart, you feel in love with everybody and everything around you. The feeling you get when you fall madly in love with a partner is now present with you at all times. Everything you give out and attract in your life is now wonderful; you are in alignment with all that is, universal love. Every frequency you give from the heart has a harmonious rhythm carrying high-vibrational emotions. You then attract others into your sphere of reality those who are also connected to the heart and who also live a wonderful, prosperous life where fear is absent. You tune into the universal stream of abundance, back into your natural state of being.

Those who reside mainly in the headspace tend to be caught up in drama, to do things they feel they 'should', even though they know deep down they don't want to. It's not much fun. A way of settling into the heart space is to train and focus your thoughts towards the things that you love, base decisions from the hearts intelligence by asking yourself 'What is best for me' and choosing the option that makes you feel amazing!

The presence experienced from meditation, conscious breathing, eating natural plant-based foods and reconnecting with nature are the most beneficial if you want to become harmonious with your heart centre.

The Biorhythms of nature are very soothing and healing; they flow through the essence of your very being aligning you with the earth's own eternal rhythm. As you work on the biggest project of your life, which is you, your awareness starts to detach from the realm of thought and into the body. Your life starts to become what you always loved and desired; confidence and self-worth grows; and you will not be easily derailed from the overpowering goodness that now flows through you.

This is not to say that you will never face difficulty again in life, but you'll understand on a deep level that challenging periods will pass and will make you a stronger, happier person too! Remember that you are the creator of your life experience. This saying expresses it perfectly:

Watch your thoughts, for they become words. Watch your words, for they become actions. Watch your actions, for they become habits. Watch your habits, for they become character. Watch your character, for it becomes your destiny.

Self-love, Acceptance & Forgiveness

Another major factor contributing to humanity's distant heart connection is that of self-love, self-acceptance and self-forgiveness. Despite all the things you think are wrong with you, love yourself for who you are and what you have achieved so far in life. Remember that many thought patterns and belief systems ultimately, are not real; there are thousands of other beliefs and thoughts with which you could label yourself. This is the beauty of the heart space—that all of these false identifications of self-cease to exist.

You cannot truly love another person with deep compassion if you fail to love yourself and accept who you are completely at the deepest level. Social conditioning contributes to the illusory layers which cover the true self. Think of it this way: your true heart/self is a rock on a beach, every time a large wave flows onto the beach, the stone is left with multiple layers of sand on top, which is not part of the rock itself. But remember, the rock is forever constant and remains intact beneath.

This metaphor can be related to external programming of the heart and mind in the way in which your true self can be covered and you are then left with illusory idealisms about yourself. For example, the television will run rampant in your mind and implant illusions on what a pretty woman or a healthy man is supposed to look like and how somebody is supposed to act. Over time, these programs can have deep subconscious impact, making you hate yourself for no reason. Remember there is absolutely nobody better than **you**.

Once you start to acknowledge deep-rooted belief systems, then it is time to work on them and bring them to the surface. Start to write things down so that your mind has more room for the solutions. Create a comparison table of the pros and cons of yourself and make small, constructive steps for self-betterment.

What can you forgive yourself for today? Holding a grudge against yourself is a silly thing to do. Again, it is like constantly holding a piece of hot coal, burning only yourself unless **you** make the decision to accept and let it go. Whatever it may be, you should practice affirmations every day for example; 'I forgive myself for saying 'I hate you' to my father right before he died when I was eight years old. I carried it around for many years and let it colour my life in a dark way.' 'I forgive myself for not being perfect.'

When you are depressed and hold self-hate, you are still living in the past, not the present. You are not present because the old, deeply rooted stories in the subconscious still come up to haunt you and take away your attention. This is the deception of the mind. Can you see the pattern of how the mind takes your attention from the true self? This is the test of life. In chapter 1, we cover the subconscious mind and steps for reprogramming, wiping away old belief systems and replacing them with the new—anybody can do it as long as the right attitude is expressed.

Deep acceptance of the past is realised when you develop an 'inner-standing' of traumas, problems, mistakes, your actions that hurt others, and others' actions that hurt you. Understanding that they are contracted within your soul and serve a much higher purpose for evolution is required. Third-density reality is tough. Let the past issues go and start healing yourself. You really have to fight for life, and, in the end, it is very worth it.

Drop the victim mentality and stop labelling/judging past situations. The only thing that is important is what you choose to do right now. Everybody is doing their best life in accordance to their level of consciousness. Try not to become attached to externals. The heart does not need anything else; it receives naturally. Forgiveness is a karmic closure to yourself and others, try not to confuse attachment with love.

'Attachment is about fear and dependency, and has nothing to do with love of self than love of another. Love without attachment is the purest love because it isn't about what others can give you because you're empty. It is about what you can give to others because you are already full.' ~ Yasmin Mogahed[25]

Optimising reality with the heart

There are so many who speak and write about the law of attraction. Highly recognised books such as *The Secret* and some of Napoleon Hill's writings are mainly focused towards creating with the mind and thoughts. These authors fail to realise that the instrument (brain) that the creation is manifested through is, in fact a polarised tool. YUSA delivers the knowledge of creation from the brain/mind but more importantly highlights the drawbacks and guides you to the heart space, in order to create from the powerful centre of spirit.

The brain is a polarised, as it deals in concepts of duality, left and right, positive and negative etc. We mention this topic briefly in chapter 1. The brain lobes go through 64 different divisions, the same 64 divisions/codons that are in the human DNA lineage. It is possible to bring towards you what you want through your intentions when creating with the mind/brain, but what you will also get is the exact and equal opposite force coming from behind what you can't see, as the law of duality is at work.

There are around 7 billion humans on planet earth, and most of them want peace; those who pray for world peace are going to get a world that is partially at peace and partially at war as long as they pray from the brain. They are always going to get the results of half peace, half war until they learn to create in a different way. There is another way, a way that many ancient people and Tibetan Buddhists speak of, which is creating from where the original stars and planets where created from, which is the heart.

If you can step out of the brain, throw it away and get out of there, you can create anything you desire and even change the world. This way, you will not get the opposite effect. Another way to explain this is that you have two heart chakras (spinning vortex of energy), one just above the sternum and another above that (the distance of your nose to your chin).

The lower chakra is connected directly to the heart, whilst the upper chakra is synchronised to the right brain and the emotional body, everybody is familiar with experiencing love, joy, hate and sadness. All of these emotions stem from the right brain and are interconnected with the higher heart chakra.

What many do not know is that there is another emotional body. Directly connected to the heart, this emotional body has no polarity, as it exists outside the realm of linear space and time, a higher-dimensional source of energy.

This is the only place where the unconditional love that many teachers talk about can be realised. Love is not from the brain (where most people get married from), where one may say something to their partner that damages their ego, and, just like that, they hate them. The love from the heart is unconditional, exactly like the unconditional love you receive from your spirit guides and soul family: no matter what you do or did, they will still love you unconditionally. Women usually get this feeling for short spaces of time, especially when giving birth.

'For as he thinketh in his heart, so is he...' (Proverbs 23:7 kjv)

I AM Realisation, stillness

The realisation of who you really are is coming to the 'inner-standing' of who you are not. Self-realisation is a realisation of one's original identity or 'oneness' with the universal creator. Self-realisation is a state where the 'I' becomes the 'He'. Self-realisation reveals that what many call God is inside one's own self. This should be interpreted as an insight of not 'my awareness,' but the 'Beings' awareness of itself in me.

Self-realisation is a process where the Jiva (as self) identifies itself with universal creator (as self). The self in man is the ultimate substance behind the world of phenomena. The highest form of yoga is the attainment of Jiva with the Supreme Self. The individual soul is merged with the absolute.

SELF-REALISATION.... AS I EXPERIENCED BY THE GRACE OF MY 'SELF' ~ by Sri Premanandaji[26]

I AM unchanging, eternal existence. I AM not body because body is changing and it is in different shapes at different phases of life. I AM not mind because mind is a bundle of thoughts that are coming and going, always changing.

I AM not emotions because sometimes I AM angry, sometimes sad and sometimes happy. They are changing all the day. I AM not father, brother, engineer, or handsome I AM not any of these labels as they are changing. I AM not this or that.... I AM not changing... I AM not birth or death... I AM Soul. What is Soul? Vedas call its pure consciousness.

What is consciousness? I don't know what it is... because it's beyond the grasping of my mind. However, searching... searching.... I remain in stillness with a question who am I? What is Soul? What is consciousness? My mind stops thinking and remains in search state. It's an 'I don't know' state. Suddenly grace happens and I know that knowingness of I am in an 'I don't know' state of consciousness.

An Ah... moment comes and truth dawns on me. I am in a state of silence... awareness... knowingness... unidentified... oneness.... remain as existence.... is....Truth.... I AM.... I AM.... I AM.... I AM.... Now I know first-hand; I AM source, I AM pure consciousness, I AM existence, I AM OM, I AM love, I AM bliss, I AM eternal, I AM, I AM....

Stillness

You can laugh at challenges when you have nothing to prove, nothing to gain and nothing to want. Why fight over scraps fallen from the table of the mind? Delusions are plentiful. Polish the jewel of your own being and you will discover your own richness. You will discover you have everything you need and more!

All power lies inside of your heart. You do not need external approval! You already possess all that you seek. There is nothing the outside world can give you that you don't already have hidden within. Find that first, and the outside will instantly reflect it back to you. Don't let others deceive you; they have the process in reverse. You have the magic wand already in your hand and are empowered beyond belief.

'Stillness is the language God speaks, and everything else is a bad translation. Stillness is really another word for space. Becoming conscious of stillness whenever we encounter it in our lives will connect us with the formless and timeless dimension within ourselves, that which is beyond thought, beyond ego. It may be the stillness that pervades the world of nature, or the stillness in your room in the early hours of the morning, or the silent gaps in between sounds. Stillness has no form – that is why through thinking we cannot become aware of it. Thought is form. Being aware of stillness means to be still. To be still is to be conscious without thought. You are never more essentially, more deeply, yourself, than when you are still. When you are still, you are who you were before you temporarily assumed this physical and mental form called a person. You are also who you will be when the form dissolves. When you are still, you are who you are beyond your temporal existence: consciousness – unconditioned, formless, and eternal' ~ Eckhart Tolle

Heart meditation

One of the easiest ways to connect with the heart is meditation. Relaxing the body and achieving stillness of the mind, encouraging full focus towards breathing into the hearts energetic centre. You can fully embrace this meditation with or without music, however if you do prefer music, it is recommended that you listen to Tibetan bowls or healing frequencies, preferably 639Hz, as this is the tone of the heart chakra. You can find these on the YUSA YouTube channel.

First find a comfortable place to sit upright; you can sit upright against your bed/wall. Ensure you place a pillow on your lower-back area so your back is slightly arched and your chest sticks out slightly. It is beneficial to have a slight curve in the lower back and the chest out, as it contributes to the opening of the heart energy centre. You can keep your legs straight or have the bottom of your feet touching each other, tucked in a diamond form. Start your music; the use of headphones is recommended to get the full effect of the frequencies.

Now, you are about to attract in the highest good of the universe and manifest abundance into your life. Start to centre yourself by inhaling through the nose and out of your mouth slowly for around **5 minutes**, this gives time for your heart rate to settle and the electromagnetic energy field to become attuned to the audio frequencies. Your Brain will then attune and balance your consciousness into the composed frequency of the heart.

After 5 minutes, start to inhale and exhale deeply and slowly through the **nose** only. As you do this, your attention slowly drifts away from the mind and thoughts. Start to feel a swirling sensation in your chest area, as you breathe deeply in through the nose, direct all of your attention towards this space. Do this for a further **5 minutes** to form a solid connection with the heart. If any thoughts try to distract you, then breathe deeper and slower. Remember to keep your chest slightly raised or out.

You are now **10 minutes** into the meditation; your heart should now be in synchronisation with the audio track, if you chose not to use an audio track then your body should be heading towards stillness and in a deeply relaxed state—**continue breathing** and upon exhalation feel your **heart chakra energy expand** all around your body, become aware of your beautiful heart, how it is opening **and spiralling outwards, grasping all positive energy** and releasing anything that no longer serves you. **Truly feel all of your negative beliefs leaving you** along with anything that may be limiting you from creating positive change in your life.

As you **release all doubts and fears** from the heart space, start **to focus on what you would like to manifest**, for the highest good. **Continue breathing in and out through the nose** and begin to truly, **deeply feel the emotion** you would have at the time your desire manifests in your life, **feel the joy, happiness, peace and serenity** of when you obtain it.

Inhale and exhale whilst **envisioning a beautiful bubble of light** just in front of your **heart chakra;** now place what you would like to have in your life inside the bubble of light, including **images, thoughts and feelings.** Hold the emotions, images and gratitude right in your heart space then bring your attention to the mid-brow region. Take **five powerful deep breaths in through** the nose and print the images of what you like (**situations, events, healing, or materials**) in vivid high-definition colour into your **third eye (mid-brow area).**

Whether its **wealth or riches**, put all of your happiness and energy into the field as you would when it is obtained. If you see money in the bubble, it is only a **symbol of the freedom it can bring.** If there is a person or ideal soul mate, **just see the outline of the beautiful person full of love,** who will love you unconditionally for who you are. Feel the bubble in your chest space grow bigger and bigger, take a deep breath in and exhale making the ball grow bigger and bigger, **charged with emotions and images.**

On every exhalation, imagine and feel the growing bubble slowly **rising up through the throat, brow and crown of the head (crown chakra)** rising up through the **ceiling and through the sky,** into the universe, up to the creator. Your bubble and manifestations are now in the god space and your **intention is complete.** Continue to feel good and **breathe slowly, giving gratitude** for your creation that is on its way to you. Try to practice this every day for **30 minutes.** Log your progress on paper for **30 days** and note the positive change in your life.

'If light is in your heart, you will find your way home.' ~Rumi

Gaia's heartbeat

Planet earth is a living being, she has a soul and an energetic construct just like humans have. The earth holds a feminine energy, and her structure is similar to yours in terms of possessing a chakra energy system that represents different spiritual factors. (The word *chakra* is Sanskrit for 'wheel' and it is used as a name for energetic centres in the body.) These energy points are located at sacred sites over the world such as:

Mt. Shasta, California, USA – Root

Lake Titicaca, Bolivia – Sacral

Ayres Rock, Australia – Solar Plexus

Glastonbury, UK – Heart

Pyramids of Giza, Egypt – Throat

Mt. Kailash, Tibet – Crown

There is also a moving chakra, which is currently at Glastonbury – Third eye

At the centre of each chakra lies a sacred site. A vortex of energy is also formed, encouraging expansion of the chakra outwardly in a circular/spiral fashion. The approximate radius for a healthy, balanced energy point is approximately 777 miles. Gaia's energy points always expand and contract, as they are living energetic organs that are dependent on the complexity of conditions that may affect them. Our ancient ancestors were well aware of this knowledge, and they built their sacred temples and monuments on top of these powerful vortexes. There are also thousands of other sites around the world with strong energy that prompted the ancients to build on them.

The earth's heartbeat is also known as the Schumann resonance, discovered by a German physicist and professor named W. O. Schumann. The ionosphere surrounding the planet is electrically positively charged, whilst the earth's surface carries a negative charge. In between this cavity are large amounts of electrical tensions, wireless, electrical energy if you will. The inside of the ionosphere layer can be used to transfer wireless information and radio waves emitted by transmitters on the earth's surface. In this way, the information can be transferred over large distances.

Nikola Tesla was the first to carry out wireless energy experiments. The experiments he conducted in Colorado Springs, in the USA, produced such powerful electrical tensions that they resulted in the creation of artificial lightning. Tesla found that these lightning flashes also produced radio waves and, because of their extremely low frequency, these waves could penetrate the earth without resistance, and, thereby, Tesla discovered the resonance frequency of the earth.

Just over a century later than Nikola Tesla's findings in 1952, German physicist W. O. Schumann[27] predicted that there are electromagnetic standing waves in the earth's atmosphere. Numerous scientific tests were conducted using ball condensers that acted as capacitors. The main aim for these scientific tests simply was to calculate the frequency between the earth and the ionosphere layer: the frequency back then was standing at 7.83 Hz. This is the electrical measurement of Gaia's heartbeat. Since entering the Photon Belt in 1987, the planetary heartbeat has increased to measurements ranging up to 12.9 Hz.

Gaia's Schumann resonance forms a natural feedback loop with the human mind and body, the underlying vibrational energy field in which your heart synchronises with, keeping all humans balanced and grounded with nature on the planet. Your vibrations are matched to the same frequency of the earth. In simple terms, humans evolve in synchronicity with the frequency or heartbeat of the earth.

The earth's heartbeat resonance is actually increasing at quite a rapid pace whilst the electromagnetic field is losing strength—we are now at the lowest point in planetary magnetics that we have been in the last 2000 years. Earth has had this experience around 14 times in the last 4.5 million years, according to the geological records, and every time it happens, it proceeds a 180-degree flip in the magnetic field, which then reverses—the South Pole becoming north and North Pole becoming south. We are in the golden age of human evolution; humanity should now be evolving/returning into the heart space, rising up in tune with the earth's resonance to maintain balance.

Your emotions, sleep patterns, perceptions of time and space, feelings about relationships and immune system response are all closely linked to the magnetic field of mother earth. The decrease in magnetics is most responsible for the volatile weather patterns around the globe today, again including what is known as 'global warming'.

The bottom line is that the fundamental heartbeat of the earth that the ancients spoke about is speeding up; the frequency measurement is slowly rising, encouraging an increase in your own brainwaves and heart's magnetic field, and, therefore, giving a sense that time in general is speeding up. Every cell in your body is always at work, constantly trying to keep up with the heartbeat of mother earth as the frequency increases. The cells are metabolising and upgrading their membrane structure, becoming crystalline in nature.

The pulse of the planet is twice as fast as it was in the mid-1980s, and nobody is sure where it is going to go. The earth's Kundalini energy is rising and heating up along with all the other planets in our solar system. The sun is due for a pole shift anytime, as it is recorded to do so every 11.2 years—you can find more information on NASA's website. Many people who are aware of these huge anomalies spend nearly all their time preparing for the moment in which the world will change.

Whether its burying boxes of food, weapons, water and so on, when you spend all your time preparing for the bad things you miss out on life itself. When frightening things happen to you, embrace the fear and transcend it into a factor for personal growth. When you work on your heart by changing your beliefs and eradicate all fear and lower-vibratory energies at the deepest levels you then become synchronised with the earth, as mentioned at the start of this section, connect back to mother earth and you will be protected. It is all a natural process and there is no dark side to it, the problem is so many are disconnected from nature, this is a major underlying factor for most suffering in the world today. Everything comes back to self.

'Everything has beauty, but not everyone sees it.' ~Confucius

Energetic disruptions & blockages in the heart field

An obstacle for many in regards to their personal connection to the heart is that of energetic disruptions and deeply rooted blockages that contribute to covering up this wonderful space. One of the main goals in life is to reconnect/live within the heart. With this being said, the universe will throw whatever problems and lessons for growth at you that are necessary in order for you to return back home to compassion.

You may experience deep trauma and a broken heart at some point in your life, and these are the two main factors that contribute towards energy blockages and soul fragmentations, leaving scars at the depth of your being. Much of this is due to non-acceptance/resistance surrounding an event or circumstance that you have no control over but still can't be at peace with. Healing a deep trauma or heartbreak can be the hardest part for some, as it involves going back to relive the event, so the unending stream of painful thoughts, tears and sadness arise once again and literally drain all of your life-force energy.

There can be scars from traumatic events that close the heart partially or completely, causing the chakra energy vortex to become off balance and distorted. Such blockages and disruptions are likely to cause illnesses which may manifest in your physical body. It is also very common for those who experience heartbreak to have very negative thoughts such as: 'I will never fully love again', 'I will never trust anyone else with my heart', 'I don't deserve love', or 'love hurts, love is pain'. These thoughts now become beliefs, seeds that have been planted in the subconscious mind that will sprout into further problems within your sphere of reality, never allowing a true healing to take place.

At the time of trauma or heartbreak, there is a fusion at the quantum level of your awareness. What happens is that part of your soul becomes fragmented and in tune with the frequency of the event. The etheric mass will then allocate itself on the heart chakra, which relates directly with your ability to give/receive love and the connection with feelings of lust, betrayal and hatred.

The frequency of the event and the thoughts you had at the time of the trauma are now embedded in your luminous energy field at a subatomic level; they then become the underlying attraction factor when it comes down to the relationships and people you bond with in the future. Holding this energetic soul fragment within your luminous energy field simply means all future relationships are going to bring the same component of heartbreak, distrust, betrayal, etc., each time energising the fragment more and more. This is the law of attraction at work, maybe you can relate this to personal experience or somebody you know.

Healing and confronting these energetic blockages is the only way forwards, to clear all past analogical experiences relating to the heartbreak and trauma at the deepest levels. This goes as deep as cleansing past-life traumas that you are not even consciously aware of, this involves the clearing all soul fragmentations, past identities and rebalancing the heart chakra in tune with the frequency of pure love. You can achieve this by working with your higher self to transmute the hearts blockages at the quantum level of your awareness. This allows a permanent healing to take place, and your frequency snaps back into harmony, allowing you to attract healthy, happy relationships.

For serious healing, you can visit a **Reiki/energy** healer, practice **heart meditation** using frequencies and tones, or visit a shaman to work with powerful healing plant medicines such as **Ayahuasca and Iboga/ibogaine.** This will allow you to open your heart again to receive and give love and to trust, the absolute key elements for a healthy, harmonious, loving and joyful relationship. To open a closed heart, the practice is to be covered and repeated over and over again, similar to how a diamond is formed. Live in your heart; it is the gateway to the divine.

'Unexpressed emotions will never die. They are buried alive and will come forth later in uglier ways.' ~ Sigmund Freud[28].

Anatomy of Fear

Fear is a very heavy burden for many. Those who live within the vibration of fear always make decisions based on what they think will be the safest decision for them. The nature of this decision-making is closely related to the lower energy chakras and the reptilian brain that ultimately deals in survival, fight or flight and animalistic behaviour.

Those who are grounded within the illusory prison of fear are operating from a vibratory frequency that is towards the lower end of the spectrum. They have lower energetic imprints in the subconscious mind, heart field and luminous energy field. Again, this could be related to past trauma, or they are simply victims of external programming, such as television and media.

Many are simply afraid of being emotionally hurt, ill, uncomfortable, lost, embarrassed, or a million other things. Their negative thinking not only limits them but also draws in negative energy from the cosmos. Feelings of worry and anxiety are simply illusory; worries about the future and holding onto the past ultimately entails one is not grounded to the present moment. This is a very dysfunctional way to live. Meditation practice can transcend all fears and false belief systems whilst slowly eradicating all fear from your being.

Until all of your fear-based negative emotions have been fully eradicated from your energy field, only then can you start to rise up the chakra system ladder, embracing higher vibratory emotions and stepping into your natural state of abundance, joy, happiness and peace.

You cannot reach success in life as long as these energetic clusters of deeply rooted fear control you; it distorts your frequency, and, therefore, you will attract only negative, fearful situations and events into your sphere of reality—again, this is the law of attraction in play. You must destroy all fear and negativity from your being and align yourself with the harmonious frequencies of universal abundance, once you do this you no longer have worries, as everything you need is swiftly provided with ease.

We delve deeper into the workings of the chakra system shortly. Below is the anatomy of fear-based emotions and the impact they have on the physical body and brain. Remember the body perceives everything as completely real alongside the subconscious mind. It is just a **belief** and a **thought form** that trigger the following:

Within seconds of perceiving a threat, the primitive Amygdala sounds a general alarm. The adrenal system promptly floods the body with adrenaline and stress hormones known as cortisol. Non-essential physiological processes then switch off, digestion stops, skin chills and blood is diverted into the muscles in preparation for a burst of emergency action. Shallow breathing now quickens; the heart races; and blood pressure skyrockets, infusing the body with oxygen whilst the liver releases glucose for quick fuel. The entire body is now in a state of fight or flight, highly alert:

Hippocampus – Cements the response to the threat into long-term memory (subconscious trauma)

Pupils – Dilate ready to relay signs of danger to the visual thalamus

Saliva – Decreases as digestion slows

Lung – Bronchioles dilate absorbing more oxygen

Body Hair – Stands on end

Thyroid Gland – Raises the resting metabolic rate

Liver – Begins to break down glycogen for instant energy to keep up with high-metabolic rate

Amygdala – Directs central and autonomic nervous systems to trigger an 'all systems' alarm, also storing memory of the threat/trauma

Hypothalamus – Incorporates the signals from organs, triggering the pituitary gland and nervous systems, causing the body's major organ systems to prepare for action

Heart – Blood pressure and heart-rate spike, infusing brain and muscles with ready fuel, distorting the hearts electromagnetic field, causing chaos in the higher ethers

Pituitary Gland – Produces thyrotropin and adrenocorticotropin, calling the thyroid and adrenal system into action

Skin – Vessels constrict causing chills and sweat

Bladder and colon – Prepare to void their contents in preparation for violent action and possible injury

Spleen – Pease ensure that you are using the same character that you use for the other similarly styled quotes.Contracts, pumping out white blood cells and platelets in preparation for physical injury

Stomach & gastrointestinal tract – Blood vessels constrict so the blood can be fed to the muscles

Adrenal medulla – Floods bloodstream with adrenaline and noradrenaline, increasing the level of blood sugar and constricting blood vessels.

You now have more of an idea of how fear delivers distortion many layers deep. All of the bodily and energetic fight-or-flight processes are triggered from a thought or belief you have in your mind that labels something as 'fearful'. Moreover, 95% of the things people fear and the stories that the mind plays out never come true.

Every time your body, energy and thoughts are subdued with fear, you transmit chaos frequencies through the universe which are delivered back to your sphere of reality in the form of circumstances and events that will, again make you feel the same way. Remember, you are the creator, and the universe is the responder.

Again, if you suffer and sometimes fall victim of such illusory fearful emotions that you want to eradicate, you can go to a Reiki energy healer or even a shaman. We delve deeper into such topics later in this section.

'Fears, even the most basic ones, can totally destroy our ambitions. Fear, if left unchecked, can destroy our lives. Fear is one of the many enemies lurking inside us.' ~ **Jim Rohn**[29]

The Chakra Energy System

We have mentioned the term *chakra* a few times already in this chapter when relating to the human energy system. Many scientists and philosophers are confronted with a great difficulty when it comes to accepting and explaining the existence of the chakras. They do not know whether the chakras are to be found in the physical body or in the subtle body. If they exist in the physical body, where are they? And of course the subtle body is not the matter of modern anatomical science.

Human beings collect energy from several different levels of vibrations, one of them being colour, and this energy is utilised in numerous ways. Throughout your luminous energy field lie formless energetic centres that are structured at the atomic and subatomic level; they form connections to major organs and glands that govern bodily functions. Each of these main energy centres is referred to as a chakra.

Chakra originates from Sanskrit language, meaning *wheel*. A chakra is a wheel-like spinning vortex that whirls in a circular motion forming a vacuum at the epicentre that draws in anything it encounters when in alignment on a particular vibratory level. Your body contains hundreds of chakras that are key to the operation of your entire being. These 'spinning energy centres' draw-in coded information from your surroundings. This information can be anything from colour vibrations to ultraviolet rays/light codes from the sun, radio/microwaves, or even another person's auric field vibrations.

Ultimately, the chakras form an alignment with the health of your environment, including the people you meet, often forming an emotional connection between the moods of others. Your chakras also radiate energetic vibrations outwardly, shaping the emotions, thoughts and feelings that another person may generate. Chakras are directly connected to, and govern the endocrine system, which in turn regulates the aging process.

Your chakras are linking mechanisms between the auric field and the meridian system within your physical body, including the etheric auric fields and higher cosmic forces. Your body contains seven **major** chakras/energy centres and many other minor chakras. Energising and balancing these chakras is the key to unlocking your true potential in all aspects of life and truly embracing states of enlightenment.

There are many chakra explanations in books and on the Internet, the systems differ depending on whether you're looking at petals, stems, roots, archetypal, elemental, or astral aspects. All in all, chakras are a complex topic. YUSA uses the tantric Kundalini terms derived from ancient India (Vedic).

In tantra and yoga, the chakras are symbolised by lotus flowers. As a symbol, the lotus is very significant. Man must pass through three clear stages in spiritual life, which represent his existence on three different levels: ignorance, aspiration/endeavour and illumination. The lotus also exists on three different levels: mud, water and air. It sprouts in the mud (ignorance), grows up through the water in an effort to reach the surface (aspiration and endeavour), and eventually reaches the air and the direct light of the sun (illumination).

Thus, the lotus symbolises man's growth from the lowest states of awareness to the higher states of consciousness. The culmination of the growth of the lotus is a beautiful flower. In the same way, the culmination of man's spiritual quest is the awakening and blossoming of the purest human potential.

Hence, each of the principal chakras can be visualised as a lotus flower with a specific colour and number of petals as follow

1. *Mooladhara*/root – 4-petalled deep-red lotus

2. *Swadhisthana*/sacral – 6-petalled vermilion/orange lotus

3. *Manipura*/solar plexus – 10-petalled bright-yellow lotus

4. *Anahata*/heart – 12-petalled green lotus

5. *Vishuddhi*/throat – 16-petalled blue lotus

6. *Ajna*/third eye – 2-petalled indigo lotus

7. *Sahasrara*/crown – 1000-petalled violet lotus

The first three chakras are recognised as the lower self, and they deal mainly in lower-vibratory emotions and patterns, relating to the material world. All chakras produce an energy vortex at the front and back of your body. A hollow tube of light runs down your spinal cord, connecting the root and higher chakras. Living purely in the lower chakra system is what can be known as 'hell'. Ignorance is the lower state of awareness/consciousness. *Heaven* and *hell* are simply metaphorical terms for where one chooses to reside in their own being, operating from the lower-vibratory end of the scale or the higher.

The **first chakra**, located at the bottom of the spine, is known as the **MOOLADHARA/ROOT CHAKRA**. Its colour is red. This chakra holds the essence of creation, elimination and grounding to the earth. Its functions are survival, self-preservation, the physical body, family, security and sense of smell. War, famine, natural disasters and any other events that threaten your basic survival are all recorded within the energies of the first chakra.

The root chakra's ruling planet is Saturn. The stones related to this energy are garnet, onyx, ruby and obsidian. Balancing this chakra energises the physical body and controls fear, greed and jealousy. The bodily functions that the root is linked to are the excretory, urinary and sexual and reproductive organs along with the adrenal glands. When poorly grounded, your spatial understanding is impaired. You may stumble around physically, mentally, spiritually and emotionally.

The root chakra is the first centre in human incarnation, but it is the highest chakra that animals have the capacity to awaken. Below this, there are other chakras that represent the evolution of the animal kingdom. They are only related to sense consciousness and not to mental awareness. The higher chakras beyond the root are not present in the psychic physiology of animals, and their nervous systems reflect this relative deficiency.

An individual with a blocked root chakra may feel fearful, anxious, insecure, frustrated, selfish and ignorant to truth. Problems like obesity, anorexia nervosa and knee troubles can occur. Root-related body parts include the hips, legs, lower back, and sexual organs. They look for material satisfaction and external comforts most of the time, such as drugs, alcohol and low-vibrational sex.

In tantra, Mooladhara is the seat of Kundalini Shakti, the basis from which the possibility of higher realisation arises. This great potential is said to be lying dormant in the form of a coiled serpent, being the latent cosmic energy or Shakti that resides in every being. When aroused, it makes its way upward through *sushumna nadi* in the spinal cord until it reaches *Sahasrara*, where the ultimate experience of enlightenment occurs.

In a man's life, his desires, his actions and his accomplishments, are controlled by sexual desires, and all externals are an expression of that lower chakra. Your lower *samskaras* and karmas are embedded there, as in lower incarnations; one's whole being is founded on the sexual personality. Sigmund Freud has also emphasised this point. He said that one's selection of clothing, food, friends, home furnishing, decor, etc., everything is influenced by his/her sexual awareness, the root chakra.

Corporations, advertisements and food industry aim to subconsciously stimulate your energetic root chakra. Companies such as KFC, McDonalds, and those behind television ads are well aware of colour therapy and mind-control tactics. They use the tone of red to stimulate the lower energy centre, along with poisonous foods, keeping you locked into the illusory lower material realm of fear and wanting.

Sanskrit name: Mooladhara, *Moola* means *root* or *foundation*, the transcendental basis of physical nature

Energies: Earth, grounding, focusing, centring

Affirmations: I AM Safe, I AM grounded, I AM fearless, & I AM centred

Foods that fuel the root chakra: Root vegetables, Beet juice, protein-rich foods and hot and peppery spices

Problems that may be related to unbalanced root chakra:

- Problems with your physical health

- Procrastination and never accomplishing your goals

- Money issues or your home a constant triggers of stress and anxiety for you

- Physically hurting yourself

- Attempts or thoughts of suicide

'To be rooted is perhaps the most important and least recognized need of the human soul.' ~Simone Weil[30]

The **second chakra**, located in the lower abdomen, is known as the **SWADHISTHANA/SACRAL CHAKRA**. Its colour is orange. This chakra holds the essence of desire, sexuality, pleasure and procreation. Its functions include emotional elimination, water regulation, sexual function/drive and sense of taste. Opening the sacral chakra isn't about enhancing sexuality, but more so about focusing primal energies upon greater awareness so that you can enjoy the flow of life.

The sacral chakra's ruling planet is Pluto. The stones related to this energy are coral, carnelian, garnet and moonstone. Balancing this chakra gives stability in your emotions, vitality, fertility, reproduction and sexual energy in general.

When this chakra is balanced, you feel full of wonder and awe for your connection to the greater cosmos.

Although Mooladhara occupies a very important place in the scheme of the chakras, Swadhisthana, which is located very near to Mooladhara, is also involved in and responsible for the awakening of Kundalini Shakti. The Swadhisthana chakra is closely related to the vegetable world, and the observance of a vegetarian diet is said to be an important practice for awakening this chakra.

Working on the sacral develops personality and self-esteem, as your body-awareness increases so does your sense of grounding and emotional intuition. The majority of people, especially in Western cultures, experience a blockage of this chakra, usually because of nature-deprivation and an overall lack of awareness surrounding the interconnectedness of all things.

When this chakra is blocked, you may feel an inability to ground yourself as well as the feelings of jealousy and guilt. You may not be able to set healthy boundaries or you might even attach too much importance on immediate gratification. Nothing seems good enough because you're never satisfied, and depression inevitably ensues. It is said that one who meditates on Kundalini in the Swadhisthana chakra is immediately freed from his internal enemies – lust, anger, greed, etc., and their nectar-like words flow in prose and verse and in well-reasoned discourse. The person becomes like the sun illuminating the darkness of ignorance.

In tantric texts, it is said that every perception of karma, experiences and associations are all recorded from your current and past lives/incarnations. When Kundalini is residing in the Swadhisthana chakra, the last vestige of karma is being thrown out and all the negative samskaras express themselves and are expelled. At this time, you may be angry, afraid, or full of sexual fantasies and passion. You may also experience lethargy, indolence, depression and all kinds of tamasic characteristics.

When no sexual desires of any kind manifest in an aspirant any more, and when there is no more personal attraction, that means that Kundalini has passed beyond the Swadhisthana chakra. Energy at different levels is known by different names. At the highest level, it is called spiritual experience. On the emotional level, it is known as love. On the physical level, it is known as sex, and at the lowest level it is known as *avidya* or ignorance. Therefore, when you talk about sex, you must understand that it is only a particular formation of energy.

Sanskrit name: Swadhisthana, *Swa* means *one's own* and *Adhisthana* means *dwelling place/residence*

Energies: Water

Affirmations: I relate to others with ease, **I FEEL** wonderful about myself, **I FEEL** my inner strength and creativity

Foods that fuel your sacral chakra: Sweet fruits, including melons, mangos, strawberries, passion fruit, oranges, coconut, honey, nuts, and spices, including cinnamon, vanilla, carob, sweet paprika, sesame seeds and caraway seeds

Problems that may be related to an unbalanced sacral chakra:

- Emotional instability

- Tendency to hide or control your feelings

- Lack of creativity and the inability to think outside the box

- Difficulties with intimacy

- Sexual issues such as impotence

- Difficulties with living in the present moment

'Do what makes you happy, be with who makes you smile, laugh as much as you breathe, and love as long as you live.' ~ **Rachel Ann Nunes**

The **third chakra**, located in the higher abdomen, is known as the **MANIPURA/SOLAR PLEXUS CHAKRA**. Its colour is yellow. This chakra holds the essence of will power, laughter, dynamism and achievement. Its functions include digestion, the assimilation of muscle groups and sense of sight. Opening the solar plexus chakra can aid in your self-esteem, self-direction, self-worth and how you honour yourself as a person. Your egoic personality, which develops during puberty, is housed in this chakra.

The solar plexus chakra's ruling planet is Mars. The stones related to this energy are amber, jasper, topaz and citrine. In opening your third chakra, you may reach deep into your own sense of self and find your balance or boundary point; this provides great foundations for growth within and without, Success in the material world is then achieved with ease.

In the same way that the sun continually radiates energy to other planets, the Manipura chakra radiates and distributes *pranic* energy (QI/CHI) throughout the entire human framework, regulating and energising the activity of the various organs, systems and processes of life. When deficient, it is more like the glowing embers of a dying fire rather than a powerful intense blaze. In this state the individual is rendered lifeless/vitality deficient and devoid of energy. They will then be hindered by poor health, depression and lack of motivation or commitment in life.

Human evolution takes place through seven planes, in the same way that Kundalini awakens in the seven chakras. When the consciousness evolves to Manipura, one acquires a spiritual perspective. When this centre is purified and awakened, the body becomes disease free and luminous; one's consciousness does not fall back into the lower states.

The solar plexus chakra is related to the digestive organs, especially the pancreas. It is associated with action, assertion, empowerment and ego mastery. Malfunctions in the navel chakra may leave you feeling tired, powerless and withdrawn. Those with an overactive solar plexus chakra may have excessive ego, excessive drive, and are often self-destructive in the amount they expect of themselves and do. Cutting down on processed sugars, caffeine and dead foods allows the solar plexus to generate energy—it is your body's main powerhouse.

Sanskrit name: Manipura, *Mani* meaning *jewel* and *Pura* meaning *city* (*city of jewels*)

Energies: Fire, energising, charging, lends energy

Affirmations: I DO embrace joy, **I DO** hold high self-worth, **I DO** have sense of direction

Foods that fuel your solar plexus chakra: Citrus (high-vibrational) fruits and juices, such as grapefruit, lemons and limes

Problems that may be related to an unbalanced solar plexus chakra:

- Having a lack of focus in life and an inability to concentrate

- Constantly worrying about what other people think

- Lacking self-esteem and self-confidence

- Feeling that your mind is often clouded mind and experiencing difficulty in making decisions

- Taking on more responsibility than you can reasonably handle

- Being often obsessed with making sure everything you do is perfect

- Finding it difficult to be alone

'What lies behind us and what lies before us are tiny matters compared to what lies within us.' ~Henry Stanley Haskins

The heart chakra ultimately deals with love and love of self, and this is the midpoint between the realms of heaven and hell in your own heart and mind, not externally. The heart chakra is the centre of your being. There are three main chakras below and three main chakras above, as above so below. A discord or imbalance in the heart chakra will adversely affect all of the other energy centres. Aspiration and endeavour lie here.

The **fourth chakra**, located in the chest area, and is known as the **ANAHATA/HEART CHAKRA**. Its colour is green. This chakra holds the essence of compassion, inner peace, self-realisation, love and acceptance. Its functions include electromagnetic-field generation, lung function, shoulders, upper back, blood pressure stabilisation, immune system/thymus regulation and sense of touch. Balancing the heart chakra is beneficial for spiritual love, compassion, universal oneness and self-love. All desires become manifested once the heart is activated.

Although Anahata is known as the heart centre, this should not be misinterpreted to mean the biological heart, the muscular pump within the chest. Although its physiological component is the cardiac plexus of nerves, the nature of this centre is far beyond the physiological dimension.

The heart chakras ruling celestial body is the sun. The stones related to this energy are rose quartz, malachite, jade and moldavite. Many issues surrounding love, paranoia, hatred, anger, jealousy, fears of betrayal, fears of letting go, loneliness and past trauma alongside the ability to heal yourself and others are centred in the fourth chakra. Related physical illnesses can include heart attack, high blood pressure, insomnia and difficulty in breathing.

It is said that in this present age, the consciousness of humanity is passing through a phase of Anahata. It means that within many people, Anahata chakra has started to function, but there is a difference between functioning and awakening. In most people, Anahata is not completely active, but it functions slightly; whereas, Mooladhara is very active and almost awake in the majority of people today.

The fourth chakra is the balance between your body and spirit. This chakra is the place where unconditional love is centred. Unconditional love is a creative and powerful energy that may guide and help you through the most impossible times. When the heart chakra is balanced, you may feel compassionate, friendly and empathetic, and you might have the desire to nurture and only see the best in others. It is imperative now that you keep your heart open and replace all judgements of others with acceptance.

It is said in many of the ancient scriptures that the heart chakra produces a sound which is non-physical and non-empirical, and transcendental in nature. This sound is endless and unbroken in the same way that the heart beats faithfully and continuously from before birth up until death.

It is also is said that the Anahata chakra is where the thoughts and desires of the individual are materialised and fulfilled, where the freedom to escape from a preordained fate and to determine one's own destiny becomes a reality. This means that as long as the consciousness is centred in the lower chakras, you will remain completely dependent on what is already enjoined for you, your fate, or destiny. Anything can be created and re-created from the heart.

For heart chakra activation, you must become extremely optimistic and positive, always full of hope. You must never dwell in the negativity of the mind. Physically, mentally and spiritually, you must be completely at peace with yourself, with people outside and with the whole community at large. Every situation is a good one for you, and the future is always bright. In all circumstances, this must be your attitude. It makes no difference whether you are amidst poverty, suffering, disease, conflict, divorce, emotional crises and discord. It is all part of the good, and therefore you accept it.

Sanskrit name: *Anahata* meaning *unstruck* or *unbeaten*

Energies: Water, calming, soothes, relaxing

Foods that fuel your heart chakra: Raw greens, broccoli, asparagus, spinach, kale, cucumber, green juices, pumpkin seeds, Spirulina and wheatgrass

Affirmations: I PRACTICE unconditional love, **I PRACTICE** non-judgement, **I PRACTICE** self-acceptance

Problems that may be related to an unbalanced heart chakra:

- Having difficulty accepting yourself the way you are or having a lack self-love

- Experiencing a lack of freedom in your life

- Having difficulty making up your mind

- Always saying *yes* to other people's demands and requests because it is difficult to say *no* to people

- Fearing rejection or abandonment

- Struggling with jealousy/finding yourself envious of others

There is also a **secondary fourth** heart chakra that is locate above the first, the distance between your chin and nose, and its colour is pink. This chakra is connected directly to the right side of the brain and is responsible for the healthy functioning of your emotional body.

It works in synchronisation with the right brain and is a powerful stream for creativity. This energy centre regulates your ability to receive love and be open to others. You can stimulate this pink chakra with the use of essential oils, such as rose, rosewood, jasmine, holly, poppy, bergamot, Melissa, pine and eucalyptus.

'If you want others to be happy, practice compassion. If you want to be happy, practice compassion.' ~ **Dalai Lama**

The **fifth, sixth** and **seventh** chakras are recognised within higher human evolution and the higher self. One has bypassed lower emotions and lives in harmony with the truth. Compassion and understanding now come forth. Reconnection with spirit, wisdom, faith and courage become strong foundations for daily living, whilst your natural state of abundance and prosperity is embraced. Illumination lies here.

The **fifth chakra**, located in the neck area, is known as the **VISHUDDHI/THROAT CHAKRA**. Its colour is blue. This chakra holds the essence of creativity, communication, following ones dreams and self-expression. Its functions include metabolism, calcium regulation, thyroid gland function and sense of hearing/sound. Opening of the throat chakra enhances speech and opens up communication areas of the brain.

The throat chakras ruling planet is Mercury. The stones related to this energy are sodalite, blue lace agate, lapis lazuli and aquamarine. It is the chakra of communication, telepathy and creative expression. Unexpressed emotions tend to constrict this energy centre. Your inner truth is your sense of what is correct and your innate tendencies and inclinations. Falsehoods and half-truths energetically pollute the throat chakra. This behaviour violates both your body and spirit.

Repressing your anger or displeasure by ignoring your feelings through evasive sweet talk or silence will manifest into imbalances such as strep throat, laryngitis, speech impediments and even nightmares of being strangled. The healthfulness of this chakra is signified by how openly and honestly, you express yourself to others. A challenge to the throat chakra is for you to express yourself in the most truthful manner.

Singing, creating, rehearsing and chanting mantras are the most powerful steps to achieve a balanced throat chakra. Opening the throat chakra creates a relationship of trust between what you want to say and what you actually deliver when communicating in the outside world.

Vishuddhi is actually the legendary 'fountain of youth'. It is said that when Kundalini is in Vishuddhi, one enjoys eternal youth. When it awakens by the practices of hatha yoga, Kundalini yoga, or tantra, then a spontaneous physical rejuvenation begins to take place.

Sanskrit name: *Vishuddhi,* meaning *purification*. Purifying and harmonising of all opposites takes place here.

Energies*:* Water, calming, soothing, relaxing

Foods that fuel your throat chakra: Liquids in general, including water, fruit juices and herbal teas; fruits, including lemons, limes, grapefruit, kiwi, apples, pears, plums, peaches, apricots, etc.; and the spices salt and lemon grass

Affirmations: I SPEAK my truth with love; **IT IS EASY** for me to speak my truth; **I EXPRESS** my truth with ease

Problems that may be related to an unbalanced throat chakra:

- Difficulty expressing yourself and your beliefs

- Lack of trust in others

- Lack of organisation in your life

- Constant worry about financial security and constant pursuit of material things

- Being shy by nature and having trouble holding a conversation with other people

'May you hear and speak truth. May your life and your creations express the fullness of who you are. May you know ever deeper levels of truth.' ~ Author Unknown

The **sixth chakra**, located at the mid-brow, is known as the **AJNA/THIRD-EYE CHAKRA**. Its colour is indigo. This chakra holds the essence of truth, vision, psychic knowledge, crystal thought, mental wellbeing, emotional intelligence and the 'sixth sense'. Its functions include hormonal/physiological regulation and pituitary and pineal functions. Connecting with the third-eye chakra brings psychic perception and creative intelligence in all that you do.

The third-eye chakras ruling planet is Jupiter. The stones related to this energy are amethyst, purple fluorite, clear quartz, moonstone, sapphire, moldavite and sugilite. The sixth chakra is the place of 'shamanic seeing'. When in balance, you have a heightened sense of intellect and can perceive information several levels deep. Ajna is the bridge that links the guru with his disciples. It represents the level at which it is possible for direct mind-to-mind communication to take place between two people.

Resonating with this centre opens the door to a reality separate from the ordinary world. Clairvoyance arises, the visual form of ESP (extrasensory perception) involving perceiving or intuiting information by way of seeing auras, colours, images, or symbols. It has also been called 'the eye of intuition', and it is the doorway through which the individual enters the astral and psychic dimension of consciousness. The mystical traditions of every age and culture make abundant references to it. It is portrayed as a psychic eye located midway between the two physical eyes. It looks inwards instead of outwards.

Your power over creative visualisation and creation lies here; whatever is visualised within the third eye is manifested into reality through the root chakra. It is interesting to note that the Ajna chakra is more active in females than it is in males. Women are more sensitive, psychic and perceptive, and they are often able to predict coming events. However, in most people, this inner eye remains closed. Although people see the events of the outside world, knowledge and understanding of truth cannot be gained. In this sense, many are blind to the real possibilities of the world, unable to view the deeper levels of human existence.

It should also be mentioned that the Ajna chakra and the pineal gland are the same thing. The pituitary gland is connected to the Sahasrara/Crown chakra and, just as the pituitary and pineal glands are intimately connected, so are Ajna and Sahasrara. We could say that Ajna is the gateway to the Sahasrara chakra. If Ajna is awakened and functioning properly, all the experiences happening in Sahasrara can be managed well.

As mentioned, in most people, the Ajna chakra, the thalamic/pineal area, is dormant. Living in Mooladhara/root and Swadhisthana/sacral for most of the time would mean that the Ajna chakra functions mainly from the medulla oblongata, the reptilian brain. Only when you stimulate and awaken the centres by yoga and detoxification can you jump levels in your nervous system and consciously awaken the higher pineal/thalamic areas and their concomitant levels of consciousness.

Physical imbalances related to the third-eye chakra include headaches, disturbed sleep/nightmares, sinus and nose congestion, eyestrain and hormonal imbalances. Your ability to separate reality from fantasy or delusion is connected to the healthfulness of this chakra. The word *Ajna* comes from the Sanskrit root which means *to know, to obey or to follow*. Literally, *Ajna* means *command* or the *monitoring centre*. In astrology, Ajna is the centre of Jupiter, which symbolises the guru or preceptor. Amongst the deities, Jupiter is represented by Brihaspati, the guru of the *devas* and preceptor of the gods. Therefore, this centre is also known as 'the guru chakra'.

Sanskrit name: Ajna meaning to perceive, follow and know spiritual guidance

Energies: Air, meditative, intuition, promotes thought

Foods that fuel your third-eye chakra: Eggplant, purple kale, concord grapes, purple carrots, blue-green algae, Guayusa tea, wheatgrass, green juices and lemon water

Affirmations: **I SEE** all truth clearly, **I SEE** my life unfold with ease, **I SEE** emotional intelligence, **I SEE** situations exactly how they are

Problems that may be related to an unbalanced third-eye chakra:

- Lacking intuition or insight in life
- Constantly hanging onto negative thoughts and having difficulty overcoming fear or anxiety
- Living in a fantasy or dream world and not in reality
- **Struggling with depression** or always feeling lonely
- Being too hard on yourself and lacking self-pride

'Intuition is a spiritual faculty and does not explain, but simply points the way.' ~Florence Scovel Shinn[31]

The **seventh chakra**, located on the top of your head, is known as the **SAHASRARA/CROWN CHAKRA**. Its colour is violet. This chakra holds the essence of psychic abilities, inner states of bliss, connection to spirit, faith and inspiration. Its functions include pineal gland balance, illumination and union with the cosmos. Sahasrara is beyond human sensory perceptions. Connecting to the violet flame awakens your connection the Christ consciousness (God Source) and transmutes negative thoughts into positive thoughts.

The crowns ruling celestial body is the moon. The stones related to this energy are amethyst, moldavite and selenite. It is the chakra of intuition, promoting thought and an inner sense of knowing. When functioning optimally, the crown chakra allows inner communications with your spiritual nature to take place.

Consciousness manifests at different levels according to the chakra that is predominantly active. Sahasrara acts through nothing and yet again, it acts through everything. Sahasrara is beyond the beyond (*paratparam*) and yet it is right here. Sahasrara is the culmination of the progressive ascension through the different chakras. It is the crown of expanded awareness. The power of the chakras does not reside in the chakras themselves, but in Sahasrara. The chakras are only switches. All the potential lies in Sahasrara.

The activation of the crown chakra (located in the same area as the soft spot on a baby's head) serves as an entryway wherein the Universal Life Force can enter your body and be dispersed downward into the lower six chakras housed below it. The individual mind or consciousness is kept in continuous touch with all types of information from the external cosmos and the understated dimensions of spiritual power. The halo depiction of Jesus in the Bible was related to the crown chakra activation and enlightenment, seventh heaven.

The violet flame stands for freedom against negative energies you are holding onto, manifesting from old karma or past negative influences. It is everything and nothing. Whatever is said about Sahasrara immediately limits and categorises it, even if we say it is infinite. It transcends logic, for logic compares one thing with another. Sahasrara is the totality, so what is there to compare it with? It transcends all concepts and yet it is the source of all concepts. It is the merging of consciousness and prana.

When Kundalini Shakti reaches Sahasrara, it is known as union between Shiva and Shakti, as Sahasrara is said to be the abode of higher consciousness or Shiva. Union between Shiva and Shakti marks the beginning of a great experience. When this union takes place, the moment of self-realisation or Samadhi begins. At this point the individual man dies, not that physical death occurs; it is death of the mundane awareness or individual awareness. It is death of the experience of name and form.

Every mystical and religious system of the world has its own way of describing this experience. Some have called it nirvana, others Samadhi, kaivalya, self-realisation, enlightenment, communion, heaven and so on. Moreover, if you read the religious and mystical poems and scriptures of the many cultures and traditions, you will find ample descriptions of Sahasrara. However, you have to read them with a different state of consciousness to understand the esoteric symbolism and terminology.

According to Yogananda, Kundalini rises and the pituitary gland secretes a yellowish fluid, and the pineal gland secretes a white fluid. When the two meet, there is a flash of light so bright this chakra is opened. Here then, the two fluids, known in the Bible as 'the land of Milk and Honey,' begin to flow down the pancreatic nerve (The River Jordan) to the third centre, which is known as the manger (where Christ Consciousness is born within you).

Sanskrit name: *Sahasrara*, meaning *thousand-fold*

Energies: Air, meditative, intuition, promotes thought

Foods that fuel your third-eye chakra: (same as third eye) Eggplant, purple kale, concord grapes, purple carrots, blue-green algae, Guayusa tea and wheatgrass, green juices and lemon water

Affirmations: I **INNERSTAND** myself, I **INNERSTAND** nature, I **INNERSTAND** that I am loved unconditionally

Problems that may be related to an unbalanced crown chakra:

- Lack of spirituality or a connection to God/universal creator
- **Lack of a sense of purpose in life**
- Lack of faith in any form of spirituality because of being too caught up with one's self, religion, or ego
- Lack the ability to let go and have faith in situations

'... The past gives you an identity and the future holds the promise of salvation, of fulfilment in whatever form. Both are illusions.' ~ Eckhart Tolle[32]

The remaining chakras hold the essence of higher intelligence, masculine/feminine balance, soul family & your connection to the universal creator. Deep connection lies here, beyond form, body and gender. These energy points are the purest of light.

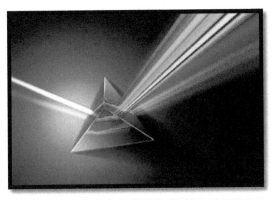

Image representation of source energy converting into the array of the colour spectrum/chakras

Activation of these etheric energy centres implies your recognition of the God's/Goddess's power within all of creation, including yourself. Beyond the mental limitations of space and time, these are higher energetics beyond the physical body that keep you connected with all life. You must activate the seven basic chakras, evolving at a slow and steady pace.

You cannot force a flower to bloom. This process is what the new age community refer to as 'ascension', not drifting off somewhere else but rising up to your true frequency/self. Climbing the energy ladder is a lengthy process; many lessons have to be learnt through many incarnations—don't be fooled by misinformation that this is an overnight job; soul evolution is timeless, it's a fight for life.

There is however, a certain problem with the awakening of the other chakras. Each one contains a store of karma or samskara, both good and bad, positive and negative, painful and pleasant. The awakening of any chakra will definitely bring to the surface an explosion or expression of the karma, and of course, not everybody is prepared or ready to face it.

Above Sahasrara/crown chakra, these energy points represent the higher divine consciousness. As Mooladhara is the highest chakra in animal evolution and the first in human evolution, Sahasrara is the highest in human evolution and the first step in the highest divine evolution.

The following chakra descriptions are mainly just for your information. The connection always remains; divert your attention towards working with the seven major energy centres with love and due care. Start working on the heart as that is the medium to all energy centres. A good start is to eat natural living foods (information in chapter 3) and meditate with crystals and a range of audio frequencies.

- The eighth chakra is located **half a foot above** the head, and it represents the soul.
- The ninth chakra is located **above the atmosphere**.
- The tenth chakra is located at the **solar centre**.
- The eleventh chakra is located at the **galactic centre**, where the earth is headed to now.
- The twelfth chakra is located at the **universal centre**.
- The thirteenth chakra is pure connection to the **universal godhead creator**.

Occult meanings of the number 13

The number 13 is feared by many, mainly because of superstition and misinformation channelled by the powers that be. This misinformation has been passed down from generation to generation, predicated by certain stories and events from a secret society called the Knights of Templar. This secret society believed that the number 13 was evil, malicious and wicked, as they were defeated in battle on Friday the 13th. Religious organisations also brand the number 13 as being evil, mainly because of there being 13 individuals portrayed at the Last Supper, 12 disciples and Jesus Christ.

The truth is that the number 13, according to occultists, spiritual sciences and metaphysics, is an extremely lucky number, high in vibration. This number represents divinity and enlightenment, and it is the number of creation as well as death. In occult and spiritual teachings, there is no death, only resurrection, ascension, reincarnation and the transformation of soul. You can choose any of these 4 routes to leave the physical plane at any time.

Thirteen is the number traditionally associated with the Divine Feminine. In ancient times, there were 13 'months' in a year, since there are 13 full moons, and therefore 13 menstrual cycles annually. The 13th letter of the alphabet is M, a letter associated with many things feminine, including mother, mom, mama, mammary glands, menstruation and one of the most powerful feminine archetypes in the world, the Virgin Mary.

There are 13 astrological signs and 13 planets in this solar system. In the lunar calendar, there are 13 cycles, where the moon moves 13 degrees across the heavens each day. The sun cycle is now present; this represents the awakening of humanity, out of the sleeping state. There are also 13 major joints and bones within in the human body. In the ancient runic alphabet, the 13th rune symbolised the end of a cycle and the new beginning that followed. Witches covens are also constructed with 13 members.

Paganism views the number 13 as the time for transition, whilst Celtic beliefs considered it as the 'coming of age' for boys. Older Celtic beliefs suggest that the number 13 is sacred because it represents the individual joining the Goddess, represented by the number 3. Numerology puts significance on the number 13 when the equation 1+3=4 is considered, 4 being the representational foundation of the circle of life, where all of creation begins.

Kundalini, the Rising Serpent Energy

The subjects of Kundalini and yoga have not been over-stood by the materialistic world for a very long time, but, as the men of science dove deeper into the mysteries of matter, they came to understand and realise that matter/form was not ultimate in the evolution of nature.

As all matter is constructed in the same manner, what applies for one form applies for all forms. When you experience the external world perceiving through your senses thoughts, feelings, cognitions and emotions, you are experiencing matter. Saying this, it implies there must be more realms of experience, opening the possibilities for you to transcend the limitations of the mind.

The construct of the human mind is matter. It is not a construct of spirit, and therefore it can be made to evolve. People have begun to realise and experience this in the last couple of decades. Everything in the universe evolves higher and higher. Nature's course spirals outwardly, infinitely represented by the number 9, the highest of single digit numbers.

Within the framework of linear time, space and objectivity there can also be a gradual evolution, limited in nature. The second form of experience can happen when the present mind expands beyond its given definitions and borders, and, when this experience occurs, old energy is released from within yourself.

Higher states of being such as nirvana, *moksha*, emancipation, self-realisation, salvation, or liberation have been spoke about by people for hundreds of years, without the full understanding being present. Many may think these levels are the end or that they are now finished, but nothing finishes; only one level of experience ends, and then another commences. Since the beginning of creation, yogis and the tantric people have always realised that there is a much greater, more potent force lying within the physical human body. A force with dynamic potential, not philosophical or transcendental—this is known as the Kundalini serpent energy/force.

What is Kundalini?

The word *Kundal* means *coil*, so Kundalini has been described as 'that which coils'. When in its dormant state, it is referred to as Shakti; upon activation, it is referred to as Devi, Kali, Durga and Lakshmi. Kundalini is known to dwell within a small gland located at the base of your spinal cord. As the evolution of man has risen above the root chakra, the gland has come to a point where it can be exploded, one being able to release the supernatural force that lies within. India's ancient traditions where built around communities organised to facilitate this explosion, but now many things are different because of the desires associated with materialism.

If you want to awaken your dormant Kundalini energy then the practice of yoga, meditation and a vegetarian diet are the main requirements. However, if it were to become a global event, then the whole social structure would have to be reorganised alongside millions of people worldwide made aware of their individual purposes for existence. The sexual interaction between man and woman would have to be reorganised if humanity wanted to experience a full awakening.

One also has to arrive at the realisation that there may be more to life than just the comforts and pleasures that satisfy basic needs. At one time, there were only a few seekers, but now millions worldwide are striving for a higher experience, and this experience is the gaining of knowledge. Once Kundalini is awakened and starts to rise throughout your energetic body, a metamorphic process occurs in the realms of nature and spirit. In turn, there is a change in your physical body and mental framework.

With the awakening of Kundalini, there is a much greater intelligence that arises, and a completely new range of creativity is brought forth. You are met with psychic and clairvoyant experiences, affecting the whole area of the mind and its behaviour. Kundalini is a biological substance that exists in the framework of your body. Once awakened, it fires electrical impulses throughout your being, and these impulses can be detected with scientific instruments.

Every person should be educated on Kundalini. In the male body, it is situated in the perineum and, in the female body; it is situated at the root of the uterus, in the cervix. As already mentioned, you can awaken this energy through the practices of pranayama breathing, kriya yoga, and meditation. Once you master the art of forcing prana into the seat of Kundalini, the energy wakes up. Upon rising, it moves up through sushumna nadi, the central nervous canal, and up to the brain. The energy ascends upwards and passes through all chakras from the root upward, as the chakras are all individually interconnected with different areas of the brain. When Kundalini reaches the brain, all of these dormant areas start blossoming, and the crown chakra's petals start to spread wide open.

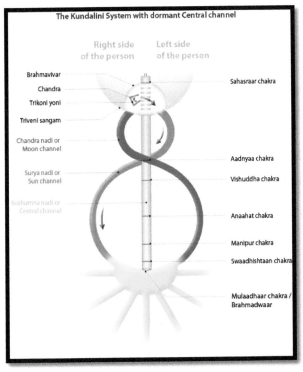

Representation of the Kundalini energy system, left and right channels[33].

Upon the awakening of Kundalini from the Mooladhara/root up to Ajna/third-eye chakra, your awareness is centred on experiencing higher things; this is not to say it is free from ego. You cannot transcend ego at the lower points of awakening. It is only when Kundalini reaches the Ajna chakra that the transcendence begins. This is where the ego is exploded into a million fragments, and the ensuing death experience occurs. As every person is at a different stage in his or her spiritual evolution, Kundalini could already be resting in Swadhisthana/the sacral, Manipura/solar plexus chakra, or Anahata/heart chakra.

In tantric scriptures, when you have awakened Kundalini but cannot handle it, it is called *Kali*. When you can handle it and you are able to use the energy for beneficial purposes it is called *Durga*. Kali is a female deity, depicted as being naked and smoky in colour. She wears a *mala* of 108 skulls, representing the past incarnations and memories of different births. In Hindu mythology, the awakening of Kali is described in detail. When Kali rises from the depths, she does so in great anger, stunning all gods and demons, keeping them all in a silent state.

In contrast, the emergence of Durga symbolises a higher, more refined symbol of the unconscious. Durga is a beautiful goddess seated on a tiger, portrayed as having eight hands, the eightfold elements of man. Durga wears a mala similar to Kali but has 52 heads that represent the 52 letters of the Sanskrit alphabet. These are outer manifestations of Brahma (the first Hindu god) in the form of sound. Durga is the remover of all evil consequences in life who gives peace and power to the one who releases it from Mooladhara.

Awakening Kundalini

The human brain has ten compartments, nine of which are dormant, whereas one is active. Everything you know and think of stems from the one portion of the brain that is active, the rest is asleep. These inactive parts of the brain are asleep simply because they have no energy or conductivity, if you will. The silent parts of the brain have prana/life force, but not consciousness.

You may ask, how does one open these dormant parts of the brain? Nearly everybody knows how to awaken a range of emotions such as fear, anxiety and passion but most are unaware of how to open more of the brain. The frontal brain lobes need to be charged with a sufficient amount of prana/life force energy, and this is done by practicing pranayama, the art of yogic breathing. The brain is an electric lamp; to turn the lamp, on you need to flick the switches—these switches are the chakras.

A genius is one who has awakened more than one part of the dormant brain, and those who have momentary flashes of genius ideas have awakened more of the brain for a few moments. A full awakening will turn you into a junior god, an incarnation of divinity in the world. If Kundalini rises to a specific chakra, then the characteristics of the certain chakra will be brought into your consciousness. For example, Swadhisthana will raise levels of joy; Manipura will raise levels of self-assertion; Anahata will expand love; and Vishuddhi will awaken wisdom and discrimination.

Awakened upon birth

If the awakening of Kundalini takes place through birth, pranayama, or tantric initiation, you don't have to know anything. Usually, one whose Kundalini is awakened at birth has parents that are highly evolved spiritually. This entails

112

that the higher faculties are fully or partially active once born, and hence the person is renowned as a saint or one of illumination, an incarnation *avatara* or son of god.

One born with active, awakened Kundalini has experiences that are very much under control, all taking form in the natural way without ever knowing that something unnatural has occurred within. A child born in this manner holds extraordinary clarity of vision, high-quality thinking, an unusually advanced philosophy/attitude towards life and the gift of detachment already within. Those born in this awakened way inner-stand that the parents were just a gateway into this realm for the work they have to do on the planet. They exhibit matured behaviour and take the middle path of life, keeping emotions under control.

Giving birth to a yogi or enlightened child is not a simple matter. In order to bring such a highly evolved soul into this world, the parental force must transform their greatest desires and aspirations into spiritual channels. In the West, it is not known that such a phenomena can take place, because of their religions and false identifications regarding the union of sex.

It is, however, possible that an entirely new race of superhuman beings can come forth onto this physical plane, radiate pure, unconditional love and strive towards the healing and reform of the planet. Through constant practice of yoga, you can transform the makeup of your genes and thereby transform their quality. You have to transform the quality of your sperm or ovaries by first transforming your whole consciousness, and this will ultimately change the elements of your body, allowing you to have children with awakened Kundalini.

The sacred spine

The back is a complex structure constructed of 33 vertebrae, over 30 muscles, numerous ligaments, multiple joints and intervertebral discs. Supporting all your upper body weight is the spine, which is made up of more than 30 small bones called vertebrae, stacked one on top of the other. A spongy piece of cartilage, called a disc, sits between each vertebra acting as shock absorbers, preventing the vertebrae from grinding against one another.

The human spine holds great importance in relation to one's spiritual growth. If you look around yourself for a moment, you may find that 70–80% of people suffer from back problems. Many live a one-sided life, neglecting the body and the spine. The most common issue with a large majority of people these days is lower-back pain, and there are good reasons for this, such as computer work, bad posture and simply an overweight upper body.

The epidemic of 'bad backs' maybe linked to a person's spiritual disorder. **Judith Harris**[34], an experienced analyst and yoga teacher defines these bodily symptoms as a reflection of one's inner state of being. The posture you may hold is either slouched in defeat or standing tall in victory; whichever it may be, it is largely unconscious and controlled by the subconscious mind. Body language of the spine is a huge indication of the quality of one's up-to-date life experience, as it is the 'backbone of life'.

In Western cultures, many have a tendency to thrust their heads and minds ahead of the rest of the physical body, always rushing and feeling like they need to be somewhere else, always, in turn, throwing the spine out of alignment. 'Getting ahead' seems to be the primary focus for the majority of people, forward-progress orientated but failing to notice how the backbone of life supports all from behind. The spine is the first dense structure that forms inside the womb, before the body, limbs and arms take form.

With this unconscious connection being recognised, it could be that back pain in an individual is symptomatic of the unconscious disconnection to everything the backbone represents, including one's spiritual connection and Kundalini awakening. This disconnection has left so many unstable and without roots, unsure of where they are, where they have come from and where they are headed to.

Your spine divides at the waist area above the sacrum. In practices such as hatha yoga, the lengthening and stretching of the spine is seen to be a crucial step for spiritual development. Aligning the spine encourages an opening throughout the entire physical body, to allow the flow of life force/QI energy to come forth and stimulate the chakra power centres, ultimately allowing the Kundalini energy to flow upwards to the apex of the brain free of blockages.

The sacrum is a curved bone consisting of five fused vertebrae, the absolute foundation of the spine supporting and rooting the entire spinal column. When you stand in correct alignment, the force of gravity flows from the head, the back of knees and down to the ankles, making the area of the sacrum the centre of gravity; for this reason, it is the focal point of your relationship to the ground and body, the centre of the root chakra.

Hatha yoga practitioners refer to the sacrum as the 'holy bone', the centre of the divine body. It is seen as the place of transformation, as it is the connecting bridge way between the lower half and upper half of your body, as above so below. The sacrum is the absolute centre of gravity; gravity will draw your feet to the floor, acting as the grounding anchor that is needed to live in the physical world, and yet it is counteracted by the tendency of all living things that encourage a sprouting and expansion growing upwards towards the sun.

Now that knowledge regarding the sacrum and its central importance has come to light, it can possibly be linked directly to lower-back pain even though a physiological cause/source may never identified. It may be so, whilst the majority of people are focused on 'getting ahead', so to speak, this area of the body has fallen into the dark, a victim of the unconscious neglect. This serves to show the number of people who have forgotten their basic roots, the balance between heaven and earth and, more importantly, those that have not yet realised the sacredness within.

Could lower-back pain be a warning sign from the body alerting your awareness, warning you of a disconnection with the true self? It is a fact that many people who suffer chronic back pains also suffer from other numerous ailments and have a serious lack of energy. As the sacrum is a large factor contributing to the rising of Kundalini, it could be that people with back pains need to seriously consider working towards reconnecting with their energetic framework before further problems manifest into illness and dis-ease.

You are now aware of the importance of the spine and the role it plays in rising Kundalini, alongside optimum energetic balance. If you feel that you have posture problems and back pains or just simply want to increase the energetic flow from the base of the spine then there is a solution. You can take up hatha yoga classes with an instructor in your area or you can get yourself a yoga trapeze swing from **www.yogabodynaturals.co.uk**[35].

All information on spinal inversion therapy (hanging upside down) is available on the website. You can set up the swing in your own home, and it only takes around 7 minutes per day to feel the maximum, rapid benefits. The greatest approach for back relief and energetic flow is traction, back and core strengthening and flexibility. The traction is a method of treatment that lengthens the spine apart (as opposed to squishing it together).

A healthy spine has full, firm and resilient disk tissues that allow for complete range of motion. This is ideal. Nevertheless, after sitting all day in an office or car, after exercising and rotating the spine at only 20% of its full potential, or after years of poor posture caused by designer shoes, it's very likely that some of your disks are not in great shape.

Mantra chants

Kundalini can also be awakened by the daily practice of daily mantra chanting. Chanting specific mantras is a highly powerful way of removing stagnant energy from your auric field and allowing the dormant energy inside of you to awaken. Once you practice a mantra daily in the correct manner, you will start to develop the vision of a higher force that gives you the power to live amidst the indifferences in life.

If you were to throw a stone into a lake, you would see the effect of circular ripples flowing outwardly from the epicentre. The sound force you emit from chanting a mantra gathers momentum in a similar way once you repeat it over and over again. The vibration occurs deeply in the ocean of your mind. Repetition of a mantra hundreds, thousands or even millions of times permeates all of the cells in your body, every part of your brain, and it purifies the physical, mental and emotional aspect of your being.

You can chant mantra aloud, softly, or in your head. The mental, psychic, physical and spiritual plane are the four main levels that encourage Kundalini to awaken systematically. When you coordinate mantra whilst breathing in through your nose, it creates a great potential in balancing your chakras and activates Mooladhara. Alongside mantra, music and frequency tones are also another tender way to enhance the awakening. All Mantra should be chanted 108 times, 100 times for yourself and eight times for everybody else and those in suffering.

A recommended mantra for anybody wanting to progress with Kundalini, spiritually or to clean the luminous energy field is **Sri Vidya.** This can be found on the YUSA YouTube channel. The Sri chakra or Sri Yantra is a diagrammatic representation like a map of the complete nerve plexus of the body (*Marma* points). It is a known fact that spiritual realisation occurs when the consciousness enters a 'hole'-like region in the heart chakra, resulting in blissful and ego-free state.

A Yantra is a pure geometric configuration, composed of basic primal shapes. These shapes are psychological symbols corresponding to inner states of human consciousness. This innate simplicity of composition is identified with spiritual presence. The use of such elementary shapes is not simplistic, but, rather, it represents the highest conception in visual terms, because the projection of the symbol is then direct and bold, so that even a small miniature can create a sense of expansiveness

This below visual is a systematic journey synchronising the movements with Khadgamala Stotram. Khadgamala Stotram is an ancient linguistic composition designed to represent systematically the journey and the various experiences and emotions that occur on the path to self-realisation. It is the story of creation and evolution in a geometric hologram.

See the diagrammatic representation of the Sri Yantra mandala below.

The Auric Field

Your auric field is simply an energetic bubble that surrounds, penetrates and extends throughout your physical body. It is electromagnetic in nature and is constructed with various types of living, intelligent vibrations and frequencies.

Every living organism has an auric field component. Whether it be plants, minerals, or humans, as well as every inanimate thing including rocks; all material objects made by man; and the earth, sun, moon and all other celestial bodies throughout the universe. The human aura has layers of physical, emotional, mental and spiritual elements. Everything throughout the universe is constructed with subatomic particles that are bound by light frequencies. Each individual particle holds electricity; therefore, the particle produces an energetic, auric field.

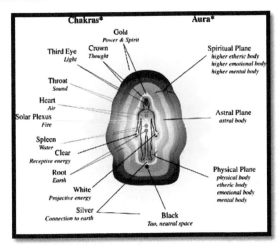

Above is a representation of the auric field and its relationship to the chakra system

Just like the chakra system, your auric field contains the primary colours of the rainbow, and it changes colour frequency upon a fluctuation in mood, thoughts and feelings. Higher vibrational thoughts and emotions such as joy peace, love and gratitude expand the energetic field and are highly conductive, which therefore give an increased sense of energy and wellbeing as well as defending you against low-vibrational disease and ailments.

Lower-vibrational thoughts and emotions, on the contrary, such as anger, hate, fear and resentment, do the opposite and encourage a contraction in your auric field. These fluctuations in your aura are caused by the charge delivered by the emotions and thoughts you emit; they are very alive with the energy and power of different vibrational frequencies.

A Russian scientist has been studying the human energy field and is claiming that people can change the world simply by using their own energy. Although this idea is not novel, not too many have taken the time to scientifically prove such ideas; however, the field of quantum physics has shed some powerful light on the topic over the years. Dr Konstantin Korotkov[36], professor of physics at St. Petersburg State Technical University, states that when you think positive and negative thoughts, each has a different impact on the surrounding environment.

Further, it is wise to keep your aura clean and in good shape. Just like you would have a daily shower to clean your physical body, it is important to pay some due care and attention to your energetic body for optimum emotional health and mental clarity. Distortions in the aura can also trigger physical disease and mental unbalance.

'We are developing the idea that our consciousness is part of the material world and that with our consciousness we can directly influence our world,' ~
Konstantin Korotkov

Importance of maintaining your energetic system

The construction of your higher-energetic soul body is very alive and very intelligent, whether you believe it or not. Each individual energy space holds vast knowledge and its own conscious awareness; it knows exactly what it needs to function at its optimum level. When your energetic system is disrupted, blocked, damaged, or slowing down then warning messages are sent to your conscious level of awareness to alert you of the imbalances.

Dependant on how strongly you embrace the connection with your higher self, the easier/harder it is for you to pick up these messages; the more you progress towards your higher spiritual connection, the easier life becomes. The emphasis of this whole chapter is to educate/help you to remember about your complete energy system so you can take control of your life and become the best you possibly can be in this lifetime. No one else is responsible for you, except you!

The majority of 'experts' in the medical industry (mainly Western) are trained primarily in observing the physical body without addressing the unseen energetic makeup and its components. As mentioned previously, your energy systems are conscious and connected with all energies in the universe, the energetic component is immortal. The physical body is an extension, and always falls in alignment with the frequency and vibration of the energy body. This is why it is important to have your higher system in balance for optimum physical health and wellbeing.

Your subatomic and electrical energy systems act as a mid-connection between the physical world and the metaphysical/spiritual world. When you look after your energy systems, you look after your deepest and most profound needs, including physical, emotional, intellectual and spiritual. We now dive into the numerous ways you can clean and maintain your higher energy systems.

The following are summaries of the physical, intellectual, emotional and spiritual ways to clear, rebalance, activate and heal your energy. All aspects are interconnected and required for healthy and vibrant living.

Sage smudging and burning: Burning sage is extremely good for cleansing negative and dark energies from your auric field, chakras and even your home. You can use a stick of white sage or use loose green sage and burn. Simply take some sage and put on a pot/plate and start to burn it; slowly blow the amber that is alight around all corners of the room with all doors and windows closed. You can sit in the room for 5–10 minutes or so.

Healing with colour: This is a very powerful method. Different colours hold a range of vibrations that affect different elements of your being. For example, green is a colour that encourages healing and calmness so if you want to focus on staying calm and supporting you're healing, wear the colour green. Green is directly related to your heart chakra, each chakra resonates with a different colour as already covered. In meditation or even when going about daily duties, visualise that you are breathing in the colour green, or decorate your room with the colour green. If you want to feel energised, do the same with the colour red. Red stimulates the root chakra, whereas violet stimulates the crown.

Giving and receiving love, self-love and expressing true emotions: Emotions left unaddressed or unexpressed remain lodged within the luminous energy field, contributing to the manifestation of blockages and chakra distortion and creating holes in your auric field. True acceptance of self and being completely happy with your present life situations and past is important for the vibrational foundations of your energetic body. For true self-acceptance and growth, you can practice urine therapy for emotional and energetic detoxification (information in chapter 3); information on this topic is found in the body section of this book. Giving and receiving love is also high on the list of importance. There is no vibrational frequency higher than unconditional love. Work on the heart, practice forgiveness and happiness, and the rest will follow.

Natural, living foods and vegetarian diet: All foods provided by Mother Nature that are organic and non-GMO (genetically modified) support your energy centres highly. This is probably the highest form of energetic regeneration alongside Ayahuasca, Iboga and urine therapy. Eat as much fruit and vegetables as you can, preferably uncooked, in their raw state. All natural and raw living foods contain Chi/QI life-force energy and hold the colour spectrum of the rainbow; this energy is unseen and formless, similar to your energy body. Consumption of fruit, vegetable and juice aids healing and elimination of stagnant energy. Cutting out meats and dairy is also a huge step towards maintaining your energy centres. Drink fruit smoothies and raw juices and stay hydrated with alkaline PH balanced water. Extensive information on these topics is given in chapter 3.

Intellectual stimulation and intellectual pursuits: These are critical elements required for a healthy energy system. The mind rests in the mental aura, and this level of the aura needs to be stimulated or it will slow down, therefore causing you to become fatigued and accelerating the aging process. You need to be learning, interested and passionate about something most of the time in your daily life. Keeping the mind active with your passions encourages growth in the mental aura and leads to an expansion of your intellectual capabilities. Creative activities such as cooking, gardening, needlework, studying, juicing, writing and singing stimulate this part of your auric field.

Grounding to the earth and regular salt baths: *Grounding*, or *earthing*, refers to connecting electrically with the Earth. A growing body of research is finding numerous health benefits because of the physical body being grounded. When you are grounded to the earth, it allows a dissipation of all negative and static energy that does not serve your being. In modern life, many have a high exposure to electromagnetic energy EMF/ELF waves.

These magnetic particles can create distortion in your energetic field causing it to become distorted. If you work with computers or in an area where the electromagnetic static is high, then it is a wise idea to get yourself a grounding cable/mat and sleep with it attached to you.

Another way to ground yourself is to go outside and place your bare feet or hands on some grass or earth, or to immerse yourself in a body of conductive water such as the sea or a mineral-rich lake. Having regular salt baths with Epsom/Dead Sea salt (www.westlab.com) is also highly beneficial in cleaning the auric field and discharging static energy that you may have picked up. There are also numerous scientifically proven health benefits related to daily grounding. You can find a cable/mat here: **www.groundology.com**[37].

Meditation, breathing and spiritual integrity: Meditation aids in quieting your busy mind so that you become open to listening, being and hearing from Universal Powers. Upon practicing for some time, you begin to step out of the mind, and balance is brought forth in to the mental auric plane. This now gives room for feeling rather than thinking—practice feeling your inner body and your heart chakra whilst breathing deeply through the nose (diaphragmatic breathing). As already mentioned, deep breathing encourages expansion and conductivity around the heart field in turn forming synchronicity with the other energy centres and brain. Your very essence and nature is of spirit; you are a spiritual being having a human experience. With this being said, it highlights the importance of being connected with your true self, the essence of spirit. Practicing the methods delivered in this book will contribute towards a rise in your level of spiritual awareness.

Ayahuasca and Iboga detox: Natures energy is very healing to human beings as humans are connected to nature on all levels. Ancient shamans in parts of Africa and South America/Amazonian regions have utilised the healing power of the plants named Ayahuasca and Iboga for generations. Many travel from all over the world to get a first-hand healing experience from ingesting the plants in a special brew form. YUSA has had extensive experience with these plants upon a visit to South Africa, where we stayed with the shamans and had deep energetic healing on multiple levels. More information on Ayahuasca and Iboga comes later in this chapter.

Physical exercise and connecting with nature: Physical exercise is an absolute must when aiming to increase your energetic vibrancy. Physical exercise not only open up the lungs, stimulates the lymphatic system and enhances perspiration levels but also encourages the rotational opening and widening of your chakras. The YUSA highly recommends the book *Science of Breath*, by **Yogi Ramacharaka** along with *Ancient Secret of the Fountain of Youth* (Book 2) by **Peter Kelder**. In these books you can find a beneficial exercise program named the **Five Tibetan Rites**.

Try to incorporate exercise 2 to 3 times each week for around 30 minutes to an hour and, most importantly, remember to stretch your muscles afterwards. Stretching and basic yoga poses have a profound positive impact on your energetic system. YUSA highly recommends the practice of tantric Kundalini yoga, a book named *A Systematic Course in the Ancient Tantric Techniques of Yoga and Kriya*, by **Swami Satyananda Saraswati,** will give the most comprehensive guidance and steps to self-realisation.

Nature, however, holds a very soothing and healing vibration with which the human heart is synchronised when exposed to clean, natural surroundings. Sunlight exposure plays a massive role in balancing your chakras and harnessing energy. It can be recognised that when you get out of the city into the countryside; you feel rejuvenated – the shades of colour, the sounds of birds, frogs, running water etc. have a soothing effect on the mind and body.

These sounds consist of vibrational frequency, which is measured in Hertz (Hz). All of these natural harmonics vibrate at 432 Hz, and it's the natural frequency of the universe. Being in tune with this universal frequency is an integral part of natural living. Try to connect with nature and the sun as much as you can; they are both conscious and hold tremendous healing power. Meditating in nature can help you connect with all that is around you. Witnessing yourself in the moment and being present delivers a subtle sense of peace and rhythmic balance.

Bill Mollison[38] said that the wild unmanaged zones are so vital: 'in Zone V, we observe and learn; it is your essential place for meditation, where we are visitors, not managers.' Moreover, this is certainly so, for in wild nature, humans deeply connect with the inner wild essential natures. Being present in and conscious of what is this moment is a simple but very profound spiritual practice. This can be done in any situation, whatever your circumstance. Even in the garden, there is a special opportunity to do this, as you can open up to a greater sense of nature.

Frequencies & Tones for Rebalancing

Your chakras are interconnected with the tones of the universe: these are called solfeggio tones. They represent the basis pitch of any sound known to man. There are seven main solfeggio frequencies that relate to each corresponding main chakra. These tones can be used in meditation, played whilst working, or even whilst going about other daily duties.

Vibration and balance is central to everything in the universe. Your body and all matter exist at different rates of vibration and have their own resonant frequencies. Therefore, sound and vibration play a fundamental role in your life by affecting physical, mental and spiritual levels of your human being. Below are the specific frequencies that stimulate and rebalance each chakra energy wheel. All of the frequencies can be found on the YUSA YouTube channel.

Some people can feel overloaded if they listen to more than 60 to 90 minutes of binaural beats in 1 day, with a rare few that can experience overload in as little as 10 minutes. During day or morning meditations, if you need to return to focus quickly, it can be best to finish a program with an Alpha track. If you have trouble with sleeping at night, it may be good to use just the Alpha and Gamma meditation during the day and morning.

Root Chakra (Red):

UT – 396 Hz: Liberating Guilt and Fear

This frequency liberates the energy, and it has beneficial effects on feelings of guilt. It cleanses the feelings of guilt, which often represent one of the basic obstacles to realisation, enabling achievement of goals in the most direct way. The 'UT' tone releases you from the feeling of guilt and fear by bringing down the defence mechanisms. The frequency of 396 Hz searches out hidden blockages, subconscious negative beliefs and ideas that have led to your present situations.

Sacral Chakra (Orange):

RE – 417 Hz: Undoing Situations & Facilitating Change

The next main tone from the solfeggio scale produces energy to bring about change. This frequency cleanses traumatic experiences and clears destructive influences of past events. When speaking of cellular processes, tone 'RE' encourages the cell and its functions in an optimal way. The frequency of 417 Hz puts you in touch with an inexhaustible source of energy that allows you to change your life.

Solar Plexus Chakra (Yellow):

MI – 528 Hz: Transformation & Miracles (DNA Repair)

Tone 'MI' is used to return human DNA to its original, perfect state. This frequency brings transformation and miracles into your life. The process of DNA reparation is followed by beneficial effects – increased amount of life energy, clarity of mind, awareness, awakened or activated creativity and ecstatic states such deep inner peace, dance and celebration. Tone 'Mi' activates your imagination, intention and intuition to operate for your highest and best purpose.

Heart Chakra (Green):

FA – 639 Hz: Connecting/Relationships

Another frequency from the sacred solfeggio scale, it enables creation of harmonious community and harmonious interpersonal relationships. Tone 'Fa' can be used for dealing with relationships problems – those in family, between partners or friends or social problems. When talking about cellular processes, 639 Hz frequency can be used to encourage the cell to communicate with its environment. This ancient solfeggio frequency enhances communication, understanding, tolerance and love.

Throat Chakra (Blue):

SOL – 741 Hz: Awakening Intuition

It cleans the cell ('Solve polluti') from the toxins. Frequent use of 741 Hz leads to a healthier, simpler life and to changes in diet towards foods that are not poisoned by various kinds of toxins. Tone 'Sol' cleans the cell from different kinds of electromagnetic radiation. Another application of this sound frequency is solving problems of any nature. The fifth frequency of the solfeggio scale will also lead you into the power of self-expression, which results in a pure and stable life.

3rd Eye Chakra (Indigo):

LA – 852 Hz: Returning to Spiritual Order

Tone 'La' is linked to your ability to see through the illusions of your life, such as the hidden agendas of people, places and things. This frequency can be used as means for opening a person up for communication with the all-embracing spirit. It raises awareness and lets you return to spiritual order. Regarding cellular processes, 852 Hz enables the cell to transform itself into a system of higher level.

Crown Chakra (Violet):

TI – 963 Hz: Solfeggio Higher-Frequency Body

This tone awakens any system to its original, perfect state. It is connected with the light and all-embracing spirit and enables the experience of returning to oneness. This frequency reconnects you with the spirit or the non-vibrational energies of the spiritual world. It will enable you to experience oneness, your true nature.

The Universal Sound, the Tone of Om/Aum

As the entire makeup of the universe is based on frequencies, tones and sounds, it is right to say that everything in creation, whether it be a planet, human, or animal, holds its own very unique frequency. In Buddhist and Hindu traditions, the mantra of **OM** is considered the primordial tone of the universe, the very vibration that forms the foundational basis of all things.

The tone Om resonates to the frequency of 136.1Hz, the frequency of the earth year (when covered digitally), lying between C and C# in Western tuning. Om or Aum is the sacred syllable, omnipotent, omnipresent and the source of all manifested existence. It runs through all life and permeates your breath/prana.

According to the Mandukya Upanishad[39], 'Om is the one eternal syllable of which all that exists. The past, the present and the future are all included in this one sound and all that exists beyond the three forms of time is also implied within it'. It is not a word but more of an intonation, similar to music, holding an ability to transcend age, race and culture. The word *Aum* is constructed by three Sanskrit letters, aa, au and ma, which when combined together produce the sound Om, absolute reality, that which encompasses the three states of waking, dreaming and deep sleep, represented by Aum. Repetition of this simple mantra is a prayer in itself; this sound permeates and resonates deeply throughout the body, penetrating the centre of your being/soul.

Chanting *Ommmmmmm* delivers peace, harmony and bliss after around 15 minutes. You create within yourself a vibration that attunes in sympathy with the cosmic vibration and you then start thinking universally. Mind moves between the opposites of silence and sound, balancing out the left and right hemispheres of the brain. Here there is no thought, only stillness. You embrace the moment of trance, a place where intellect and mind are transcended whilst you embrace the infinite self in a moment of realisation—this is the power of Om.

A very powerful and healing Om mantra you can listen to on the YUSA YouTube channel is called **Mahamrityunjaya mantra** (maha-mrityun-jaya); it is one of the more potent of the ancient Sanskrit mantras. Mahamrityunjaya is a call for enlightenment and is a practice of purifying the karma of the soul at deep levels. It is also said to be very beneficial for mental, emotional and physical health. It is recommended that you listen to this mantra daily for 40 days. The translation for the mantra is below.

Tryambakam: *Trya* means *three*. *Ambakam* means *eyes*. It means the *three eyes of the Absolute*, which are the processes of creation, existence and dissolution, as well as the other triads, which are part of Aum. The three 'eyes' means experiencing these 3 stages and triads at one time, from the higher, all pervasive vantage point of the Absolute.

Yajamahe: We rejoice in meditation on all of this.

Sugandhim: The word means *fragrance*. Like a spreading fragrance, all of this permeates the whole of existence, whilst at the same time being that existence.

Pushtivardhanam: The word means *that which sustains and nourishes all*. Thus, the fragrance that permeates all is the sustainer of all beings, whilst also the essence of all beings.

Urvarukamiva: *Urva* means *big and powerful*. *Arukam* means *disease*, like the spiritual diseases of ignorance and untruth, which are like the death of Wisdom or Truth.

Bandhanan: The word means *bound down*, as in bound down to the ignorance and untruth.

Mrityor: The word means *ignorance and untruth*.

Mukshiya: The word means *liberation from the cycles of physical, mental and spiritual death*.

Maamritat: The word means *please give me rejuvenating nectar, to have this liberation, like the process of severing the cucumber from the creeping vine.*

Below is comparison of the similarities between the Sri Yantra mandala and a Tonoscope picture/cymatics of the sound of Om. The Sri Yantra is thousands of years old.

Sri Yantra (OM) Mandala   OM sound on a Tonoscope

'Om is not just a sound or vibration. It is not just a symbol. It is the entire cosmos, whatever we can see, touch, hear and feel. Moreover, it is all that is within our perception and all that is beyond our perception. It is the core of our very existence. If you think of Om only as a sound, a technique or a symbol of the Divine, you will miss it altogether. Om is the mysterious cosmic energy that is the substratum of all the things and all the beings of the entire universe. It is an eternal song of the Divine. It is continuously resounding in silence on the background of everything that exists.' ~ **Amit Ray**

Tibetan singing bowls for sound therapy

According to Tibetan oral tradition, the existence of singing bowls dates back to the time of the historical Buddha Shakyamuni (560–480 B.C.). The tradition was brought from India to Tibet, along with the teachings of the Buddha, by the great tantric master Padmasambhava, in the 8th century A.D.

The use of Tibetan bowls produces a powerful form of vibrational sound healing, an effective and proven modality is centred on the use of alternate pure vibrations to reduce stress, create a deep sense of peace, alter consciousness and promote enhanced health and sense of wellbeing.

During your waking state, the Beta brainwave frequency is mainly dominant. The use of sound therapy and listening to Tibetan bowls can entrain your brainwaves into deeper Alpha and Theta frequencies, inducing deep meditative peaceful states, enhanced mental clarity and increased intuition. This type of sound therapy creates a sacred space within a person, encouraging healing from pain, depression and emotional disorders.

The ancient instrument of Tibetan singing bowls is played in a specific rhythmic pattern that creates a sound frequency of Aum or Om. This is the sound wave of perfection affecting your nervous system as it synchronises the hemispheres of the brain. Listening to the frequencies of the bowls also promotes chakra healing and balancing.

The oldest Tibetan bowls have been metallurgical tested by the British Museum of London, where they found the bowls to consist of a 12-metal alloy consisting of silver, nickel, copper, zinc, antimony, tin, lead, cobalt, bismuth, arsenic, cadmium and iron. This is now a lost art, as it appears that this type of quality cannot be reproduced in today's age.

There is a Tibetan bowl playlist on the YUSA YouTube channel, you can choose to sit and meditate whilst listening to these bowls or simply play the audios when going about other duties. It is recommended that you listen 30 minutes a day to nourish your mind, body and spirit.

The Luminous Energy Field, the blueprint Of Life

The Western world differentiates greatly between curing and healing. Curing is the business of medicine and eliminating symptoms, whereas healing is dealing with the deeply rooted issues that have caused a certain illness to manifest; it is a much more thorough practice, claiming recognition of the underlying issue. Healing has to do with an experience of infinity, an experience of the self, which exists outside of time. This part of the self can never experience illness and can never be touched by disease.

There are ancient healing methodologies that have been in existence for over 50,000 years, proven effective. Taught from teacher to student, grandmother to granddaughter, grandfather to grandson, these methodologies hold great importance in many traditions, including shamanic. These methodologies are rarely spoken about or even known by people in the Western world. They are known as the luminous healing practices of the shamanic Americas.

The word *shaman* is a Siberian word meaning *'one who knows'*. The shaman is one who works midway between the physical world and the spiritual world, trained in a very specific manner, not by another person, but by nature and the plant world. Their role is to provide certain healing practices to an individual at the energetic plane of their being, healing and balancing the chakras, luminous energy field, heart, DNA structure and more.

As mentioned previously, a high percentage of illnesses and imbalances are due to the physical manifestation of distorted/deeply rooted energy lodged in the chakra system that account for disrupting ones natural energy flow. Past traumatic events, negative thinking and toxic emotions are also to blame. The shamanic teachings are slowly crossing over to practitioners worldwide, filling the missing pieces of the puzzle, allowing more and more people to experience a fulfilled healing, which in turn allow more love to be spread between people and across the world.

Western medicine disregards this knowledge, with the primary focus aimed at attacking the body with medication, often allowing only a temporary release from whatever health troubles one may be experiencing. The problem with this is that the underlying, non-physical issue still remains energetically imprinted within the luminous body and can always manifest into something physical at a later time until it is eradicated completely.

The makeup of the luminous energy field

The luminous energy body is the essence or soul construct within every single person, and it survives death and experiences immortality. The luminous energy field takes a shape similar to a doughnut's, and it has a narrow axis or tunnel; earlier on in this section, it was briefly described as the hearts toroidal field. It is a very complex design created by a higher force of intelligence that decided to give your life consciousness. It is interconnected with the heart field, auric field and the chakra system and is perceived as an aura of electromagnetic light energy that informs the physical body.

There is an infinite flow throughout the luminous energy field. The flow moves clockwise around the physical body as well as a vertically up the spinal cord through the root chakra and out through the crown. The energy field consists of four main layers which are causal (spirit), psychic (soul), mental-emotional (mind) and physical (body). This energy field serves as a defensive cocoon in the same manner as the skin does to the physical body.

The luminous energy field is a potent reservoir of vital force, a sea of energy that is alive and as indispensable to your health as nutrients, minerals and oxygen, the purest and most precious energies for life. When your energetic body becomes depleted by environmental pollutants, ill health, bad diet, negative thoughts and emotions, or stress, then disease is likely to manifest on the physical level/physical body. You can live a truly optimised, energised and healthy life just by ensuring this energy field is replenished and taken care of. Many people do not have a clue what they are beyond the physical body, purely because they cannot see and are unaware of the inner workings of their being.

Tibetan and Indian mystics described the luminous energy as a halo that surrounds the physical body; this was documented thousands of years ago. The Buddhists depicted the luminous energy field in mandala pictures as Buddha enveloped by blue and gold bands of fire. Native American elders speak of persons who shimmer in the night as if illuminated by an inner sun.

'You are not the limitations that have been spoken over you. Your energetic signature is infinite. And as a vibrational being nothing can limit you.' ~
Panache Desai[40]

YUSA's experience with the shamans

Earlier in 2013, YUSA travelled to South Africa to stay with our good shaman friends in order to learn more about the human energetic structure and to attend some workshops surrounding soul evolution and emotional healing. The shamans, we had the privilege of working with, understood that everybody has a unique luminous energy body surrounding the physical one that informs and organises the physical body in the same way that the energy fields of a magnet will organise iron filings on a piece of glass.

The shamans taught us that it is vital for every person to take control and intervene at the level of the luminous energy field, the level of the blueprint, rather than just treating the physical body with drugs or surgery, as whatever condition one may be suffering from could later re-express itself. They also mentioned that the energetic field/Torus is healthiest and expanded when in nature. When you are in a city or close to electrical equipment, however, the energy field becomes depleted and squashed, forming a tight cocoon around the physical body.

We learnt that the luminous energy field contains a variety of emotional data, such as early life experiences, genetically inherited illnesses and past-life memories before birth. The luminous energy field is a storage centre for previous events both positive and negative. It came to our realisation that when you can perceive the absolute nature of this energetic field, you can perceive the nature of life itself. The visual spectrum that the human eye can see is very narrow, within the band of the electromagnetic spectrum, but most of what is happening in the universe is happening outside of this visual spectrum.

Spending a lot of time with the shamans and experiencing extensive personal healing work with the aid of medicinal plants really triggered some deeper expansive thinking which allowed us to recognise with our inner eyes, the interconnectedness and sacredness within all life. To perceive the luminous energy field you have to remove the veil so to speak, breakout of the cultural trance many are under in this day and age, which so many have been educated into and which defines the nature of reality in a very limiting way.

We also learnt that if the luminous energy field becomes toxic when you experience and are unable to process toxic emotions, they begin to build like sludge, weakening and debilitating the flows in the field. This is a main cause of lethargy, tiredness and unconsciousness, and it ultimately leads to suffering and illness. The emotions and thoughts one has at the time of deep trauma form energetic matter onto the luminous energy field and do not leave until they are healed at the same level. This is the metaphysical reason why a person may never being able to get over a traumatic event and why the memory of the event may revisit him or her in later life.

Luminous energy field & trauma

The luminous energy field literally organises your reality. It will choreograph life experiences that recreate the original wounding in order to give a fresh opportunity to heal. Dependant on the person, a recreation of a traumatic event may be too much to handle and may end up strengthening the imprint within the field. Therefore, the person is left needing greater core healing from the medicinal plants and shamans. The way an imprint works is that if you don't learn the lessons and heal, you can end up 'marrying' it. This is seen all over the world today in different aspects of people's lives.

For example, a woman at the age of 32 had several significant relationships in her past. She found that they all ended up in the same tragic manner of betrayal, cheating and heartbreak. Her luminous energy field carried an imprint that was centred on the theme of abandonment and betrayal. She realised that she had had the same relationship but with several different men, repeating it over and over again. It was not until she erased and healed the energetic stamp that was she able to experience a fulfilling and wholesome relationship with another person.

As mentioned earlier in this chapter and in the mind chapter, thoughts and emotions are atomic energy and are very much alive. We explained that energy cannot be destroyed, only transformed, and form the basis and operation of the universal law of attraction. By having an energetic blueprint attached to your energy field that is charged with traumatic emotion from the past, it gravitates towards itself the same vibration of events, in turn creating circumstances and events within your reality that will make you feel the same way. The luminous energy field is 5000 times stronger than the mind; this field is the main attraction source, with the mind and thoughts coming secondary. Many people fail to deliver the importance of this topic in their books and courses.

The shamans explained that the emotional blueprint actually forms itself to the walls of the luminous energy field becoming permanent energetic stain, similar to a fingerprint but with an electrical charge. Not only does an imprint hold energy, but it also contains information regarding the circumstances surrounding the original wounding. Whenever the stagnant imprint is triggered, the information is transmitted to the corresponding chakra and dominates the central nervous system, recreating the emotional chaos and pushing the imprint deeper and deeper.

An original imprint can be formed upon experiencing feelings/events such as child abuse, losing a partner or family member, a sense of feeling unloved, past-life trauma (even the way you could have died), bullying experiences and feeling left out, unloved, or neglected. Most often, in the earliest part of life, energetic imprints can also take form, even whilst still in the womb.

When you do not take control and program your luminous energy field with your own dreams and desires that you wish to create, then it is left open for programming by outside sources. When you connect with the subtle vibrations of nature, a healing balance in your luminous field is brought forth, allowing there to be a replenishment by sources that are not limited to the self. Your chakras are the organs of the luminous energy field, just as the stomach, liver etc. is to the physical body.

When the luminous energy field become highly toxic, you are no longer able to recycle emotional waste, and the chakra organs become clogged and backed up. The chakras metabolise energy and feed you in a very essential way; when they are clogged up, the quality of the fuel is reduced, causing mood swings, depression and activation of genetic blueprints. For example, suppose that a pair of twin brothers carry a genetic imprint of prostate cancer in their energy field. One brother who has a toxic energy field and emotions falls ill and has to undergo surgery. He is slightly confused, as his physical health and diet are good. The other brother who has a clean energy field does not pick up the illness, even though his physical lifestyle is not as clean.

An increase of energetic toxicity within the luminous energy field will eventually overload and directly affect the workings of the immune system, communicating degraded conditions to the body. Emotionally, depression kicks in; physically, it is a lack of vital energy, an inability to sleep well, decreased nutrient absorption from food and the expression of various diseases and ailments.

Modalities of healing and intrusive energies/entities

There are four modalities of healing when a shaman is working with the luminous energy field; the first one being the illumination process. This core healing process involving the clearing and erasing old imprints in the luminous energy field and assisting the client into experiencing infinity, stepping outside of time into their infinite nature up to the 8th chakra that exists outside of the physical body. The illumination process erases imprints from the luminous energy field, alongside the clearing and metabolising of any old energy within the chakras so they can energetically vibrate again at their optimum and natural state in order for you to acquire the rainbow body.

The second process involves working with intrusive energies or entities. In the West, it is assumed that all of the energies and emotions you experience belong to you alone. In traditional societies, they understand that there are energies that do not belong to you that are intrusive in nature. There are two kinds of intrusive energies.

The first one being thought forms; these are energies that are being directed at you if someone feels you have betrayed them or done them wrong. These types of energies are mainly from people who you were once close with, maybe one who thinks you left them and destroyed their lives because you where the love of their life. The resentment and anger they produce towards you can penetrate into your energy field, but they are not perceived as being foreign as you shared deep experiences with that specific person in the past.

The thought form intrusions are 'psychic darts' that can actually embed themselves within the body and eventually begin to transmit their poisons in the form of anger and fear, the two most deadly poisons in the world. The second type of intrusive energy is one that is spiritual/energetic in nature, an actual spirit force attached to your etheric body hosting and draining your energy.

As mentioned earlier, you only see a small percentage of the electromagnetic spectrum with your eyes in this dimensional reality. There are forces all around you, and the luminous energy field acts as a shield: the stronger the field, the more effective protection it can form against outside entities. When people are possessed, they have energy latching onto their luminous field. Somebody with weak energy at any given time (mainly whilst ill or drunk from alcohol) can have an energetic force attached to their luminous body, causing them to act strange, violent, or angry.

The third process the shamans work with is called the soul retrieval process. The healer will journey on behalf of the client to help them to recover a soul part that was lost in times of deep trauma and pain. The process of a soul retrieval can accomplish in a couple of sessions, that which can literally take years in psychotherapy. In psychotherapy, you are retrieving the 'whys' and the 'hows' of the event, whilst a soul retrieval process is recovering quantum energy full of life force, then re-installing it into ones psyche for essential resources the person needs in order to heal.

The fourth and final process is the death rites. This is forgotten in the West, but there is no greater gift you could give to somebody than to assist them in their greatest journey. The death rites allow you to be a moment of calm in the middle of a storm for somebody who is afraid and about to pass over, somebody who does not understand what will happen. Few people in their lives have practiced stillness, surrender, acceptance and love; these practices are required for you to die consciously.

The death rites assist in helping a loved one at the time of transition, playing a big part in the disengagement of the luminous energy field so that the luminous body does not remain attached to the physical body after death. The chakras also need to be sealed so the luminous body cannot re-enter the physical body.

In assisting a loved one into coming to peace with their life history, illuminating the chakras and helping them let go of past events, what they may have inflicted on others or vice versa, contributes largely to the lifting of all karma so that nothing is left. If one dies unconsciously, full of fear and non-acceptance, then their soul body can become trapped in a lower part of the astral realm; they are then known as 'lost souls' and will gravitate to the most spiritually open person in the family, acting as an intrusion to their luminous energy body until they can be put to rest with shamanic practices.

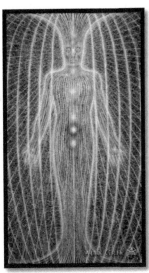

The above images display energetic workings of the etheric body and energetic hosts. Images sourced from painter Alex Grey[41]

133

The luminous energy field at the time of death

In the West, it is possible that many luminous bodies get trapped upon death, especially those who are religious and have a priest around them upon the time of passing. Instead of aiding the person and releasing their chakras from the physical body, a priest will make the symbol of a cross upon the forehead. This is the region for the third-eye/Ajna chakra, and crossing over this spiritual centre seals the chakras within the physical body ritualistically, keeping the chakras attached to the physical, causing great suffering for the one who is trying to leave this plane of existence. This can ultimately lead to the person being caught in a realm between the worlds.

Upon physical death, the soul prepares for its transition back home, where the death can then become a prolonged process if the energy field and emotions are very toxic. When the luminous body disengages from the physical in the correct manner, the 8th chakra completely envelops the other seven chakras, forming an egg-shaped orb. This orb travels up the centre of the toroidal field. Eastern scriptures indicate the orb will leave through the most developed chakra of that lifetime. Your soul has achieved immortality and has no need to return to earth unless you choose to reincarnate, it is now time to review the life and lessons for that incarnation.

To help somebody who is in the transition process, it is good to tell them that it is OK to let go. Giving a person permission to pass is one of the most important things that you could give to somebody on their journey. The state of infinity is everybody's birth right, but it is not a given. It is only those who step up to life and attain the wisdom through reincarnation that really get to experience infinity and never die again. For a soul that doesn't 'make it' through multiple lifetimes and may have fragmented due to suffering, the molecules and atoms of the luminous body will be reabsorbed into the creator, no longer holding individual consciousness.

Practice the arts of love, acceptance and surrender in life and let go of attachments. This will ensure a conscious death process with the least pain and suffering. Upon a panoramic life review, all emotions from life's situations are brought to the surface and this can be traumatic for the soul. Practice these arts in your life and accept whatever has been and gone; do not hold onto circumstances; let them flow through you and out of you, the principle practices of Zen Buddhism.

Alongside the various ancient methodologies of healing which the shamans adhere to, there are also specific techniques which involve sacred plants that are thousands and thousands of years old. These plants hold the innate ability to transform, detoxify and awaken one to their upmost life potential. In comparing the shamanic plants Iboga and Ayahuasca, the most difficult part is finding any common ground at all. They are as different as two experiences could be; though each of them is a master medicine in its own right.

YUSA has extensive first-hand experience with both of these magnificent healing plants and the results are so outstanding we have to share with those who are searching for psychological assistance. These medicines both have psychedelic effects and carry high vibratory spiritual energy, with Ayahuasca, being the feminine, and Iboga, being the masculine.

We travelled to Cape Town, South Africa to do an extensive 3-day Iboga detox flood, where the root was ingested (in powdered form), and a great healing took place for around 12 hours. A nurse was present, giving regular blood pressure checks and watching over, 24 hours per day. Ayahuasca, however, was prepared in a ceremony at the shaman's residence outside of Johannesburg. This was an in-depth ceremony that involved firstly clearing our energies with white sage and flower sprays; then we drank the prepared medicine, the shamans sang to summon the Aya spirit and the healing started. Detailed descriptions of each are below.

Iboga: The stern father

The Iboga experience is unique in the realm of psychedelics, almost to the point where it should be a part of a different category. Around 1 hour upon ingesting the Iboga, there is a sensation of falling deeper into oneself; it basically connects you with your higher self and the realm of thought becomes one of a higher nature. The reason for doing a full Iboga flood was to clear out old imprints in the luminous energy field and let go of old traumas and past conditioning buried deep.

To cut a long story short, Iboga makes the person revisit old traumatic events which have been stored within the energy body and subconscious mind. It may be uncomfortable for a while but it ensures a very in-depth removal of stagnant energy and past pain. It is like meeting the stern father so to speak, looking back on life in a loving way, letting go of all that no longer serves you.

Whereas most psychedelics either heighten normal senses or make them seem to disappear altogether, during the Iboga experience you are acutely aware of the physical discomfort of the body: rapid heart rate, intense dizziness, buzzing in the ears and the stern voice of the truth, lasting for 12 strong hours. Iboga will also put you in the shoes of those you have treated badly in your life; this can be quite a distressing lesson.

When the Iboga experience starts to smooth out a little, a superior sense of mental clarity arises, one that has never been felt before probably in your entire life. Your head actually feels lighter as if all the useless thought forms have been removed from the mental realm whilst a clearing of deeply rooted fears and anxiety forms have been removed from the luminous energy field. You feel like you are ready for a new approach to life and have literally been reborn.

Whilst present within the Iboga experience there is no translation issue because it is you talking to yourself. If you can't understand yourself you are in big trouble. People have called Iboga your 'stern father' and this is due to the nature of what Iboga tells you. It will very bluntly explain to you how you have been messing up, put you in the shoes of others you may of hurt and tell you to shape up! And for many, that may sound like your father, but in reality it is your higher self-directing your mind in line with what would be best for your soul evolution.

Iboga completely re-tunes your physical body and can eliminate drug cravings. It is known that cancers, viruses and illnesses reside at a different frequency compared to the healthy cells in the body. This makes sense, as these pathogens are rapidly dividing and devouring at a hyperactive rate. Iboga helps your entire body to adapt to a new frequency. Iboga is known to provide an all-natural full-body cellular detoxification and overall cleansing which is essential for a proper functioning body and mind. Patents are currently pending on Iboga alkaloids to reverse or treat dementia, Alzheimer's, depression and attention deficit hyperactivity disorder (ADHD), certain mental illnesses and psychiatric conditions whilst the compound is widely respected as an effective agent in treating serious drug addictions.

During your detox (about 12-24 hours), Iboga will clear your body of all unnatural substances and chemicals and you start feeling your true organic self with no toxins effecting your thought processes or physical body. In the case of addition you overcome you physical dependence of drugs or alcohol with very little if no withdrawal effects. Ibogaine has been found to activate a growth factor (Glial cell line-derived Neurotropic Factor) that regenerates dopamine neurons suppressed by excessive drug use, states of depression and also back-signals the cell nuclei to express more GDNF by effectively creating a loop mechanism.

In addition, one needs to receive a spiritual journey to detox his or her mind and make a full recovery to connect back to the true self, or soul. This type of therapy allows intellectual introspection into psychological, emotional and spiritual concerns. Iboga has the power to enter the brain and re-tune neuropathways, resetting and polishing the receptors in the brain that are constructed through substance dependency.

Tapping into your own database of memories, memes and anchor points, the spirit of Iboga crystallises momentous visuals on your inner chalk board, whilst many also hear a telepathic voice of truth both answering questions and pointing out blind spots over the course of a single session, which can last up to 36 hours depending on your sensitivity, dose and current state of consciousness.

During this time, arrows of truth incessantly pierce your dream-like bubbles, but these arrows are coated with love's varnish and shot by an omniscient bowman who already knows what you are ready to see. Your emotional body is also temporarily relieved through this experience so that you can observe and process past trauma in a near instant and a smoother process without getting caught up in old triggers and tears. This allows you to glide fast through the multitude of blocks you may have, for there is always work to be done.

Iboga is a true miracle plant, but it is banned/ illegal in many countries; maybe this is because it can relieve so many mental problems and is known to be more effective than having 10 years of psychotherapy in one session. This is a very old practice done by the Bwiti shamans in central Africa. In Bwiti, if a teenager misbehaved or were arrested by police, instead of them being sent to jail, they were sent to visit Iboga.

The Iboga Bwiti shamans speak of going deeper rather than further. They believe that their medicine accesses the infinite nature of the soul inside of you, and the soul's infinite knowledge extends all the way to the beginning of time. In the entire 24-hour encounter with truth, there was never the feeling of accessing anything externally. It was simply the self that was accessed; it was virtually omniscient and had our best interest at heart!

Iboga has been used by people with the following problems.

Mental problems: Depression, anxiety, bipolar disorder, depersonalisation disorder, body dysmorphic disorder, mental/emotional abuse issues, mood disorders, post-traumatic stress disorder (PTSD), severe mental blocks, ADHD and childhood emotional trauma.

Physical problems: Hepatitis, herpes, chronic fatigue syndrome, Auto-immune conditions, human papilomavirus (HPV), chronic infections, aerotoxic syndrome, chemical toxicity, heavy metal toxicity, arthritis, physical stress, eczema, lupus, blood clots, Parkinson's disease, multiple sclerosis's and infertility

Spiritual cleansing: Iboga aids in discovering your true self, in finding your life's blueprint, connecting with ancestors, asking questions, getting answers, healing the root of illness, aligning with spirit, experiencing rebirth, awakening, finding passion, rapidly evolving emotionally and learning the truth of universal existence.

Just to wrap things up, Iboga has a unique ability of detoxifying the luminous energy field, the chakra system and the subconscious mind, healing you greatly on the formless level, far beyond the physical. As mentioned, it is at these levels where all disease and mental issues start; modern medicine does not come anywhere close to this type of healing.

Every human has blind spots, distractions and some level of denial or the ability to lie to themselves about their own life and the universe. When you are fortunate enough to get into the spiritual realm with the help of a shaman, Iboga will show you the truth. You will find deep meaningful answers. You can find out information that you would not have otherwise had any way of knowing.

Iboga in its raw, natural plant form. Today it is the most potent plant for purposes of naturally treating drug addictions

Ayahuasca: The Vine of the Soul

Ayahuasca arrives with a warm buzz; it brings the fireworks, a purge, and then 8–10 hours later, a peaceful connectedness that allows you a full night's sleep. Looked at this way, Ayahuasca may seem preferable; however, the sheer psychobytes of content downloaded from Iboga is unrivalled.

Ayahuasca is an Amazonian plant mixture prepared from a combination of plants and chemicals that varies in potency, depending on the maker. The brew is a traditional South American preparation most commonly made by combining the Banisteriopsis caapi vine and Psychotria viridis leaves (DMT). This drink is widely employed throughout Amazonian Perú, Ecuador, Colombia, Bolivia and western Brazil, and it is used mainly as a medicine for healing under the guidance of an experienced shaman.

Upon consuming the concentrated formula, it can take anywhere between 5 and 30 minutes until you start to feel its effects. How shamans first discovered Ayahuasca is still debated to this day, but it was obvious that they spoke to the plants and the plants spoke back. Ayahuasca is used traditionally as a spiritual medicine to heal people in a unique and loving way; shamans used it to gain insight about the land, hunting information and also to receive guidance from the other side. Shamans also explained how Amazonians used Ayahuasca to see where their enemies hide out in the jungle.

Ayahuasca brew is illegal in the USA and UK right now because of its DMT content. DMT is a schedule 1 drug in the USA under the Religious Freedom Restoration Act, even though the chemical DMT is naturally produced by the pineal gland, and it is gaining momentum as a legitimate religious practice.

The Ayahuasquero shamans speak of going father, exploring dimensions beyond what you can see and feel, and this may well be a function of the DMT. With the strong correlation between the natural DMT released during physical death, DMT seems to be a gateway to the realms beyond the physical.

Ayahuasca is becoming increasingly popular in the medical world for its powerful treatment effects for substance dependency, whilst gaining ground from those people in the West searching for a legitimate spiritual path. Maybe people want to go further than a guru's; perhaps with the growing consciousness shift and the hype surrounding 2012 onward, these people are hungry for more immediate results and a first-hand experience of what is actually going on.

When Ayahuasca is used properly under the guidance of trained shamans, the experience is deeply healing on a soul level. It is said that a few Ayahuasca ceremonies are as effective on one's psyche as 5 years of western psychotherapy. The reasons for needing a shaman to conduct a ceremony with Aya and not Iboga is because Ayahuasca opens up your universe, chakra system and luminous energy field, and therefore it needs holding together on the etheric levels by the shaman. This is so that no outside forces can host your energetic body. Iboga is slightly different; the spirit of Iboga forms a vortex around your energy field so that you are fully protected at all times. It is not advised to drink Ayahuasca without a shaman.

However, some spiritual circles and new age communities frown upon the use of shamanic plants with their argument being 'it's an easy way out'. This is mainly due to the lack of education surrounding these topics, a lot of misinformation around Ayahuasca has people thinking it's simply another hallucinogenic, feel good, new age experience. This is nothing like LSD, mushrooms or ecstasy. To compare them is simply inappropriate and very disrespectful.

From YUSA's experience it is hard work, plain and simple. When Ayahuasca is used in conjunction with your meditation, raw food/detoxification, yoga, exercise, or any other mindfulness based practices, it can change your life for the better. Many think that love is synonymous with good feelings, but the love that Ayahuasca pours over your being is other worldly. She gives you the opportunity to see the rawness of reality and your ego and essence clearly, with no filters or apologies.

Ayahuasca is not for everyone, only for those who are very, very serious about waking up to the truth of who you are. If you participate in ceremony more than once and welcome Aya into your life, you will be shown more than you can ever imagine, worlds beyond worlds. All of the painful, dark and hidden truths about yourself, past lives, soul contracts, your childhood, cosmic love and insights into your own future. Once you start work with her on a regular basis, you can potentially burn through and remove your psychological blocks and obstacles.

However, the benefits that come from Aya come at a high price. Not in monetary terms but in terms of your personality and how it can suffer throughout the ceremony whilst you see parts of yourself that may literally make you want to vomit. Everything you have ever avoided feeling will surface. Everything you ever dismissed and pushed away, alongside emotions of everyone you have ever judged, blamed, hurt or ridiculed will course through your entire body. This is a huge clearing process for the higher good.

As far as ritual and pageantry, nothing that quite compares to the transfixing magic of an Ayahuasca ceremony. The music of Ayahuasca is known as the Icaros sung by the shaman him/herself. They are sometimes haunting, often beautiful melodies passed down from generation to generation, taught initially by the plants themselves they say.

The shaman works with rattles made of leaves, tobacco, and cinnamon rose water, and pours his energy into the ceremony, carrying you to the realms beyond death, partly by the sweat of his labour. His physical manipulations throughout the ceremony have a direct and dramatic effect. You feel indelibly part of something mystical. The plants encourage the unlocking of your DNA.

One's experience with Ayahuasca can depend on a few different factors. A small percentage of people who go into ceremony and ingest Ayahuasca for the first time have been known to experience the hardest night of their life. Many have reported vomiting, diarrhoea, upset stomach and experiencing a psychotic break, where all references of 'me' where non-existent.

Deep terror can hit you for a while, and an inferno of kaleidoscopic visions depicting sacred geometry may entrance your mind. All of this is a cleanout process. The intensity of the clean-up process is dependent on what previous detox work you have already done. With Ayahuasca you feel like there is a little clean-up crew at work in your organs, squeezing out all of the bad stuff, the decay, the bacteria and then pushing that back into your bowels and stomach to be disposed of.

YUSA's experience was not so dramatic; we attended around six Ayahuasca ceremonies, and all were very relaxing and profoundly peaceful. This is mainly due to the amount of physical detoxification we went through for around a year prior. This detoxification involved juicing fruits and vegetables, fasting and a raw food diet. We also did the Iboga full flood around 3 weeks prior to the first Ayahuasca experience, which cleansed most of the bad energies from the luminous energy field and mind. Whatever state Ayahuasca puts you in, remember it is for the greater good and a deep clearing of old energies, the death of one's ego and a spiritual emergence. Her love is unwavering and as big as all the cosmos combined.

If you are going to make the commitment to explore the depths of your mind, soul and the infinite universe, both of these medicines are the best things you can do for yourself. If you are in pain and your inner intuition is guiding you towards a complete cleanout then take the time out to get some serious healing and clear out deep underlying issues that are in the way of your happiness and success. When you are clean energetically, physically and on a mental level, it leaves space for mental clarity and for you to reprogram your being from scratch, giving you optimal creation power for the life you desire!

YUSA recommends the Iboga treatment first before Ayahuasca; they work brilliantly hand in hand, but all depends on your personal experience and what you want to achieve alongside the level of detoxification you may want to experience. Here are some questions you should ask yourself before deciding; the level of spiritual realisation is profound. Either way, they are both great investments towards the deeper inner-standing of yourself.

1. Do you have an addiction problem, eating disorder, or self-limiting mental issue? If the answer is yes, then seek **Iboga** for sure.

2. Would you prefer to know the answers to your questions, or feel and see the answers to your questions? To know, choose **Iboga** to feel and to see choose **Ayahuasca**.

3. Do you want an experience unlike anything you can find in the physical plane? Something wholly other? Choose **Ayahuasca.**

4. Do you want to make peace/communicate with deceased family members/friends? Choose **Iboga.**

5. Is your mind the root of your physical illness or your body? For mind, choose Iboga; for body choose **Ayahuasca** (except in the case of physical drug dependency, for which Iboga is well suited).

6. Do you want a rapid energetic cleanse of the subconscious and luminous energy field? A sense of alignment and rebirth so you can reprogram your mind and energy from fresh? Choose **Iboga.**

For more information regarding the Ayahuasca and Iboga retreats, there are two trusted sources below. When looking for retreats online make sure you do plenty of research and lookup reviews etc., as there are some retreats that are run by bad shamans. If you have any questions about Iboga or Ayahuasca, e-mail YUSA, and we may be able to help. Never mix these plants with alcohol.

'You cannot transcend what you do not know. To go beyond yourself, you must know yourself' ~ Sri Nisargadatta Maharaj[42]

Ayahuasca retreats, initiation courses, seminars and healings: www.ayahuascaassociation.org[43].

Ibogaine flood, Cape Town, SA: www.iboga.co.za[44]

The preparation of Banisteriopsis caapi vine and Psychotria viridis leaves

Sacred geometry: The geometrical laws of creation

The study of sacred geometry involves the observation of highly intelligent universal patterns that construct the foundations within everything in reality and the universe. In creation, there exists a multitude of shapes and numbers partly recognised as the 'divine proportion'. These patterns are no accident, and they are presented with such accuracy that they could only be the workings of something much greater: the result of the omnipotent, most powerful and greatly intelligent.

Physicists send probes into space, historians attempt to piece together scattered fragments from the past and botanists study nature's secrets. It is agreed that life, if nothing else, is endlessly mysterious. There exists a variety of different forms and rhythms; they capture patterns, relationships and tell-tale signs towards the very nature of existence. Certain ratios and shapes find themselves repeating throughout the universe, and these geometric shapes and figures seem to radiate intense positivity.

The evidence and research suggest that these geometrical/mathematical ratios, harmonics and proportions that are found in music, nature, the human body, light and cosmology can be understood as a complex system of inter-dimensional symbols and structures leading beyond space, time and form. According to this view, these basic patterns of existence are perceived as being sacred. It unites the mind and the heart, spirit and matter, science and spirituality. The ancients knew that these patterns were codes symbolic of your own inner realm and that the experience of sacred geometry was essential to the education of the soul.

By connecting and studying the nature of the patterns form and relationship to all life, one may contemplate the great mysteries and mind-blowing design of the universe, encouraging an expanded view on the laws that fabricate your very existence. The purpose of this section is to deliver a much greater realisation and enhance your awareness of the laws of life and the intricately designed mathematical base to all creation. This goes to proves that human existence is no accident and that humans are a product of something beautiful and much greater than what the powers that be have led the world to believe.

Sacred geometry in nature

The geometric shapes, spirals numbers and evidence of the divine proportion are embedded within all aspects of nature. Their symmetry, beauty and mathematical preciseness can direct one towards a relationship of balance, harmony and symmetry that is quite uncanny. The strands of your DNA, the cornea of our eye, snowflakes, pinecones, flower petals, diamond crystals, the branching of trees, a nautilus shell, the star we spin around, the galaxy we spiral within, the air you breathe and all life forms, as we know them, emerge out of timeless geometric codes. Below are some examples of this pattern within nature.

The head of a flower is made up of small seeds which are produced at the centre, and then migrate towards the outside to fill eventually all the space (as for the sunflower but on a much smaller level). Each new seed appears at a certain angle in relation to the preceding one. For example, if the angle is 90 degrees, that is 1/4 of a turn. Sunflowers, which have opposing spirals of seeds, utilise the Fibonacci sequence to distribute most efficiently their seeds in the most compact space.

The chambered nautilus is a living fossil that has survived in earth's oceans for the last 500 million years. A cross-section of the shell of the nautilus will show the cycles of its growth as a series of chambers arranged in a precise olden mean spiral. The Golden Mean is represented by Fibonacci, the Greek letter phi (with the decimal representation of 1.6180...) is one of those mysterious natural numbers that seems to arise out of the basic structure of the cosmos.

Below is a simple red cabbage that has been cut in half displaying the spiral pattern from its root which it took form. Every vegetable and plant has a mathematical pattern basis it grows into; the proportion remains consistent throughout and is infinite in nature. This pattern is known as the Fibonacci ratio.

The aloe Vera plant and acorn are seen as both following and display classic Fibonacci structure. Spiralling outwards from the source, again infinite in nature, this outward pattern is represented by the number 9, always expanding never contracting, this is the nature of the universe itself manifested into plant form—everything is interconnected and alive!

It is the opinion of many that this anomaly is evidence of the universal creator showing the uniqueness of planet earth in relationship to the whole cosmos. It also accomplishes another fact, for this 'anomaly' shatters the big bang and nebular hypothesis; for if all the planets formed from a whirling cloud of dust and atoms, this feature would not be present. To think that the timings of the revolutions of the planets around the sun correlates with the arrangement of leaves around stems on plants is also an amazing phenomenon.

The Fibonacci sequence

There is a special numerical ratio that can be related to the proportions of everything, from nature's smallest building blocks, such as atoms, to the most advanced patterns in the universe, such as unimaginably large celestial bodies.

The Fibonacci numbering sequence is a pattern discovered around A.D. 1200 by **Leonardo Pisa** [45](historically known as Fibonacci). The proportion is derived from something known as the Fibonacci sequence. An arrangement of numbers wherein each succeeding term is simply the sum of the two preceding terms (1, 1, 2, 3, 5, 8, 13, etc.)

The Fibonacci sequence forms the basis for the Golden Ratio 1.618 (the division of the two preceding terms) a proportion that reoccurs with amazing consistency throughout the natural world. The Fibonacci sequence, also known as the Golden Mean, Phi, or the divine proportion, has fuelled the imagination of artists, mystics and mathematicians for centuries.

As shown below, the spiral diagram forming within perfection of the Fibonacci sequence

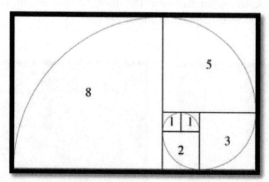

'The spiral of creation is not static. It is a living, evolving, emergent system of extreme creativity. Seek out those fine souls who are also on the inner journey. Share, support, and learn from each other. Be the infinite explorer.' ~
Neil Kramer[46]

Drawing a golden spiral of Fibonacci on paper only begins to describe the infinite pattern that nature creates, one that embodies the dynamic principles of regeneration and whose imprint in life is of a symmetrical and balanced growth. Life is either expanding, growing, being drawn out, or its diminishing, dissolving, or collapsing. Seeing the beauty of an unfolding leaf or the patterning of petals in a rose, one immediately recognises the perfect and delicate spiral.

Hurricane Bonnie approaching the eastern seaboard of the USA on August 15, 1998. The spiralling cloud was twice as tall as Mount Everest. Mathematicians call the golden spiral's eye an 'asymptote', a place always approached but never reached. The calm eye of a storm is the centre of gravity around which wind and water are expanding and contracting, around which the whole storm is balanced. The eye of every spiral is a dynamic place where all opposites meet and where life and death are one phenomenon. All the forces that create growth and keep it in balance are at work in the eye, the source.

Geometry in the human body

As humans are connected with nature and synchronise with the biorhythms of the earth, the sacred pattern also creates the foundations for which your body adheres to and takes form from. Nature has designed the human body so that its members (arms, legs etc.) are duly proportioned to the frame as a whole.

Below is an interesting drawing from Leonardo Da Vinci. What he is showing in this sketch is how the human body 'squares the circle'. He inscribed the human body into a circle and a square, the two figures considered images of mathematical perfection.

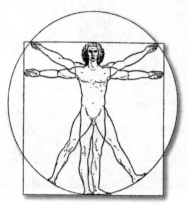

When man stretches his arms and holds them horizontally, man's body will perfectly fit into the square. On the other hand, when he spreads his legs and raises his arms as in the sketch, man's body can be perfectly circumscribed by a circle. The circumference of the square 'equals' that of the circle. Hermetic tradition tells us that the human body can be regarded as a blueprint for the universe by means of all the ratios that are found within the body.

The cochlea inside a human ear is encased within a hard shell and filled with liquid. Around the central column is a rail of sensitive hairs that decrease in thickness as the column winds upward.

Sound vibrations enter the whirlpool of the outer ear and tap at the cochlea's base, travelling in waves up and around the inner liquid. It's two and three quarter spiral turns allow humans to hear approximately ten octaves of sound. Other mammals have different numbers of turns explaining why they can hear different frequencies of sound.

Sacred geometrical imagery and the flower of life

Through consciously engaging with the geometries, you can introduce healthy working systems into your reality. The more you understand universal law the more you can apply the harmony that is apparent in nature as a more powerful force in your own life.

The geometries can also be a great synthesiser of the left and right hemispheres of the brain. The rational, analytical aspects of the patterns are processed through the left hemisphere, whereas the visual beauty and profound implications are processed through the right, therefore implementing whole brain consciousness and expanded awareness.

It is a gradual process but when used in a mindful and purposeful way the vibrational patterns of the geometries generate a resonance that can have a calming and transformative effect right down to the level of your RNA/DNA. Currently humans use only 3% of the current 2-strand DNA.

According to some esoteric teachings, however, the original divine blueprint of human DNA contains an additional eleven etheric strands, which are fused together and contained within the two perceptible strands.

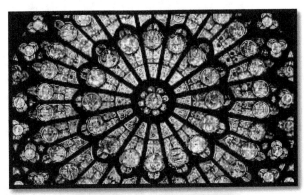

Star-Tetrahedron MER-KA-BA. The vehicle of ascension

149

The below image, the flower of life, is the modern name given to the ancient geometrical figure composed of multiple evenly spaced, overlapping circles. It is considered by many to contain ancient, religious value depicting the fundamental forms of space and time. Found in the palace of an Assyrian King, the oldest flower of life design dates back to 645 BC. If you want to learn more about sacred geometry, Google **Secrets in plain sight** by Scott Onstott[47].

Below, to the left is an image of an embryo in the womb taking spiral form outwardly from the cellular structure of the third embryonic division which also represents the flower of life. To the right is an X-ray image of a left hand, you can see the mathematical principle representing the Fibonacci ratio. (1,2,3,5,8) this pattern is evident within all the body's major bone and DNA structure.

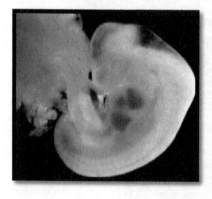
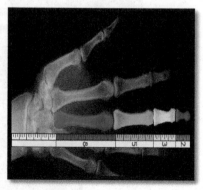

DNA Activation

The complex topic of human DNA is one that is overlooked by many and misunderstood by the studies of science. Scientists have long believed that DNA only instructs the cells on how to make and organise specific proteins. Nevertheless, the recent discovery of a new, second DNA code (Encyclopaedia of DNA Elements Project) suggests the body speaks two different languages, proteins and higher genetics (non-physical).

Many new agers speak on the topic of DNA activation but only half-heartedly. There is no magical way to activate your DNA; it is an ongoing evolutionary process and a result of a natural, balanced lifestyle, the one that was always intended for and designed for humanity to follow, in alignment with Mother Earth. This book covers a range of topics that when put into practice, will definitely encourage you to remember and activate higher strands of DNA.

DNA is the 'blueprint of life' and is located within each and every cell of the body. In addition to each chromosome's DNA helix of two strands, there are an additional ten etheric strands available to each human being on the planet that have been dormant since 'the fall' of man. Each additional DNA strand possesses attributes that permit the individual to perform greater human accomplishments.

Scientists acknowledge that humans currently only use 3% of the current 2-strand DNA! Thus, we live in a society where people are sick, unhappy, stressed out, create wars, have difficulty experiencing love and are very disconnected with the true self, nature and the universe.

According to this research, the 12 strands of DNA facilitate 12 levels of consciousness, seven higher senses, 13 chakras and 12 chemical nucleotide bases (compared to the current four), allowing a shift to 144 chromosomes (compared to the current 64). This etheric DNA that every human has lying dormant within is known to contain information about your spiritual nature and heritage. As you start to unlock these DNA codes, your consciousness expands and you start to **remember** who you are, where you came from and what your spiritual path entails.

The 12 attributes and evolutionary traits of DNA

Strand 1: Courage to move ahead and integrate your fears

Strand 2: Ability to focus on something and follow it to completion

Strand 3: Maintaining gender balance between male/female power

Strand 4: Balance between your energy field and the physical body

Strand 5: Living peacefully in a state of acceptance

Strand 6: Strength to stand in one's truth regardless of the outcome

Strand 7: Ability to accept both your dark and light sides

Strand 8: Ability to hold personal boundaries regardless of outcomes

Strand 9: Ability to accept and live within a diverse community

Strand 10: Ability to tune into and listen to one's soul or higher self

Strand 11: Power to envision, create and manifest these visions in 3D

Strand 12: Ability to be accepting, kind and appreciate the value in all things

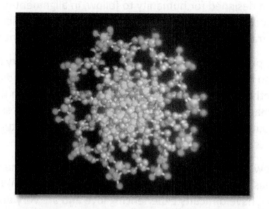

Diagrammatic representation of the double helix DNA

DNA & human evolution

You as a human being now have such under-developed DNA potential that you couldn't even imagine. Remember you have only two strands of DNA active whilst inhabiting your human body, it is just like having a car that has 12 cylinders but is running on just two. Wouldn't you be curious to see how it may run on maybe three or three and a half cylinders? And how to do so?

Three of your DNA strands represent and govern over the **physical** body, another three are concerned with the **emotional** body, another three with the **mental** body and the remaining three with the **spiritual** body. All of these aspects are represented in your body as neural pathways to the brain. There is a direct connection between the luminous energy field, chakra system, nervous system and your DNA. The workings of your being is a highly complex and intelligent system.

The neural connections are connected and nourished through the endocrine system of ductless glands. These glands work in tandem with the chakras.

When all neural pathways are working in harmony with your chakra system, they will provide the frequency conduit of higher realms, resulting in your consciousness expansion, multidimensional in nature.

Terrain modification holds great importance; being intelligently selective of what you decide to put into your body. This modification includes transitioning from a dietary lifestyle where dead, processed and animal foods are dominant into a plant-based lifestyle bursting with life, living enzymes and chlorophyll. The body chapter delivers the education and practical guidance regarding terrain modification so your physical body can remain within a harmonious balance with your mind and spirit.

DNA activation is of high importance now. If you have energetic blockages, auric attachments, karmic imprints, chakra distortions, or unnatural energetic seals, then it makes it harder to speed up the particles and accrete the frequencies necessary to advance in this worldwide shift. You may also be noticing how your awareness of time is speeding up.

There is a major evolutionary shift happening now on the planet as the earth's heartbeat and Kundalini energy is rising. It is the same for humans, but the majority of humans are behind. A lot of detoxification and returning to the self is the only way forward. There is an infinite power within you; you have to prepare your body to be a place where that power can reside.

Awareness and attitude are the two fundamental factors in this equation. Modern day science agrees that all humans really need to do is tiny little micro adjustments in every single cell (and you can do it yourself from the inside), the way you eat, the way you think and the way you feel.

Think of yourself as a mythological 'self', you really don't know about the inner depths of yourself and have this undeveloped DNA, but if you can be smart enough to work towards unravelling it, it may show to you what you have planned for yourself in this incarnation. You must realise that you came to the planet with all of your programs temporarily erased, did you know how to do anything when you came to the planet? No.

Think of your soul as a seed, this seed is planted in the soil of life by intelligence. This seed has received some external conditioning and programming causing a superficial layer to be constructed and you need to remove that. Detox, detach and deprogram! Remove the programs that construct the bubble around you and re-harmonise with the spirit and nature within yourself.

The key is to find out what's optimum to nourish your body and your mind. Your body is the key to your mind, and the temple on the whole can only be understood once you get the body and mind in equanimity. Your body can be compared to a car for example, when you put enhanced fuels into your car, keep the filters clean and nourish the supercomputer (brain) then you have the absolute infinite potential of top performance.

Your DNA activates in cycles, as mentioned previously, DNA is interconnected with the nervous system, luminous energy field and chakra system, and they all work in tandem. Starting from the root area being 6Hz/cycles, sacral being 7Hz/cycles, solar plexus being 8Hz/cycles, heart being 9Hz/cycles, throat being 10Hz/cycles, third eye being 11Hz/cycles, crown being 12Hz/cycles and soul centre being 13Hz/cycles. Your body and mind have an equanimity that has to stay in tune with the planetary energetics and the sun.

Every planet in the solar system is now being 'stepped up' meaning energetic frequencies are on the increase. This is a natural process of evolution that occurs every 25,920 (approx.) years. Therefore, if the earth and sun are being stepped up, it means that every single organism that is living within its terrain, including your body and energy system, has to be modified to stay in tune.

You can look up into the sky at night time and see that Venus, Mars and Jupiter are brighter than they ever have been. All planets are heating up not just earth; this is mainly due to the sun moving into an area of the galaxy that has a supercharged energy field. You can go on NASA website and review the scientific evidence of this theory.

Humans are being energetically stepped up on the planet; earlier in this chapter is a description of the Schumann resonance. Back in 1980, the natural heartbeat of the earth was at 7.83 cycles which correlates with the human solar plexus centre (9cycles) meaning that at that time humans should have been near enough ready to awaken the heart. The open heart means that the mind is no longer on its own; it has a filter, opening the awareness that's sees the beauty within everything.

The mind is filtered in accordance to which energetic centre/chakra is most active. For instance, the root chakra of 6 Hz/cycle deals with sexual desires, (this energy centre actually measures at 6.66Hz/cycles could this '666' be metaphorical for the lower self?). The sacral energy centre/chakra deals with food desires, with this being said, when one is operating from these lower centres the mind is mainly fixated on sexual and food pleasures, temporary in nature.

The earths cycle/heartbeat is currently measuring above 12Hz, this entails that humanity should be operating from the higher DNA activated energy centres. DNA activation is a natural process, humans need to harmonise and remain in tune with the earth and the sun.

The body needs a lot of space, you need to give it what it needs and take away what it doesn't need. If the mind is too corrupted and is always doing, doing, doing and doing it doesn't get time to rest unless you are asleep and for many, that is not rest. The mind is so overactive for some people that they have to numb themselves with hyper toxicity. Many sleep but do not get down to the deep theta or deep delta states of relaxation, meaning the consciousness cannot move beyond the lower astral realm.

When you start cleaning yourself of the toxicity in your blood, the filth that is going through your mind, and the bizarre chemicals that are distorting cellular structure, you can then start to rebuild and harmonise with the natural cycles. Start practicing diaphragmatic breathing and entertaining bigger thoughts and visions of yourself in the world, work towards success, not monetarily but the success of being a bigger, more wholesome character within.

To wrap things up it has been established that 97% of your DNA operates in the realms of Bioelectric and bio-acoustic signalling. Only 3% of your DNA is responsible for protein manufacture, whilst the other 97% of your DNA is metaphysical, which is why it is so easily influenced by frequencies, sounds and vibrations.

To activate your DNA is to activate higher-dimensional states of awareness, frequencies and vibrations of the 97%, which is commonly known as JUNK DNA in Western science, only until recently has this changed. The only way to activate your DNA is to awaken the Kundalini energy, awaken all seven chakras and reconnect back to nature. As you start to rise up and unlock DNA codons, you start to remember the truth about your existence. Use the information in this book to assist the purification of your body and mind, ultimately reconnecting back to self!

'Yesterday I was clever so I changed the world, Today I am wise so I AM changing myself' ~Rumi

Soul evolution & the shift in consciousness

In the beginning of 'time', it is said that the universal creator or 'God' if you like, was in all places, residing in a pure state. This state of purity contained a void, purely dark matter without any specific consciousness. The creator did not know itself and its greater 'beingness' so patterns of creation where instituted, solid planets where created alongside empty space/formlessness and the creator stepped into its own creation. The plan was that every part/ soul would know every over part, by experience.

The soul can be seen as a step-down transformer from the universal creator power, a co-creator or extension of the divine if you will. Every soul is given the opportunity to experience all levels starting from the lowest dimensional state of consciousness, planes and realms of experience. The soul has free will and can inhabit any form it wishes, its reason for being is so that it can experience as much as it can on every level, ultimately leading to the growth of awareness surrounding its own divine nature.

The reality of the Soul's evolutionary path is quite complex. Within the universe, there are five main realms, which are known as the lower/negative planes. In this sense negative does not mean 'bad', but rather, negative like the pole of a battery. A battery has negative and positive poles; together they create the charge that produces power. The planes of existence also have negative and positive poles and are directly linked to the different bodies that are present in your luminous energy field. The soul actually has to step down into the negative realms of duality, as the soul itself is whole, just like the creator.

The etheric realm is related to the unconscious level of man's consciousness.

The mental realm is related to the mind of man.

The causal realm is related to the emotional level of man.

The astral realm is related to the imaginative level of man.

The physical realm is related to the material substance of man's experience.

Every soul has a home in the soul realm from which it came from, free from pain and suffering. In the lower negative realms, the soul is just a stranger, a wanderer if you will and always holds a desire to go back home. The soul chooses to incarnate into the lower realms, so it can gain experience of those parts of the universal creator/god. When incarnating into the physical form there are several levels of consciousness that are the souls essential tools for life. **These tools are as follows:**

An unconsciousness mind – Where memory is stored, where dreams originate from, where your whole life experience is stored, and where many behaviour patterns become automatic habits.

A conscious mind - Used to record events, make intellectual decisions and record/play back information, it can easily get distracted by the glamour, illusions and pleasures of the world.

Emotions - Where energy is generated and stored, to be directed towards the manifestation of desires.

An imagination - The expressions of which can be labelled positive or negative, enhancing or blocking one's experience.

Conscious self - Which gets up in the morning, drives the car to work, reads the newspaper, studies the reports, talks to friends, etc.

A basic self – Controls the bodily functions, directs the body in well-learnt habit patterns, and much like a five-year-old child, asserts its desires and wishes upon the conscious self.

A higher self – It functions as your personal guardian, directing the conscious self towards those experiences that will be for its greatest good. Holds vast intelligence and knowledge of your life's destiny within the physical form and is always attempting to direct your conscious awareness towards your lessons/people with which you have soul contracts. Many people have lost the connection with the higher self. The focus of writing this book was to ultimately guide and educate others towards forming a reconnection with their higher self so they can start to find their spiritual path in life that they came here to follow.

Once the soul reaches home, it resides in a group constructed by formless energetic matter, this known as the soul group. The soul upon leaving the physical body or any other state of form then travels back to this group and becomes one again until it decides to branch out to seek more experience.

Think of this soul group as a hard drive storage device, and this device contains a bunch of movies. You want to play a movie so you plug the storage device into your computer, you then play the movie until it is finished and you then unplug the storage device until you want to experience another. The soul plays out a movie/life and takes the experience back home, learning and attaining wisdom and experience from the process.

There are a large number of souls within your personal soul group, some teacher's state 144,000 but no figure can really be specified. Your soul family has always been and always ever will be. When people speak of the term 'soul mates', it describes the connection between another soul that resides in the same group/home as your own, connected at heart for eternity. Your soul family love you unconditionally and reside in the natural state of joy and abundance. The soul has no gender, race, age etc. as these constructs only exist in the lower realms of polarity/duality. As mentioned earlier in this chapter, the heart resides in the realm of soul, outside the boundaries of duality/space and time.

You must realise that everything in your life is just a learning experience for your soul, every experience, every person you meet and all suffering is predetermined before you are born. There are so many distractions out here on the planet, obstacles or tests if you will that are designed to distract your conscious awareness away from your higher self, ultimately steering you off track. As the soul goes through human life, imbalances are created, mainly when a person is in an unconscious state.

When it's time for the body to pass over and the soul to transform, there are often karmic situations that have never been cleared or balanced, thus the soul at a later time embodies again/reincarnates into form so it can clear its debts, right the wrongs to bring back balance and harmony for the higher good. It's the soul's nature to want to incarnate into the physical plane for experience but it is the role of karma, (the creation and the release) that is responsible for the re-embodiment into form.

Many people have lived hundreds of lives on earth and are still in the learning process and attempting to gain an understanding of karma so they can be released from the wheel of reincarnation. This is so the appreciation for the upmost freedom of their soul can be felt, master this realm and transcend to higher realms.

Free will is always present in this equation, more so for the people who die consciously with no attachments and have practiced the arts of surrender, acceptance and unconditional love throughout their lives. Many people who are disconnected with nature and their higher self, hold on to fears and illusory attachments at the time of death. They do not understand what is going to happen once they pass over and fall victim to the wheel of reincarnation, dying unconsciously and not having the free will of choosing the family, lessons and so forth for the next life. The soul is then reincarnated into a body's circumstances and events in accordance to what fears and beliefs are held in the subconscious mind and luminous energy field.

Those who die unconsciously did not learn the lesson of unconditional love, realise their true power within the heart and held a fear-based vibration throughout their lives. The universe will put the soul in rough places until the lesson is learnt! It is important not to get trapped by the illusions of the world as it could cost you more than a few lifetimes. It's all a learning curve for the higher good. Everybody wants to go to heaven, but nobody wants to die.

'A human being is part of the whole called by us, the universe. A part limited by time and space. He experiences himself, his thoughts and feelings as something separated from the rest, a kind of optical delusion of his consciousness. The delusion is a kind of prison for us, restricting us to our

personal desires and affection for a few persons nearest to us. Our task must be to free ourselves from this prison, by widening our circle of compassion to enhance all living creatures and the whole of nature in its beauty' ~ **Albert Einstein**

Soul contracts

The soul understands that transforming into physical form (body) is temporary in nature and it adheres to certain contracts and lessons before being born into the physical world. It is highly possible that you may have asked yourself once or maybe even numerous times; 'what is my purpose or what the whole point of my existence is?' An 'old soul' is just a person who has maintained their essence through lifetimes. A 'new soul' is a more fragmented person, who isn't their true self/essence constantly.

In your life you may have met somebody or had a friend who came across as if their whole life had been mapped out for them, having a complete sense of what it is they would like to do in life whilst being surrounded by helpful people. You may have asked yourself why this is so, is it purely down to luck? It is spoken of by many metaphysical teachers that each and every person is guided by a sacred contract that the soul constructed (with other souls) before you were born.

The contract is known to contain a wide range of agreements regarding what kind of work you need to do in this current life, what you are intended to learn and the key relationships with the people who agreed to assist you in learning the lessons. You also plan your parents, choose the talents and abilities you will have and any other life situations that will help you evolve spiritually which you can learn from. You also decide on the situations that will bring you together with people in relationships that will give you the opportunity to fulfil karmic debts from your past existences. A great deal of this information can be found in your personal astrological natal chart.

Having contracts that ultimately plan your life's circumstances and events doesn't necessarily mean that you have no free will. At any given time your contract may provide you with an opportunity for growth, maybe in the form of challengers at the workplace, solving past grudges and coming to peace with an old partner or maybe something completely new. One way of viewing your contract is the healthfulness of your overall relationship with your personal power and spiritual power.

It determines how you work with your energy and to whom you give it. These contracts are very intellectual and complex in nature, they go beyond the human minds understanding and any computer system built by man. Fulfilling your sacred contracts also depend on how much you are willing to surrender to divine timings. Having absolute faith in 'what is', and allowing your higher self to intervene subconsciously to reach your level of awareness, guiding you to be in a certain place at a certain time with another person and so forth.

Every person, every event or circumstance that you encounter and experience holds great significance and has an agreed role in your learning experience on planet earth. The same goes for yourself having contracts to helping others learn, whether it's through painful times or joyful times. Within the sacred contracts you choose your teachers for the current incarnation that could be somebody on the Internet or even your pets! A lot of the time it is difficult as you may not surrender and accept a painful situation and the ego may get involved. It could take a long time before you see the reasons for it and the lesson may be pushed forwards to a later date until it is learnt.

The sooner you start to accept and embrace challenging situations that arise in the moment, the less painful it becomes. In time, you can learn to accept each event as it happens without struggling against it and prolonging your mental, emotional and physical suffering. Naturally, you can't be expected to see everything immediately, or in advance. But if you have a way of looking at the symbolic meaning of your experiences, you will be better prepared to accept the inevitable changes to your life. Fighting change builds up emotional energetic scar tissue. Surrendering to the divine allows you to accept the changes and allow life to flow.

The Bible quotes; 'As a man thinketh in his heart, he becomes.' This expresses a lot of truth when perceived from the mystical consciousness. This works both ways positive and negative. You may say, 'The thing that I feared most has come upon me.'

That would certainly make sense because the thing that you fear most, you think about. You give energy into it. You dwell on it and think: 'What would happen if...?' and you create that which you fear and it appears. You create it. You bring it forwards. Then you say, 'Why me, universe?' If you can get the universe to communicate, it may answer, 'Why not? You created it; you're responsible for it.' You might just as well take a deep breath, mark it up as an experience and a lesson and go on. In reality, there is not much else you can do. Learn all you can from every experience and just continue smiling.

The universe is always speaking to you, sending small messages, causing coincidences and serendipities. Reminding you to stop, look around, to believe in something else, something more!

When anybody becomes alienated from soul, your inner nature, all respect for outer nature is disregarded, resulting in the pollution and degradation of the environment. Many keep looking for things on the outside to heal, which is backwards. We go inside temples, churches and mosques instead of inside ourselves. Everybody has the choice and power to make life so much easier,

160

hopefully you can use this information as a tool for searching for the light in the darkest of times.

Below are descriptions of the main states/dimensions of creation, this is just so you can have a better understanding regarding the levels and realms that the soul experiences. You are currently experiencing the 3rd, 4th and 5th states of elementary school, you have already experienced the mineral, plant and animal kingdom.

Twelve density states of creation

First – Minerals (rocks and soil) and oil, original thought

Second – Plants, worms and microbes, awareness of being

Third – Animals and lower human, cause and effect/duality

Fourth – Higher-frequency humans, Evolutionary Bridge

Fifth – Light body status human, unity consciousness

Sixth – soul energy body, higher self and celestial body, Unconditional love

Seventh – Over soul energy body, Creative expression

Eighth – Angels and composite higher self, Universal Travellers

Ninth – Archangels and monad realm, Spiritual Complex

Tenth – Creator gods, Upper creation realm

Eleventh – Universal god realm, Servants of creation

Twelfth – Godhead founders and Elohim (Hebrew)

Thirteenth – The void, un-manifested creation

'We are all the same, all the same, Longing to find our way back; Back to the one, back to the only one.' ~ **Rumi**

The Universal Shift

Every soul inhabiting a human body is designed to evolve, and that evolution is directly and intimately tied in with the earths. The elemental particles that give substance to your cells come from the earth and stars. The cells are imbued within your divine consciousness, forming a union of spirit and matter. In this context, you as a human are the progeny of Mother Earth and Father Sky, spiritual beings embodied with the elements of terra firma (solid earth)

It is very important to mention that one of the worst propagandas in the spiritual community is that there is a **mass awakening happening on the planet within everybody**. There is opportunity for it, but it is not a given, the next few pages have been written to give you more of an understanding in regards to the evolution of consciousness that **some** people are embracing now on the planet. Please bear this in mind whilst reading. The consciousness shift is like a train and it is completely up to the individual to jump on board.

Since 1987 when the consciousness shift stepped up a gear, there have been profound changes found by modern science in human DNA. As the earth's electrical field gets weaker and its magnetic system gets stronger, the high frequency solar flares from the sun have been emitting very high-vibrational light particles throughout planet earth and all inhabitants. In humans, evolutionary activation occurs as torsion waves that stimulate or 'jump DNA' to rewrite the genetic code, a phenomenon supported by a considerable amount of scientific evidence.

Scientific research and many others suggest that an energy source (Photon Belt) emanating from galactic centre is activating DNA and setting in motion the process of accelerated evolution, it is not known what the outcome may be but it is a beautiful time for humanity. As the energy is dissipated onto the planet, it starts to activate and attune the higher energy centres within each and every human being.

When you become naturally attuned to higher consciousness, you become synchronised to the harmonies of the cosmos; on the mundane level, sacred geometry, meditation, frequencies, tones, mantras, breathing, natural foods and medicinal plants are to be used as a tool to help lead you back towards a sense of attunement and unity, a process known through the ages as 'the journey home'.

By raising your own frequency and harnessing more vibrational light within your energy field, humans as a collective consciousness can assist the whole of humanity along the path of evolution and personal energetic ascension. As individuals work on themselves and make the shift to unconditional love from within, that love will soon spread to other people's energy fields and plant the seeds for change.

When the majority of humans on the planet start to embrace and operate from the heart space, mass creativity is born and solutions to all planetary problems can easily come forth. People start working with each other rather than against each other and the collective ego/pain body starts to crumble.

Many are falling sick on the planet and feeling uncomfortable. The energy is attuning your chakras, DNA and luminous energy field as a result of the increase in vibrational frequencies. Many are experiencing headaches, stomach pains, feelings of depression, uncertainty, changes in sleep patterns and mood swings. This is all-natural but indicates you are out of alignment, you must raise the energetic frequency of the physical body and eat less dense foods so it can stay in balance with your energetic self. Nutrition and detox is essential not television and medication!

Attributes of consciousness that can be attained throughout the shift, Consciousness relates to awareness or a state of knowing, a perceived degree of existing reality. Reality in terms of perceived truth is relative to the experience since individual truths are constantly changing

1. The first level of third DMC is dependency on others.

2. Next, you gain trust and respect for yourself and others.

3. Then you strive within yourself to become self-dependant and/or self-sufficient.

4. At this point, you understand the importance of self-love.

5. Then implement the use of love so that it works in your life.

6. Once you really love yourself you develop a love for others and control yourself centred ego.

7. By continually loving yourself and others, you become mentally and emotionally stable.

8. Then you seek out new knowledge and helpful information to bring balance back into your life.

9. Then a desire and willingness comes into your consciousness, to love and be responsible for yourself and others.

10. Now you commit time and understanding to who you really are, you use your multidimensionality and you know where you are going.

11. When other souls request help, or you observe an imbalance in nature, you use the tools of Love to assist.

12. You now fully accept your responsibility to help create a better world, develop spirituality, become multidimensional and prepare to shift your consciousness into the fourth DMC and beyond.

Within the divine vibration of love during this turning of cycles, humanity no longer has to live under oppression and below the veil. Every single soul receives a call for awakening, but the problem is that not everybody picks up. Humanity on the whole as 'spirit' is destined to achieve more of a perfect union in solidarity with the grand purpose and plan of heaven on earth. This state can only be achieved upon the recognition of the kingdom of heaven within yourself.

Every soul is subject to the larger scheme of this 25,920-year cycle. For many souls, it is believed that they have been on the earth the whole time, constantly reincarnating into form, learning and evolving all the way from the dark ages. This goes for the spirit of the earth too, the feminine energy of planet earth is also part of the greater evolutionary cycle that has had to endure and sustain all human life and suffering for the longest.

Many refer to these times as 'the return of Christ', remember that Christ consciousness is within you; this is the activation of your seven chakras and raising Kundalini. The Christ consciousness is realised when you are in alignment with mother earth's heartbeat, connecting at the 13-Hz cycle. By now, you should have an understanding of how your energy is directly interconnected with the earths and your own evolution. Remember not everybody is ready to raise Kundalini; it can be very dangerous for some people: 95% of the population would die or go mad if Kundalini started awakening—everybody at their own pace.

Everything within the nature of evolution is measured in cycles; the return of Christ is the return of your full infinite nature, the return of pure love and compassion. The universal creator expresses itself through everything, its decided to experience its own creation directly so it's consciousness dropped down to the lowest state, this is known as Melchizedek consciousness. Now consciousness is about to make the journey back to source. Melchizedek consciousness is within everybody; everybody is an explorer, equally valued but just holds different levels of wisdom.

Not everybody is ready to embrace the shift, only a small percentage of people are ready, this is how it was designed to be, it is those who are connected with nature and have found peace within themselves, those who have completed most of their soul lessons and balanced out their karma. This is not to say some are better than others are.

Everybody is at a different level in his or her soul evolution; there is a divine plan for each individual, as you are loved greatly. Nobody is quite sure what exactly may happen, but it is surely time to start detaching from the engineered illusions and start to focusing on yourself. Small acts, when multiplied by millions of people, can indeed transform the whole world.

This is the time where the false illusory system start to crumble and the rebirth of anew comes forth, only if humans work together and work towards self-sustainability. A lot of pain and suffering will arise for many people; this is all a natural process. Many people may want their old jobs back, old comforts etc., but this is just the universe testing you. You must look within and let go of all attachments, use any painful times to practice the arts of acceptance and surrender, hold the faith that something beautiful will come of it all. There is now a mass rebirth and cleansing-process is taking place—do not be a victim of the distractions from government and media.

The powers that be are well aware of the planetary changes and the shift, not to go into the conspiracy side of things but they have been systematically attacking humans on a variety of levels for a long period of time, mainly to keep consciousness in a low state. From controlling the food supply, educational system, fraudulent banking system, water supply, the media and television just to name a few. As people awaken back into compassion and realise this system is nothing more than a scam that caters only a few, you will see more people fight back and start to slowly modify the foundations to which the system operates.

Instead of looking at the powers that be in absolute disgust for what they are provoking towards humanity and nature, instead look at them as obstacles for growth, the balancing of your karma if you will. Without the power structure, the way it is and if the world was in a perfect state, there wouldn't be much reason to incarnate here as it would just be like a holiday.

One huge step you can take in regards to personal growth is to drop all any anger and resentment for what they are causing and embrace the realisation that they are helping humanity for the higher good, allowing many souls to accomplish their life lessons. At the end of the day the real 'you' can never be harmed, the same goes for the spirit of the earth. Saying this there is no longer a need to feed the unwanted, try your best to detach from the current system and work towards building a self-sustaining reality.

'There is a global awakening blooming all around this trembling earth. A thirst for justice, for equality, for harmony, for sustainability, for creativity, for compassion- for love. It's a tsunami of transformation. And it cannot be stopped. A global super movement is emerging, rooted in interdependence. Heart by heart, we can transform this world, from the bottom up. We aren't asking for permission. We are doing this. Now'

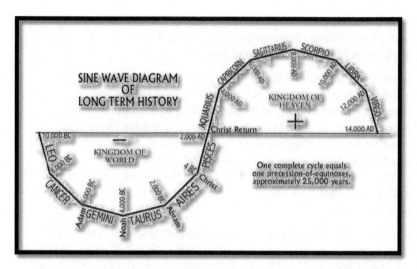

A diagrammatic representation of the platonic year. The period of one complete cycle of the equinoxes around the ecliptic. (Defined by NASA)

Planetary changes in the solar system

Many ancient prophecies spoke of the great shift that planet earth, in fact the entire galaxy, is experiencing right now. These prophecies predict that the current third-dimensional reality is transitioning into fourth and fifth-dimensional states of being. The planet has just entered into the Age of Aquarius from Pisces indication that the feminine energy is now dominant. This shift encourages a heightened consciousness in humanity and a shifting of the earth's magnetic field (poles). (Higher Vibrational energy)

The Native Americans, the Hopi and the Zulu tribe in Africa believe in the coming change. The Maya believe (by the prophecy of their elders and the 'Sixth Sun') that the Seventh Sun is coming.

To give you an example of the difference between these 3 consciousness states, we will consider how a human reacts when involved in a traffic accident:

1. When the car of a **third-dimensional consciousness** individual is damaged, that human most frequently reacts with anger, abuse and blame towards the one they thought caused the damage.

2. **A fourth dimensional consciousness** individual would relate this accident to karma and accept what has happened as a balancing process. This individual senses that he was on the other side of a similar accident. Thus, the accident has occurred repeatedly to help him develop patience without judgement.

3. **The fifth-dimensional consciousness** individual would react with acceptance and love for the other person and send grace to help them calm their nerves and to relieve their concern about the damaged car. Also this human may state, since no one was killed lets be thankful for this experience.

Before we continue, it is wise to highlight the actual, real date that the ancients where in alignment with. Currently we are in the year 2014 on the **Gregorian calendar**, whilst the ancients worked with the **Ethiopian/Ethiopic calendar.** The Ethiopic calendar lags some 8 years behind the Gregorian calendar, the conversion from **January 2014** to the Ethiopic calendar gives the month of **April 2006.** Therefore, in reality, 2012 has not yet arrived; the real 2012 will be 2020 in relation to the Gregorian calendar.

You can go and research this information for yourself; it is a subject that most people fail to address when they write, blog, or speak about the ideology behind 2012. As mentioned earlier, the Ethiopian Calendar lags some 8 years behind the Gregorian calendar. Meaning Ethiopians celebrated the 2000 millennium eight years after the countries following the Gregorian calendar and most parts of the world did.

The Ethiopian Calendar is also composed of 13 months, different from the 12 months in the Gregorian calendar, in which the 13th month (Pagumé) lasts 5 days and 6 days in a leap year. September the 11th is the New Year on this calendar.

The whole purpose of developing and/or keeping a calendar is to predict future events based upon the cyclical nature of the world, to keep such things as agriculture in line with the seasons or inform out-of-line politicians when their terms of office are up for reconsideration. Many may shout 2012 is the 'end' of the world; this is just ignorant as nothing ever ends throughout the universe. The idea that everything is coming to some sort of completion, i.e. the end of cycles, the end of days and the end period, just doesn't compute when it comes to the idea of a calendar.

Every human being is a co-creator, the shift is just not 'happening' to humanity but humanity is also creating the shift right in the moment. There is a collective unconscious that looms over everybody, a collective storage of thoughts, emotions and imagery that needs to be converted into a vibration of love rather than one of fear and gloom. Unfortunately the majority of humans have been programmed by controlled externals and live in a fear-based state. As each person seeks the truth and transforms himself or herself from within, changes can slowly come about in the collective unconscious.

An example of mass programming of the collective unconscious is the workings behind the film called '2012'. This film was created and cost over 200million dollars, money that could have easily been distributed to those in need. This film was put out to instil fear and an illusory story into the masses subliminally that will be replayed in the mind and hearts of many people. After reading thus far in this book, you understand how powerful thoughts and emotions are, stories of fear and destruction planted into millions of people is just an attempt to slow down the planetary shift, but that will not be allowed to happen.

'The goal of life is to make your heartbeat match the beat of the universe, to match your nature with nature' ~ **Joseph Campbell**

Planetary Changes

Many are programmed to believe that the earth alone is going through a rapid phase of warming up, volatile weather patterns and 'natural' disasters. Research suggests that earth is not experiencing these anomalies alone and every other planet in the solar system is undergoing huge change. Below are short descriptions regarding other planets that are undergoing some type of change, and this information was mainly sourced from NASA website, but we encourage you to do your own research.

SUN: The Sun's magnetic field is more than 230% stronger than it was at the beginning of the 1900s. Its overall energetic activity has sizeably increased, creating a frenzy of activity that continues to embarrass NASA's official predictions.

VENUS: Is now glowing in the dark. Venus crossed the path of the sun, marking the beginning of an 8-year Venus cycle that ended on June 6th of 2012 (Gregorian).This transit released very powerful energies to harmonise the masculine or patriarchal forces of the Sun with the heartful, loving energies associated with Venus. Many indigenous people consider the eight-year cycle as an evolutionary doorway or gestational period for the release of new ideas and world change. Potential anniversary dates that might trigger other events on earth

EARTH: Beginning about 1960, earth's surface grew dimmer by 4–6%. About 1994 it began brightening again, which scientists believe may be accelerating global warming and the greenhouse effect. During the last 30 years, the icecaps have thinned out by as much as 40%. For reasons that scientists are unable to explain, in 1997 the structure of the earth began shifting from being more egg-shaped, elongated at the poles, to being more pumpkin-shaped, or flattened at the poles.

MARS: NASA's close-up images of Mars shows how its icecaps virtually melted within just one year, causing 50% changes in surface features and its atmospheric density has risen by 200% since 1997.

JUPITER: Jupiter has become so highly energised that it is now surrounded by a visibly glowing doughnut tube of energy in the path of the moon, which now glows in the dark. The size of Jupiter's magnetic field has more than doubled since 1992.

SATURN: Saturn's Polar Regions have been noticeably brightening, and its magnetic field strength has been increasing. Between 1980 and 1996, the speed of rotation for Saturn's clouds at the equator reduced by a whopping 58.2%, which was an unexpected and dramatic change in its weather patterns.

URANUS: In 1999, NASA articles were referring to Uranus as being hit by Huge Storms, making it a dynamic world with the brightest clouds in the outer solar system. NASA also said that if springtime on earth were anything like it would be on Uranus, we would be experiencing waves of massive storms, each one covering the country from Kansas to New York, with temperatures of 300 degrees below zero. NASA's Voyager II space probe indicates that both Uranus and Neptune appear to have had recent magnetic pole shifts – 60 degrees for Uranus and 50 for Neptune.

NEPTUNE: Since 1996, Neptune has become 40% brighter on the infrared scale and is 100% brighter in certain areas of its surface. Neptune's moon Triton has had a 'very large percentage increase' in atmospheric pressure and temperature that is comparable to an increase on Earth of 22-degrees Fahrenheit.

PLUTO: As of September 2002, Pluto has experienced a 300% increase in its atmospheric pressure in the last 14 years, has also become noticeably darker in colour.

Many people fear these earthly changes. Connect back to the heart at the deepest levels and you will be safe! Simple as that. There is no destruction and suffering in the universe, it is illusory and temporary for the higher evolution of your soul. This earth and everything that happens here is just a micro segment of 'real life'.

Remember! You are currently on a 4.5billion year old spaceship, a self-sufficient, organic, complex spaceship. You are orbiting a power source that is a million times larger than your ship. There are 200 billion more power sources, possibly like yours, in your group. There are 40 more groups in your particular neighbourhood. Your neighbourhood is moving at 2 million miles per hour to an object that is 150 million light years away. Welcome to life. It's more exciting than you think on a larger scale!

Universal Laws

The universe is perfectly balanced by natural and moral laws with regulatory vibrations to maintain order. When you work within the laws, you can be assured of an eventual positive outcome. When the laws are transgressed, you can be assured of suffering. The only purpose of this is to teach you a better way. These laws are an extract from Dick Sutphen's[48] book *lighting the Light Within*.

1. The Law of Harmony. This law supersedes even the fundamental law of karma, for harmony is the supreme potential of balance. The purpose of Karma is to attain harmony. If you throw a rock into a pond, you disturb the harmony of the pond. You are the cause, and the effect is the splash and the ripples that flow out and back until harmony is restored. Similarly, your disharmonious actions flow out into the Universe and back onto you, lifetime after lifetime, until eventually, your own harmony is restored.

2. The Law of Reincarnation and Karma. Until you have resolved your Karma and fulfilled your Dharma, which are the deeds you must do, you will continue to reincarnate into sequential lifetime upon the earth. Neither universal creator nor the Lords of Karma bestow suffering upon you during these lives. You and you alone decide what you most need to learn in your earthly sojourns. Thus for each life experience you seek out other souls, often with shared histories, with karmic configurations that match your needs. Whenever you act with intention, you create karma. Actions are considered thoughts, emotions, words and deeds, and the motive, desire and intent behind each. Disharmonious acts must be balanced in the future in this life or in a future lifetime, to have soul growth.

3. The Law of Wisdom. Wisdom erases karma. If you have the wisdom to learn your lessons through love and wisdom, you can mitigate your suffering. Sadly, we seem to learn the fastest through pain, through directly experiencing the consequences of our actions. As an example, you greedily take from others, and instead of learning through wisdom and love that this is wrong, you have to experience from others someone greedily taking from you, whether later in this life or in a future lifetime.

Example 1: In your last life you were married to a Soul who is your mate today, and whom you cruelly left for another in that previous lifetime. Before you were born into your current life, you agreed to be left by your mate, under similar circumstances—this will allow you to balance your Karma—and directly experience the pain of abandonment. If through the wisdom of Master-Life-Awareness, it is easier to detach consciously from the relationship with love, you will ease the pain of parting while also passing your own test and thus absolving karma and evolving from within.

Example 2. Assume that you have astrologically destined a severe relationship test for May of your 35th year. If you have learnt through past-life awareness, as well as present life learning, to be positive, non-judgmental and without expectations in your relationship, you may only experience an argument with your mate on that fateful day in May, but if you haven't learnt your past lessons and have intensified your disharmony during your relationship, you might experience a divorce in May of your 35th year.

4. The Law of Grace. Karma can be experienced to the letter of the law or in mercy and grace. In other words if you give love, mercy and grace to others, you will receive the same in return.

5. The Law of Soul Evolution. All people on Earth shares the goal of soul evolution whether they realise it or not. We have reincarnated because we desire to evolve spiritually. By rising above all of your fear-based emotions and in so doing learning how to express unconditional love, we raise our vibrational rate and move closer to a state of harmony. Even where it appears that we are not evolving we are in reality making progress. We learn through the pain of our disharmonious acts, which can be viewed as our mistakes or failures. This is the law of Soul evolution.

6. The Law of Bodhisattva. Bodhisattva is a Sanskrit term commonly accepted by most Metaphysical adepts today. It means one who has transcended the need of Earthly incarnations but who has chosen to return to the earth to support others in achieving enlightenment. A Bodhisattva knows he will never really be free until all Souls are free. Most serious students of metaphysics have entered the Bodhisattva Development Stage of their evolution.

7. The Law of Vibrational Attainment. The entire Universe operates on the same principle of vibrational energy. When Einstein discovered that 'matter is energy', he unlocked the door to emerging science and metaphysics. Scientists have proven that energy cannot die, it can only transform (reincarnate), and, by its very nature, energy must go forwards or backwards; it cannot stand still, for it to do so is stagnation, resulting in transformation. You are energy. Your skin, which appears solid, is actually trillions of swiftly moving molecules orbiting each other at a specific vibrational rate; a physical life rate you have earned in the past as a result of how harmoniously—or disharmoniously you have lived your past lives and your current life up until this moment in time. When you are harmonious for a lifetime, you will have attained the highest vibrational rate—the God level.

8. The Law of Free Will. The law of free will operates in the three following ways.

1. Although many of the major events in your life are astrologically predestined, you always have free will to mitigate the impact of the event, or to transcend it entirely. This will result from how you live your life up to the

situation you have destined for yourself to experience. If you show grace and mercy to others, are positive, loving, compassionate and demonstrate by your action that you have learnt past lessons, you can minimise disharmonious experiences!

2. As you obtain Master of Life awareness and develop conscious detachment, you will be far less affected by worldly events than in the past. A Master of Life enjoys all the warmth and joy that life has to offer, but detaches from the negativity by allowing it to flow through him without affecting him.

3. You always have free will in how you respond to any situation. If you respond with positive emotions, compassion and integrity, you have probably learnt your karmic lessons and will not have to experience a similar situation in the future.

9. The Law of One. Every Soul, living and discarnate, is connected at the level of the collective unconscious, deep within the higher self. You are interconnected and a part of a great energy gestalt called God/universal creator, and because you are part of God, you are God. It is the goal of the gestalt to move the energy forwards, creating more energy. So, in living harmoniously, you increase your vibrational rate and intensify the vibration of the entire gestalt. When you are disharmonious, you decrease the vibration of the entire gestalt, because all are one. Everything you think, say and do, affects every other Soul.

10. The Law of Manifestation. Everything manifest begins as a thought, an idea. Ideas and experiences create beliefs, which in turn, create your reality. If you are unhappy with your current reality, you must change your beliefs and your behaviour. Beliefs can be changed once you identify those that are not working for you, and begin programming what will create success and harmony in your life. The unlimited creative power of your mind, through dedication, awareness and training, can be the wisdom to rise above your karma. Within physical and spiritual laws, you can manifest any reality you desire to experience. Concerning changing your behaviour, you must decide which disharmonious behaviour you want to eliminate. Then be aware that you don't have to change how you feel about something to affect it, if you are willing to change what you are doing.

11. The Law of Conscious Detachment. Buddha's early teachings are best summarised with one of his statements, 'It is your resistance to what is that causes your suffering.' and by suffering, he meant everything that doesn't work in your life; relationship problems, loss of loved ones, loneliness, sickness, accidents, guilt, monetary hardship, unfulfilled desires and so on. When you accept what is, you accept the unalterable realities in your life without resisting them. Some things are facts. They exist, and, no matter how much you resist them, there is nothing you can do about them. Change what you can change, but have the wisdom to accept unalterable situations as they are, without wasting mental or physical energy attempting to change what you cannot change. Out of acceptance comes involved detachment, which is the ability to enjoy all the positive aspects of life, but to allow the negative to flow through you without resistance and without affecting you.

12. The Law of Gratitude. From the perspective of Karma and the Law of One, the more you give, the more you will receive. The more you assist others, the more you will assist yourself. The power of this Law also works in your day-to-day life.

13. The Law of Fellowship. When two or more people of similar vibration are gathered for a shared purpose, their combined energy directed to the attainment of that purpose is doubled, tripled, quadrupled or more. This esoteric awareness has been used by covens, esoteric religions, healing groups and recently, worldwide meditations for world peace.

14. The Law of Resistance. That which you resist, you draw to you, and you will perpetuate its influence upon your life. Resistance is fear, so it is something you need to resolve karmically. The Law of Resistance assures that you let go of the fear by encountering it until you are forced to deal with it by learning conscious detachment.

Example: You may have a strong resistance towards people of Asia or Africa, of Jewish people or your mother-in-law. Your resistance is fear. The quickest way to overcome that which you fear is through direct experience, thus you will reincarnate as an Asian, Black, Jew, or mother in-law in a future lifetime. When you attain Master of Life awareness and stop resisting [your fear] by consciously detaching from the negativity, the problem will be resolved. Most disharmonious situations are solved through a change in your viewpoint. By changing your perspective, you can usually eliminate the effects of a problem, and if you are no longer affected by a problem, you no longer have a problem, although nothing about the problem situation may have changed. Another aspect of the Law of Resistance states, 'That which you resist, you become, if not in this lifetime, then in a future incarnation.'

15. The Law of Attraction. 'Where your attention goes, your energy flows'. You attract what you are and that which you concentrate upon. If you are negative, you draw in and experience negativity. If you are loving, you draw in and experience love. You can attract to you only those qualities you possess. So, if you want peace and harmony in your life, you must become peaceful and harmonious.

16. The Law of Reflection. This Law says that the traits you respond to in others, you recognise in yourself, both positive and negative. It has four primary manifestations:

That which you admire in others, you recognise as existing within yourself. **That** which you resist and react to strongly in others is sure to be found within yourself. **That** which you resist and react to in others is something that you are afraid exists within you and **that** which you resist in yourself, you will dislike in others.

In other words, you have chosen to incarnate upon the manifest plane to learn to rise above the effect of fear. Those fears will always be reflected in your reactions to others. Thus, your goals are very obvious once you recognise how to perceive them. As you let go of the fear, you automatically open to expressing more unconditional love.

17. The Law of Unconditional Love. The expression of unconditional love will eventually result in harmony. Unconditional love is not romantic love. It is the acceptance of others as they are without judgement or expectations. It is total acceptance of others without attempting to change them, except by your own positive example. The Law of Unconditional love says, 'If you go out of your way to express unconditional love, you automatically rise above fear, and as you transcend your fears, you automatically open yourself to unconditional love.

18. The Law of Magnetic Affinities. By astrologically choosing the time and place of your birth, you determine the nature or the affects you will experience in your life. On the other side, before you're born, you make decisions about the lifetime we will be entering into. You chose your parents, other souls to interact with you, and the astrological configurations of your birth, which determine your character, personality, abilities, restrictions and timing for strengths and weaknesses—If all of this seems too complicated to be real, be aware that you are only using 5 to 10% of the capacity of your brain. In addition, the brain-mind researchers say the human brain has 200,000 times the capacity of the greatest computer ever built. Such calculations as just described would be no problem for such a computer.

19. The Law of Abundance. You have within yourself everything required to make your earthly incarnation a paradise if you choose to accept that which is your divine birth right. We live in a Universe of abundance, although the majority of those populating our planet appear to view it as a Universe of scarcity.

20. The Law of Divine Order. If you seek to understand the Law of Divine Order, study the natural balance of nature, for it works very much the same way. Everything is as it should be, although humankind (the energy gestalt) is far from experiencing its potential of total harmony. There are no accidents. Your energy, translated into thoughts, words, emotions and deeds, causes all your experiences. This assures that you always have the learning opportunities you require to resolve your karma, and, as with you, the collective thoughts, words, emotions and deeds of humankind create the environment for all. If enough souls focus their energy upon peace, all will have peace. If the majority of souls are filled with anger, all may have to experience war. We are all one, and like the many sub-personalities within you, the dominant traits of humankind (the entire gestalt) will emerge to resolve our group karma.

It is mentioned within these 20 laws that your life is astrologically predestined. Before you are born into this physical reality, you choose your lessons and experiences then a life blueprint is created. This blueprint is then hidden from you, (bit of a cruel joke you may say). This blueprint is an astrological natal chart, which is constructed from your details of birth; it shows all planetary influences and alignments that have an impact on your life's circumstances and events. You can get yourself a natal reading here: www.13signsastrology.com/astrology-readings

Changing the Karma

Karma, everybody has heard of it. Even though it's been a part of everyday vocabulary since the 1960'2, most people only have a vague idea about it. Many may already have a slight idea regarding karma and how it actually works, although they may not refer to it as 'karma' but maybe 'manifesting' or 'the power of positive thinking' or even 'conscious creation'.

Karma is actually a Sanskrit word, just like 'chakra'. Sanskrit is the language of the ancients, and most importantly is the language of a spiritual culture – the Vedic culture of ancient India. After millennia of being shrouded in mystery the east is giving up its secrets, and complete understanding of karma is available to the entire world.

The Sanskrit language actually contains many words that have no direct equivalent in western languages. Together these words describe an entire worldview, a spiritual worldview, which stands in sharp contrast to the modern western (now global) worldview. Thus taking one word from it, such as yoga, or karma, cannot give a complete understanding since it must be over stood in the context of the entire worldview. Karma on the whole can be summed up in one word: reaction. **The general features of karma are:**

- Karma is a law of the universe, just like the laws of physics. Chemistry or gravity, and operates with the same infallible dependability.
- Every desire you have, every action you perform generates a karmic reaction that eventually **must** be fulfilled.
- Actions that generate karma are akin to planting seeds that will fructify at some future. In this life or **in a future life.**
- Karma operates on two levels, individual and group/collective karma.

- You are born into circumstances that will facilitate the fulfilment of your karmic destiny.
- 'Good' karma gives us desirable results, while 'bad' karma gives us pain, suffering and trouble.

The karma of all collective and personal actions in the past is now coming back to haunt everybody on the planet. As mentioned, a huge cleansing and rebirth process is indeed upon humanity and we must be cleansed for the higher good. Most often in the form of temporary suffering. Karma in itself implies that it's not the politicians, not the bankers, not the foreigners taking all the jobs, not any of the people whom we want to point the finger. Instead, it's someone who we hardly ever point the finger at-ourselves.

Every human on the planet is indeed responsible for this huge debt, and it is one which must, and will be paid. The good news is that the suffering can be averted because karma can be changed. One of the most important things about karma is that every desire will be fulfilled. Every karmic reaction must be received-however long it takes, regardless of how many lifetimes one must be born again. Indeed, it's the reaction of karma that generates future births in the world.

Acts of karma are like planting seeds that will fructify in time.

Economic issues can be individual or widespread affecting a large number of people, such as during an economic crisis, or war, such widespread suffering is understood to be collective karma. Humans can also have good group or collective karma- such as when there is peaceful coexistence, good relations, universal education, a high standard of living, widespread abundance, widespread happiness, satisfaction etc. Collective karma is generated by a group of people who together engage in 'good' or 'bad' karmic reactions.

You're born into circumstances that fulfil your karmic destiny

It's not by chance that you are born into a specific family, at a specific time and place. You are given a birth that will allow yourself to receive the karma generated in previous lifetimes, good and bad. Remember that karma is a universal law just like the law of attraction which makes no mistakes. The circumstances you are born into are a result of previous work, like it or not. By the same token you are creating in the current life the circumstances that will define the next life. Understanding the principle should be motivation to always do well and be good!

Children across the world are born into poverty or wealth, sickness or health, pleasant or unpleasant circumstances and many wonder why in the world could the universal creator or 'god' be so unjust. What did an unfortunate child do to deserve suffering in life? But the laws of the universe are not unjust.

Every one of us have lived before and created the present circumstances of the current life out of free will. There is a higher power that controls this world, and all humans should be mindful that each and every soul on the planet can live a happy life if one lives in complete harmony with the laws of nature. So the question is, are you doing things in this life that will create a fortunate situation in the next birth, or are you contributing towards the actions, thoughts and feelings that will cause suffering? Everything is noted and everybody will reap what they have sown.

Karma generates both desirable and undesirable qualities

If in the current life you generate predominantly 'good' karma, then in the next life you will have an attractive and desirable personal qualities such as physical beauty, good health and strength, a good education and intelligence, fame, various natural skills, or perhaps even be a prodigy. 'Bad' karma on the other hand results in undesirable qualities in bodily appearance, bad health, lack of intelligence or poor education, lack of ability, and legal and financial problems. Understanding this unfailing law of the universe can give strong motivating to act with kindness from the heart not mind, following the golden rule that we should do unto others as we would like them to do to us.

The spiritually equal nature of all living beings

The universe is the creator of all life, therefore each and every being is equal – regardless of their position in this world. The 'important' people, the political leaders, company presidents have no more value than the street beggars. Each is a spiritual being and each has an equal place in relationship to the absolute.

When we say 'living beings' what exactly do we mean? Just people? Or plants, animals, insects and fish? Actually every living thing, because it is a spiritual spark, or soul that gives absolute life to every one of them-whether a bird, a tree, a cow, a human being, or even a germ-the life principle is the same. It is the spirit soul that is life, and that gives life to any material body.

The spirit soul wears the material body just like a suit of clothes, or rather uses the material body as a machine to fulfil its desires. The body is alive because life is present in the body in the form of spirit soul, but when the soul leaves the body, the body becomes lifeless, or dead. Actually the body is just matter, a bunch of chemicals, and is always 'dead'. It is the soul that activates the body so the body itself appears to have life. Life comes from the soul; life is the soul. It's not that you have a soul, you **are** the soul!

You are the life that comes and goes in countless bodies, changing one after another. The soul passes into another body at the time of death if reincarnation is chosen. Every aspect of creation is very deliberate and perfectly arranged and understanding how that is so allows you to cooperate with the plan of the universal creator so circumstances and events can run as smoothly as they can. Due to not understanding and not accepting this principle many ignorantly act against the laws of nature and often make a mess of things, which is what is happening right now, and bringing karmic reactions in the form of suffering through economic, social and political problems.

If humanity wants to over stand the scale of karmic debt, we all must be willing to acknowledge the scale of injustice that modern society creates and which all of us participate. But to do so the boundaries and mental limitations of society must be overlooked and nature must be considered above all.

The same ancient texts that explain karma also tell us of another world, a spiritual divine world where everyone is beautiful, and happy. In that world there is no suffering, no disease, eternal youth and no one ever dies. Life goes on there eternally in complete harmony. That perfect place is the spiritual world.

As a spiritual being you have the option to live either in this world you are in, or in that one, and amazingly, it's the same actions of karma that bind many to the current world and carry many to the other one. Karma is based on desire. By hearing about and desiring to enter the spiritual world one can transfer themselves there but must first learn to do the things that are done there. You must become qualified to enter there by engaging in spiritual activities.

Just as the material body requires food for sustenance, your spiritual body requires sustenance as well. But not fully over standing this will in fact neglect to feed the soul and therefore results in emptiness deep within- a longing and hankering for something fulfilling and meaningful. However you may try to fulfil this need with various types of material enjoyments, the emptiness continues. Maybe the point of despair is reached even if everything the world has to offer is in ones grasp.

The supreme universal creator cannot be seen and is transcendental to this material realm and is therefore beyond human ability to see with material eyes. But it is known that that the creator can be reached through the waves of sound and will be ever present, providing the spiritual sustenance. Each and every day practice the mantra below for heart purification, karma purification and to gain a deeper sense of self.

Repeat 108 times:

    Ommmmm/Aimmmmmm

    KA, E, I, LA, HRIM

    HA, SA, KA, HA, LA, HRIM

    SA, KA, LA, HRIM

The Warrior of the Light by Paulo Coelho

Every warrior of the light has been afraid to enter a combat. Every warrior of the light has betrayed and lied in the past.

Every warrior of the light has lost faith in the future. Every warrior of the light has trodden a path which is not his own.

Every warrior of the light has suffered because of unimportant things. Every warrior of the light has doubted that he is a warrior of the light.

Every warrior of the light has failed in his spiritual obligations. Every warrior of the light has said yes when he meant no. and every warrior of the light has hurt someone he loved.

This is why he and she are warriors of the light . . . They had endured all this without losing hope to improve.

A loving heart is the key to health and success in this life. Love is your true nature and the underlying essence of everything in the universe. In love, all is one. The opposite of love is fear, which leads to anger, shame and guilt and these are the obstructions to health, harmony and peace. In order to be truly healthy you must learn to experience, accept, take responsibility and release the fear that has plagued many since the beginning of life. This is the way to true balance.

This is the path to peace everlasting. Be courageous today. Go inward. Be honest. Allow this life to humble you. Serve all. Expect nothing in return. Give and give and give of yourself until your last breathe. Your rewards do not come from this world. Open your heart, let the fear dissipate by experiencing it out and be a courageous channel of Divine Love. Courage is not the absence of fear, courage is moving ahead in spite of it. Love those who hate you. Criticise no one. You are a warrior of light, you are bigger and more expanded than that and you are appreciated. Let your light shine bright. Shrink your Self for no one.

Your courage and faith is inspirational. You are brilliant. You are so awesome and magnificent. Words cannot express your uniqueness or how beautiful you are. Give your gifts and feel whole and complete in so doing.

'There do exist enquiring minds, which long for the truth of the heart, seek it, strive to solve the problems set by life, try to penetrate to the essence of things and phenomena and to penetrate into themselves. If a man reasons and thinks soundly, no matter which path he follows in solving these problems, he must inevitably arrive back at himself, and begin with the solution of the problem of what he is himself and what his place is in the world around him.' G. I. Gurdjieff[49]

Chapter 3, The body.

It is important to ask yourself—is your food **energising you or poisoning you**? The eating habits of modern man are centred on fast stimulation rather than soul gratification. In the Western world, people have been led astray with misinformation regarding which foods are naturally compatible with the human organism. The culprits responsible for the widespread misinformation, propaganda and deep-rooted deception are the major corporations who hold dominion over the majority of the world's food supplies, pharmaceutical companies and media advertisement industries.

We unquestionably live in a toxic food environment. You can find a fast food restaurant located on every other corner, hosting cheap advertisements for highly processed foods with little to no nutritional value. These so-called foods not only unleash toxicity into the human body but can also cause an imbalance in clarity of mind and sensory perceptions, ultimately permeating chaos throughout the higher energetic structure of your being.

There are currently over 15,000 actively used chemicals in major food supplies. This section provides information needed to become conscious of what you are ingesting. More than half of the US population is overweight or clinically obese, mainly due to a high-toxicity diet, over-consumption of animal products and genetically modified foods (GMOs).

Over 1,000 million prescription items were dispensed in the United Kingdom overall in 2012, a 4.1 per cent increase (39.0 million items) from the previous year and a 62.2 per cent increase (383.5 million items) since 2002. Why such an increase in such a short amount of time? A large factor is the subliminal social programming of the population's collective consciousness via television, radio, institutions, parents and society. Many people's decision making processes have been left to external sources. Overall, the connection between humans and nature has been forgotten, and a large percentage of what is eaten consists of merely food-like products.

What can we do to help reverse this imbalance between man and nature? We can work to spread real information and knowledge, start to eat what is right and that which is provided by nature. Natural food, i.e., fruits, vegetables, nuts, seeds and superfoods, all hold energetic auras. Digesting them brings life to every cell in the human body, delivering adequate nutrition, enhanced energy and an increase in oxygen. Not only do raw, natural foods feed your mind and soul, but they also help prevent disease on a physical level.

Scientifically, the mind is VIBRATION and the human body is ENERGY. When you nourish both, something magical happens. VIBRATION + ENERGY = CONSCIOUSNESS. Blockages in your energy field can start to be discharged because the food you are eating is no longer dead; it is alive with vibration, hydration and most importantly, conductivity. Living foods are packed full of nutrients, enzymes and life force that contribute to the expansion and growth in your conscious awareness.

In this chapter, we expand on the most vital aspects of health and how to truly nourish the temple you reside in—your one true home. We highlight the dangerous chemical additives in everyday food products, the most nutrient dense superfoods on the planet, guides to detoxification and regeneration, the vegetarian/vegan natural way of life, benefits of fasting, juice recipes and more. With this information, you can start to make steps that will go hand in hand with the other two chapters of this booklet, bringing ultimate balance into your life.

Why Are We So Sick?

There is a high probability that you know somebody who is suffering from an illness or who has to consume regular prescription medications. In the year 2014, we are supposedly at the pinnacle of technology, but in reality humans have gone from the dominant species on the planet to the sickest, in just one century.

The world is currently in the midst of a pandemic of chronic illness, crippling many cultures and societies. For the last five decades, the amount of money spent year upon year on medications, medical doctors, surgery, nurses and hospitals has only increased. Throughout those same fifty years, the monetary expense of pharmaceutical drugs, along with the overall number of prescriptions, has increased by around sixty times on average for each person

The number of people suffering from some form chronic illness is on a consistent incline alongside obesity rates, which are rising and have shot up by around 400 per cent in the last decade alone. Type 2 diabetes had to be renamed 'adult onset diabetes', but it was 'on-setting' for so many children that they could no longer name it 'adult onset'.

The population has been led to believe that solutions to their health problems are going to come from drugs and surgery alone. People have been led to believe that sometime in the future, scientists will discover a cure-all drug that will fix all of the world's health problems; therefore, it is believed that there is no need to pay attention to the other underlying factors that are in one's own control.

The current medical system clearly is not working. But is it not working because the right drug and surgery hasn't been found yet? Is it not working because people are not getting treatment quickly enough? Or is it not working because it takes the wrong approach and will never work? The most important question we should be asking ourselves as a species is—why are we so sick?

If we do not find out why we are so sick, then we are unlikely to find the solution to the problem of how to get and stay well. According to the prevailing allopathic sickness and treatment systems, many fall sick because of predetermined genetics and inherent weaknesses that encourage pathological cell function, leading to heart disease, cancer, diabetes, stroke, depression and ADHD, among others. Due to this belief, they feel that the most rational approach is to override the body's innate ability to self-heal and self-regulate with pharmaceutical drugs.

For many people, their lives are as busy as the world. A large majority often do not get the time to focus on themselves, consume diet high in nutrition, or to quiet the mind throughout the day. There is a wide range of factors that contribute to one's sickness, such as acidic blood, acidic thoughts, holding onto past pain, lack of oxygen/shallow breathing, dehydration, mineral deficiency, white sugar/animal/processed foods and the intake of harmful chemicals found in a large majority of the 'food like' products many are consuming.

A medical doctor's theory is that you can obtain all the minerals and nutrients required from a balanced diet alone, but there are some underlying factors that extend beyond this solution. Depending upon where you live, even if you are eating a plant-based diet there is a high probability you are still not obtaining all the necessary minerals needed to keep the body and brain in equanimity.

For example, if there is no boron and no copper present in the soils, they are not being absorbed into the food; therefore, logically minimal minerals are reaching the body. Even the healthiest, raw-conscious eaters can be deficient in minerals, so whatever your diet may be, it is wise to supplement. This world is dirty, filthy and toxic—it is therefore crucial to educate yourself, enhance your awareness and spread the truth in order to live to your upmost potential.

Geoengineering, chemtrails and weather modification are on the need-to-know list if you want to preserve your health. You will have to do your own research on these topics, as we only provide the solutions. The heavy metal toxicity in the environment tends to accumulate in the brain and nerves—in the electrical system of the body, which attracts nanoparticulate metals. These metals can cause havoc in the body, inflammation and pain arise along with the shutdown of major glands such as the thyroid and adrenals.

Fast food restaurants alongside the meat and dairy industry pack their products with artificial chemicals, such as aspartame and MSG. Such chemicals program your taste buds and cause you to become neurologically addicted, making it very challenging to break the unhealthy habit of consuming such foods. When your taste buds are programmed a certain way, healthy food may taste horrific, as you are used to all the processed, artificial junk.

However, it may take only a small period of time to reprogram. These types of foods are addictive and stimulate dopamine receptors in the brain similar to drugs, alcohol and television. For this reason, they are consumed excessively when a person is overweight, bored, angry, in pain or residing in a lower level of consciousness, ultimately seeking external comfort.

As mentioned, a lack of oxygen intake also encourages low-level consciousness and illness. Can your body get sick if there is enough oxygen in each cell? With good water intake and avoidance of chronic dehydration, all mineral needs are met alongside the synergy and the conductivity (coming from the relationship between the micro and macro nutrients), then oxygen levels do not pose a problem, and the nutritional tools are optimised and at work in the body. Green foods and juices contain chlorophyll; the chemical structure varies by just one molecule (from haemoglobin the iron-containing oxygen-transporting metalloproteinase within the red blood cells of all vertebrates).

Green juices and superfoods, such as Spirulina and wheatgrass, are absolutely key for delivering chlorophyll into the system, which is crucial for supporting the utilisation of oxygen and purifying the blood within the human organism.

This supplementation alone makes it much more difficult for illnesses to manifest in the physical body; also remember that many illnesses can also stem from unresolved emotional issues and past trauma that are still integrated within the luminous energy field that was discussed previously.

A plan must be put in place to detoxify the barrage of heavy metal toxicity, as well as the high levels of other kinds of toxicity in the environment, water and beauty products. Birds, insects, trees, plants, fish and humans are all dying. If you want to survive and thrive, then it is crucial to make use of fruits and vegetables, which is nature's medicine. Antioxidants, bioflavonoids, polyphenols, essential oils and other anti-inflammatory, acid-neutralising properties from juices and raw food work wonders in the body.

The human race is destroying the planet; every person is engaged in this process, but if you climb up the ladder of society, the destruction of the environment becomes an even greater conspiracy. Too many in today's society are deficient in love, truth and energy. This chapter delves deep into many topics surrounding health and regeneration of your physical temple.

A large number of people are exhausted and simply stressed out due to the high demands of modern day life. Many people simply do not have enough free time available, but it is vital for you as a co-creator to look after your own body, mind and consciousness, as there is nothing else more important in the whole world. When you nourish your mind, body and spirit, external living snaps into balance; therefore, creating the reality you desire is a lot easier.

At 29 years old, a person should not be suffering with chronic fatigue syndrome, but if you are drinking tap water, not supplementing with minerals, and eating mainly dead foods, then you will not see a lot of improvement. Raw living foods—fruits, herbs, vegetables, nuts and seeds—can be soaked and brought to life. Absorb those bio-available minerals, vitamins, antioxidants and fibres. Allowing them to move throughout your system for optimum cellular function, communication and conductivity.

The fluoride in the water may put everybody to sleep; the dense foods make it harder for you to embrace creative energy, and the glands do not function efficiently while energy from the sexual organs does not travel through the body in a wasteful manner. Start by modifying small things in your daily life and implementing some of the knowledge presented in this chapter. Eliminate some of the denser foods, get hydrated, get to bed earlier and eliminate stress!

One of the greatest things you can do if you're trying to heal yourself is to continue to expand your consciousness with some kind of spiritual practice. Elevating your state of consciousness has been clinically shown to be a major factor in healing disease and depression at a much more rapid pace.

The people who are willing to meditate, spend time in nature and ultimately embrace a higher field of energy/love are the ones who see efficient results a lot faster than those who do not. This will return one to the natural state of being— sickness was never intended for the human race.

There are a range of factors around physical health, but it is always better to work towards disease prevention than having to visit your doctor numerous times each month, residing in a low vibrational state of being. It is possible to work on your own personal awakening and be inspired. Making a radical choice for better health is not about fear of sickness or death—it's about quality of life, longevity and shining from the inside out.

The body's connection to spiritual developments

The human body is a very complex temple, an alchemical laboratory made up of a digestive, nervous, cardiovascular, musculosketal, lymphatic, endocrine, immune, reproductive, respiratory and excretory systems.

If you keep your temple clean and pure with good habits, you can restore it to perfect health and reconnect with your spiritual essence and higher self. In the Bible, the human body is referred to as 'the temple of god,' otherwise known as Solomon's temple (the soul of man's temple).

On a purely organic level, there truly is no separation between your thoughts, emotions and physical body. For so long, the Western world has been trained to view mind, body and spirit as separate, so on an energetic level these spheres have learnt to function separately. Even now, most people in the general population are cut off from their bodies and are unaware of what is happening inside; this goes for those people who are relatively 'awake', as well.

This mind, body, spirit disconnection has manifested over the course of the last few centuries when human consciousness became divided. On the whole, humans as a species are quite divided from one another; as long as body disconnection is present, it is difficult to receive the warning signs of physical ailment or disease in the course of manifestation. This information stays buried and you remain unaware that something is terribly amiss, until it is too late and you become seriously ill.

Some people do receive the body's cry out for help, want to do something but just do not know where to start. A large percentage of disease is caused by chronic stress alone, which is due to subconscious thought programs and belief systems that you may not have the ability to comprehend. Without an awareness of the thoughts and beliefs that drive your behaviour, you cannot change internally.

As planet Earth and her inhabitants move in tandem with the energetic shift that is widening throughout the entire solar system, old patterns of separating and splitting up the mind, the body and the spirit are being broken up, bringing back the unity consciousness with which humans were once connected. The downside to this breakup is that many people are getting sick and feeling down as the three spheres of mind, body and spirit are brought back into equanimity.

For this reason it is highly important for your own conscious evolution that you focus on the body as much as the mind and spirit aspects of your being. If your physical body is plugged with poisons and toxins, it is difficult to stay in synchronicity with the higher energies that are enhancing the formless aspects of your mind and spirit. For the first time, many are receiving information about taking place within themselves alongside the external environment.

The small percentage of people on the planet that are very sensitive energetically have always had these pathways open, alongside a stronger synchronicity between mind, body and spirit. They tend to feel everything and find it quite difficult to process toxins. Whether it's environmental, pharmaceutical or emotional, they can react strongly to such infiltrations.

These sensitive people have an instantaneous feedback loop, which means when a troubling thought arises that may lead to an uncomfortable emotion, immediately it is felt within the body. It acts as a teaching mechanism to guide the person into living consciously, awake and mindfully.

If this feedback loop is not functioning within your being, then its absence acts as an incentive to clean up your act. The ones who are living in ignorance and are holding deep-rooted issues will be forced to accept, adapt and surrender as the whole transition into the new energies. People cannot be acting heartlessly anymore, as the heart knows what is best for your evolutionary development and will respond to your negative actions very loudly and very clearly, often in the form of pain and suffering.

It is important to be aware that if you're experiencing these fluctuating symptoms, it is a natural process towards your awakening. It was known that in the past that spiritual awakening only happened at the etheric, spiritual level, with only a fraction of the energy filtering down into the emotional, mental and physical realm. It can be uncomfortable for many, especially the ones out of balance, but ultimately it is all for the higher good.

As you awaken spiritually and start to heal yourself, you must remember that your physicality is also being upgraded, configured and rewired. This also includes your emotions and DNA. It is possible that you could experience a shutdown for long periods of time in such a dramatic process; it could come in a form of illness, an accident or something completely random and mysterious. Many will lose their bearings and feel disoriented in their day-to-day life.

This is all a natural process and going through an important stage of recreation. If confusion sets in, just rest and remember it's all for the best. As you embrace the awakening, so will others who find themselves in your energetic sphere.

With all this being said, it's highly important for you to detoxify your body and bring it back into balance with the mind and spirit. In this section is a range information that is vital for your own self-education in terms of what to feed your own body so it can run optimally and so you can raise your own cellular vibration.

Genetically Modified Organisms (GMOs) & Poisons in Foods

Genetically modified organisms (GMOs) are organisms such as plants, animals and microorganisms, whose genetic characteristics have been altered in a way that does not occur naturally by mating and/or natural recombination (mainly formed in laboratories). Food and feed that contain or consist of such GMOs (or are produced from GMOs) are called genetically modified (GM) food/feed.

The European legislation on Genetically Modified Organisms (GMOs) has been in place since the early 1990s and aims to ensure that GMOs and GMO-derived products that are produced or marketed within the EU meet the highest safety standards whilst ensuring harmonised regulation, thereby ensuring the effective functioning of the internal market.

Genetically modified foods are absolutely everywhere, and only a small minority are aware of what's occurring behind the scenes of the food industry. There are a handful of corporations at work tampering with the food supply, crossing genetics and DNA, which in turn destroys the natural food chain. It is crucial that human beings consume the most natural foods for the evolution of DNA and genetic coding, as explained in the previous chapter. Mixing these modified foods within the cellular structure of the human organism will wreak havoc on your natural genetic code and can trigger genetic imbalances and inherited weaknesses.

The long term effects of consuming genetically modified foods and crops is unknown. The public serve as the guinea pigs of GMO experimentation. There have not been sufficient studies about medium- or long-term health, as there has not been enough time since the first commercial sales of genetically modified produce. The very first commercial sale of genetically modified foods took place only twenty years ago, in the year 1994.

That being said, there is absolutely no possibility that the health authorities can test every single outcome on a large enough population of people, over a long enough period of time, to determine that GMO foods are harmless. One geneticist, David Suzuki[50], recently expressed his concern for the number of genetically modified products people are consuming. He claims that human beings are actually part of a 'massive genetic experiment' and have been for many years; this will only worsen, as the foods the majority of uneducated people are eating are also saturated with toxic chemicals, which we will discuss shortly.

As genome sciences have advanced over the last few years, it has been revealed that a variety of living organisms can share their genes. Beforehand it was recognised that only the genes between individual members of a species could be shared through reproduction, geneticists followed the inheritance of a species genes in what they called a 'vertical fashion'. This involves breeding a male and a female and doing the same with their offspring. As the sciences moved forward it has come to light that genes can be shared with not only members of the same species, but it is possible to cross different species such as animals, humans, crops and fruits. This is known as horizontal gene transfer.

This is not to say that a human being mates with an apple, banana or a plant. Instead, the biotechnology and biotech corporations such as Monsanto have allowed the transfer of genes from one species to the other without any regard for natural biological limitations and constraints.

This is a large problem, as it is based on very irresponsible science—the rules that applied to 'vertical' gene transfer do not necessarily apply to 'horizontal' gene transfer. Biotech sciences have made the assumption that these principles are acceptable to work with, which demonstrates that GMOs should be subjected to a long period of testing and rigorous research before people can continue to consume them.

The safety assessment of GM foods generally investigates the following: the direct health effects (toxicity), tendencies to provoke allergic reaction (allergenicity), specific components thought to have nutritional or toxic properties, the stability of the inserted gene, nutritional effects associated with genetic modification and any unintended effects that could result from the gene insertion.

'One small mutation in a human being can determine so much, the point is when you move a gene, one gene, one tiny gene out of an organism into a different one, you completely change its context. There is no way to predict how it's going to behave and what the outcome will be. We think that we design these life forms, but it's like taking the Toronto orchestra prepared to play a Beethoven symphony and then you take some random drummers from 'here' and flip them in with the Toronto symphony and you say, play music.

What comes out is going to be something very, very different. Publicists say that there is good intention behind GMOs, but the fact of the matter is, it's driven by money.' – David Suzuki

With this simple observation of carelessness brought to the surface, it now seems untenable that the governing health authorities and the FDA (Food and Drug Administration) have the power to approve these foods as safe. It is almost as if they simply told everybody they were safe and the population took it as truth without questioning it. However, now things are changing, as more and more start to wake up and question the world around them.

'GMOs aren't meant to feed the world, they're designed to sell Monsanto's herbicide roundup' ~Organic Consumer's Association[51]

Why are GM foods produced?

Genetically modified foods are produced and marketed because there is a perceived advantage to the producer or consumer. This is supposed to translate into a lower price and a greater nutritional benefit value, but this is not actually the case.

The initial objective for developing plants based on GM organisms was to improve crop protection. The GM crops currently on the market are mainly aimed at increasing the levels of crop protection through the introduction of plant disease resistance caused by insects, viruses or increased tolerance of herbicides.

According to the FDA and the United States Department of Agriculture (USDA), there are over 40 plant varieties that have completed all of the federal requirements for commercialization. Some examples of these plants include tomatoes and cantaloupe melons (which have modified ripening characteristics), soybeans and sugar beets (which are resistant to herbicides) and corn and cotton plants (which have increased resistance to insect pests).

Not all of these products are currently available in supermarkets; however, the prevalence of GM foods in U.S. and European grocery stores is more widespread than is commonly thought. While there are very few genetically-modified whole fruits and vegetables available on produce stands, highly processed foods, such as vegetable oils or breakfast cereals, most likely contain some percentage of genetically-modified ingredients because the raw ingredients have been pooled into one processing stream from a number of different sources.

Insect resistance is achieved by incorporating the gene into the food/plant the for toxin production from the bacterium Bacillus thuringiensis. This toxin is currently used as a conventional insecticide in agriculture and is safe for human consumption. GM crops that permanently produce this toxin have been shown to require lower quantities of insecticides in specific situations, e.g., where pest pressure is high.

Virus resistance is achieved through the introduction of a gene from certain viruses that cause disease in plants. Virus resistance makes plants less susceptible to diseases caused by such viruses, resulting in higher crop yields.

Herbicide tolerance is achieved through the introduction of a gene from a bacterium conveying resistance to some herbicides. In situations where weed pressure is high, the use of such crops has resulted in a reduction in the quantity of the herbicides used.

There are some logical reasons for the manufacturing of genetically modified foods and crops. Many countries need to be nutritionally sustained as their population rate increases, but nature can sustain every single person on this planet the natural way, with the correct resources and education. Even though GM has its benefits, the biotech industries are going too far. Are they in it for the profit only, or is there some other kind of goal they want to achieve?

If you do your research, it becomes apparent that the owners of the major corporations working alongside the biotech industries also hold major shares and investment in the pharmaceutical companies. This book is not about identifying conspiracies, but about observing that there is a painful cycle at work here.

For example, you consume the modified foods, you then become ill for no apparent reason; you visit the local doctor and are prescribed prescription medications, and ultimately your consciousness suffers and your energetic frequency remains in a dull, worn-out state. We leave these suggestions in your hands to decide, but it is undeniable that only a small handful truly benefit from this cycle.

The harmful effects of GMOs within the human organism

GMOs are literally reshaping people's bodies and making many terribly sick. Many countries have forbidden GMOs, and the monetary value of their stocks is declining. The US and the United Kingdom are two of the last frontiers for lining the pockets of these biotech companies. Every time you buy unlabelled foods, you are highly likely to be buying GMOs and supporting the small group who are destroying the population's natural food supply and ecosystem.

There is evidence based on animal studies that eating genetically modified foods causes a wide variety of problems—so many, in fact, that tracing the source of the problem is difficult, especially over time. As mentioned previously, there is not enough data to show the long-term effects of eating the foods that have been genetically altered. Some scientists predict that GMOs are one of the root causes of epidemics that now plague the United States' health problems, including obesity, diabetes, asthma, fertility problems, food allergies and even cancer, ADHD and autism. There are many conditions that are on the rise, coinciding with the introduction of changes in the population's food system over time.

Those who are against GMOs' scientific research are adamant that GMOs cause allergies, infertility and reproductive problems, organ damage, insulin regulation problems, accelerated aging, immune problems and changes to the gastrointestinal system.

Many organizations and scientists agree that not enough data have been gathered about the long-term side effects of ingesting GMOs. It seems too much of a coincidence that since the first commercial productions and sales of GMO foods in the 1990s, the world has experienced the largest pandemic of disease and illness ever recorded in history.

There are studies showing that when humans or animals digest genetically modified foods, the artificially created genes transfer into the beneficial bacteria in the intestinal wall, in turn altering its character. If the gene that creates Bt-toxin in GM corn were to transfer, it might turn your intestinal bacteria into living pesticide and parasite factories; altering intestinal bacteria is also known to encourage mental illness and depression.

Researchers report that the microbes found in the small bowel of people with ileostomy are capable of acquiring and harbouring DNA sequences in a negative way. It is also pretty clear that the damaged DNA from food can and does end up within animal tissues and the milk products that people consume.

It is also important to note that the gene transfer among genetically engineered agricultural crops and surrounding native species has given rise to a highly resistant species called super weeds. These super weeds are treated with toxic chemicals such as Glyphosate and Endosulfan, the active ingredients found in the weed killer globally known as 'Roundup'. These herbicides are so toxic to the human body that the workers spraying it onto the food have to wear a full body suit and oxygen mask. So what makes it acceptable to consume?

There is a growing global awareness within the farming industry regarding the harmful effects of poisonous sprays and modified crops. A 38-year old Latin American farmer named 'Jose Pizarro Montoya[52]' is now an ex-GMO farmer after reporting a large number of dead rats on his roadside, all which had eaten the maize grains from his fields. This led him to Internet research where he found the truth regarding the biotech company Monsanto and its criminal background. He won a lawsuit with the GMO company for breaching health and safety contracts and stated that he never wants another farmer to go through the same process. Jose is now working to expose the harm posed by the transnational corporation to the rest of his country.

The human bloodstream is considered to be an environment separated from the outside world and the digestive tract. According to the standard paradigm of science, large macromolecules consumed within foods are unable to pass directly through the circulatory system. DNA and proteins are thought to be degraded into small constituents (amino acids and nucleic acids) then to go on to be absorbed and distributed to various parts of the body.

Genetically modified foods contain meal derived from DNA fragments that contain cross-genetic coding that are large enough to carry complete genes and avoid the natural process of degrading, therefore entering the circulation system via an unknown mechanism. Because the modified genetics cannot be broken down into amino acids and proteins, they then linger in the blood stream outweighing the natural human DNA.

A mixed bag of plant/animal DNA is now dormant within the human organism. This is very dangerous, as it causes malfunctions in the blood plasma and can ultimately lead to genetic and cellular mutation, destroying the crystalline structure that is essential for the evolution of your consciousness.

"Suppressing dialogue, retracing studies and not doing follow-up research is anti-science. Thus, personal attacks and attempts to discredit those with different opinion are part of the arsenal used by the leading biotech industry to push their agenda on an unwitting population. Promoting the GMOs with claims that they will help us feed the world or prevent blindness is inaccurate and misleading'~ Carole Bartolotto, registered dietician

The American Academy of Environmental Medicine issued a report listing the health risks associated with genetically modified foods. The report cautions physicians to educate their patients by providing reading material about the risk factors associated with GMOs and how to avoid GMOs whenever possible. The report concludes by asking physicians to consider genetically modified foods as a possible cause of a patient's symptoms (responsibletechnology.org).

In part, the report states that GMOs can cause:

- antibiotic resistance when you are ill;
- accelerated aging;
- infertility;
- problems with regulating the body's insulin;
- changes in your major organs (enzyme mutation);
- gastrointestinal problems, including bleeding ulcers and leaky gut syndrome;

- allergies to milk and other foods;
- long-term nutritional deficiencies;
- excessive cell growth which can lead to cancer;
- gluten sensitivity and
- autoimmune diseases.

Conclusions, warnings and the future for GMOs

It is evident that the biotech giant Monsanto does not want to feed the world; they want to control the world's food supply. It has got to the point where many people have fallen sick due to consuming unlabelled, toxic 'everyday' foods and produce. However, awareness is rising at a rapid pace and these companies are slowly losing ground.

Would you really want to eat a food-like product that has been modified in a laboratory? Doing so detaches you from nature, as you are no longer nourishing the body with natural living enzymes but transforming your cellular structure and creating a radical imbalance within your DNA and personal energetic blueprint.

To bring balance and harmony back to the planet, humans have to transform internally first. How are we expected to live in a sane world when a large percentage of the population has the genes and DNA structure of animals active in their bloodstreams? Awareness and information needs to be spread throughout communities, families and friend networks. There is too much suffering and illness on the planet, but that can and will be changed with the right attitude.

Much-needed awareness of what is really happening with the food supply is not widely known, as the general population is distracted constantly by unimportant things such as television shows and sports games. Too many are living in ignorance and not taking responsibility for their own health and state of consciousness. How much suffering will it take for humanity to rise up and wise up?

The chances are very high that at least seven out of ten items you have purchased from your standard supermarket or grocery store are GM foods. If you care about your well-being and don't want to end up like Frankenstein's monster, then you must be more vigilant whilst shopping for food.

The future for GMOs will not look so bright as long as the population educate themselves, share knowledge and take a stand against the major corporations who are literally killing everybody. There have been mass protests worldwide against Monsanto and their biotech counterparts but the media pays no attention as they are also owned by the same group of so-called 'elites'.

According to extensive research Monsanto and the production/distribution of GMOs have been completely banned by France, Switzerland, South Australia, Russia, New Zealand, Peru, Luxembourg, Madeira, Ireland, Japan, Costa Rica, Germany, Greece, Bulgaria, Austria and South Africa (currently fighting). As awareness is cultivated, more and more farmers and local people are working together to grow their own foods and share with each other. This is how it should be done—organically with compassion for others.

The US and the UK are currently still asleep from eating too many GMOs and need to take a stand. Many talk about the zombie apocalypse, but the zombies are already here, on our own doorstep. The chemicals that people are consuming are literally putting the body, brain and nervous system into a sleep state.

You now know, from reading the last chapter, how important the current times are for your personal spiritual growth and awakening. Could it be that the so-called elite are aware of the mass changes in our solar system and physical bodies? Either way, you will need to start detoxifying your bodies and return to the natural state of being.

There are many studies online from independent researchers and victims of the GMO industry that serve as sources of information. Below are some things to look for. Remember it takes a conscious effort to awaken from sleep mode

Which foods are genetically modified and what to look for on labels

It is mind-blowing how much of the food supply is modified genetically and saturated with useless chemical additives. It will at first seem a daunting task to avoid GMOs; however, it is understood you cannot completely rule out every GMO chemical, but it's a start on the right path.

Genetically modified food figures

- **93 per cent** of soybean fields in the United States are genetically modified, 77 per cent worldwide

- **85 per cent** of corn in the United States is genetically modified, 26 per cent worldwide

(Affecting products that contain **canola oil, corn syrup, cornmeal, xanthan gum, corn starch**)

- **95 per cent** of sugar beet crops grown in the US in 2010 were genetically engineered, 9 per cent worldwide

- **93 per cent** of cotton is modified, 49 per cent worldwide (Affecting cottonseed oil)

- **80 per cent** Hawaiian papaya is genetically altered

- **70–90 per cent** of processed foods on grocery store shelves contain GM foods and chemicals

- Majority of livestock are fed GM foods

(affects meat, milk and eggs)

'We are poisoning ourselves with highly processed, nutrient deficient foods.' ~
Dr Ian Brighthope

Corporations are currently gaining slow control over the majority by using chemicals in our everyday foods, thereby affecting us internally, creating illnesses, lowering IQ and effectively dumbing down the consumer to a point where mass control seems to be an easy conquest. This section first exposes you to would be the most commonly used chemicals in our everyday foods that you should instinctively avoid. We encourage your own further research on these poisons.

Keywords to look out for on food packaging:

- Vanillin.

- Amino acids.

- Aspartame (which goes by the trade names **Equal**, **NutraSweet** and **AminoSweet**, produced using GM bacterial strains of E. coli). Found in sugar free products but poses more harm whilst encouraging hyper-toxicity in the brain and nervous system.

- Hydrolysed vegetable protein, which is made from corn and soy

- Xanthan gum.

- Ascorbic acid – is not real Vitamin C; nearly all ascorbic acid comes from GM corn.

- Sodium ascorbate.

- Citric acid.

- Lactic acid.

- Maltodextrins – starch made from corn, used as filler, sweetener and non-caking agent.

- Milled or modified soy (**flour, lecithin, proteins, powder, meal, syrup**).

- Milled or modified corn (**starch, flour, meal, malt, syrup, oil**).

- Fructose as in high fructose corn syrup (used in many products and causes many health risks).

- MSG – **monosodium glutamate,** added to most foods, extremely addictive and neurotoxic.

- Yeast extract.

- Gluten: could be the cause of many of your health problems. This common compound in many foods can trigger chronic disease. Everybody is gluten intolerant, as the stomach cannot process it.

- Emulsified or emulsifiers.

- Sucrose-based: sucrose is sugar. If it is based on sugar, what did they do to it?

- 'From concentrate': means not from real food.

- Syrup: anything that is a syrup has gone through processing with one of the GMO grains.

- Avoid any dairy products that are non-organic, or that do not contain a '**No rBGH**' label. Unless a dairy product is specifically labelled as being certified organic, or as not containing the artificial growth hormone **rBGH**, which is sometimes labelled as **rBST**, it likely contains GMOs. Short for recombinant bovine growth hormone, **rBGH** is created using GMO E. coli just like aspartame, and is used in conventional cattle unless otherwise labelled.

Steps to take in avoiding harmful products

Start by eliminating processed, fake foods. Nearly 75 per cent of all processed foods contain a high amount of genetically modified ingredients and chemicals. Much of the processed, dead junk foods contain trans-fats, acrylamide and little to no nutritional value. Avoiding processed food will not only help cut back on your GMO intake but will also boost your health. Processing destroys the enzyme structure within the food, therefore making it lifeless and useless to the cellular structure of the body.

As mentioned, you should now make a conscious effort for you to check food labels and packaging whilst shopping. GM soybeans and corn make up the largest portion of genetically modified crops. When looking at a product label, if any ingredients such as corn flour and meal, dextrin, gluten starch, soy sauce, margarine and tofu (to name a few) are listed, there's a good chance it has come from GM corn or soy, unless it's listed as organic.

Check the small stickers on the fruit and vegetables. They show different PLU codes, indicting if the fruit was organically grown, conventionally grown or genetically modified. The PLU code for conventionally grown fruit consists of four numbers, organically grown fruit has five numbers prefaced by the number nine and GM fruit has five numbers prefaced by the number eight.

Do the best you can to buy locally sourced and organic produce. By definition, food that is certified organic must be free from all GM organisms, produced without artificial pesticides, fertilizers and from an animal reared without the routine use of antibiotics, growth promoters or other drugs. Start to support local farmers and markets.

The Dirty Dozen (buy these organic where possible)

Source: Environmental Working Group (EWG):

1. Apples
2. Celery
3. Sweet bell peppers
4. Cranberries (**six suspected hormone disruptors where found on cranberries. Chemicals linked to cancers, obesity and developmental disorders**)
5. Strawberries (**Around fourteen different pesticide values can be found in the standard strawberry. Around 94 per cent have been known to contain toxic residues**)
6. Nectarines (imported)
7. Grapes
8. Spinach
9. Lettuce (**can contain over 51 pesticide residues, twelve known carcinogens, 29 hormone disruptors, nine neurotoxins, ten development toxins**)
10. Cucumbers
11. Blueberries (**14 of the 52 pesticide residues found in blueberries are neurotoxins that harm brain development and contributes to falling IQs.**)
12. Potatoes
Other 'dirty' produce: green beans and kale/Greens may contain residues of special concern.

The Clean 15 (lowest in pesticides):
1. Onions
2. Sweet Corn
3. Pineapples
4. Avocado
5. Cabbage
6. Sweet peas

7. Asparagus
8. Mangos
9. Eggplant
10. Kiwi
11. Cantaloupe – domestic
12. Sweet Potatoes
13. Grapefruit
14. Watermelon
15. Mushrooms

Other important notes

When buying organic food, the costs can be a little higher. This is because organic farmers get no government hand-outs or subsidies, but you can feel good about contributing to a better world. High-quality food is grown without pesticides, chemical fertilisers and not sprayed with roundup weed killer.

The main aspect for body regeneration and increasing cellular vibration is consuming living foods only. For optimum bodily function and mind, body and spiritual balance, it is vital to avoid fake foods! You are an organic counterpart of nature and should not be consuming the unnatural. The next few pages are written to raise awareness, and we delve into the detoxification and regeneration information later on.

There are large corporations who are trying to stop the correct labelling of GMO foods, such as Coca Cola, Nestle, Kellogg's, Mars, Wrigley, Ocean spray, Monsanto, Heinz, McCain's and many more. These companies are also encouraging other forms of geo-engineering (cloud seeding, chemtrails, sky dimming, solar radiation management, ocean fertilisation and stratospheric aerosols) that are destroying planet earth at a rapid pace.

Deforestation – Decline of the bee population and other vital pollinators (bees are dying in the millions due to GMOs, massively impacting the natural food chain), tree decline, fungus rise, oxygen reduction, mass animal extinction and flora decline. **Those benefiting:** GM farming, GM agriculture and depopulation programs.

Weather manipulation – Floods, droughts, earthquakes, tsunami, violent storms, natural disasters, freezing temperatures. Research: HAARP. **Those benefiting:** Disaster insurances, banking, utility companies, property developers, GM drought and flood resistant crop production, weather warfare weapons (HAARP)

Sky darkening – A loss of clean energy investment such as solar power and renewable energy sources, vitamin D deficiency, depression, rickets, paranoia, mental illness. **Those benefiting:** Utility companies, pharmaceutical companies, nuclear power companies and private healthcare.

Air pollution – Hay fever, cancer increase, seasonal manipulated FLU, Alzheimer's, Parkinson's, multiple sclerosis and autism. **Those benefiting:** Private healthcare and 'Big Pharma' pharmaceuticals.

Soil contamination – Organic crop crisis, acidification of the soils, aluminium and heavy metal oxidised soils, fauna decline, water pollution and river pollution. **Those benefiting:** GMO agricultural based production and aluminium resistant GMO seeds.

Biotech companies are destroying the environment and aim to take control of the food supply and create a robot world, full of sick and stupid people. We cannot allow this to happen. If you want to learn more about the destructive effects of geo-engineering on planet Earth, it is recommended you purchase a book called *'Deep Green Resistance'* **(www.deepgreenresistance.org).**

'Only when the last tree has died, the last river been poisoned and the last fish has been caught will we realise we cannot eat money' ~ **Cree Indian Proverb**

GMO Food Documentaries:

Food Matters – Food Matters is a feature length documentary film on the best choices you can make for you and your family's health. It contains a collection of interviews with leading nutritionists, naturopaths, scientists, doctors and medical journalists.

Genetic Roulette –Never-before-seen evidence points to genetically engineered foods as a major contributor to rising disease rates in the US population, especially among children. Monsanto's strong arm tactics, the FDA's fraudulent policies and the USDA's disregard for the growing health emergency are also laid bare. This sometimes shocking film may change your diet, help you protect your family and accelerate the consumer tipping point against GMOs.

Factory Farming in the Animal Product Industry

Here are some major facts surrounding the meat and dairy industry that are never mentioned mainstream and are often suppressed unless one decides to delve deeper and personally research these subjects. This information is not intended to force anybody or to manipulate one's opinion surrounding animal product consumption. This book is all about self-betterment and building foundations for enhancing one's life and the truth is that to live optimally, no other being needs to be harmed.

A factory farm is a large-scale industrial operation that houses thousands of animals raised for food, such as chickens, turkeys, cows and pigs. For the factory farming system to work, it needs high volumes of cheap animal feed as well as antibiotics and pesticides to mitigate the spread of disease exacerbated by the overcrowded living conditions. Animals are often confined to small areas and physically restrained to control or limit movement. Food is supplied inside and is characterised by high concentrations of protein.

The meat and dairy industry is no longer what it used to be. Organic farming that consists of naturally fed animals alongside the use of natural substances is now very hard to find. This is mainly due to biotech corporations squeezing smaller, organic farmers out of the market with their corrupt legal powers and sinister tactics to bring local family farming to its knees. Smaller farms frequently have little option but to either intensify their own production or go out of business.

Claims that we need to massively increase the amount of food we produce to feed a growing world population are increasingly common. But these claims have been based on inaccurate calculations and assumptions about further increasing unhealthy levels of meat and dairy consumption.

A wide variety of methods are used to maintain factory-farmed animal health, including growth hormones and antimicrobial agents. Often these systems employ breeding programs to produce more productive animals suited to the cruel, confined conditions.

Some facts, main issues and effects of factory farming[53]:

- Animals are fed and sprayed with huge amounts of pesticides and antibiotics, which can remain in their bodies and are passed on to the people who eat them, creating serious health hazards for humans.
- The beaks of chickens, turkeys and ducks are often removed in factory farms to reduce the excessive feather pecking and cannibalism seen among stressed, overcrowded birds.
- A typical supermarket chicken today contains more than twice the fat, and about a third less protein than 40 years ago.

- Two out of every three farm animals in the world are now factory farmed.
- Confining so many animals in one place produces much more waste than the surrounding land can handle. As a result, factory farms are associated with various environmental hazards, such as water, land and air pollution.
- The pollution from animal waste is known to cause respiratory problems, skin infections, nausea, depression and even death for people who live near factory farms.
- Dairy cows typically live to their third lactation before being culled. Naturally, a cow can live for 20 years.
- Pig, chicken and cattle waste has polluted 35,000 miles of rivers in 22 American states and contaminated groundwater in 17 states.
- Egg-laying hens are sometimes starved for up to fourteen days, exposed to changing light patterns and given no water in order to shock their bodies into moulting, a usually natural process by which worn feathers are replaced. It's common for 5–10 per cent of hens to die during the forced moulting process.
- Worldwide, about 70 billion farm animals are now reared for food each year.

In addition to poisoning your own body with foreign substances and GMO strains of bacteria, the support of factory farming is destroying and polluting the planet, not to mention the funding of your own oppression and keeping corporations in power.

Factory farming has adverse effects, as it encourages a high demand for synthetic substances such as GM soy protein feed (for animal bulking) and other oil-based products. Livestock production uses 70 per cent of all available agricultural land, consumes around 40 per cent of the world's grain harvest and uses eight per cent of the global human water supply.

Most of the animal breeds used in factory farming are specifically bred to produce large quantities of meat and dairy. Producing 1kg of meat through typical industrial methods, for example, requires 20kg of feed for beef, 7.3kg for pork and 4.5kg for chicken. The feed is so modified and toxic that a large majority of the animals develop organ failure, liver cancers and tumours with no testing or thought for the effects on human health

A recent United Nations report concluded that a global shift toward a vegan diet is necessary to combat the worst effects of climate change. The UN is not alone in its analysis: a staggering 51 per cent or more of global greenhouse-gas emissions are caused by animal agriculture, according to a report published by the World watch Institute.

Researchers at the University of Chicago concluded that switching from a standard American diet to a vegan diet is more effective in the fight against climate change than switching from a standard American car to a hybrid. A German study conducted in 2008 concluded that a meat-eater's diet is responsible for more than seven times as much greenhouse-gas emissions as a vegan's diet is (Source:www.peta.org).

Dairy farming and the reality behind cow's milk

Cows and humans alike both produce milk for one reason—to nourish their young. But think about it—humans are the only species that still drink milk after nursing. Can this be due to human intelligence bypassing natures pre-programming, or have we been programmed by external forces to consume another species' milk for reasons other than any self-benefit?

Perhaps it's because the government tells the masses to. Today's processed milk is far from healthy and is essentially a dead liquid, devoid of any real nutritional value. Raw milk is a step up in nutrition since it's not put through the violent heating stages of its conventional counterpart and retains the nutrient values that nature intended. However, do we really need to drink any milk of any kind from another species besides our own? Many like to regurgitate the false information that humans can only get calcium from milk, but this is untrue.

Raw milk drinkers definitely have an edge in the nutrition department because at least they drink a beverage that has the potential to prevent disease. Unlike conventional, pasteurised milk, which is known to cause heart-disease and diabetes, raw milk can actually prevent these conditions. However, raw milk drinkers should know their cows intimately before making consumer purchases of raw milk.

It is the dairy industry's fairy tale that pasteurised milk builds strong bones, when actually it has the reverse effect and is known to encourage osteoporosis. The false belief that the calcium component found in cow's milk builds strong bones is absolutely ingrained throughout society. This statement has no basis in reality, because calcium is only one of many minerals your body needs for building strong bones. Pasteurised cow milk encourages mucus within the gastrointestinal tract of the human body.

The pasteurisation process only creates calcium carbonate, which has no way of entering the body's cells without a chelating agent. The body has to then find a way to pull the calcium from the bones and other tissues in order to buffer and balance the calcium carbonate in the blood. This process encourages osteoporosis. Pasteurised milk is definitely harmful and toxic to the body.

One glass of milk can contain:

- 135 million pus cells;
- bovine growth hormones (BVG);
- antibiotics;
- traces of faeces;
- 51 milligrams of cholesterol;
- 300 calories;
- 16 grams of fat;
- acidic leeching protein and
- Calcium from your own bones.

Factory farm operators have to force cows to produce the milk continuously. This is achieved by impregnating them using artificial insemination then the calves are taken from their mothers around a day after being born. Males are destined for barren lots or veal crates, where they will be fed GMO feed and fattened for beef production. Each and every female awaits the same fate as their mothers.

The cows are hooked up several times a day, genetically manipulated, inseminated and pumped with growth hormone, so they can produce anywhere between 3–5 times as more milk as they would naturally to feed their calves. The growth hormone BVG has been banned in some countries due to its toxic harmful effects on cow and human health.

A cow in the dairy industry is normally killed after 4–5 years of slavery; their bodies are processed into animal food and low-grade hamburger meats. It seems that this whole industry is quite pointless as the product the consumer receives is riddled with harmful substances and an added energetic component of fear and suffering. There are other milk choices that taste a lot better and have wider benefits to your health.

'Man serves the interests of no creature except himself.' ~ George Orwell

Three healthier, non-suffering milk substitutes

Hemp milk

Made from hemp seeds that are soaked and ground into water, yielding a creamy nutty beverage. It contains 10 essential amino acids and a three-to-one ratio of omega-6 and omega-3 essential fatty acids; other nutrients include magnesium, phytosterols, ascorbic acid, beta-carotene, calcium, fibre, iron, potassium, phosphorus, riboflavin, niacin and thiamin. If you would like some health in glass, this is a great choice.

Coconut milk

From the grated meat of a coconut and probably the tastiest of all milks. The colour and rich taste of coconut milk can be attributed to the high-oil content which is easily one of the healthiest oils in the world. Most of the fat is saturated fat, but it is this fat that leads to its anti-viral, anti-bacterial and anti-protozoa properties. Coconut oil contains the highest level of auric acid of any substance on earth.

Compared to cow's milk it's easier to digest because the body uses treeless enzymes for its digestion as opposed to cow's milk. It also contains a high level of omega 3, 6 and 9 fats along with high amounts of amino acids. This excellent combination of fats and amino acids makes it a complete meal in and of itself. The high level of omega 3, 6 and 9 fats and protein in this milk are more bio-available to humans compared to all other animal fats and most vegetable fats. This bio-availability results in the body's ability to assimilate all its nutrients.

Almond milk

Contains about three grams of fat per eight ounce serving. Its fat content is equivalent to rice milk. Because it contains so many great natural components that almond milk does not need to be fortified. Almond milk delivers muscle power in abundance as part of an organised dietary programme, which is superb for bodybuilders and even athletes.

Your muscles will benefit greatly thanks to the riboflavin and protein resulting in increased vitamin B and iron. Almond milk is lower in both fat and calories than reduced-fat cow's milk. One cup of vanilla-flavoured or sweetened almond milk contains about 90 calories and 2.5 grams of fat (compared to the 120 calories and five grams of fat in 1 cup of cow's milk).

Soy milk—mostly harmful

Many vegetarians and those people who are lactose intolerant choose soy milk as a substitute, but soy is GMO 80 per cent of the time. Soy contains high levels of phytic acid and phytoestrogens, which are known for withdrawing nutrients from the body at the time of assimilation. Phytoestrogens are plant-derived xenoestrogens, not generated within the human endocrine system but consumed by eating phytoestrogen plants.

Because of its phytoestrogen content, soy has been linked to endocrine disruption, infertility and hypothyroidism. Diets that are high in phytic acid can cause growth problems in children, infants on genetically modified soy milk substitutes receive the estrogenic equivalent of four birth control pills per day. Many baby formulas are soy-based and genetically modified, but most mothers are aware of this. GMO soy was recently found to have high residues of glyphosate, the active ingredient of roundup weed killer.

Overconsumption of pork

Many people across the world consume three square meals per day with the intention of fuelling their bodies and absorbing nutrition that is adequate for their vitality. The problem is that these three meals are increasingly becoming more processed and less natural. Who said the human organism needs three dense meals to run optimally? The truth is that many people are actually eating themselves to death.

The results can easily be seen within the explosion of sickness and disease figures becoming like a plague on the planet. Many are not in good health and fail to make the connection between what they eat and their health; they are therefore destined to a life of ill health and fatigue. Much of this problem is due to ignorance of diet, health and the human body; people fail to realise that they are much more than just a body and are running around chasing externals in search of a better life.

Medical sciences and doctors have only been able to accomplish the curing of some diseases, but the underlying root problem is never really addressed. Western medicine is designed to react to an illness instead of helping one prevent an illness, treating the effect rather than the cause (where the problem lies). Most people recognise what poisons do to the body; for example, if you were to consume cyanide, you would die. Many parents will tell their kids to eat their vegetables but the broader connection to the long term effects of nutritionally poor diets is never established.

Even in the Bible, a set of dietary rules were established, setting the basis for which creatures were designed to be eaten and which were meant for other purposes. In the world today, there is an excessive overconsumption of dead animal products and modified meats, one of these meats being pork. Swine constitutes a large portion of menus in the UK and USA, bacon and pork chops being a large part of the standard diet.

A lot of insight into a pig can be ascertained by observing what they eat and how they are raised. You may have heard the expression 'you are what you eat', and if you knew what a pig ate, you might find it a bit disturbing. The factory farmed pig is fed harmful genetically modified feed and pumped with antibiotics to stop it from getting sick from the cannibalism it endures when stuffed in overcrowded surroundings. Farmed pigs are literally chewing each other to pieces as a result of their fear and stress.

The digestive system of a pig differs slightly to that of a cow as its system is not designed to filter out the toxins consumed. Instead, any harmful toxins work their way through the animal and are then deposited into the animals flesh, especially in its fat.

The pig is actually able to sustain a very high amount of toxicity, and for this reason the farmers/corporations purchase garbage such as rotting meat and vegetables to feed them, as they can easily be sustained with it. The pig has no detoxification mechanism within the digestive system that can remove consumed toxins and the host of parasites that thrive internally.

The metabolism and assimilation of a pig's digestive system is much faster than other animals. A cow can assimilate and digest foods in around 12–24 hours, giving time for detoxification, which in turn prevents harmful parasites from infiltrating the bloodstream and burying into the flesh. Because of the pigs' fast assimilation process, most of the flesh takes form as fat, because muscles cannot gain the adequate nutrition needed for growth.

Every animal has its unique purpose, and scavengers such as pigs are not designed to be eaten. They have been designed as natural vacuum cleaners that will eat their own faeces, urine, carcasses and garbage. Consumption of such causes no harm to the animals, as that's what nature intended for them to do! Under the pigs hooves are sores that are designed to expel poisons from the pig's body, which is why pigs are able to eat poisonous snakes. If these ducts become plugged, then the pig will have to be slaughtered and sent to market before it contaminates other animals.

Inside the pig is an abundance of parasites. For instance, the animal can sustain 19 different kinds of worms in its body. Some have minor effects on humans, but others are very harmful. The pork worm itself is contracted when you consume meat that contains trichinae larva, once this meat is being digested in the intestine, the larvae hatch and grow into adult roundworms and hold the capability to produce offspring and can burrow in the intestinal wall. The danger here is that these worms can be transported around the body via the lymphatic system and even bury themselves for years within the brain.

Those infected with trichinosis can experience a wide range of symptoms: abdominal discomfort, cramping, diarrhoea, muscle pain (especially muscle pain with breathing, chewing or using large muscles) and fever. If the damage to the tissue is severe, the long-term problems are never-ending.

So-called experts argue that properly cooking pork at 167 degrees Fahrenheit will destroy the bacteria and parasites present. Most who cook pork, however, are not as careful as those conducting a laboratory study. Simple organisms such as these worms are remarkably resilient, so just cooking the meat does not necessarily make it safe. Inspection and governmental seals on pork do not remove the danger of the worms, yet it is classed as safe for consumption.

Within the factory farming business, piglets are torn from their distraught mothers after just a few weeks. Their tails and ends of their teeth are snipped off with pliers whilst the males are castrated. No painkillers are given to ease their suffering. The pigs then spend their entire lives in extremely crowded pens on tiny slabs of filthy concrete.

When the time comes for pig's slaughter, many are forced onto transport trucks that travel for many miles through all weather extremes. Many die of heat exhaustion in the summer or arrive frozen to the inside of the truck in the winter. According to industry reports, more than 1 million pigs die in transport each year and an additional 420,000 are crippled by the time they arrive at the slaughterhouse.

'It appears to be a legitimate demand that, when a man exchanges dollars for pork, he should not do it, on the basis that he may be purchasing his death warrant.' -- **Dr. Maurice C. Carter** *(zoology chief at the United States Bureau of Animal Industry)*

The organic and free-range myth

Everybody is familiar with the organic labelling on animal produce throughout stores worldwide. These 'organic' packages are often decorated with friendly-looking, happy images of animals pictured on open grassland, but in reality, a large percentage of the time these animals are not treated well, and the consumer is sadly mistaken.

Companies lead the population into believing that products that are labelled 'free-roaming/range' are derived from well-looked-after outdoor animals who spend their lives enjoying the fresh air and sunshine alongside others. However, the reality is that a large majority of the 'so-called' organic and free-range farms cram the animals together in sheds or mud-filled lots. These animals are still victim to mutilations such as de-beaking, dehorning and castration without painkillers.

For instance 'organically raised' cows are sent to factory-farm feedlots tube fattened prior to slaughter, caked with faeces and mud. However, those who are fattened on feedlots can still be labelled organic as long as they are given organic, non-GM feed. Organically bred chickens can often suffer even higher mortality rates than those who are drugged, due to the lack of tolerance to overcrowded conditions and internal parasites.

Ultimately, at the end of their distressed lives, the animals who survive the ordeals of organic farming are then shipped onto trucks throughout weather extremes without food, water or rest in many cases. They are hung upside down in the same slaughterhouses used by the factory farming industry, whilst their throats are cut as, still conscious, they struggle to escape. Thus, their flesh is subject to the same potential for bacterial contamination from unsanitary conditions.

The USDA and FDA cautions consumers that the 'organic' label should not be confused with or likened to 'natural' or any other label and it makes no claims that organically produced food is safer or more nutritious than conventionally (factory-) produced food. There are certain tricks and regulations the food agencies use to fool the consumer; just like the 'free-range' label, the 'organic' label does not guarantee that animals were treated any better than animals raised in conventional factory farms.

The main advantage in choosing an organically labelled package of meat is that it may not contain antibiotics, hormones or any other arsenic-based additives that may be found within non-organic produce. The reality is that even though organic or so-called 'natural' meat, eggs and dairy foods maybe somewhat safer of that from drugged animals, they are still laden with artery-clogging saturated fats and cholesterol, as all products are that are derived from farm animals alike.

The last point to note is the techniques used to preserve meats and dairy produce so they do not rot or 'go off' in the supermarkets. Straight from the cow, milk starts to separate and deteriorate within hours. To enable it to survive in the shop and then your fridge, ordinary fresh milk has its fat levels altered and is then pasteurised to remove bacteria (heated to more than 70 degrees Centigrade). However, this process destroys vitamin C and many of the nutrients present in 'raw' milk.

Some supermarkets and butchers treat meat with carbon monoxide and sodium/potassium salts to preserve or mask the age and possible spoilage of the meat, as they understand that retailers always look for the fresh red colour in raw meat products. Most of the meat takes 2–4 weeks to reach the supermarket from the slaughterhouse, and beef is often processed with something known as 'pink slime'. This slime was once only used in dog food and cooking oil.

The pink slime processing filler is a cheap substitute added into meat produce, consisting of waste animal fat trimmings, cartilage, sinew and organs that are heated at a low temperature to separate fat from muscle, spun in a centrifuge, sprayed with ammonia then finally frozen into blocks ready for the consumer. This filler does not have to appear on the packaging, as the USDA and FDA state it is pink, therefore it is meat. It is most often found in cheap hamburgers, hotdogs and fast food chains.

As mentioned previously, the meat and dairy industries are not what they used to be 50–100 years ago. It is dominated by greed and suffering with no real care about the consumers. Do your own research, but remember that pathogens, parasites, fungus, viruses, bacteria, toxins and other groups of micro bacteria living inside you are virtually the cause of most diseases.

A metaphysical concept of animal product consumption

There is much controversy and debate over whether or not the human organism was designed for consuming meat and animal products. Either way, one thing is for certain; the link between the overconsumption of processed, toxic animal products and the dramatic rising figures of those who are falling sick.

There is more to consuming factory farmed animals than to what meets the eye. As you know from reading the spirit chapter, humans and animals alike have an energetic blueprint, an energetic body counterpart that is not visible within the spectrum of human sight. Many seem to think that the lower species of animals do not have a soul like humans, but this is unfounded.

Even though it is the higher species of humans who seek an 'above the physical' understanding for life, energetically and metaphysically, the animal and human being have similar characteristics. The animal eats, you eat; the animal sleeps, you sleep; the animal mates, you mate; the animal defends, you defend. Many animals hold high amounts of compassion towards humans and have similar emotions such as fear, love, resentment and pain.

Whilst animals experience the inhumane slaughtering processes of factory farming, they tolerate copious amounts of fear, which are stored energetically within their being alongside the release of stress hormones that are not in the best interests of humans to consume. All of the painful lower vibratory emotions an animal experiences throughout slaughter are transferred into their energetic bodies and stored in the flesh. For this reason, many religious communities pray over their meat to remove the distorted spiritual aspect before consuming, but in the West this is rare.

As if the consumption of chemical laden animal products were not enough, this painful energetic counterpart that that the average person may not consider or can comprehend is also present in this equation. What does this mean for those who are consuming meat on a regular basis? Eating meats that are saturated with the energetic component of suffering and fear means that low vibrational energy is constantly being transferred into your own energy body and state of being, therefore acting as a heavy anchor on your vibration. Energy is never destroyed and can only be transferred.

An important goal in your personal development is working towards gaining mastery over and transcending lower vibratory emotions and fear-based states of being that you may face. Your natural state is complete fearlessness and love, but regaining that state is a challenging task every human being on the planet has to embrace. When you are consistently consuming foods that hold a low negative vibration, your body and spirit cannot experience the finer and more subtle vibrations. Your luminous energy body becomes burdened whilst the physical becomes denser.

Everybody has an innate sense that some food is inherently heavy while other food is light. This goes beyond how it feels in your stomach. Plant foods are directly synthesised from sunlight. The further you move from this process, the lower in vibrational energy the food gets. Thus, freshly picked fruits, vegetables and nuts are generally high in vibration, while meat from animals is lower. The closer food is to a living state, the higher its vibration, so it may surprise vegetarians to know that bread, pasta and other processed foods are typically of a vibration lower than meat.

Of course, eating high vibration food does encourage a higher physical cellular vibration. That doesn't mean that you can't set your own tone and have a high vibration while eating low-vibration foods; it just means that it will take more conscious effort and energy to overcome the low vibrations you ingest. This is also true of all influences, of course: if you surround ourselves with spiritual people and peaceful circumstances, we will naturally grow more spiritual and peaceful. This doesn't mean you can't be spiritual and peaceful in chaotic, disharmonious situations, but doing so will take more conscious effort on your own part.

In summary, while eating whole, fresh plant foods encourages a high vibration, good health also supports a high vibration, so it is wise to listen to your body and feed it accordingly. While meat has a lower vibration than fresh plant foods, you are still better off eating humanely raised and slaughtered meat than the processed, dead energy of refined carbohydrates that form the bulk of the modern diet.

Above all, you must listen to your inner knowledge in all you do. Life is a personal, individual journey, so there is no one right answer for all people. There are certain habits and attitudes that tend to support and nourish us regardless of the individual choices you make.

If humans were truly meant to eat meat, then meats would be eaten raw and bloody. The thought of eating such meat makes one's stomach turn. Humans are conditioned to believe that animal flesh is beneficial and that everybody is meant to consume it for survival and health purposes. Cooking your meat (destroying enzymes) and seasoning it with salt, ketchup, mayo, mustard or tabasco sauce only disguises the awful taste of flesh. This is the only way humans would eat meat, because we refuse to eat it raw and bloody like real carnivores.

A popular argument of meat eaters is that 'In the wild, animals kill other animals for food. It's a part of nature.' First of all, we are not in the wild.

Second, anybody can easily live without eating meat and killing. The entire population and planet would be much healthier living in such a manner.

The Karmic debt of the dinner table

Together as a whole, humanity is responsible for a lot of death that does indeed carry a massive karmic price tag. The statistics are staggering:

10 Billion Animals slaughtered every year in Europe-not counting fish and other aquatic creatures. Every **day** some:

- 94,000 cattle are killed (more than 1 every second; 34.4 million cattle per year)
- 25,000,000 chickens are killed (14,000 per minute; 9 Billion per year-not counting the male chicks that are literally shredded as soon as they are born)
- 2,600 calves are killed (956,600 per year)
- 320,000+ pigs are killed (116,500,000+million per year)
- 10,000+ turkeys are killed (3,672,000 per year)

Alongside these European figures, Americans are responsible for at least another 10 Billion or so. Worldwide figures total more than 55 Billion animals killed annually. That is approximately 8 lives taken for every human being on the planet, every year, and this is still insignificant if we take into account the unlimited numbers of living beings killed in a culture that prefers death as the solution to many problems.

For example, the modern approach to food production, the source of humanities life energy is to kill billions of animals, and to feed them weeds are killed with herbicides, insects with insecticides, pathogens with antibiotics and then finally killing off the bacteria that festers in those caucuses by cooking it, etc.

If humanities approach to food production is laden with death at every step is it a surprise that the overall orientation to the remainder of life is to eliminate others, of any species, that are in one's way or presents itself as a problem? Too often the modern approach to solving problems is to kill something or someone, and a karmic debt is created for every living being that is killed. Killing begets killing. Slaughter on the battlefields of man will continue as long as the slaughterhouses remain open.

YUSA's soul intention is to raise the awareness of the suffering and death meted to others mainly in western culture. Of course tallying the numbers cannot convey the horror and suffering experienced by the victims. One can only imagine the mental and physical distress experienced by these people and animals. Lives are taken and wasted without any consideration of their plight.

211

And all of that stress, suffering and death contributes to the staggering debt to be paid – by humanities own suffering and death. It doesn't have to be this way.

Greatly reducing and one day eliminating all animal deaths is the only way to clear up the Karmic debt being served at the dinner table. Not only killing is eliminated, but total resource use is also diminished as flesh foods are not only unnecessary for health, but waste huge amounts of resources. Consider the following facts of resource use and waste;

- Livestock production uses more than half of all water used for all purposes in the United States alone.
- Only 25 gallons of water are needed to produce a pound of wheat, but 5,000 gallons of water needed to produce one pound of beef. The amount of water used by a cow raised for slaughter is sufficient to float a warship.
- Oil depletion is hastened by food. 78 calories of fossil fuels are used to produce only 1 calorie of protein from beef.
- 33 percent of all raw materials (base products of farming, forestry and mining, including fossil fuels) are consumed in the production of livestock.
- But only 2 percent of all raw materials would be consumed by the U.S if everyone ate a complete vegetarian diet.
- The number of people worldwide who will die as a result of malnutrition each year is around 20 million.
- Number of people who could be adequately fed using land freed if only Americans, or Europeans reduced their intake of meat by just 10%: 10 Million.
- 16 pounds of grain and soybeans are needed to produce just one pound of edible flesh from feedlot beef!
- Thus 90 percent of all protein produced is wasted by cycling grain through livestock.
- 70% of all antibiotics are given to healthy animals to increase weight gain, resulting in reduced potency of the antibiotics to control infectious diseases.
- 400,000 pounds of potatoes can be grown on an acre of land, but only 250 pounds of beef can be produced on the same acre.

The list goes on, it is very evident that all beings on the planet can live in absolute harmony where suffering is non-existent. It appears the corporations in control of these slaughterhouses and meat industries etc. would not like it if humans went back to providing for themselves and have conditioned the masses that this is the real and only way to live. But this is false.

Factory farming documentaries

Food Inc[54]. – Filmmaker Robert Kenner lifts the veil on the US nation's food industry, exposing the highly mechanised underbelly that has been hidden from the American consumer with the consent of government's regulatory agencies, USDA and FDA. America's food supply is now controlled by a handful of corporations that often put profit ahead of consumer health, the livelihood of the American farmer, the safety of workers and their own environment. We have bigger-breasted chickens, the perfect pork chop, herbicide-resistant soybean seeds, even tomatoes that won't go bad, but we also have new strains of E. coli—the harmful bacteria that causes illness for an estimated 73,000 Americans annually.

Forks over Knives[55]–A 2011 American documentary film directed by American independent filmmaker Lee Fulkerson that advocates a low-fat, whole-food, plant-based diet as a means of combating a number of diseases.

Earthlings[56]–Documentary film about humankind's complete economic dependence on animals raised for food, clothing, entertainment, scientific research and as pets. Using hidden cameras and never-before-seen footage, *Earthlings* chronicles the day-to-day practices of the largest industries in the world, all of which rely entirely on animals for profit. Powerful, informative, controversial and thought-provoking, *Earthlings* is by far the most comprehensive documentary ever produced on the correlation between nature, animals and human economic interests.

Recommended EBook read –'The China Study[57]' – Startling implications for diet, weight loss and long-term health.

Acid & Alkaline States of Being

This chapter is centred on food awareness and physical regeneration. The population has definitely been bamboozled by the food makers, drug companies, government etc. with their primary investment being; not letting you know the truth. Not only is there that but you also have your own self to deal with which has been heavily programmed and for many, the belief that it is actually possible to get well is non-existent.

The human body consists of trillions of cells that are bathed in fluids; these fluids need to be alkaline in order for the cells to function at optimum level. In society, the majority do not even understand the acid/alkaline balance of the body, as it is not something you are made aware of even though it is one of the most important factors for human health.

Nearly everything is acidic: acidic thoughts, acidic violence, acidic relationships and acidic foods. Meats, dairy, white breads, sugars and alcohol are major factors for humanity's inflammation, congestion and acidosis, making a large number of people unwell and unbalanced.

Today's stressful, modern environment is not one which supports the 45 litres of fluid (approximately) within the human organism that are acid, alkaline or neutral. All these fluids perform certain functions, but only if they are operating within their desired parameters. When it comes to blood, it is very specific in the way in which it operates, as it is bound to a very narrow range of PH, which borders on the alkaline.

If the blood PH moves outside the designated range, it can begin to setup an environment of rapid decline. In terms of the logarithmic PH scale, a PH of 7.0 is a neutral state, anything above 7.0 is considered alkaline whilst anything below 7.0 is considered acidic. The blood tends to sit in a very narrow range of 7.36–7.42. PH comes from Latin meaning, Potential Hydrogen.

PH controls every biochemical and bioelectrical function in the body. It is a control mechanism for the speed at which these two functions work whilst regulating enzyme activity. An alkaline PH enables more resistance flow whilst supplying a cool and slow energy, Acidic, on the other hand, supplies a hot and fast energy with less resistance flow. This lower resistance is due to the lower number of hydrogen Ions present in the bodily fluids.

In an alkaline environment there is a greater amount of resistance, meaning the electrical and chemical activities are going to be slower therefore, there will be less aging, burnout and oxidation stress/damage on the skin (fewer wrinkles). This is key for longevity. The higher the PH, the more alkaline- and oxygen-rich the blood and cells become; the lower the PH, the more acidic and oxygen deprived they become.

Take a car battery, for example. An acid battery's main function is to provide sudden, powerful bursts of energy in order to overcome the friction of a stable car engine to start up. An acid battery's energy is immediate and powerful (rapid aging), whilst an alkaline battery (biochemically speaking) is cool and slow, with a longer-lasting shelf life (longevity).

Oxygen is carried by haemoglobin within the blood, but the amount of oxygen that can be carried is strictly under the control of the PH. Cellular degeneration is a disease of cellular suffocation; when a cell receives less than 40 per cent of its natural oxygen requirement, it must either adapt or die.

When your urine drops below a PH reading of 6.0, the body will start to extract sodium from the stomach and calcium from the bones to neutralise the blood. The difference between a PH at 6.0 and a PH at 7.0 is the electrical speed. The bio-electrical speed between 6.0 and 7.0 differs by a factor of 10, meaning the speeds are ten times faster than they would be at 7.0. If the PH were at 5.0,then the electrical and chemical speeds would be running 100 times faster than they would if they were at 7.0 (10 times 10). The body's oxygen levels can also suffer if the body's PH balance is low: for example, if your body's PH is 6.0, the oxygen circulation is also reduced by a factor of ten.

When your body falls into the range of acidic PH balance, the excessive acidity creates more stress, encourages lower energy levels, digestion depletion and increased levels of fatigue. It also promotes excess weight gain alongside bodily aches and pains and ultimately more serious disorders. The body will pull the alkaline/acidic fluids from the different organs in order to keep the blood in equanimity and to adapt to its environment.

When an alkaline environment is maintained in the body, metabolic, enzymatic, and immunologic, repair mechanisms function at their best. The acid-forming metabolic of stress and inflammation caused by high-fat and high-protein foods are adequately and effectively neutralised only when sufficient mineral-buffering reserves are present. Mineral-buffering reserves are the gift that alkaline-forming foods give to your body. A diet that is predominantly alkaline-forming is essential to the maintenance of sustained health.

Most vegetables and fruits contain higher proportions of alkaline-forming elements than other foods. These foods promote a more alkaline environment in the body. For example, commercial corn, barley, soybeans and legumes are acid-forming. This may reflect breeding selection in the last fifty years that favoured higher carbohydrate and fat content. What would happen if the population started to eat a lot more raw fruits and vegetables? There wouldn't be as many people profiting, and many more people would be hydrated, mineralised and alkalised, thereby living more energised lives.

Acidity and sickness

There have been many independent studies surrounding the topic of high acidity levels within the human organism and its overall relation to sickness and ill health. One of these independent researchers was named Dr. Otto Warburg[58], a 1931German physiologist, medical doctor and Nobel laureate. Warburg was one of the 20th century's leading biochemists and was awarded a Nobel peace prize for his research into cancer and the body's PH balance.

Otto Warburg made the discovery that cancer cells find it extremely difficult to thrive and survive in a PH of 7.0 or above and that cell degeneration is simply a result of 'cell suffocation'. After much study and research, Warburg came to the conclusion that cancerous tissues are acidic in nature whilst healthy tissues are much more alkaline. Water divides itself into H+ and OH-negative Ions: an excess of H+ is acidic whilst an excess of OH-negative Ions is alkaline.

When healthy cells are bathing in bodily fluids that are rich in OH-negative Ions, then the slowest form (most resistance) of bio-electrical activity will take place, meaning the multiplication and cellular communication between diseased cells, viruses and any other foreign bodies become slower to non-existent.

With this being said, when these OH-negative ions start to deplete because of toxicity, chemical-laden foods, stress, negative emotions and thoughts, then the cells can actually start to become hypoxic (a condition in which the body or a region of the body is deprived of adequate oxygen supply). If this is the case, then cellular function starts to deplete, which has a negative impact on well-being.

Alongside Warburg's discovery that cancer cells thrive in a low PH environment (one as low as 5.0–5.5 due to the lactic acid production (by the cells) which elevates carbon dioxide levels), It is also important to remember that in a lower PH environment you have less oxygen and faster bio-chemical processes. (Meaning that something is going to rapidly multiply along with faster bio-electrical processes therefore enhancing the signalling of the rapid multiplication, speeding it up).

PH is the dividing line between health and disease. In this day and age it is wise for you to be conscious of the daily fluctuations of the PH levels within your own body if you want to experience optimal health or want to get well from an illness or diseased state. It may be wise for you to start testing your PH levels so you can get in tune with your body and how it fluctuates around different environmental factors and with what you ingest.

A healthy body has PH levels around 6.75–7.75. Just as you can get sick and have bodily disturbances when you are too acidic, the same goes for a body that is too alkaline in nature--there must be a balance, as with everything in life. Oxygen follows PH, and the higher the PH, the higher oxygen levels that are transported by haemoglobin. As mentioned previously, someone with a PH of 7.0 has ten times more oxygen in their system than a person with a PH of 6.0 and 100 times more than a person with a PH of 5.Acidosis and hypoxia (lack of oxygen) are two sides of the same coin; where you have one, you have the other.

Balancing acidity with nutrition

Maintaining proper PH with health and nutrition is not a guarantee of perfect health. It simply means you give yourself opportunity to avoid disease. A constant supply of nutrition and nutrients are needed for a healthy body, including: amino acids, chlorophyll, mineral salts, trace minerals and living enzymes.

In this society, acidic diets and attitudes are dominant. People experience low levels of energy, exhausting easily, and some people are quick to temper, always running hot and fast. The majority of food commercials encourage acidity consumption such as pro-inflammatory coffee for breakfast, pro-inflammatory bread and pro-inflammatory burgers for lunch, washed down with acidic soft drinks full of sugar.

There are varying pH levels within your body that also need to be maintained, but have greater fluctuation, like urine. They directly reflect the food we consume. A poor diet is very taxing on your body as it has to constantly maintain homeostasis(which it undergoes at all times), struggling to obtain alkalising nutrients from organs and bones, thus depleting their necessary stores.

Top methods of alkalising the body:

- **Eating vegetables, mainly green–** Veggies are whole foods without extreme processed sugars that feed disease. Organic vegetables are packed with the minerals and nutrients from the soil, which are meant to be transferred to our bodies via our crops. It is best to consume a proportion around 80 per cent of your veggies either raw, **lightly cooked, blended or juiced** for greater amounts of energy and mental clarity. Superfoods also assist in alkalising the body—more on that later in this chapter.

- **Low-sugar fruits and herbs –** Lemons, limes, grapefruit berries and avocados are the most ideal fruits to consume, alongside herbs such as parsley, cilantro, bok choy, celery and kale. Sugar feeds disease, so moderation is necessary to maintain health. Enjoy other fruits as an occasional treat to minimise your intake, and avoid fruit juice from cartons altogether unless it is freshly pressed in small quantities on occasion.

- Do your best and try to only consume **20 per cent of acidic foods each day –** This should represent only whole unprocessed foods including plant and organic animal protein, whole grains (preferably sprouted), nuts, seeds and some fruit.

- **Alkaline water –** By increasing your water intake each and every day, you will increase all body functions that all require water in some way. If this water is pure and alkalised it will optimise these functions and increase OH-Negative ions. Flushing and detoxifying is vitally important and without water elimination struggles to take place and toxins become lodged and can cause problems. You can also purchase an **alkaline water stick** at amazon.com and add some sole Himalayan salt minerals to your water (instructions in next topic).

- **Lemon, ginger and lime water** – Aside from green juice, lemon, lime and ginger water is the most potent detoxifying, alkalising drinks you can introduce into your daily routine. On the outside of our body, a lemon is acidic, but once consumed it leaves an alkaline ash that supports body functions within. Lemon flushes and tightens the cells whilst the ginger soothes inflammation. This drink is an excellent replacement for morning coffee.

- **Reduce your stress**– Erase and confront any negative thought patterns and emotions. Your thought vibrations have that ability to program bodily fluids. Practice meditation and exercise on a regular basis to balance excess cortisol and eradicate negative energies.

Harmful and processed junk to avoid

- **White processed sugar** – One of the most acidic things to the body is sugar, which is a poison that kills as it has been depleted of its life forces, vitamins and minerals. Sugar taken every day produces a continuously overacidic condition, whilst more and more minerals are required from deep in the body in the attempt to rectify the imbalance.

- **Animal and dairy products** – Such products are very mucous-forming and tend to encourage mucous production in cellular fluids. If you eat a lot of acid and mucous-forming foods, your body produces a layer of mucous as a protection barrier against the onslaught of toxic foods that the body does not recognise as natural. In the rare case that one could acquire raw dairy one might argue its benefits, but realistically humans shouldn't be drinking the milk of other animals that is meant to nurture the lives of its offspring, as the enzymes that break it down properly are non-existent in the body after the age of two. Animal protein is one of the most metabolically acidic foods humans eat. It creates conditions of acidity within the body after ingestion, again forcing the body to seek to return to an alkaline state through demineralisation of the bones and the cells.

- **Stimulants** – Coffee, alcohol, fizzy drinks, processed chocolate and sugar should be avoided altogether for those in a disease state and used only on occasion otherwise. It takes 32 glasses of alkaline water to balance 1 can of pop, and eight glasses for one glass of wine and coffee. The body has to put in a lot of energy and effort to balance itself after consumption of such products.

- **Processed foods** – Since the introduction of processed foods in the 1950s, disease rates have been climbing steadily, especially the top two fatal ones like cancer and heart disease. As tempting as they may be, packaged foods are mostly poison, filled with non-food and chemicals. Do your best to only shop the outside of the grocery store and minimise your purchases of packages. Your cart should be mostly filled with veggies and whole foods. In a restaurant setting, do your best to include a salad and/or veggies in your choices.

- **Unhappiness and stress**- Living in a constant state of stress, anxiety and fear can wreak havoc on the body's PH balance due to the overactive hormonal messengers. Only you can change your life, and those who choose not to improve their situations are the ones who are susceptible to disease and illness.

Antacids: If you have to take any form of antacid, the natural solution is quite simple. There is no reason to be acidic if you eat properly and flush your body regularly with plenty of water. Foods that neutralise are important to consume, such as greens and bananas. The human organism has a hard time breaking down meat in the stomach, and when it sits for a while it becomes painful as it rots in the intestines and colon.

Be aware of what your body is telling you. Heartburn or burping excessively can mean that you have an excess built-up of acid. If you get this after eating certain foods then stop eating them. Your body is crying out for help, letting you know it is way too acidic; masking the process by pills will not help the circumstances. An ulcer is formed when you choose to ignore your body's signs over and over and remain in your regular eating patterns. Remember, when you are acidic you are more prone to disease and flu. Acidity weakens your body if you do not learn to neutralise it.

Eat whole, unrefined organic foods to protect yourself from the difficulties, complications and deficiencies that arise from processed foods. Fresh fruits and leafy green vegetables should comprise the majority of the human diet. The simpler you eat, the better you will digest. When digestion is compromised by stress or bad food combinations, the mind gets cloudy. The GI tract and the mind are intimately connected by a series of nerves. When your guts are fermenting or filled with rancid food particles, parasites and viruses can proliferate and when they leave their excrement behind it is very acidic, irritating and inflammatory. Clear intestines equal a clear mind and serenity in the body.

Introducing as many new raw plant based foods into your consumption will be rewarding to your body. Health was made to be quite simple. Mother Earth provides minerals, nutrients, plenty of digestible protein and vitamins in raw nuts, seeds, legumes, grains, vegetables and fruits.

'I don't understand why asking people to eat a well-balanced plant based diet is considered drastic, while it is medically conservative to cut people open and put them on cholesterol-lowering drugs for the rest of their lives. ~ Gandhi

Acid and alkaline food comparison chart- Acidic to alkaline states of everyday foods sourced from bodybykale.ning.com

Hydration, Minerals & Cellular Conductivity

Dehydration and low mineral/electrolytic conductivity within the body are the highest triggers for disease and illness on the planet today. Dehydration occurs when the body loses more water than what is taken in. It is often accompanied by disturbances in the body's mineral salt or electrolyte balance, especially disturbances in the concentrations of sodium and potassium.

The body tends to lose around 1.5–2.5 litres of bodily fluids daily; the body can compensate for a temporary loss in fluids by shifting water from the cells into the blood vessels. These fluids need to be replaced, or else the body can suffer some serious consequences. The body loses fluids through a combination of processes such as urinating, vomiting, breathing and sweating.

Hydrate by drinking lots of water; better still, drink fruit and vegetable juices, as they contain a dense saturation of minerals that have been absorbed from the soils. Just by keeping hydrated the quality of your joints and skin can be enhanced greatly. Many people often mistake thirst for hunger, so the next time you think you're hungry (if you are trying to lose weight or eliminate some kind of pain/inflammation from the body), try drinking a litre of alkalised/lemon water. In this way you can give your body time to properly digest previously eaten foods before the next meal.

Programming has led the population into believing that 3–4 meals per day are absolutely essential for the body to absorb adequate nutrition. Eating so many meals per day, especially processed, dead foods, causes sickness, as you cannot possibly be cleanly digesting so much without the body leaving behind metabolic waste that gets trapped in the joints, lymphatic system, sinuses and kidneys. Humans are clogged.

Two meals a day is best, with a potential fruit/green juice or fruit snack. Oranges, watermelons, celery, grapes and cucumbers are real high-water, highly nourishing hydrating foods. Maximum energisation is embraced from your soul self; you can tap into that through meditation regardless of your religion, as the energy is all the same.

Protoplasmic energy, on the other hand, is derived from the minerals and sugars from fruit and vegetables. Fruit vibrates higher than any other food, creating a resonant energy that when consumed adds great energy to your electromagnetic self. You will attract other people, and you will attract good things into your life as the high vibrational fruit energy will allow you to attract love, prosperity and abundance into your sphere of reality.

Consuming fruit delivers hydration and mineralisation to the body; the fruit acids are also amazing solvents that clean out the body's pipework. You want as much energy as possible flowing through the pipes, such as blood vessels, nerve vessels and lymph vessels. When you start to hydrate, mineralise and alkalise the body, everything can begin to disperse. The reason why human beings have pain, inflammation, stiffness, chronic and acute illnesses is because of the waste matter that has built up within the organism, causing cellular dysfunction. These three methodologies are vital for higher cellular function.

There are various types of inflammation, but there are also acids that have accumulated within the body that need to be dispersed with a constant flow of water and mineral salts. This ensures a consistent flow of the lymphatic system and kidneys in order to clear out the starchy carbohydrate residues that are left behind from processed and inorganic breads, cakes, grains and dairy.

Alongside carbohydrate residue is uric acid that is stored within the body from the consumption of animal proteins. If you're going to eat a diet high in animal products and proteins, it is wise to neutralise the acids with leafy greens, preferably in the form of green juices.

The three types of dehydration

If the body loses bodily fluids at a level of more than one per cent of your body weight, reductions in physical and cognitive performance can occur and may cause impairment of thermoregulation (ability of an organism to keep its body temperature within certain boundaries) and cardiovascular functions. With fluid deficits of four per cent, severe performance decrements may be observed as well as difficulties in concentration, headaches, irritability and sleepiness and even increases in respiratory rates. Dehydration that causes a loss of ten per cent or more of body weight can be fatal.

Hypotonic dehydration

Hypotonic dehydration is when there is a larger loss of sodium in the body than there is water. High sweat instances, gastro-intestinal water losses or electrolyte deficits can be characterised by an osmotic shift of fluids from the **extracellular** area to the **intracellular**. This can occur from excessive intake of plain water that has little to no mineral content, such as certain bottled waters and tap water. This complication can be life-threatening if swelling causes pressure on the brain (cerebral oedema). This is called hyponatremia (An electrolyte disturbance in which the sodium Ion concentration in the blood plasma).

Hypertonic dehydration

Hypertonic dehydration is when water loss exceeds mineral salt loss, more water than sodium is lost. This is triggered by inadequate water intake, excessive sweating, osmotic diuresis and drugs. Hypotonic dehydration is characterised by an osmotic shift of water from the **intracellular** fluids to the **extracellular** fluid, most common for those people who are diabetic accounting for 5% of paediatric cases of dehydration.

Isotonic dehydration

Isotonic dehydration is characterised by a loss of both water and mineral salts from the extracellular fluids, both reduced in equivalent amounts. This can be induced through vomiting, sickness, diarrhoea or simply through inadequate intake. There is no osmotic shift of water from the intracellular space to the extracellular space. This type of dehydration accounts for cases of dehydration in young children.

Mineral salts and electrolytes

The study of biochemistry is the study of the chemistry of life, the study of the union between organic and inorganic substances whereby new compounds are formed. In relation to so-called disease, biochemical systems focus on the levels of inorganic cell salts and tissue builders present in the body.

The constituent parts of your body are principles, such as oxygen, hydrogen, carbon, lime, iron, potash, soda, silica and magnesium, just to name a few. These elements and gases are perfect in their molecular structures but may be endlessly diversified in combination, like the wood, bricks, mortar and stones that can be used to erect a building.

The human body is a receptacle, a container in which much is stored; it is a storage battery that will always run on charge if the chemicals are present in the proper quantity and combination, similar to how a car would run when charged and supplied with the necessary ingredients for it to vibrate and cause motion. The cell salts are found in foods (mainly natural) and are carried into the blood after digestion, where they carry the process of life and, by the law of chemical affinity, ensure that the human form and bodily functions are materialised.

When a deficiency occurs in any of the electrolyte or mineral workers due to a non-assimilation of food, poor liver functioning or digestion processes then dematerialisation of the body commences. It can be said that disease is a deficiency of some of the chemical constituents that carry on the chemistry of life, and not an entity in itself. Once you learn that disease is not a thing, but a cry out for help from the body due to conditions that lack some inorganic constituents of the blood, it follows logically that the proper method of curing is to supply the blood that it lacks.

Electrolytes (also known as ions) are minerals in your blood and other body fluids that carry an electric charge. Electrolytes affect the amount of water in your body, the acidity of your blood (pH), your muscle function and other important processes. You lose electrolytes when you sweat. You must replace them by drinking fluids as they are highly important for the communication between cells and carry voltages across cell membranes.

Charged electrolytes are primarily composed of the minerals sodium, magnesium, calcium, potassium, chloride, phosphates and sulphates and are regulated by the liver. Your body is made up of the same minerals that are in the Earth, as human beings are a part of nature, directly connected physically, spiritually and energetically. When you're healthy, you actually take on the same form as nature does. What works for the plants will work for humans.

Ions and minerals provide the body with balance and encourage a higher cellular vibratory rate within the physical body. Just as you can clean and enhance your luminous energy field and auric body (as was discussed in the previous chapter), the same is true for your physical body at a cellular level.

Just as minerals provide balance in your body, they help make things 'go'. They keep your bones strong and your immune system healthy; they support your nervous system, produce energy and create cells. They work with the vitamins consumed and can be potent antioxidants, those which destroy free radicals.

Minerals and electrolytes are the gateway to a higher cellular vibratory rate, a higher vibrational field of energy within the physical body which, in turn, keeps equanimity with your energetic body/ self. Once you detoxify the layers of mucous from the cell membranes and start to nourish them with high water, high mineral and high alkalising foods, your body can reach a higher vibratory rate, one in which disease may find it nearly impossible to thrive in and systemic energy levels can run at peak performance.

Systemic energy differs somewhat from the temporary 'high' kind of energy that you may feel from consuming coffee or an excess of sugar foods. Systemic energy is the energetic force at the deepest cellular level, right down to the atomic structure of your being, which arises when you detoxify and nourish this microcosmic part of yourself, the negatively charged electrons and the positively charged protons (the parts of the nucleus) form a perfectly balanced whole.

If the system is clean and undisturbed, both parts of the atom are electrically neutral and reside in close relationship; these subsystems vibrate with high velocity. The dynamic balance between the protons and electrons at the deepest energy level is known as the normal state of the atom. With this being said, it is crucial for somebody who is in ill health or who wants to have more energy and feel better to target this area. Detoxification, alkalisation and regeneration at the deepest levels can save somebody's life and restore that person to perfect health. We will delve deeper into detoxification later on.

Main minerals, vitamins and their roles within the body

Calcium -- Vital for strong bones, liver function and teeth health, needed for muscles to contract and relax properly; assists in healthy nerve function. **Source:** barley grass, Brazil nuts, spinach, sesame seeds

Chromium -- Key component of glucose tolerance factor (GTF) which works with insulin to regulate blood-sugar levels. **Source:** green peppers, bananas, parsnips, apples, sweet potatoes

Copper – Involved in the making of red blood cells, bone production and general body tissue maintenance. Also important for various chemicals in the nervous system. **Source:** Kale, sesame seeds, brown rice, chickpeas

Iodine – Needed for the proper function of the thyroid gland and thyroid hormones. **Source:** Blue green algae and seaweeds

Iron – Prevents anaemia and helps with haemoglobin production which carries oxygen around the body. **Source:** Green leafy vegetables, legumes, lentils, pumpkin seeds, dried fruits

Magnesium – Essential for healthy bones and teeth and plays an important role in enzyme systems that help the body make use of the energy stored in the tissues. Magnesium is needed to assist vitamins B1 & B6 work efficiently whilst transmitting nerve impulses and aiding muscle contraction. **Source:** almonds, cashews, butternut squash, brown rice, bananas, spinach

Manganese – Important for healthy cellular communication, bone development and efficient protein and fat metabolism. **Source:** almonds, curly kale, brown rice, blackberries, pine nuts

Phosphorous – Plays a vital role in the release and use of energy from consumed foods. An important building block for various proteins, carbohydrates and fats. **Source:** brown rice, lentils, bean sprouts, spring greens

Potassium -- Important for maintaining fluid balance, muscle and nerve functioning. Involved in the maintenance of normal blood sugar levels whilst helping control blood pressure. **Source:** avocado, bananas, fresh fruits, courgettes, butter beans, Swiss chard

Selenium – Enhances the functioning of the blood cells whilst acting as a powerful antioxidant, also protects against heart disease. **Source:** Brazil nuts, lentils, dried apricots and peaches, celery, potatoes

Sodium – Important for maintaining correct amounts of bodily fluids and also plays a large role in muscle and nerve functions alongside potassium. **Source:** olives, rye bread, Swiss chard, spinach, pistachio nuts

Zinc – Component of insulin and is required for blood sugar control. Vital for proper taste and hearing whilst playing an important role in wound healing and enzyme activation. Zinc is highly important for male fertility, hormone function, growth, liver function and the immune system. **Source:** Lentils, peas, chickpeas, dried seaweeds, pumpkin seeds, raw cacao

Vitamin A – Helps maintain healthy skin, eyes and bones. Boosts immune system and is essential for the development and growth of cells. **Source:** Dark green leafy vegetables like broccoli, spinach, watercress, kale, beet greens and deep orange fruits such as oranges, carrots, mangoes and papayas.

Beta-carotene -- Converted into vitamin when necessary by the body. Acts as a powerful antioxidant whilst promoting faster healing within mucous membranes, works in favour of cardiovascular health and supports healthy skin. **Source:** Kale, spinach, carrots, watercress, broccoli, asparagus, pumpkins, watermelons, cantaloupes and chard.

Thiamin / Vitamin B1 -- Assists with the release of energy from carbohydrates and is important for brain and nerves which use glucose for their energy needs. **Source:** Yeast extracts, brown rice, rye bread, nuts, seeds and green vegetables

Vitamin B2 – Aids in normal growth of bodily tissues and supports healthy nerve function, skin and vision. **Source:** Kale, parsley, broccoli, beet greens, almonds, avocados, asparagus and prunes

Vitamin B3 / Niacin – Absorbs and releases slow assimilating energy from all types of foods, maintains skin, brain and nerve function, like the other B vitamins and enhances mental functions. **Source:** Broad beans, peas, peanuts, brown rice, red peppers, spring onions and dried peaches.

Vitamin B6 -- Assists in forming red blood cells, hormones and antibodies. Anti-anxiety vitamin for women, especially. **Source:** turnip greens, kale, avocados, wheatgrass, cauliflower, prunes, bananas and carrots

Vitamin B12 -- Vital for healthy nervous system and prevents pernicious anaemia (a condition of too few red blood cells than normal). **Source:** Seaweed, Spirulina and blue green algae

Vitamin C -- Increases activity of the white blood cells. The cells are needed to protect the immune system, helping to resist against infections. **Source:** Strawberries, blackcurrants, broccoli, kiwis, lemons, oranges, tomatoes, spinach and mixed peppers.

Vitamin D -- Regulates the activities of calcium, which, in turn, protects and supports strong bones, teeth and healthy joints. **Source:** sunflower seeds.

Vitamin E -- Assists with the growth and repair of the inner lining of arterial walls. An anti-inflammatory that improves circulation. Promotes healing alongside regulating the levels of stomach acid. **Source:** Watercress, spinach, almonds, sunflower seeds, asparagus and carrots

Vitamin K -- Vital for blood clotting when you cut or injure yourself. **Source:** Broccoli, dried seaweeds, Brussels sprouts, kale and cabbage.

Folic acid -- Protects against anaemia, great for blood cell support and preventing birth defects. **Source:** Green leafy vegetables, fruits, nuts, oats, dried fruits and citrus fruits.

Conductivity in the body

There are around 75 different types of minerals in the ocean. A plant needs 15 minerals for its existence alongside water and sunshine. The planet is made up of minerals. The human body is also made of minerals, the most abundant being calcium (around 3.6 per cent of your body weight within the skeletal system).

With all of the convenience foods that many are eating and drinking alongside the evolution of technological advancements, in the last 50 years or so, you would think that the population would be some kind of superhuman race. But, you can see, if you go to a major supermarket, that the majority of the herd most definitely have a lot of fat accumulation, which is also known as body fat. The primary factor for this accumulations that of plugged skin pores alongside the lack of minerals within the body that make it difficult for cellular regeneration and proper functioning.

Conductivity is not health; it's a construct of what you are, a being that is electromagnetic in nature. The standard diet holds little to no mineral value; half of it is processed and saturated in chemicals (hence why it tastes so good). Vitamins encourage reactions in the body whilst minerals give absolute life. As you can see, the food pyramid on the following page displays the range of foods consumed in today's world from the standard diet up to the medicinal, superfoods-rich diet.

The chart displays the relation between PH levels (acid to alkaline), levels of consciousness and the variables of foods ranging from sickness up to health. It's a clear guide as to where you want to be heading if your desire is to experience enhanced states of health and well-being. The conductivity and mineral content gets higher as you start to climb up the pyramid. It is important to remember that you cannot jump over any levels; you must work slowly in order to allow your body to detoxify from the old lifestyle and configure to the new lifestyle, removing the toxins present in the standard diet so you can start to merge into higher levels of lighter foods.

You must climb the stairs one stair at a time. Mineral conductivity is light: light means vitality and vitality is measured by the number of creatures and parasites that live in your body. If you are in sickness and ill health, you are living at the bottom of the food pyramid. If you endure heavy loads of stress and anger, your conductivity lessens, as stress promotes acidity. On the other hand, if you're living in bliss and happiness, the vitality and conductivity levels within your body will be higher as these emotions are high vibrational in nature.

It is also important to note the correlation between the levels of the food pyramid and the chakra energy system. This is the mind-body connection that starts to enhance as you feed the physical body with mineralised, high-vibrational foods. Colourful, natural foods enhance the nervous system and stimulate the chakras. Everybody is in transition but once you find out you actually get healthier eating a plant based diet than you do on a meat-eating diet you can start to optimise your health and wellness and experiment with what works for you.

You can switch to a vegan or plant based diet, but if there are no minerals in the foods then you can really start to suffer with lethargy, motivational issues and vitality. This book does not aim to tell you what to do or what to eat, but, rather, to guide you along the path of identifying higher value foods and for you to begin removing toxic and contaminated foods that have no benefit for your evolution and well-being. The body is a machine and it runs off certain types of fuels. The fuels it runs on are calcium, potassium, sodium, magnesium, zinc, boron and silicon. It does not run on aluminium, cadmium, mercury, lead, arsenic, stainless steel, insecticides, pesticides, herbicides and plasticisers.

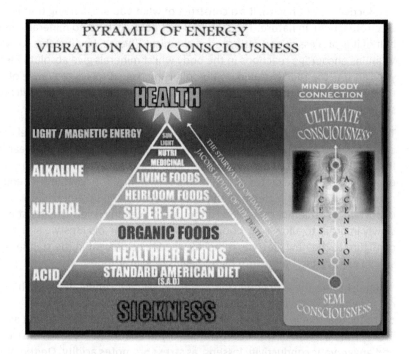

ENERGY+VIBRATION=CONSCIOUSNESS

The pyramid of energy. Sourced from Dr. Robert Cassar

Supplements & methods to mineralise your body

Mineral deficiency is undermining the health of many people worldwide. There is a range of factors responsible for whether or not you get the minerals needed to support cellular communication and conductivity within the body. The two main factors are the presence or absence of minerals within the soil that the foods are grown and the biochemical individuality within a person which determines the specific need for nutrients. Some people naturally need more than others.

Man has exploited a large range of minerals from the Earth from the beginnings of civilisation such as gems for barter, iron for tools and uranium for weapons alongside zinc, copper and others for industrial use. These are all crude applications compared to the delicate synchronicities of minerals that take place within the billions of cells in your body every moment of the day.

The most impressive quality of minerals is that they are able to lend their atomic energy to the active enzymes within your body. They act as co-factors in the speeding process of the chemical reactions responsible for life. Without the minerals assisting the enzymes, the reactions the enzymes endure by themselves would not encourage life, as they would be too slow.

Minerals and enzyme activity within the body is directly connected with what foods you consume. Modern food technology and the intensive farming methods have drastically reduced the mineral content within the foods that are most commonly available to the public. Artificial fertilisers pesticides and other chemicals that are commonly used only provide nitrates, not the ninety or so vital minerals needed for plants to grow optimally (conventionally grown fruits and vegetables are known to contain only three minerals). This form of food production depletes the soil further and reduces the availability of life giving elements.

On top of these processes, the already depleted plants are refined in such a manner that your body cannot get accustomed to them. This becomes a problem, as many people think they are absorbing their daily requirement for the vital nutrients but this is not the case as the resultant substance no longer has the ability to sustain life. Standard food may taste wonderful but, in reality, it is not nourishing the human organism. Cooking food at temperatures higher than42 degrees Celsius further depletes its mineral content because the living enzymes and minerals leach out into cooking water or fat, later to be discarded. More than 75 per cent of the minerals in food can be lost in this way.

One of the deep secrets of spiritual nutrition is the secret of minerals. They are frequencies of light and information. They are the building blocks of creation for the material world and universe. They activate the vitamins and organ structures. They are the catalysts for the enzymatic reactions within the body.

They are the frequency rates in the system. They are not necessarily the energy makers, however. The human body is composed entirely of minerals and water.

Fulvic acid – As mentioned, modern farming and food processing techniques often destroy a large per cent of the nutrients and minerals needed for humans to survive. In this day and age, it is wise to supplement yourself with minerals, regardless of your diet, in order to absorb necessary nutrients.

Minerals such as magnesium, calcium and potassium are most easily consumed because they are found more frequently in a regular diet, compared to trace minerals. Trace minerals include iron, zinc manganese copper, molybdenum, iodine, chromium and selenium. Fulvic acid can enhance the absorption rate of nutrients, minerals, vitamins and herbal supplements/superfoods.

Just by consuming a few drops of Fulvic solution each day you can make up for any mineral deficiencies as a result of eating a poor diet or as a result of ill health. Fulvic acid is recommended to anybody --even those eating healthy, organic foods -- to ensure they receive all of the trace minerals they may be lacking.

Fulvic minerals found at **www.purefulvicminerals.com**come from one of the richest sources of Fulvic acid and trace minerals known to man. This Fulvic mineral deposit is rich in minerals that have developed naturally for over 60 million years, since the end of the Cretaceous Period. During that time, prehistoric plant life broke down into Fulvic acids and trace minerals in the form of preserved sea plant material, called 'Fulvic shale' by geologists.

Magnesium chloride -- Magnesium deficiencies in humans can be mild or severe. Studies suggest that such deficiencies are more and more common. Reports published by the World Health Organisation have estimated that three quarters of Americans do not meet the Recommended Daily Intake (RDI) of magnesium.

Magnesium is nothing short of a miracle mineral. It possesses healing effects on a wide range of diseases and it also has the ability to rejuvenate the aging body. Magnesium is essential for many enzyme reactions, especially in regards to cellular energy production. The health of the brain, nervous system, teeth and bones all depend on magnesium. Magnesium chloride it is also an impressive infection fighter.

Magnesium has a calming effect on the nervous system. It is frequently used to promote good sleep. But, more importantly, it can be used to calm irritated and over-excited nerves. This is especially useful when treating epileptic seizures, convulsions in pregnant women and the 'shakes' in alcoholics.

Adequate levels of magnesium are essential for the heart muscle. Those who die from heart attacks are known to have very low magnesium and very high calcium levels in their heart muscles. Patients with coronary heart disease and who were treated with large amounts of magnesium survived better than those patients given standard drug treatment. Magnesium dilates the arteries of the heart and lowers cholesterol and fat levels.

In addition to its anti-microbial and immune-stimulating properties, both magnesium and chloride have other important functions in keeping people young and healthy. Chloride, of course, is required to produce a large quantity of gastric acid each day and is also needed to stimulate starch-digesting enzymes. Magnesium is the mineral of rejuvenation and prevents the calcification of organs and tissues that is characteristic of old-age-related degeneration.

Ancient Minerals™ magnesium products offer a convenient form of transdermal magnesium, absorbed through the skin for those who prefer to avoid the hassle of taking pills and the difficulties inherent with poorly tolerated oral supplements.**www.ancient-minerals.com**

Silica Minerals -Silica is the most common mineral in the world. Silica accounts for 27.8 per cent of the earth's weight, making it the second principal component of the earth's crust after oxygen. Its crystallised and amorphous forms are found in a variety of rocks, including sandstone and various forms of granite.

Organic silica is found in different parts of the body such as the spleen, liver, pancreas, lungs, heart, brain, super-renal glands, skin, hair and nails. Organic silica is found in all the cells of the body, in different proportions. It is also found, in trace amounts, in different skeletal structures, including the teeth and bones.

Organic silica forms a significant component of the most common tissue in the body, connective tissue. It also facilitates the electrical impulses on the cell membranes, thus encouraging the flow of systemic energy throughout the body. Silica enhances intercellular communication and regulates the electric potential in the cell membranes. It also has important vibratory and reactive powers that contribute to energetic vibration.

All people are born with adequate organic silica in their bodies, but this important mineral gradually gets depleted with age. The body loses its ability to absorb organic silica with time but it still continuously uses the mineral. Therefore, it becomes important to supply more of the mineral nutritionally through supplementation.

Silica, found at **www.silalive.com,** can aid with a number of common health problems such as abnormal cell growth, imbalances in sugar alongside difficulties with memory and cholesterol. This forgotten mineral helps the body by prohibiting unhealthy and diseased cells from growing whilst it strengthens healthy cells and allows them to live longer. One health benefit offered by silica is improved absorption of essential nutrients. It softens heart valves, cleanses the arteries, blood, colon, lungs and stomach and increases vascular flexibility and the flushing of heavy metals. It eliminates harmful bacteria and viruses, while increasing flexibility, joint mobility, arthritis relief. Silica also reduces acne parasites and fungi.

Sole salt mix (Himalayan pink salt) -- Sole (pronounced Solay) is a Himalayan salt infusion that promotes health and wellness. Sole is essentially water that has been fully saturated with a natural salt. This is not just a small amount of salt dissolved in water, but water that has absorbed as much natural salt as it is able to absorb (26 per cent).

Consuming Sole on a regular basis can help with hydration and electrolytes, detoxification (antibacterial properties) and energy. It improves digestion (promotes food absorption and stimulates the intestinal tract), eliminates muscle cramps, promotes healthy bones, skin, hair and nails. It encourages weight loss by nourishing at the cellular level and healthier veins.

This mixture is high in magnesium, silicon, B vitamins, amino acids and phytonutrients. It is very alkaline; it can hold a DC current charge, making it a superconductive salt mixture. All you need is some distilled water, Himalayan pink salt and a glass jar 32oz or glass bottle.

Instructions

-- Fill the jar about ¼ of the way with Himalayan salt
-- Add filtered/distilled water to the jar, leaving about an inch of space at the top
-- Put on the plastic lid and shake the jar gently
-- Leave on the counter overnight to let the salt dissolve.
-- The next day, if there is still some salt on the bottom of the jar, the water has absorbed its maximum amount of salt and the Sole is ready to use.

To use: Mix 1 tsp of the Sole in to a glass of water and consume every morning on an empty stomach. Do not use a metal utensil to measure or touch the Sole as it can destroy electrolytic content. You can also add the mixture into a juice or smoothie for added minerals.

Himalayan Pink Salt, found at **www.westlab.com,** is one of the purest salts available for culinary, therapeutic and cosmetic use. This delectable salt has beautifully formed crystals that range in colour from off-white to a lustrous pink. This deep colour indicates a quantifiable amount of 84 trace elements and iron. The benefits are endless, but Himalayan Pink Salt is primarily used for gourmet cooking and in bath preparations. Ensure the salt is hand mined and organic.

Epsom/Dead sea bath salt –Epsom salt is not actually a salt; it is a naturally occurring pure mineral compound consisting of magnesium and sulfate. Long known as a natural remedy for a number of ailments, Epsom salt has numerous health benefits, as well as many beauty, household and gardening-related uses.

Studies have shown that magnesium and sulfate are both readily absorbed through the skin: baths in Epsom salt, therefore, are an easy and ideal way to enjoy its amazing health benefits. Magnesium plays a number of roles in the body including regulating the activity of over 325 enzymes, reducing inflammation, helping muscle and nerve function and preventing artery hardening. Sulfates also help improve the absorption of nutrients, flush toxins and ease migraine headaches.

The sulfates in Epsom salt help flush toxins and heavy metals from the cells. They also ease muscle pain by helping the body eliminate harmful substances. Your skin is a highly porous membrane; adding the right minerals to your bathwater triggers a process called reverse osmosis, which pulls salt out of your body and harmful toxins along with it. For a detoxifying bath, at least once weekly, add two cups of Ultra Epsom Salts to the water in a bathtub and soak for 10 minutes.

Dead Sea salt is salt from the Dead Sea, which is located between Jordan and Israel. The Dead Sea is technically a lake and is the lowest point on Earth. It has been recognised for centuries as a centre for wellness and health, thanks to the low levels of air pollution and the temperate climate.

Soaking in Dead Sea salt does wonders for your body. Skin problems such as rashes, sores, hives and itching can be treated by soaking in a hot bath filled with these amazing salts. Dead Sea salt contains large amounts of magnesium and bromide, which cleanse and disinfect your skin, making you less susceptible to skin-related allergies. Dead Sea salt also treats acne, psoriasis, dermatitis, eczema, dandruff, scabies and seborrhoea. Dead Sea salt is also effective in combating hair loss, water retention and cellulite.

Stress, an ailment that affects many, can be greatly reduced when you take regular baths with Dead Sea salt. As your circulation improves, your heart rate decreases. The warm water and the minerals in the salt work together to relax your mind, body and spirit. After a long bath, you feel rejuvenated and refreshed. You will be relaxed from the inside out, and you'll sleep better than ever before. Because of this, Dead Sea salt is also a fabulous treatment for insomnia.

www.westlab.com salts are the highest quality natural Epsom and Dead Sea salts available, high magnesium, high grade salts sourced from the Dead Sea and cleaned using a natural, chemical-free process.

Coconut water --Coconut water is the fluid from a ripe coconut. Its reputation is gained from its naturally low sugar content (6 grams per cup) and its mineral rich rehydration delivery. Coconut water has gained popularity with many athletes who strive to maintain balanced electrolyte levels whilst avoiding mainstream junk sports drinks that contain chemicals, caffeine and other harmful substances.

As previously mentioned, electrolytes are minerals like potassium, sodium, magnesium and chloride that help maintain proper fluid levels in the body and regulate muscle function. For athletes, the most obvious symptom of electrolyte imbalance is muscle cramping, but other signs can include weakness, dizziness or heart palpitations.

Coconut water contains even more potassium per serving than the famously potassium-potent banana, delivering about 600 milligrams per cup (versus 362 milligrams in a medium banana). Potassium depletion is often to blame if you experience muscle cramping during exercise.

One cup of coconut water provides more than 252 milligrams of sodium. Sodium works to maintain your body's fluid balance; a low sodium level, or hyponatremia, is 'the most common electrolyte disorder worldwide[59]'.Extreme hyponatremia is a potentially fatal condition caused when cells in the brain absorb too much fluid and the brain swells within the confines of the skull.

According to the UN, coconut water's chemical profile is so similar to blood plasma that it has been used intravenously to save lives in developing countries and during World War II. In the Pacific, it was siphoned directly from the nut to provide emergency transfusions for wounded soldiers. It is also used as a home remedy for dehydration-related ailments such as cholera and gastroenteritis[60].

Coconut water seems to be a cure-all for a range of digestive and urinary ailments and has been used in the tropics to treat stomach flu, dysentery, indigestion, constipation, intestinal worms, bladder infections and malfunctioning kidneys. It's a natural diuretic and is said to prevent urinary tract infections (UTIs) and kidney stones. Research from the Philippines found drinking coconut water up to three times a week may reduce kidney stone size and the need for surgery.

Superfood Supplements for Enhanced Well-Being & Detoxification

Superfoods are a unique and diverse category of foods produced by nature. They are calorie sparse and nutrient dense, meaning they pack a large amount of power for their weight as far as nutritional goodness goes. They are superior sources of essential nutrients, minerals and anti-oxidants. These nutrients are vital for your well-being but the human body cannot make them by itself.

The simple things in life are the ones most often overlooked. The correct approach to radiant health and abundant energy is so simple because it is simply common sense. In spite of all of the negatives in the world, we are living in incredible times. The accessibility to the most amazing foods from around the world is at its peak. These foods are capable of reversing humanity's current nutritional catastrophe whilst healing, energising and inspiring people to actualise their full potential as citizens of the Earth.

Superfoods are derived from the highest vibrational, energetic points of the earth such as the Himalayas, Andes Mountains, Amazon rainforest, palm beaches of the Philippines, African landscape and so forth. When you experiment with raw, living superfoods and start to cleanse your body, you are tapping into the ancient food knowledge from cultures around the globe, experiencing the greatest expression of food technology whilst living in harmony with nature.

Simply put, there is no real substitute for these whole foods. Superfoods are complete whole food supplements, these are the most mineral- and nutrient-rich foods on the planet. These are not fractionalised supplements that you may find in the local supermarket. All superfood minerals, vitamins and nutrients are easily absorbed by the body, vibrating at a completely unique and higher level altogether, claiming their rightful place at the top of the food pyramid.

Plants feed on the minerals provided by Mother Earth and humans feed on the plants. This is the way nature intended things and it is self-evident in the fact that 95 per cent of absorbable minerals come from plants. Most people are disconnected from nature; this is one of the main reasons people are suffering.' If you walk two steps towards Nature, Nature would come four steps towards you'.

The superfood lifestyle is about playing the game at the highest of levels. The aim is not too supposedly 'feel fine' but not be able to drag yourself out of bed in the morning. The goal, instead, is to feel spectacular, amazing and extraordinary—bouncing with energy, embracing new opportunities and expanding your mind, your awareness and enhancing levels of consciousness.

All in all, superfoods have a unique ability to eliminate and push out the bad metabolic waste that is stored within your body. Consuming superfoods packed with nutrients satisfy hunger cravings at a deep level, providing your body with what it has been searching for, thus reducing mental food cravings and the habit of overeating.

Many people who follow erroneous mainstream information tend to think that healthy eating and so-called 'dieting' is centred on the denial of certain foods. To an extent, it is based on abstaining from contaminated foods, but, in reality, it is about enjoying natural foods whilst feeding the body with what it wants so there is no longer a need to eat nutrient-deficient foods. Once you start to eat a natural, high nutrition diet, your body will take form into its natural shape/size as toxins are eradicated and cellular regeneration is enhanced.

Before we continue, it is important to note that this entire publication seeks only to demonstrate the beneficial applications of superfoods and dietary enhancements for various disorders in the human organism. In no way should this book, or the contents therein, substitute for personal supervision by qualified medical personnel. The opinions and information surrounding all health alternatives are solely the opinions of the author and those of extensive research and experience. People with health problems should visit their physician. **Below are the main types of superfoods and their traditional uses:**

Green Superfoods

Leafy green vegetables are excellent, but green superfoods are even better. These types of superfoods hold the highest, most potent concentrations of easily digestible nutrients, vitamins, minerals, fat burning compounds and living enzymes. All of these components work towards protecting and healing the body.

Green superfoods contain a wide array of beneficial substances including proteins, protective photo-chemicals and healthy bacteria which help you to build cleaner muscles and tissues, aid your digestive system function and more effectively protect against disease and illness. Green superfoods are extremely rich in chlorophyll. Chlorophyll is the pigment that gives plants their natural green colour and the molecular structure of chlorophyll is very similar to human haemoglobin. Science has shown that when a person increases their intake of chlorophyll-rich foods, the body's production of haemoglobin is greatly increased. Higher amounts of haemoglobin in the bloodstream mean more oxygen-rich blood, which is the first and most important element that cells need to thrive and combat disease.

Wheatgrass – Wheatgrass is the sprouted grass of a wheat seed. Unlike the whole wheat grain, because it has been sprouted wheatgrass no longer contains gluten or other common allergic agents. Wheatgrass is super alkalising and is excellent for promoting healthy blood. It causes the thyroid gland to stimulate metabolism, thus assisting in digestion and promoting weight loss. Its high enzyme content also has a cleansing effect.

Wheatgrass increases red blood-cell count and lowers blood pressure. It cleanses the blood, organs and the gastrointestinal tract of debris.

It is a powerful liver and blood detoxifier and protector. The enzymes and amino acids found in wheatgrass can protect you from carcinogens like no other food or medicine. It strengthens your cells by neutralising environmental pollutants.

Wheatgrass is known to combat tumours and neutralise toxins. Recent studies show that wheatgrass juice has a powerful ability to fight tumours without the usual toxicity of drugs that also inhibit cell-destroying agents. The many active compounds found in wheatgrass juice cleanse the blood and neutralise and digest toxins in our cells. You can grow your own wheatgrass at home and juice it into one-shot servings or buy it as freeze dried powder. Be careful when first taking wheatgrass, as it can send you into detox shock if your body may not be accustomed to it!

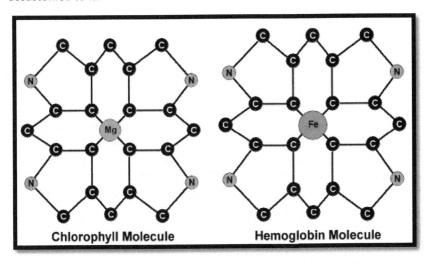

Molecular comparison between chlorophyll and haemoglobin. Magnesium and Iron is what differentiates the two. Sourced from: www.ajpip.com

The many active compounds found in wheatgrass juice cleanse the blood and neutralise and digest toxins in our cells. You can grow your own wheatgrass at home and juice it into one-shot servings or buy it as freeze dried powder. Be careful when first taking wheatgrass, as it can send you into detox shock if you are not used to it as when you remove a toxin from your system, (gluten, sugar, cigarettes, meat, dairy, etc.) your body will go through a detoxing process to rid itself of the toxins. This can cause headaches, lethargy, joint pain, acne, skin rash, painful periods, muscle soreness, depression, anxiety, weight loss, hormonal swings, bloating, nausea, sore throat, and a bunch of other unpleasant symptoms.

Barley grass – Barley grass has eleven times more calcium than cow's milk, five times more iron than spinach and seven times more Vitamin C and bio-flavonoids than orange juice. It contains significant amounts of Vitamin B12, which is very important in a vegetarian diet. Barley grass juice has anti-viral properties and neutralises heavy metals such as mercury in the blood.

Barley grass is very high in organic sodium, which dissolves calcium deposits on the joints and replenishes organic sodium in the lining of the stomach. This aids digestion by improving the production of hydrochloric acid in the stomach. People with arthritis have used celery juice for years because of the organic sodium it contains (28mg per 100grms), but the amount of organic sodium in barley grass is much higher (775mg per 100 grams)

Blue green algae/Spirulina – Algae was the first form of life on Earth and its power is immense. Wild blue-green algae is a phyto-plankton and contains virtually every nutrient. With a 60 per cent protein content and a more complete amino acid profile than beef or soy beans, it also contains one of the best known sources of beta carotene, B vitamins and chlorophyll. It has been shown to improve brain function and memory, strengthen the immune system and help with viruses, colds and flu.

Spirulina is a cultivated micro-algae which has been consumed for thousands of years by the indigenous peoples in Mexico and Africa. It contains 70 per cent *complete* protein, towering over steak, which consists of only 25 per cent protein once cooked. Studies have shown that Spirulina can help control blood sugar levels and curb sugar cravings, making it a key food for diabetics. It can also be used to assist in weight loss and as a general nutritional supplement.

Blue-green algae and Spirulina are rich in vitamins A, C, E and the B-complex vitamins, including vitamins B12 and B6. Since these vitamins are packaged in their natural form, they are in a highly usable state; that makes them far superior to modern vitamin supplements. (It should be noted that some experts don't consider the vitamin B12 in Spirulina to be bioavailable; others disagree.)

These foods are rich in natural minerals like calcium, magnesium and iron. They are also an excellent source of the trace minerals commonly lacking in today's standard diet. Many of these vitamins and minerals exhibit antioxidant properties which aid in the elimination of toxins and free-radicals, helping the body fight disease and stay healthy. These elements also fight cancer -- in fact, preliminary studies point to Spirulina as a natural anti-cancer agent.

Spirulina contains a variety of amino acids. There is a lot of confusion over amino acids, so we have listed the main ones below and their benefits:

-- **Isoleucine (4.13 per cent):** Needed for growth, brain development and nitrogen balance within the body. Also assists with synthesising other non-essential amino acids.

-- **Leucine (5.8 per cent):** Helps increase muscular energy levels and stimulate brain function.

-- **Lysine (4.0 per cent):** Used for forming blood antibodies; improves the circulatory system and promotes cell growth.

-- **Methionine (2.17 per cent):** Vital for metabolising the fats and lipids that maintain a healthy liver. Also helps calm the nerves.

-- **Phenylalanine (3.95 per cent):** Used by the thyroid for the production of thyroxin which, in turn, governs metabolic rate.

-- **Threonine (4.17 per cent):** Improves competence of the intestines and, thus, aids digestion.

-- **Tryptophane (1.13 per cent):** Enhances the use of B group vitamins and improves nerve fibres. This contributes to emotional stability and calmness.

-- **Valine (6.0 per cent):** Assists with the co-ordination of the muscular system as well as contributing to improved mental capacity.

Non-essential amino acids are a group of twelve amino acids. Spirulina doesn't have all of them, but it does contain ten. 'Non-essential', in this context, means that, if not naturally present in normal foods, the amino acids can be synthesised. It does *not* mean that the body has no need of them. Again, the following list is that of the non-essential amino acids that are provided by Spirulina:

– **Alanine (5.82 per cent):** Strengthens the walls of cells.

– **Arginine (5.98 per cent):** Important for the production of seminal fluid which is about

 Arginine (80 per cent): Assists in keeping the blood clean.

– **Aspartic Acid (6.34 per cent):** Helps with the transformation of carbohydrates into energy.

– **Cysteine (0.67 per cent):** Aids with pancreatic health and stabilises blood sugar. May help alleviate food allergies.

– **Glutamic Acid (8.94 per cent):** Along with glucose, it fuels the brain cells. Can reduce the craving for alcohol and stabilise mental health.

– **Glycine (3.5 per cent):** Promoter of energy.

– **Histidine (1.08 per cent):** Improves nerve relays, especially in the hearing organs. Has even been used as a remedy for deafness.

– **Proline (2.97 per cent):** A precursor of Glutamic acid.

– **Serine (4.0 per cent):** Helps with the formation of the fatty sheath surrounding nerve fibres.

– **Tyrosine (4.6 per cent):** Known to slow the ageing of cells and to suppress hunger. Involved in the colouration of hair and skin and also helps with sunburn protection.

In spite of their nutritional punch, blue-green algae and Spirulina do not pack a lot of calories. This makes it effortless to incorporate these superfoods into your diet regardless of your nutritional needs and preferences. It is important to find a quality source of blue-green algae or Spirulina. Poor quality supplements may contain heavy metal contaminants and other toxins. Be sure to examine the source of your blue-green algae and Spirulina carefully before buying.

Chlorella – Chlorella is a fresh water algae and, like its other algae cousins, it contains a complete protein profile, all the B vitamins, vitamin C and E and many minerals. It is amazing for the immune system and for reducing cholesterol and preventing the hardening of the arteries, precursors to heart attacks and strokes. Chlorella is known to be the densest chlorophyll-rich food on the planet.

Adding chlorella to your diet will contribute to your recommended daily fibre intake. 10g of Chlorella will provide you with about 2.1g of fibre (two times more than brown bread). Chlorella supports weight loss, when used in combination with exercise, because it contains Vitamins B2, B3, B12, iron and magnesium, which all contribute to a reduction of tiredness and fatigue.

Chlorella promotes digestive health because it contains zinc. Zinc contributes to a normal, acid-base metabolism, normal carbohydrate metabolism, normal macronutrient metabolism, normal metabolism of fatty acids and normal absorption of vitamin A. For sexual health, zinc contributes to normal fertility and reproduction. Vitamins B1, B2, B3, B6, B12 and magnesium elevate overall physical health by contributing to the normal function of the nervous system.

Green Vibrance Superfood powder – Green Vibrance powder was first formulated over 20 years ago and has remained at the forefront of quality 'green Superfood nutrition' since then. It is a dynamic product with new ingredients of value being added regularly to maintain its position as the greens product of choice. The quality of the product has been reflected in the awards it has received over the years. It is the one supplement (although we prefer to regard it as food) that everyone should consider adding to their diet, especially for those who are in ill health.

Green Vibrance was developed by Vibrant Health[61] to support the four foundations of health, nutrition, digestion, circulation and immunity with total-body benefits. It delivers a host of trace nutrients that may be deficient in our modern diets.

Green Vibrance powder contains concentrated green vegetables, grass juice powders, algae and sea vegetables, antioxidant and phyto-nutrient-rich botanicals, digestive enzymes, concentrated probiotics and Vitamin D3. The blend gives very dense nutrition with a huge variety of trace nutrients. It is easy to take: just add a scoop of powder to water or juice and drink daily. It is available in four different sizes, in addition to sachets and capsules.

Your vitality is the sum total of the health of each cell. To reach optimal health, the immune system must be strong, a robust gastro-intestinal tract must draw in complete nutrition and the liver must operate at peak efficiency. Those nutrients must, in turn, be delivered to all of the cells in the body, even those at the very edge of your fingers and toes. Green Vibrance is a concentrated superfood with a purpose: to make you healthier and stronger. Green Vibrance feeds each cell what it needs to run at its best.

There are a lot of ingredients in Green Vibrance, found at **www.greenvibrance.com**. There are seventy-three in all. They were put together with care in order to maximise the synergy among the nutrients. The result delivers healthful nutritional support to the eleven body systems. Concentrated in nutrition, it provides immunity, bone health, circulatory and antioxidant support, liver support, probiotics and digestion support. Please visit the website for a more in-depth description of the product.

Fruit and nut superfoods

The following fruit and nut superfoods contain high levels of antioxidant properties that assist in fighting free radicals within the body. Free radicals are, in part, a natural occurrence of the metabolism, but sometimes extra and unnecessary loads can put extra stress on your body and generate too many free radicals. External factors such as smoking, environmental pollution, radiation, deep fried fats/hydrogenated oils, burned foods and too much cooked food can cause free radicals to invade the immune system. The results can be problematic. This is when you need antioxidants to build up the immune system and fight off the free radicals in the form of superfoods or supplements.

Raw cacao – The raw cacao bean is possibly the world's most concentrated food source of antioxidants provided by nature, holding an antioxidant (ORAC-oxygen radical absorbance capacity) score of 95,500. To put that into perspective, that is fourteen times more flavonoids (antioxidants) than red wine and 21 times more than green tea. Antioxidants are important to stop the body from 'rusting', so to speak, as oxidisation makes you feel and look old.

These beans are extremely high in magnesium and contain 21 per cent of the RDA serving of iron. Cacao is a great source of serotonin, dopamine and phenylethylamine, three well-studied neurotransmitters, which help to alleviate depression and are associated with feelings of well-being. Cacao contains monoamine oxidase inhibitors (MAO Inhibitors) that improve our mood because they allow serotonin and dopamine to remain in the bloodstream longer before being broken down.

Cacao has been celebrated for centuries throughout Mexican, Central and South American cultures due to its delicious taste and exceptional nutritional profile. Aztecs once used cacao beans as currency in ancient times. Several Mayan rituals, festivals and celebrations were devoted to honouring cacao, and its Latin name translates to 'Food of the Gods'. Be sure to attain certified, organic and raw cacao in either powder, nib or whole bean form. (The temperature will have never been allowed to exceed 40 degrees while processing the raw cacao, therefore allowing all of the heat sensitive vitamins, minerals and antioxidants to remain intact.)

Goji berries – Goji berries are grown on vines mainly in the protected valleys of Inner Mongolia and Tibet. These distinctively flavoured red berries are a very rich source of vitamin C, having 500 times more vitamin C per ounce than oranges and, actually, more than any other fruit. They are a superb source of vitamins A, B1, B2, B6 and E and contain a full complement of protein with 18 amino acids and 21 trace minerals. Most of all, they are an excellent antioxidant and an ideal natural whole food for reversing aging and protecting against disease.

Goji berries play an important role in traditional Chinese medicine (TCM). They are believed to enhance immune system function, help eyesight, protect the liver, boost sperm production and improve circulation, among other effects. In TCM terms, Goji berries are sweet in taste and neutral in nature; they act on the liver, lung and kidney channels and enrich *yin*. Goji berries can be eaten raw, brewed into a tea, blended into a smoothie, or prepared as a tincture.

Goji Berries contain complex phyto-nutrients and bio flavonoids:

– **Betaine:** Used by the liver to produce choline, a compound that calms nervousness, enhances memory, promotes muscle growth and protects against fatty liver disease

– **Physalin:** Active against all major types of leukaemia. It has also been used as a treatment for Hepatitis B

– **Solavetivone:** A powerful anti-fungal and anti-bacterial compound

– **Beta-Sitoserol:** An anti-inflammatory agent. It has been used to treat sexual impotence and prostate enlargement. It also has a cholesterol lowering effect

– **Cyperone:** Sesquiterpene benefits the heart and helps maintain normal blood pressure. It has also been used in the treatment of cervical cancer.

Coconut oil – The fat obtained from coconut oil is digested very easily and utilised in a different manner by the body than saturated fats such as those in butter, meat, eggs and dairy, because it is part of the medium-chain fatty acid variety.

Whereas harmful saturated fats are stored in the body's cells, medium chain fatty acids are utilised directly by the liver and immediately converted into energy. Coconut oil encourages faster metabolism rates, so your body will burn more calories, lose weight and detoxify.

The health benefits of coconut oil include hair care, skin care, stress relief, cholesterol level maintenance, weight loss, a boosted immune system, proper digestion and regulated metabolism. It also provides relief from kidney problems, heart diseases, high blood pressure, diabetes, HIV and cancer, while helping to improve dental quality and bone strength.

Coconut oil is extensively used on the Indian sub-continent for hair care. Most of the people in those countries apply coconut oil on their hair every day after bathing or showering. It is an excellent conditioner and helps the re-growth process of damaged hair. It also provides the essential proteins required for nourishing and healing damaged hair.

Coconut oil is strongly recommended for a number of other benefits that are explained below. Using coconut oil has been shown to mildly help the following:

– Liver: The presence of medium chain triglycerides and fatty acids helps in preventing various liver diseases because those substances are easily converted into energy when they reach the liver. This reduces the work load of the liver and also prevents the accumulation of fat. The liver regenerates every 30 days, so coconut oil ensures the liver's optimum vitality with enzyme support

– Kidney: Coconut oil helps in preventing kidney and gall bladder diseases. It also helps to dissolve kidney stones

– Pancreatitis: Coconut oil is also believed to be useful in treating pancreatitis

– Stress relief: Coconut oil is very soothing and, hence, it helps in removing stress. Applying coconut oil to the head, followed by a gentle massage, helps to eliminate mental fatigue

– Diabetes: Coconut oil helps in controlling blood sugar and improves the secretion of insulin. It also promotes the effective utilisation of blood glucose, thereby preventing and treating diabetes

– Bones: As mentioned earlier, coconut oil improves the ability of the body to absorb important minerals. These include calcium and magnesium, which are necessary for the development of bones. Thus, coconut oil is very useful to women who are prone to osteoporosis after middle age.

– Dental care and oil pulling: Calcium is an important component of your teeth. Since coconut oil facilitates absorption of calcium by the body, it helps in developing strong teeth. Coconut oil also stops tooth decay as it diminishes harmful bacteria.

Oil pulling with coconut oil is extremely beneficial for oral health and detoxification. Simply take a tablespoon of oil and swill in your mouth for 20 minutes. Oil pulling reduces the amount of S. mutans (germ) count in the teeth plaque and mouth saliva. Scientists believe that the lipids in the oil both pull out bacteria and stop bacteria from sticking to the walls of the oral cavity. Many health practitioners believe that there are many other benefits to be gained from oil pulling.

These benefits of oil can be attributed to the presence of lauric acid, capric acid and caprylic acid. All of these acids have antimicrobial, antioxidant, anti-fungal, antibacterial properties. Pacific Islanders deem coconut oil to be the soothing, cure-all gift from nature for many ailments.

Coconut oil comes in various forms such as pure, refined (which is bad), virgin and organic. Be sure to buy raw, cold pressed, organic coconut oil. You can use coconut oil as a replacement for any other cooking oils and you can never use too much of it. Add a tablespoon of raw coconut oil to your favourite smoothie for added goodness.

Mucunapruriens powder – A shrub traditionally used in Ayurvedic medicine. The powder is made from ground seeds. Mucuna is an excellent source of naturally occurring 5Htp (a natural supplement that converts into the brain chemical serotonin), DMT and boosts dopamine in the brain. Due to its potency, it is important to use Mucuna sparingly.

L-Dopa is the amino acid compound from which your body produces dopamine. As a regular part of a healthy diet, Mucunapruriens provides many benefits. Among the long list are enhanced libido and sexual capacity, increased testosterone production and improved mood and energy.

Low dopamine levels are associated with addiction, depression, psychosis, schizophrenia and Attention Deficit Disorder (ADD). Since dopamine itself cannot cross the blood-brain barrier, it is delivered in a precursor state, a form which causes the brain to produce dopamine. L-Dopa is just such a precursor. L-Dopa has been found to be effective in alleviating depression, increasing focus and in treating Parkinson's disease.

Depression and Dopamine – Depression affects everyone differently. However, common symptoms include; a lack of motivation, lowered self-esteem, depressed mood, irritability, lack of interest in activities, insomnia, body aches and loss of appetite. Researchers believe a combination of factors, including imbalances in neurotransmitters and unconscious energetic imprints, can contribute to symptoms of depression.

Most research has focused on the effects of imbalances in the neurotransmitters known as serotonin and noradrenaline. However, research published in the Oct. 1, 2002, issue of the journal *Biological Psychiatry* explains that mesolimbic dopamine deficiency plays an important role in the development of specific symptoms of depression, especially anhedonia (anhedonia is the inability to experience pleasure and extreme loss of motivation).

If you intend to consume more than a teaspoon of mucunain a day, please consult a registered healthcare practitioner first. Mucuna has been shown to lower blood sugar; therefore, it should be avoided by diabetics. It is also not recommended for pregnant women as it may act as a uterine stimulant. You are, however, encouraged to do your own research on this superfood and how it could benefit you, personally.

Maca root powder – Maca is a flavourful ancient superfood derived from Peru. It has been cultivated for at least 2,000 years and was known to be consumed by Inca warriors to increase endurance and strength. Maca powder is highly nutritious in nature and is traditionally used to gain energy, promote sexual desire, enhance immune system function and support fertility. It continues to be a significant medicinal plant and staple food for the Peruvian people and is widely available worldwide as a powerful whole food.

Maca is a Peruvian root vegetable containing a variety of nutrients such as vitamins, minerals, enzymes and every essential amino acid. Maca powder is perfect in smoothies, juices and protein drinks. (Maca contains 13.2g protein per 100g serving). It is recommended that you abstain from Maca powder consumption for one week of every month when enjoying on a daily basis, as this significantly intensifies the product's benefits.

– Healthy energy levels: Maca powder consists of two groups of unique compounds: macamides and macaenes, believed to be directly responsible for its energy-boosting effects. Maca powder is high in phosphorus, manganese and iron. Iron promotes oxygen transport, helping fight fatigue and exhaustion.

– Stabilises hormone levels: Maca powder contains bioactive compounds, plant sterols and prostaglandins that help regulate the endocrine system. Its helps normalise your steroid hormones like testosterone, progesterone and oestrogen.

– Relief from PMS/Menopausal Discomfort: Studies showed that women taking maca had substantial reduction of PMS symptoms and menopausal discomfort, as maca acts as a hormonal regulator.

– Sexual health: In multiple studies, maca powder has been shown to boost sexual desire in both men and women without any adverse effects on sexual hormones. Studies also confirmed sperm count and motility were improved in men taking maca powder.

Guayusa Tea – Guayusa is a rare, naturally caffeinated herbal tea produced from the leaves of a holly tree (*Ilex Guayusa*). Guayusa can be found growing in the Amazon rainforest regions of Ecuador, Peru and Colombia.

It is estimated that over 98 per cent of the guayusa trees in the world are located in Ecuador, making it the epicentre of guayusa habitat on the planet. This is where the plant grows in abundance. The leaves of the holly tree are picked by the farmers and laid out to be dried in the sun, avoiding the use of any solvents, pesticides and harmful chemicals. The end product reaches the consumer in its purest natural state.

Guayusa has been part of Amazonian culture for over 2,000 years and is treasured for its unique balance of caffeine, antioxidants, vitamins and amino acids that awaken the mind and fortify the body. Guayusa is a botanical cousin to Yerba Mate (ilex paraguariensis) which has gained amazing popularity throughout the world in recent years for its health benefits and energising effects.

What sets Guayusa apart from all other teas is its foremost extremely smooth flavour. It is less bitter than many teas and has a delicious earthy and floral flavour. Guayusa also exceeds many other teas and foods for its energising effects and health benefiting qualities (also gaining popularity for its ability to enhance lucid dreaming). Truly, guayusa is a superfood. Guayusa is great, served hot or cold, with lemon or honey. In addition, the leaves may be boiled and steeped many times without losing their flavour.

Average caffeine content of guayusa is 90mg per 8oz cup, which is second to coffee at 120mg per 8oz cup. The main factor that separates guayusa tea from coffee is the molecular caffeine structure differs so it does not encourage a crash or anxious jitters from coffee drinking. This makes it a healthy coffee substitute.

Bee superfoods

Our ancient Khemetian and Hindu Indian ancestors used bee-derived superfoods in their ceremonies in 1,000BC. Even the Babylonians were said to have used them in their medicinal practices. The Western world discovered the benefits of Mother Nature's bee superfoods during an investigation of native Russian beekeepers who, on average, lived over 100 years. These beekeepers were known to consume raw honey, rich in bee pollen, on a daily basis.

Bee pollen/raw honey – Pollen is harvested by bees from flowering plants and then formed into granules. Bee pollen is a natural allergy fighting antidote (particularly hay fever and sinusitis). Bee pollen is up there with the most complete foods found in nature, holding seven times more protein than beef. This compound is extremely beneficial for the extra nutritional and energetic needs of athletes as well as those recovering from illness. Research shows that pollen counteracts the signs of aging and increases both mental and physical capability.

Bees package their pollen with nectar and enzymes, which produces a powerful superfood. In fact, bee pollen contains thousands of enzymes and co-enzymes which are necessary for true vitality. Bee pollen also contains 22 amino acids, including the eight essential ones. It is, in essence, a complete protein. You'll also find dozens of vitamins and minerals in bee pollen, as well as natural hormones and important fatty acids.

While science has yet to thoroughly examine bee pollen and raw honey for its benefits, many people have successfully used it to treat a variety of ailments, including:

– Indigestion, diarrhoea, constipation and other digestive issues
– Anaemia & Asthma
– Low energy and fatigue
– Depression
– Skin conditions such as acne
– Sexual problems
– Haemorrhoids
– Obesity
– Rheumatism and arthritis

Bee pollen is known to be an accelerator of human growth. It regulates the action of the intestinal functions, especially in cases of chronic constipation or diarrhoea that have been resistant to antibiotic treatment. Pollen self-digests and aids the digestion of other foods. A natural occurrence with bee pollen is weight control. Taken into your digestive system, there is a speedy combustion, which makes fats burn faster and increases the rate of burned calories.

Bee pollen can be taken in liquid form (extract or tea), capsule, chewable tablet, granules or powder. Add 1 teaspoon of bee pollen granules to your smoothie or protein drink. Raw honey can be ingested the same way.

Herbal and seaweed superfoods

Seaweeds are true wonder foods, whilst herbs offer the body unique nourishment and nutrients that may not be otherwise offered, due to poor diet or environmental deficiencies in the air and soil. Seaweed superfoods are the most nutritionally dense superfoods on the planet because they have access to all of the nutrients and minerals within the ocean.

Herbs, as medicine, are essential body balancers that work with the body functions so that it can heal and regulate itself. Herbs have been used for centuries as part of wise, natural healing methods. Herbs are best used in their whole form rather than isolating effective plant constituents so-called 'active ingredients'.

Aloe Vera – Aloe vera juice contains leaf pulp that is rich in natural nutrients and fibre. This well-known herbal remedy for the skin also has many benefits for internal healing, cleansing and repair when ingested as a nutritional drink. However, it can cause also adverse side effects and reactions and should only be taken as directed. Do not consume aloe vera that is not made for internal use and consult your doctor before self-medicating for any reason.

The aloe vera plant is a perennial succulent that grows in the wild and thrives in tropical and sub-tropical areas. Aloe vera has been used since the times of Kemet as skin moisturiser and burn healer. It is also effective for treating cuts, bruises, acne and eczema. Aloe has been deemed a superfood after research which suggests it contains over seventy healing compounds such as natural steroids, antibiotic agents, amino acids, minerals and enzymes.

Aloe vera may also have similar benefits on the lining of the digestive tract, when ingested as a drink. A review published in the *British Journal of General Practice* notes that aloe vera decreases irritation and enhances healing and repair of ulcers in the stomach and intestines. Aloe vera juice also helps to decrease inflammation in irritable bowel syndrome, colitis and other inflammatory disorders of the gut. Additionally, aloe vera can increase healthy bacteria in the intestines that aid digestion. This is mostly due to the high concentration of natural sulphur (MSM) that it contains. Aloe juices alkalises the digestive tract, preventing over-acidity, a common cause of indigestion, acid reflux, heartburn and ulcers.

Taking aloe vera internally may also help improve blood circulation in the body. A clinical study published in the medical journal *Angiology* reported that aloe vera may help decrease total fat levels in patients with high cholesterol. This helps to reduce fatty deposits and blood clots in the arteries of the heart.[62]

Nettle – This plant is extremely effective in removing unwanted pounds. A cup of nettle tea every morning is ideal for bowel movements. Nettle is best known as a stinging plant, but when the nettle leaves are dried and then eaten, the sting is neutralised by the saliva in your mouth.

Nettle leaves increase thyroid function, increase metabolism and release mucus in the colon, allowing for the flushing of excess wastes and aiding in detoxification. Nettle has been used for centuries to treat allergy symptoms, particularly hay fever, which is the most common allergy problem. Decongestants, antihistamines, allergy shots and even prescription medications such as Allegra and Claritin treat only the symptoms of allergies and tend to lose effectiveness over a period of time. They can also cause drowsiness, dry sinuses, insomnia and high blood pressure. Nettle has none of these side effects. It can be used on a regular basis and has an impressive number of other benefits, most notably as a treatment for prostate enlargement.

An infusion of the plant is very valuable in stemming internal bleeding. It is also used to treat anaemia, excessive menstruation, haemorrhoids, and arthritis, rheumatism and skin complaints like eczema. Externally, the plant is used to treat skin complaints, arthritic pain, gout, sciatica, neuralgia, haemorrhoids and hair problems. You can visit a homeopath, drink nettle tea or simply go and pick wild nettles and add them into your favourite fresh green juice!

Kelp – Also known as brown algae, kelp is the most common seaweed found along the ocean shores. Its thick leaves make it perfect for a hot seaweed bath. It is also available in supplement form.

Excellent source of vitamins and minerals: kelp has been shown to contain 46 minerals, 16 amino acids (the building blocks of protein) and eleven different vitamins. Prominent among the minerals are iodine, salt, iron, potassium, phosphorus and calcium. The lead vitamins in kelp are vitamin A and niacin.

– **Helps in thyroid gland regulation:** Due to kelp's high levels of natural iodine, it is essential in regulating your thyroid hormones and therefore our metabolism and energy levels.

– **Helps with hydration:** This may be particularly important to note when you have been ill or exposed to too much heat and sun. Make a soup or broth with kelp in order to rehydrate quickly.

– **Assists in weight management and weight loss**: Due to kelp's iodine content and its role in thyroid function, one of kelp's benefits is improving metabolism and energy. An iodine deficiency can slow your metabolic function by as much at 50 per cent, so including kelp can naturally and significantly improve weight loss and other associated health problems.

– **Improves body pH:** Kelp is an alkaline food and therefore an essential part of maintaining acid-base balance in the body and an effective component in a healthy acid-alkaline diet.

– Protects against radiation poisoning: Once again, due to kelp's high natural iodine levels, it prevents the thyroid from up-taking harmful levels of radioactive iodine present after a nuclear disaster. This has been particularly important since the recent nuclear fallout in Japan in 2011.

– Cancer prevention: Kelp prevents cancer particularly in estrogenic sensitive cancers such as breast, endometrial and ovarian cancers.

Why does this little-known plant work so well? Dr. D.C. Jarvis, author of Folk Medicine (Galahad, 1996), points out that the composition of the human body and of seawater are the same. It's only practical, he suggests, that people should turn to the sea to supplement mineral needs.

Dulse –A red seaweed that can be bought either whole or as flakes. Dulse sold as flakes does not need to be soaked and can be added straight to any meal. Whole dulse is better soaked, drained of water and sliced before adding to your dish. It is great to use as seasoning on salads, vegetables and soups.

Dulse is considered a superfood because of its high iodine and potassium content, in addition to its long list of micro-nutrients and phytochemicals. Many herbalists prefer dulse over kelp in green superfood recipes because of its neutral flavour. Found primarily in cold waters off the Atlantic coast of Canada, Ireland and Norway, dulse has been used traditionally to control parasites, treat scurvy and improve thyroid function. Dulse is a scientifically proven antioxidant, a source of plant protein and is often suggested as a part of healing protocols to correct hypothyroid issues.

Dulse may be best known for its high iodine content. A natural source of iodine is critical for patients suffering from hypothyroid symptoms. According to the Mayo Clinic, hypothyroid symptoms include:

- Fatigue
- Dry skin and face
- Muscle aches and pains
- Chest pains
- Unusual sensitivity to cold temperatures
- A lower-than-normal basal body temperature
- Headaches and migraines
- Constipation
- Depression
- Hair loss
- Brittle and peeling nails
- High blood cholesterol
- Weight gain or obesity
- Heavy periods in females

This seaweed has also been demonstrated to inhibit the growth of lipid (fat) cells in laboratory conditions. This is extremely important, as environmental toxins are believed to be causing an increase in a host of auto-immune diseases, such as multiple sclerosis, lupus and rheumatoid arthritis.

The combination of constant stress, environmental pathogens and malnutrition is burning out many people's immune systems. Utilising dulse and other antioxidants helps to repair compromised body tissues.

Bentonite clay and psyllium husk – Healing clays that have been used by cultures throughout history have been largely forgotten in recent times. Certain clays were renowned for their helpful nutrient base and their unique ability to squeeze and attract toxins out of the body. Many animals are known to turn to eating dirt and clay to assist the toxin and poison removal from their systems during times of distress and illness.

In recent times, healing clays such as bentonite and herbs such as psyllium husk have once again been gaining popularity for their superior uses of internal and external detoxification. These two superfoods work best when used together.

Psyllium husk – Psyllium is the husk of the seed of the plantain (mostly found in India) and is a top herb used in weight control and for general intestinal health. It contains a spongy fibre that reduces appetite, improves digestion and cleanses the system, making it an excellent choice for healthy dieting. Psyllium can provide the fibre that is missing on low carbohydrate diets. Every 100 grams of psyllium provides 71 grams of soluble fibre; a similar amount of oat bran would contain only five grams of soluble fibre.

Psyllium has also been used for irritable bowel syndrome (a stress-related disorder with alternating bouts of diarrhoea and constipation). Because it will produce easy bowel movements with a loose stool, psyllium is used by patients with anal fissures (cracks in the skin near the anus) and haemorrhoids. It is often recommended following anal or rectal surgery, during pregnancy and as a secondary treatment in certain types of diarrhoea.

In a study of people with ulcerative colitis (a type of inflammatory bowel disorder), psyllium seeds were as shown to be as effective as the prescription drug mesalamine in decreasing recurrences of the disease. In addition, a physician may recommend the use of psyllium as a bulking agent for mild to moderate cases of diarrhoea from either ulcerative colitis or Crohn's disease (another type of inflammatory bowel disorder).

Psyllium husk is a bulking fibre, which means once ingested it expands and forms a gelatin-like mass in the colon by drawing in water. Once this occurs, the husks are able to 'scrub' the intestines clean and transport waste through the intestinal tract. Used in conjunction with bentonite clay, it can remove waste after detoxification that is stored in the lower area of the body.

Bentonite clay – Bentonite clay is composed of aged volcanic ash. The name comes from the largest known deposit of bentonite clay, located in Fort Benton, Wyoming.

Bentonite is one of the most effective and powerful healing clays. A good-quality bentonite should be grey or cream in colour. It has a very fine, velvety texture and is odourless and non-staining. Bentonite can be used externally as a clay poultice, mud pack or in the bath and in skin care recipes.

This special clay holds a unique ability to produce an 'electrical charge' when it comes into contact with hydration. Bentonite's electrical components change when it comes into contact with fluids giving it the ability to absorb and attract toxins which can then be expelled from the body. Toxins include impurities, chemicals and heavy metals making this product one of the best for detoxification. Healing clays like Bentonite have a high concentration of minerals including silica, calcium, magnesium, sodium, iron and potassium.

Bentonite is a swelling clay. Once it comes into contact with water, it swells rapidly like a highly porous sponge, allowing its negative charge to attract any harmful substances that hold a positive charge. From there, the positively charged toxins and chemicals are drawn into and bound to the sponge electrically. Bentonite will absorb the toxin, chemical or heavy metals whilst releasing its beneficial minerals for the body to utilise. The clay cannot be digested by the stomach, so it assists in pulling excess hydrogen from within the body allowing the cells to replace it with oxygen.

Bentonite clay is a common ingredient in many detox and cleansing products. It has an alkalising effect on the body and when taken correctly, it can help balance gut bacteria. Bentonite clay helps with:

- digestive disturbances like acid reflux, constipation, bloating, gas, etc. (Kaolin clay was common ingredient in medicines like Maalox and Rolaids for years);
- skin and allergy issues;
- providing minerals for the body;
- speedy recovery from vomiting and diarrhoea;
- detoxification;
- in oral health preparations and
- externally for all types of skin problems and to speed healing.

The water activates its electromagnetic charge. Be sure to not to use a metallic spoon to stir the water. Preparing the glassful before bed is a good habit. The longer the clay sits in the water, the more it imparts its electromagnetic charge into the water, turning the water into medicine. The whole glass gets charged, so you don't need very much of the physicality of the clay itself to draw toxins. A good drink to have daily is bentonite and psyllium husk. Add 1 teaspoon of each into the blender and fill up with 32oz of water, blend for 30 seconds and consume.

Hemp superfoods –Raw organic hemp has many uses, traditionally used as a muscle builder and energy booster. This ancient food can be traced back thousands of years to Chinese, Egyptian, Persian and other cultures, where it was a highly revered food source. Hemp seed contains all the essential amino acids and fatty acids and is considered to be a complete food.

At 30 per cent protein content, hemp protein powder is the answer for anyone looking for a raw, vegan and organic muscle and energy booster. It is also essential for overall health maintenance; it contains a wide array of nutrients, antioxidants and fibre. Hemp has been long overlooked as a superfood for its misunderstood association with marijuana. Hemp seeds will not get you high, as they do not contain THC.

Proteins serve a variety of functions in the human body. The main function of dietary protein is to supply amino acids for the growth and maintenance of body tissue. Digestion disassembles proteins into their basic building blocks -- the amino acids. Hemp protein contains all 20 known amino acids including the nine essential amino acids (EAAs) our bodies cannot produce.

Proteins are considered complete when they contain all nine essential amino acids in a sufficient quantity and ratio to meet the body's needs. Hemp seeds contain an adequate supply of these high quality proteins encouraging a well-balanced diet. Hemp protein is free of the trypsin inhibitors that block protein absorption and free of oligosaccharides, which cause stomach upset and gas.

Approximately 65 per cent of the protein in hempseeds is made up of the globulin protein edestin and is found only in hemp seed. Edestin aids digestion, is relatively phosphorus-free and considered the backbone of the cell's DNA. The other one third of hemp seed protein is albumin, another high quality globulin protein similar to that found in egg whites.

The globulin known as edestin, contained in hemp seed, closely resembles the globulin in blood plasma and is compatible with the human digestive system. It is vital to the maintenance of a healthy immune system and is also used to manufacture antibodies.

Other health benefits of hemp include:

- A 1.5-tablespoon serving of hemp seeds contains five grams of protein, 86 milligrams of magnesium, 10 per cent daily value of iron, 1245 milligrams of Omega-3 fatty acids and 436 milligrams of Omega-6 fatty acids!
- One of the Omega-6 acids, gamma linolenic acid (GLA), is an excellent source of anti-inflammatory hormone balancing agents that also supports a healthy metabolism and good skin, hair and nails.
- Like flaxseeds, hemp seeds contain all ten of the essential amino acids.
- Its protein source is much more digestible than others and won't leave you feeling bloated.
- Hemp seeds contain anti-aging antioxidants such as vitamin E.
- They're also rich in other minerals such as zinc and phosphorus.

Hempseed oil – The aliphatic alcohols contained in hempseed oil have also been known to lower cholesterol and reduce platelet aggregation. One of these alcohols, phytol, is associated with antioxidant and anticancer benefits and can also be found in healthy foods such as spinach, beans, raw vegetables and asparagus.

Another antioxidant in hempseed oil is tocopherol, which is known to be beneficial against degenerative diseases, such as atherosclerosis and Alzheimer's. Among other benefits, hempseed oil has also shown a positive effect on dermatological diseases and lipid metabolism (the process by which fatty acids are broken down in the body).

Hempseed oil also has high levels of vitamins A, C and E and β-carotene, and it is rich in minerals like phosphorus, potassium, magnesium, sulphur and calcium. As a food, hempseed oil is nutritious – it contains an excellent balance of polyunsaturated fatty acids

The power of raw seed sprouting

Sprouting raw nuts and seeds is not a something that is widely discussed or shared in today's modern world. Germinating raw nuts, seeds, grains and even beans is one of the most efficient ways to pack a diverse group of nutrients into your body in just one or two handfuls. The nutritional and living enzyme components found within raw, soaked seeds multiplies tenfold once you offer them life and hydration.

Soaking and rinsing seeds will remove the outer layer of enzyme inhibitors, allowing the seed to break down and begin the process of germination. The seeds then begin to break down all of the resting nutrition into its simplest components. The proteins break down into amino acids and the complex starches break down into simple carbs. The seeds' nutrient contents then start to multiply as it prepared to become a full size plant resulting in fibre rich food packed with vitamins, minerals alongside proteins and essential fatty acids

Germinated sprouts are an incredible source of nutrition, especially if you are vegetarian/vegan or if you are an athletic type who does vigorous, regular exercise. Remarkable levels of vitamin C, E, B and A have been identified within sprouted seeds. (Sprouts have up to twelve times the original/un-sprouted content). Many refer to sprouts as being 'pre-digested' due to the early life breaking down processes. This enables the sprouts to be easily absorbed with minimum energy input from the digestive system. The heightened quantity of enzymes is another factor that aids in their digestion. Sprouts can be eaten at any meal to help the digestive process along and keep raw living nutrition pumping through your blood.

The most practical and beneficial way to gain the super nutrients and goodness from these seeds is to get savvy and do it yourself at home. By doing it yourself the seeds lose no nutrition on their trip to the sprouting jar into the refrigerator but sprouts that are harvested and left at room temperature will dry up and lose their nutritional value within 1–2 hours. Sprouting is a very simple thing to do whilst being inexpensive, sprouts are an excellent addition in one's diet who is recovering or suffering from illness as they bring absolute life to the human organism.

You can find a range of sprouters (jar or tray) at: **www.ukjuicers.com** along with organic seeds with the most beneficial being (quoted from their website):

Alfalfa seeds – The ubiquitous alfalfa sprout is probably the easiest of all to grow. This ever popular, delicious salad sprout is very high in protein (40 per cent) and helps lower bad cholesterol. A good supplier of vitamin B complex, vitamins A,C,D,E and K, along with phosphorous, calcium, potassium, magnesium, iron, selenium and zinc.

Broccoli seeds – Broccoli sprouts are absolutely delicious and are believed to have even more potent anti-cancer properties than the fully grown vegetable. Also a great immune booster, broccoli sprouts contain high levels of vitamins, A, C, B and E, potassium and calcium.

Lentil seeds – Lentil sprouts are very high in protein (25 per cent) and mineral salts (Ca, Fe, Mg, K, Se, Zn and Na). Prized for both their high nutritional value and excellent flavour, these sprouts are excellent in soups and salads.

Sunflower seeds --Sunflower greens are renowned for being delicious in taste. They are high in protein and natural sugars and help maintain a healthy nervous system. The Sprouts are rich in Vitamin B-Complex, A, E, C & D, as well as Calcium, Iron, Phosphorous, Potassium, Magnesium and Selenium.

Living enzymes, the fountain of vibrant life

Enzymes are the sparks of life that spark the fires within your digestive system. They keep you alive whilst ones enzyme activity is an accurate way to measure the life force of the individual. Humans are alive due to the thousands of enzymes that work towards regulating the overall life processes. Enzymes are the physical agents of life holding essential roles in digestion, detoxification from internal/external pollution and for immune system, metabolic and regenerative processes.

It is known that cooking or boiling food anywhere above 42 degrees Celsius for half an hour or more will destroy 100 per cent of the plant enzymes. In other words, any type of cooking, boiling, baking, canning, food irradiation, frying and microwave cooking kills enzymes. Even boiling food for three minutes will take away a large percentage of the enzymes' vital force. Enzyme levels are indicative of your state of health and there is enough research backing to say that one's enzyme reserve is a direct link to longevity and vitality.

Enzymes are known to contain two key concepts:

(1) Enzymes are living, biochemical factors that activate and carry out the biological processes in the body. This includes all digestive activities, detoxification on physical levels, nerve impulses, healing the body and the functioning of RNA/DNA.
(2) The capacity of an organism to make enzymes is exhaustible. Therefore on the biological level, how enzyme resources are utilised and replenished will be a measure of your overall health, longevity and energetic vibration.

When you make the conscious decision to consume more plant based, nutrient dense foods (which are filled with *prana* life force energy derived straight from nature) you then begin to maintain continuous exogenous enzyme structure within your body. This ultimately means there will be a decrease in the endogenous (produced within or caused by factors within the organism) enzyme structure. You can go ahead and research the scientific studies online. They all suggest that excess enzymes released from enzyme-rich, living foods are absorbed into the body, therefore increasing your systemic energy flow and allowing you to experience higher states of health, happiness and well-being.

It is medically observed that in the most degenerative diseases and bodily functions there is an underlying factor directly connected to the body being nutritionally depleted and enzyme-exhausted, leading to an incomplete metabolism. The more workable and energised enzyme systems you maintain, the more opportunities are open for you to receive energisation and rejuvenation. All undigested food within the body must be eliminated as toxins or to prevent a build-up of acidosis. Consuming dead foods slowly depletes the enzyme energy within the body as all of the life force is used for digestion purposes and eliminating waste. A direct link can be drawn, therefore, between the number of people falling sick and the number of people consuming contaminated, dead foods.

If you pay conscious attention, remaining aware to what you are consuming and start to replenish lost enzymes, nutrients and minerals through utilising the information presented in this book, then you will definitely experience healthier states of biological functioning. This, in turn, will reverse and minimise the aging process as you now have an abundance of living enzymes that are more available to enhance other bodily processes. You will also feel more content within yourself.

Consuming foods and using herbs that are still fresh and full of the *prana* life-force is one of the best ways to enhance your body's enzyme reserve. Doing so diminishes the physiological ageing process and maximising the rejuvenation process. 95 per cent of foods that take up the supermarket shelves are void of enzymes, in other words contain no 'plant life force'. Every time you have a burger, bun, pizza, fast-food meal or anything else that comes in a packet, tin or can, your body has to dip into its own enzyme resources to make up for the shortfall.

Enzymes are lost through stress, alcohol and processed foods. You can't get them back from Diet Coke, hot dogs or coffee. You can only replace them with raw, whole foods, including juices.

Other Important bodily factors enzymes assist with:

- They increase your general energy level and vitality
- They aid in detoxifying the body
- They are catalyses that make digestion and all metabolic processes work
- They are living proteins that direct the life-force into our basic biochemical and metabolic process
- They repair your DNA/RNA
- They transform and store vital life force/Chi energy within the cellular structure and energetic counterpart of the physical body
- They make encourage active hormone production
- They balance and enhance many aspects of our immune system by decreasing and minimising the immune-mediated inflammation of joints
- They prevent blood clots and almost all vascular disease
- They have anti-inflammatory and analgesic effect and so decrease pain

Enzymes are substances that make life possible. They are needed for every chemical reaction that takes place in the human body. No mineral, vitamin, or hormone can do any work without enzymes. Our bodies, all our organs, tissues and cells are run by metabolic enzymes.'-Dr. Edward Howell[63], 'Enzyme Nutrition'

YUSA Juicing for Detoxification & Regeneration

Raw, living foods pack tremendous power. Undoubtedly, there is far too much pain, far too much suffering, far too much stiffness and far too many issues that people are experiencing within society. It is not too difficult to eliminate the better part of those once you gain a little bit of understanding, knowledge and a small amount of gentle, loving discipline. YUSA aims to encourage you to make positive choices that will allow you to thrive in life.

Your body naturally detoxifies everyday as part of a normal body process. Detoxification is one of the body's most basic automatic functions of eliminating and neutralising toxins through the colon, liver, kidneys, lungs, lymph and skin.

Regular juicing is transformational, especially in the spring/summer as these periods are really good for obtaining the highly mineralised fruit and vegetables that are brilliant for cleansing, flushing, healing and regenerating the body. Pain, stiffness, lymphatic blockages, headaches, problems in the colon and problems with the skin can start to be released and cleared up with ease.

The good news is that it is absolutely possible for you to be emotionally free, mentally clear, physically energetic and spiritually connected. Start walking along the path of consuming these living foods and detoxifying the old waste debris that lays stagnant in the body. The knowledge and importance of consuming raw living foods has escaped the vast majority of human beings and if you do not look after your own body, you will indeed have nowhere to live.

'I know that if I do not drink a sufficient quantity of fresh raw vegetable juices every day then, as likely as not, my full quota of nourishment enzymes is missing from my body' ~ Dr. Norman Walker[64]

It is important to note that what you eat, alongside your emotional and mental state, has absolute dominion over the flow of the divine knowing within every human being. The aim is to clear out anything that is in the way of the divine life force flow. It is important to incorporate all aspects: physical, emotional, mental and spiritual, in order to live an abundant life that is divine whilst here on Earth.

Even when the going gets tough, you're doing it right, things are happening and you have the universe at your back. The pendulum is going to keep swinging, so do not stop! the more intent you are on your growth, the more negatives and mental programs which are buried deep inside of you will rise to the surface and you will have remain strong in dealing with them. You will have to work your way out of the attachment to the things that make you and many others comfortably miserable. It will take a lot of honesty, deep integrity and humility. It will be worth it in the long run and will provide you with the ability to be yourself and authentic.

When you start to detoxify your body, you will experience tiredness and mood swings as the toxicity gets eliminated. Some days you are up, some days you are down. The only way to get through these periods is to have lots of rest and embrace the moment, embracing the now and acceptance in the times of change and detoxification is highly rewarding as it allows there to be less friction in the process. When you start resisting and saying to yourself 'things should be different than what they are', then you are telling the whole universe no and you cannot tell the universe no without hitting a brick wall.

Allow the universe, the conditions, the environment, your thoughts, your heart and your emotions simply be and it is promised that all will come well in your phase of transformation. Everybody wants to feel their own self-worth, their own value and can only do so if the work is put in separate to any externals. There is only one person that can do this and that is you. Get on the raw foods, get on the juices, keep cleansing and keep going. There is always light at the end of every tunnel. Remember, it is all about the minerals, the enzymes and nutrients that create the conductivity within the organs, glands and tissues.

Nutritionally developing the brain, endocrine and nervous system is the key for to you becoming a superconductor of the divine energies that allow you to embrace pure radiance and be used by the universe, so you can lead a very fulfilling life alongside assisting others on their journey in the most powerful and positive way possible. This information and practice methodologies are such an important spokes on the wheel of growth, but is overlooked because junk food like pizza tastes so good. YUSA is not 'anti' any foods but it is pro living, raw fruits, vegetables, herbs, nuts and seeds!

Consuming raw foods and juicing is important for anybody who wants to improve their life. As mentioned, you may have to go through some rough times at first because people are just so clogged up. But, when you get clean and can just have a jar of juice and your body really can harness every bit of it and provide energy that lasts all day long, you have done it. At this stage, mental clarity arises, emotional well-being comes forth and conductivity awakens cellular functioning. No longer can those old stagnant ways of being stick around.

Have the courage to move through what you're afraid to face. Too many people get stuck and remain stuck for their entire lifetime -- if not lifetime after lifetime. Pain is fear leaving the body; don't try to suppress your feelings with alcohol, drugs or junk food. Become a master of being with what is. The life of happiness, peace, joy and bliss is yours for the taking; it all starts with self-love. This is mandatory for growth and for truly loving others. Loving others is actually loving yourself, as others are you. It is a high spiritual understanding: everything is interconnected and nothing is separated.

Juicing is a powerful way to increase the energy, synergy and flow of life, therefore enabling you to have more energy for breathing, talking, exercising and digesting. Extracting the fibres, sugars and minerals from the fresh living fruit and vegetables is delivering pure electricity right into the bloodstream and the brain. Junk, debris, colourings, additives, preservatives can no longer stick to the cell membranes and the lymphatic system slowing down the systemic synergy flow alongside the abundant flow of information and knowledge.

Juice as medicine

You may have heard the quote 'let food be thy medicine' from Hippocrates (also known as 'the father of medicine'). We doubt that Hippocrates was referring to burgers, fries, pizzas and so forth. Only the juices of natural, life-force-producing foods act as medicine for the body.

The freshly extracted juices from organically grown fruits and vegetables have been widely used in the treatment and prevention of just about every disease known to man. A medical doctor named Max Gerson[65] put 50 of his cancer patients through a juice therapy regime and all of them showed great progress in recovery and many were healed.

This is not to say that juicing can definitely cure cancer, as everybody is different, but Gerson's juice experiment had extremely remarkable results. He wasn't the first person to use freshly extracted juices to feed life force back into the cells in order to treat and prevent disease. It is recommended that anybody suffering from disease check out Gerson's book, *A Cancer Therapy: Results of Fifty Cases*.

There is nothing more therapeutic than the healing and health benefits of juicing. All life on Earth emanates from the green (chlorophyll) of the plant. Having a couple of glasses of freshly extracted juice daily is one of the most powerful ways of preventing and treating disease, as well as clearing out junk from the internal system. The best way to fight cancer and any other disease is not to poison the body and weaken it further but to feed it the right nutrients.

It is clear that there are millions of different factors that contribute to disease and there is no question that, in many cases, medical intervention and treatments can play beneficial roles to ease suffering. Often, though, relief is temporary. However, it needs to be made crystal clear that the life giving juice that is trapped within the fibres of nature's finest foods is what the body craves for optimum well-being. It is illegal to advertise the fact that any foods can help with disease. A conspiracy theorist may say that the pharmaceutical companies and the government have some kind of vested interest in giving the impression that nature's foods cannot heal or prevent disease, making people think that drugs are the only way. But, this is not true.

Never underestimate the healing power of nature. Once you start to remove the GMO poisons and chemically laden foods out of your diet, your hair will start to shine, your eyes start to sparkle, your skin begins to glow, and your energy heightens. If you need to lose weight it just falls off as all the toxicity is eliminated. If you were to put yourself on a plan of consuming only freshly extracted vegetable and fruit juices, you would lose around 1–2Lbs of weight every 2–3 weeks. This is known as fasting but more about that later.

A fast is where no food at all is consumed. The juices contained within the fibres of the raw fruits and vegetables is a meal in itself due to the high nutritional and mineral content, liquid food that flows through the body and feeds the cells with incredible ease. Freshly extracted juice can be called liquid gold for the body and mind and you can feel the living goodness nourish your body within minutes of consuming, it is important to note that the juices you will make at home is in a completely different league to the bottled, canned and cartoned versions you find in shops that have no enzymes whatsoever.

Remember that humans are a part of nature and nature is always there for you, as mentioned; humans are sick because they have lost the connection with the Mother. Things must be brought back into balance. There is a very interesting and inspiring documentary that you can watch online so you can witness the ultimate power of nature's juices as a methodology for healing called: *Fat, Sick and Nearly Dead* by **Joe Cross**. It can be found on YouTube or his website: **www.fatsickandnearlydead.com**

'100 pounds overweight, loaded up on steroids and suffering from a debilitating autoimmune disease, Joe Cross is at the end of his rope and the end of his hope. In the mirror he saw a 310lb man whose gut was bigger than a beach ball and a path laid out before him that wouldn't end well— with one foot already in the grave, the other wasn't far behind. Fat, Sick and Nearly Dead *is an inspiring film that chronicles Joe's personal mission to regain his health.*

With doctors and conventional medicines unable to help long- term, Joe turns to the only option left, the body's ability to heal itself. He trades in the junk food and hits the road with juicer and generator in tow, vowing only to drink fresh fruit and vegetable juice for the next 60 days. Across 3,000 miles Joe has one goal in mind: To get off his pills and achieve a balanced lifestyle.

While talking to more than 500 Americans about food, health and longevity, it's at a truck stop in Arizona where Joe meets a truck driver who suffers from the same rare condition. Phil Staples is morbidly obese weighing in at 429 lbs; a cheeseburger away from a heart-attack. As Joe is recovering his health, Phil begins his own epic journey to get well.

What emerges is nothing short of amazing – an inspiring tale of healing and human connection.

Part road trip, part self-help manifesto, Fat, Sick and Nearly Dead defies the traditional documentary format to present an unconventional and uplifting story of two men from different worlds who each realize that the only person who can save them is themselves'.

Raw energy, chlorophyll and digestion

Although fruit and vegetables hold great healing power, you cannot beat the power of raw nutrition in the form of a liquid. As mentioned previously, once you start to apply heat to vegetables the enzyme life content is immediately destroyed.

Upon consuming the machine extracted juice you can be absolutely sure that every single drop of life force reaches parts of the body that the vegetables you eat cannot. This is not to say stop eating slightly cooked/steamed vegetables altogether; the fibre is brilliant for the system. It just means that the raw juices (preferably green) also need to be included to optimise your well-being.

Green vegetables contain a substance called chlorophyll, also known as 'concentrated sunshine', this is sunlight energy trapped within the fibres of the plant. This concentrated sunshine is extremely beneficial for your body and is able to improve the functioning of the heart, liver. It cleans the intestines, improves oxygen flow and cardiovascular health, alkalises the body, helps strengthen the immune system and is able to reduce blood pressure. Chlorophyll is vital and will assist you on your path of spiritual growth.

One of the most energy-consuming processes that the human body undertakes is the elimination, assimilation and digestion of foods and it can be especially energy consuming if you are eating the wrong kind of foods, which are dead, have little to no nutritional value and have no living enzyme contents. You may have experienced feeling very tired and just want to go to sleep after eating a large meal that consisted mainly of cooked and processed foods.

The body cannot provide enough systemic energy to keep you awake and digest food at the same time! In order for the body to turn a heap of semi-dead foods into some sort of useable body fuel, it needs to shut down other areas. Usually, eyesight, hearing and consciousness are the first senses to go. The process of dead food digestion, elimination and assimilation can take hours, days, weeks and even months! Leaving behind dehydrated metabolic waste residue that over time covers the cell membrane in mucous and slows down bodily functioning ultimately leading to disease and the need for serious detoxification.

You have over 30 feet of intestinal tract. It was designed to digest and extract enzymes, minerals and nutrition from natural foods rich in hydration. There are many pockets and twists within the intestines and that is where you will find some of the undigested foods that were eaten days, months and even years ago. Consuming denatured foods on a daily basis is very taxing on the body and bits of food are often left undigested in the colon. Many people have clogged their systems so much that they have a build-up of waste matter that has gradually hardened and reduced the 6–7cm wide tunnel to one as narrow as a few millimetres.

This contributes as a major foundation for disease for so many people, a clogged up, backed up system. Just as you would ensure the best fuels go into your car and a regular service is carried out to maintain the internal pipework. The same care and attention needs to be given to your body. Many are suffering with different ailments and diseases for which they then go and run to a doctor for help, only treating the surface problem leaving the underlying issue unattended to.

Minerals and enzymes are the building blocks to life, which nourish the body at a cellular level. If the system and the body's own 'juice extractor' is clogged up with metabolic waste, it can no longer be as effective compared to if it were clean. Backed up pipework within the body makes it 100 times harder for the living components within eaten foods to be absorbed. This is why consuming raw fruit and vegetable juices is so beneficial: you have effectively already done the body's digestion work and provided the cells with the raw living enzymes that are vital for you to thrive and survive.

A regular flow of juice will start to break down and remove the metabolic, cement-like waste that clogs your digestive system, allowing the life giving substances to be readily absorbed and physical regeneration to take place. A clogged-up body cannot absorb nutrients, which tends to lead to illness. All people are in need of is a good detox. You cannot have a body full of dirt and debris without it affecting your mind: the bacteria within the intestinal tract are closely related to depression and emotional balance.

Life is about having the physical and mental vibrancy to tackle any of life's challenges with greater ease, waking up in the mornings and actually feeling awake! This can only be achieved through having a clean system that is able to absorb the nutritious building blocks of life that not only feed your body but also enhance your consciousness and awareness.

'If you put juice in your body today, you'll have a much better tomorrow.' ~
Jack LaLanne

Motivation for change

There is nothing stopping anyone from getting the body and energy levels they desire apart from excuses and limited belief systems. But, in reality, there is nothing stopping you from taking the steps necessary. Sadly, fear will cause many people will come up with a million excuses as to why they cannot do it at the time.

Many others say 'I would do, but I don't have the time', but these are the people who are able to tell you absolutely everything about 'Coronation Street', 'Emmerdale' and 'Big Brother'. They have the time to watch TV but don't have the time to exercise or prepare a few apples.

You must ask yourself just how important you regard your health and well-being and where it fits into your priorities of life. Health and fitness should be at the top of your list as health is wealth. Too many people look to externals to get ahead in life, not understanding that you attract circumstances that match your energetic vibration. It is important to start from within and clean-up your physical and energetic body in order to achieve success, well-being and happiness.

When health is concerned, you cannot afford not to put the work in. What price would you put on your heart or liver? Or even your life? There is no price that can be attached and money means nothing compared with your health. Your number one priority should be to ensure there is a quality flow of 'live' nutrients throughout your body on a daily basis regardless of cost. If you put the self-work in that is presented in this book you can quite easily attract and manifest the resources that are beneficial to your well-being. Remember that your natural soul state is abundant in nature.

Despite what you may think, it doesn't cost any more to be healthy than it does to be sick. You can support your local farmers and nourish your body with the foods nature left for you to enjoy or eat chemical-laden, fake foods produced by biotech companies. The choice is yours.

The same people who say they cannot afford to eat well are the ones who seem to find money for cigarettes, alcohol and junk food. The average drinker will spend around £80,000 on alcohol in their lifetime and an average 20-a-day cigarette smoker will spend around £50,000. Despite what the population has been conditioned to believe, the average person does not require a large quantity of food to thrive. Too many people are overeating because their bodies are laden with parasites, suffering from malnutrition and false hunger.

When you decide to burden your system with copious amounts of junk food, your body will be working hard to extract what it can in order to survive. This is extremely hard for the body if the foods are low in enzymes and minerals and is only a matter of time until the body cries out for more. When you start feeding your body with live nutrients it craves, you will find that you are satisfied even though you have eaten much less.

Without the correct nutrition and a good supply of oxygen, you cannot perform at your best within or without. Many people in today's world are money rich and health poor, what's the point of earning all that money if it gives you a heart attack in the process? It is understandable that obtaining free time for many is becoming harder but, realistically, how long does it take to prepare a fresh juice, blend a smoothie, peel a banana or prepare some veggies?. How much time does it take to go for a walk, run, lift some weights, or jump on a rebounder?

Juicing recipes and top juicers

There are hundreds of juicers on the market but only a few of them are worth the price you pay. There are a range of different types of juicers but the two most common juicers are known as 'centrifugal' and 'masticating'. The juicers and blender listed can be found online.

Centrifugal juicer – If you are on a budget and/or just wanting to give juicing a shot without making a larger financial commitment. A centrifugal juicer can save you a lot of time when it comes to the preparation and juicing of your fruit and vegetables. It can also save money. If a centrifugal juicer is what you can afford, then it is going to be a much better choice than not buying a juicer at all.

'Breville JE98XL Juice Fountain Plus 850-Watt Juice Extractor' is the juicer that Joe Cross used in the documentary *Fat, Sick and Nearly Dead*. The Breville JE98XL Juice Fountain Plus 850-Watt Juice Extractor is also more affordable than other higher-priced juicers and gets the job done! Many people use this juicer and are very happy with it.

Masticating juicer – Masticating juicers use a single gear or auger to literally chew up the fibre of fruit and vegetables. The cell walls of the fruits or vegetables are broken down through a grinding motion. The juice is then squeezed and separated from the pulp by crushing the produce against a screen. The leftover pulp and the juice come out of the juicer through separate exits and can both be collected by containers or whatever means you wish to use.

The **'Omega 8006 Nutrition Centre Masticating Juicer'**'s what is recommended if you want to spend that extra money and are serious about juicing. The quality of the juice is much higher compared to a centrifugal, they do not heat up half as much and you will be getting more out of your fruit and vegetables over time. This type of juicer is brilliant for juicing wheatgrass and fine herbs. The downside to this juicer is that it may make a little longer to complete the juicing process and you may have to cut the fruit and vegetables up.

Blending

Unlike juices, smoothies consist of the entire fruit or vegetable, skin and all and contain all of the fibre from the vegetables. However, the blending process breaks the fibre apart (which makes the fruit and vegetables easier to digest) but also helps create a slow, even release of nutrients into the blood stream and avoids blood sugar spikes. Smoothies tend to be more filling, because of the fibre and generally faster to make than juice, so they can be great to drink first thing in the morning as your breakfast, or for snacks throughout the day. The recommended blender is the **'Hi-Blend Multi Speed Super Blender';** it is absolutely brilliant for producing a balanced mix of all ingredients especially superfood powders, nuts and seeds.

Juicing recipes

Below are the most potent juice recipes and smoothies that you can put together yourself in the kitchen. It is recommended and quite important that you purchase the fresh fruits and vegetables from a local supplier or farmers market for the highest quality juices.

Lemon coffee alternative

- 6 lemons
- 3 limes (optional)
- 1 thumb of ginger
- 2 Thumbs of turmeric

Peel half the rind of each one of the lemons and limes and juice them alongside the thumb size piece of ginger and turmeric. The science of ginger for cancer is now rapidly advancing. Lab studies confirm the potent activity against multiple cancers including lung, pancreatic, colon, breast cancer and leukaemia. Store the juices in a jar and keep in the refrigerator. This light potent mixture helps to flush the system of impurities and tighten the cells while supplying the body with essential nutrients. Add the mixture to a litre bottle of water and shake to your desired strength. For added power, add some cayenne pepper for a stronger detox.

Citrus Punch

-   6 oranges (peeled)
-   4 carrots
-   2 grapefruits (peeled)
-   1 lemon
-   Mint leaves (optional)

This juice is packed with beta carotene, which helps mop up the harmful free radicals within the body and strengthens the immune system. Oranges are rich in vitamin C, folic acid and hold an array of minerals such as potassium, which are depleted by excessive alcohol consumption. The healthy bacteria in the fruits help replenish healthy bacteria in the gut, eradicating nausea and an upset stomach. Natural sugars assist in raising the depleted blood sugars and rehydrating the system. This juice is brilliant for weight loss because the mint works towards eliminating toxins from the fatty tissues.

Beetroot Booster

-   4 raw beets(washed)
-   1 full head of celery
-   1 lemon
-   1 thumb of ginger
-   4 apples
-   1/2 bunch of parsley
-   2 inches of broccoli stem

Parsley is one of nature's finest super herbs. It expels worms, relieves gas, freshens breath, stimulates the digestive system, assists kidneys, liver, lungs, stomach and thyroid function. Celery assists with flushing the body of excessive carbon dioxide and reduces any acidity in the system. Beetroot is amazing at cleaning the bloodstream and works well with lemon at cleaning the kidneys and liver.

Lemon Ginger Blast

-   1 thumb of Ginger & 1 lemon
-   1 fennel bulb
-   Kale leaves
-   1 whole, peeled cucumber
-   1/2 bunch of parsley
-   4 apples

- 1 full head of celery
- 1 TSP Spirulina/Green Vibrance powder

This juice works wonders for general detoxification and fighting disease. It is amazing at removing heavy metals that are clogging the bloodstream and nervous system. The magnesium in the leafy green vegetables helps with hyperglycaemia and blood circulation. The enormous quantity of anti-oxidants and minerals will help build your natural defences whilst the Green Vibrance and Spirulina deliver super powerful amounts of chlorophyll and amino acids.

Superfood smoothies

The following smoothie recipes are not for the faint hearted! These smoothies consist of the most potent superfoods on the planet and should be implemented into your daily lifestyle slowly and carefully. The following recipes are brilliant for anybody who is in ill health, needs energy, feels depressed. It is also good for the athletic type who want a complete source of protein and amino acids.

Mood-enhancing, mineralising protein shake

- 1 TBS Maca powder
- 1 TBS Macuna powder
- 1 TBS cacao powder
- 1 TSP coconut oil
- 1 TSP Green Vibrance/Spirulina powder
- 750ML almond milk/coconut water/filtered water
- 1 TBS walnuts (optional)
- 1 TBS sunflower seeds (optional)
- 1 TBS pea/brown rice protein powder
- organic blueberries & 2 bananas

Blueberries contain some of nature's most powerful antioxidants and anti-ageing phytonutrients. Coconut oil, Maca, Macuna, cacao and Spirulina powders have their numerous benefits as already listed. Walnuts and sunflower seeds deliver complete proteins and essential fats that feed the brain, glands and nervous system. Pea/brown rice protein is an organic, non-GMO protein source that works very well with almond milk or coconut water. This is an excellent mix for assisting with depression, mineral deficiencies, and illness alongside gaining clean, lean muscle mass.

Gorilla Milk

To juice:

- 1 bunch of kale
- 1 peeled, whole cucumber
- 1 bunch of parsley
- 1 bunch of cilantro
- 1 apple
- 1 full head of celery
- 1 TSP Spirulina/ Green Vibrance powder (optional)
- 1 lemon

To Blend:

- 3 handfuls of soaked almonds (soak in water for 24 hours prior)
- 3 large pieces of coconut meat from 1–2 coconuts
- Few dashes of Himalayan salt
- 750ML of coconut water/ filtered water
- 1 TBS Maca powder

This gorilla milk recipe consists of two parts, one part juiced and one part blended. This mixture is high in vibration and is excellent for regeneration of the body from the cellular level all the way up to muscle and strength building.

Once you have blended the ingredients, make sure to filter the mixture as the almonds can leave behind lumpy bits, you should then be left with smooth, super powered milk. Add the juiced mixture into the blender with the filtered milk and mix for 60 seconds. (You can also choose your own ratios and pour into a glass by hand)

The juiced ingredients are now combined with the almond and coconut milk. Drink as much as you like; doing so will supercharge the body, heal tissues and greatly assist in detoxifying harmful toxins and disease. You can also fast on gorilla milk if you are a first timer as it is so packed with goodness it does not starve the body.

This drink most definitely accelerates the healing and regeneration processes of the body. Drinking this on a regular basis will replenish the enzymes and minerals that are needed for your optimum health and well-being.

Intestinal and colon cleanse

- 1 TBS bentonite clay
- 1 TSP psyllium husk
- 500 ML water

This simple combination is a great detoxification drink that will clean up the intestinal tract and colon. Simply add 1 tablespoon of Psyllium husk flakes and 1 teaspoon of bentonite clay into the blender with some water, blend and drink as fast as possible as the clay will start to expand once it comes into contact with moisture.

This drink is best consumed on an empty stomach so it can get to work absorbing the toxins, heavy metals and free radicals and eliminate them from your system. Drink one large glass in the morning and one large glass before bed; it works well alongside juice fasting and detoxing.

The six liquids of vitality

Vitality is important as vitality makes everything better in life. If you have vitality in anything you do, it means that there is a lot of forward motion at work. The liquids below are super-hydrating fluids and they are all made with water as the main base. You can head over to: **www.earthshiftproject.com** for more information, quality ingredients and steps. **The liquids of vitality are as follows:**

1. Standard, alkalised filtered high PH water – Alkalises and neutralises accumulated acids within the body.
2. Blue-green algae violet prism water – Superfood packed with minerals, vitamins and monoamine oxidase inhibitors that feed the brain.
3. Burgundy hibiscus water – Diuretic that promotes detox and the production of urine alongside strong immune system.
4. Cayenne lemon water – Super fat dissolvent and detoxifier. Recipe previously mentioned.
5. Kombucha – Ancient Chinese solution bursting with enzymes, hyaluronic and glucuronic acid, which are vital for regeneration
6. Fulvic acid plant mineral complex liquid – Remineralisation drink that eats up junk, containing Fulvic and humic acid

Liver and kidney detox

A large percentage of the 'stuff' many people are eating is not exactly pure. As mentioned previously, plants are sprayed with chemicals, animals are injected with hormones and antibiotics, whilst genetically modified foods are on the rise. This means that there are a variety of toxins entering the body that are potentially destroying tissues and harming cells.

The liver and kidneys perform a huge role in the body and are mainly responsible for the filtering and elimination of the toxic chemicals that are consumed on a daily basis within the foods many people assume to be safe and normal to eat. Rows of liver cells are separated by space acting like a sieve, which is where the blood flows. This sieve can be compared to a customs agent finding out what illegal goods are being brought across the border, removing toxic substances from the bloodstream.

There are special cells that keep guard, known as 'Kupffer cells'. These are the guardians which eat up and break down toxins, chemicals and microorganisms that are not supposed to be passing through. Kupffer cells disarm the toxins by converting a dangerous chemical to a less harmful one or by packaging them for easier disposal through your bile or urine.

The liver is the largest organ in the body second to the skin and performs over 500 different functions, a lot more than any other organ in the body. It is extremely hard to recover from illness without a strong, healthy functioning liver. If the liver is unable to carry out its basic functions it will become clogged, weak and congested therefore having a negative impact on the other organs.

Preparation

It is recommended that you repeat the cleanse every 6–8 weeks, as it is believed that you may have to release up to 2,000 stones to eliminate any allergies that are related to liver congestion. The cleanse is most effective if you eat an alkaline, natural diet low in fats for at least 3–5 days before the flush and you may also want to drink lots of apple juice daily for seven days prior in order to soften the stones that are stored in the kidneys.

Ingredients

- 4 TBS Epsom salts (magnesium sulphate)
- Organic olive oil (125 ML/ half a cup
- 6 lemons (juiced)
- 1 litre bottle/jar
- Freshly squeezed apple juice for the morning after (6–8 apples juiced)
- 2 Niacin pills (vitamin B3)

Instructions

Choose two days where you are not busy so you can get plenty of rest the day after. Make sure you take no medicines, pills or vitamins that you can do without and eat a light breakfast that does not consist of fat preferably just fruits up to 2:00 P<M.

Starting at 2:00 PM in the afternoon – Do not eat or drink after 2:00 PM. If you break this rule you could feel quite ill later. Prepare your Epsom salts.

Mix four TBS of Epsom salt with three cups / 750 ML of water and pour this into a container or jar. This makes four servings, ¾ cup (185 ml) each. Leave the jar in the refrigerator for later on. (You can also prepare the lemon and olive oil 9:45 PM drink beforehand).

It is recommended that you prepare the liquids at your last meal to prevent you from getting hungry in between 2:00 PM and 6:00 PM and giving into any temptation of eating.

6:00 PM – It is time to drink your first serving of Epsom salts and water. Drink 1/4 of the premixed solution (3/4 pint glass). It does not taste very nice, so you may want to hold your nose. Remember that if you need to go to the bathroom at any time it is okay!

If you did not prepare this ahead of time, mix 1 tbs. in ¾ cup water now. You may add 1/4 fresh squeezed lemon to improve the taste. You may also drink a few mouthfuls of water afterwards or rinse your mouth.

8:00 PM – Repeat by drinking your second 3/4 pint glass (185 ml) of Epsom salts and water. Get anything you need to do out of the way for that evening as the timing is critical for success.

9:45 PM – Pour 1/2 cup of olive oil into the pint jar or bottle. Juice 2 lemons through a juicer so the highest quality liquid is extracted, filter the pulp and add to the bottle of olive oil. Ensure there is ½ a cup of lemon if not simply juice more lemons. Close the jar or bottle and shake hard until watery. Don't drink it just yet. Swallow the two Niacin pills, they help to expand the bile duct.

10:00 PM –It is now time to drink the lemon and olive oil mixture. Drink it standing up and try to do so in 5–-15 minutes next to your bed so you can jump in straight after.

Time to lie down – The sooner you lie down after drinking the lemon and olive oil mix, the better the cleansing process will be. As soon as the drink is down walk to your bed and lie down on your right side with your knees pulled up close to your chest. Try to keep perfectly still for at least 20 minutes. You may feel a train of stones travelling along the bile ducts like marbles. There is no pain because the bile duct valves are open due to the Epsom salts. Try to go to sleep as soon as possible.

6:00 AM awakening – Set your alarm to wake at 6:00 AM and immediately drink the third dose of water mixed with Epsom salts. If you feel a bit nauseous, just wait a little while before drinking. Ensure you drink the salts between 6:00 AM and 7:00 AM; do not drink before 6:00 AM.

8:00 AM – (two hours later) drink your fourth (the last) dose of the Epsom salts and water and you may go back to bed again. Go to the bathroom when appropriate. After two hours from your fourth and final glass of Epsom salts, it is advised you drink the freshly squeezed apple juice as it will assist in dissolving the gallstones and is a nice transition back to normal eating. Fruit is then advised up to around 12 PM.

You will be able to see how well you did in accordance with your bowel movement. If you are doing this for the first time, expect a heavy flow of garbage and poisons to be released from the kidneys, liver, gall bladder and colon and expect to pass hundreds of cholesterol filled gallstones. This flush is absolutely safe and effective for detoxification of these major organs so they can process toxins and clean the blood in a more efficient manner.

Weight loss

The term 'weight loss' is one of the most widely searched terms punched into the Internet search engines today. There is so much error and misinformation surrounding weight loss and the information regarding exactly what excess body weight really is.

Many people tend to think that consuming the foods that are labelled 'low fat' is all that needs to be done to lose weight, but this is inaccurate as the majority of the foods available are full of chemicals that were designed to keep you from being able to say no to them. Alongside the harmful chemicals, there are the hormonal aspects that work on preventing the brain and stomach registering connection that lets you know when you are no longer hungry.

The engineered chemicals simply make you want to eat more and more and more! If you were to go from the standard cooked diet to eating more cooked, whole foods such as brown rice, vegetables and whole wheat bread, you may start to see some differences in weight over a long period of time, but nothing overly substantial.

The raw, living, hydrating foods are where you will find rapid, sustainable results. When you consume the living foods, with the living light and the living water, you can start to dissolve the accumulations of the cholesterol, the mucous, the saturated fats, the hydrogenated fats and the complex starchy, cooked, over processed carbohydrates that stick to your cells and stay there.

These fats will accumulate in the body and remain stagnant unless you do something about it and alkalise the body. Cellulite is a protecting agent made up of cholesterol and water that sticks to body tissues in order to protect your body by surrounding the foreign toxicity matter and chemicals, storing them so they cannot enter the bloodstream and cause huge problems.

So, each time you eat toxic foods, the storage areas get larger and larger as the toxicity builds up in the body, ultimately leading to weight gain. The underlying issue of toxicity needs to be addressed and eradicated if you want to see improvements in your physique. The immediate acidosis needs to be dealt with along with the immediate invaders. It is only logical that consuming the poisonous processed foods are a big *no* and all that is required is some simple hydration and bodily plumbing.

For the large food companies, making people addicted to their foods is a strict line of business. They have shareholders that need to be made happy at the end of the day, but the downside is that they are destroying people's lives and making many people unhappy with themselves. It is the same companies that make the natural cures and healthy alternatives discreet to the public eye and have more security at the food processing factories than Fort Knox does.

There are integrity foods and non-integrity foods. Consuming the non-integrity foods will ultimately damage the body, create toxicity and shut off the nervous system. It is a very subtle process and people need to wake up to these facts right now if they want the most out of life. The aim here is to encourage you and give you the foundational steps to detox and reach new levels of happiness through nourishing your body and feeling the best just as you deserve.

The most effective way of stripping the underlying toxicity from the cells is by consuming leafy green vegetables loaded with chlorophyll alongside the removal of such chemical laden foods by using the information at the start of this chapter and being more vigilant when out shopping. Juicing and juice fasting is the most effective way, combined with eating lots of fruit. This will not only flush the cells but energise them too. It is recommended you watch the 'Fat, Sick and Nearly Dead' documentary to see how powerful nature's foods really are at bringing back the balance and equanimity into the physical body.

Remember, alkalising the body delivers tremendous oxygen delivery so the body can start to breathe and function at its optimal levels. Out there in the weight loss world not many are actually thinking about the functionality of the trillions of cells that make up the body. You want every single cell in your body functioning at the highest rate possible for ultimate vibration and energy flow, detoxifying the junk will lead to the strengthening and protection of the body over some time.

A lack of education and the conditioning to eat junk by the food companies is leading to havoc in people's lives. Many are experiencing their thyroids shutting down, having their gall bladders and stomachs cut out: it is pure insanity. You do not have to be 100 per cent raw or take on any extreme diet plan that all the fake magazines are infiltrating your mind with but simply return to nature and start juicing! Get yourself a juicer, get yourself some fruit, make small steps and do your research. Get some fresh air, eliminate the poisons, mineralise, alkalise and nourish the body with living foods and you are on your way. If you don't have your health, you do not have anything because you cannot enjoy the life you were given.

Fasting for Physical, Emotional & Spiritual Well-Being

Fasting is the most powerful form of detoxification that can be practised. It cleans out and give birth to the regeneration of the physical body whilst purifying the mind and spirit. Fasting and dietary practices can be used as a model and a medium for enhanced awareness, consciousness alongside embracing a rising sensitivity to the light within.

Fasting is a period of abstinence from all foods where only fluids are consumed (in sufficient quantities) to cleanse the body and satisfy the physiologic requirements. When the body does not have to digest solid food, the energy is systematically focused towards cleansing itself of everything apart from the vital tissues. A person fasting even 30–40 days on water alone will not suffer a deficiency of minerals, vitamins fatty acids or protein as the body gathers all essential substances in an extraordinary manner upon the breakdown of unhealthy cells.

There is a fear for some people that strength will diminish from the catabolism of the muscle fibres, but starvation will occur only when the body is forced to use vital tissue to survive. Even during long fasts, the number of muscle fibres remains the same. Although the healthy cells may be reduced in size and strength for a time, they remain perfectly sound and are quickly replenished thereafter.

A well-nourished and healthy man can live up to 50–70 days without food if he is in the right surroundings where harsh elements and emotional stress cannot be a catalyst for disruption. Most people have sufficient fat reserves that are able to sustain them for many weeks but the major factor in regards to the healing principles of fasting is the resting phase.

Resting is understood to be a vital factor towards enhancing the recovery process when fasting, because the body is then able to direct most of its energy towards the mechanical and chemical processes of detoxification. The recovery rates from illness and bodily dysfunctions are swifter than normal upon fasting as the body is re-organising itself from the atomic level, working to rid the system of toxicity and excess waste matter and as the toxic load is reduced and eliminated, the functioning of every cell is enhanced.

During this deep and profound rest, toxin intake and production are reduced to a minimum while autolysins and elimination proceed unchecked. Anabolic processes such as tissue and bone healing also proceed at a maximal rate during the fast! It is great to include one bentonite and psyllium husk drink once a day whilst fasting for maximum detoxification and elimination.

There are many methods the body uses for the elimination of foreign substances and waste such as the liver, lungs, kidneys and colon etc. but when these become backed up and overloaded, the body then resorts to extra ordinary methods of elimination and ailments can start to manifest such as boils, mucous, sweats, vomiting, diarrhoea and other forms of illness and discharges. A toxic overload can build storage forms in the joints, vessels, muscles, organs and almost any tissue in the body.

The first stages of cleansing can be quite emotional and challenging, as large quantities of waste matter and digestive residues are stripped and removed from the body. You may feel quite ill due to the quantities of waste that are passing through the bloodstream, whilst the tongue becomes coated and foul-smelling as the body proceeds into hyper detoxification, pushing toxicity through every opening. Keep going, lie down, meditate, breathe deeply and relax. It only gets better.

After day three of fasting, there is little to no desire for food. It then becomes evident that it is only the mind that craves food as a form of contentment and temporary satisfaction. The second stage involves the cleansing of mucous, fat, diseased and dying cells and the more easily removable toxins. Your energy starts to heighten to the point where you do not even need much sleep and mental clarity starts to sharpen alongside a subtle sense of peace.

The final stage of liquid fasting involves the deep cleansing and removal of the toxins that have accumulated in your cellular tissue all the way from the day you were born alongside the cleansing of the microscopic tubes that carry vital elements to the brain. Cleansing of these last layers is possible through any combination of water fasting and juice fasting. Urine fasting is the most powerful. A raw, high mineralised diet and lifestyle also has similar effects to fasting but will take a longer period of time to match the magnificent healing results.

To summarise, during extended fasts the body is able to remove dead, dying and diseased cells, unwanted fatty tissues, trans-fatty acids, hardened coatings of mucous on the intestinal wall, toxins in the spleen, liver and kidneys, toxic waste matter in the lymphatic system and bloodstream, mucous from the lungs and sinuses, heavy metals, eradication of yeast, mould and fungus, removal of imbedded toxins within the cellular fibres and deeper organ tissues and waste deposits in the microscopic tubes responsible for nourishing brain cells.

A large percentage of the bodily anomalies mentioned above are responsible for a huge number of diseases and ailments. Many people run to the medical industry to get assistance with these issues, not treating the underlying issue but just temporarily masking it with other harmful chemicals and substances. To overcome a number of severe diseases, it is important to continue through a series of fasts, to the point where the full scouring action of catabolism removes the disease from the tissues.

So many people who have successfully completed a fast agree that they have way no hunger and much more energy than they would have normally. Once you experience this for yourself, it is indeed deeply liberating to find that if you surrender and have the faith in the process. It becomes the fastest and most simple process of discovering every human being has deep power and freedom to heal and take control of their own bodies

Emotional & spiritual benefits of fasting

When you pay attention to what you put into your mouth, it can lead to what's going on in your mind. Fasting allows the physical body to embrace the assimilation of *pranic* energy rather than the biochemical energy. Fasting and purifying the body allows you to become a better conductor of Kundalini energy and a vessel for your inner light to shine through.

Embracing the *pranic* energy improves the balance and alignment of the chakras and subtle energetic bodies. Through repeated fasts you will also become a clearer channel for the assimilation of the cosmic energy flow into your system, further increasing the sensitivities to the movement of Kundalini. The more you embrace these forces, the easier it will become to be motivated to continue to enhance personal development on many levels.

Many of these spiritual aspects of yourself that have been waiting for a long period of time will finally be able to shine through as the system detoxifies the junk and external programming which has been conditioned into the masses since birth. Fasting in a calm, serene and peaceful environment will allow you to express and deal with the new spiritual phenomena in a beneficial and positive way. As previously mentioned, meditation and relaxing with audios can also assist greatly.

Other fasting benefits

Another interesting phenomenon worth noting is that the years of taste bud and bodily conditioning, which have been made to tolerate the unhealthy processed foods, are reversed. You will feel satisfied with smaller amounts of food and be more sensitive to tiredness and sluggishness when you have overeaten. Going back to rich foods full of fat, processed sugars and salts will cause nausea, headaches and weakness to the body as the cells will be so clean they are very susceptible to any form of junk that should not be in the body.

After a fast, it is necessary in order to slowly and carefully return to a normal and natural eating pattern. You should take at least one week to gradually and carefully readjust your eating habits. The best way to end a fast is to stop drinking liquids at the end of the afternoon. After one hour, drink a glass of orange juice, lemon juice with water, grape juice or apple juice. The next day, drink another glass of fruit juice during lunch. From this time on, start eating juicy fruits.

After a fast, your body is clean, and has far less tolerance for the poisonous foods that you were used to eating previously. Feeling sick when eating poison is a sign that your body is functioning normally. Select your food carefully, even though it is not possible to avoid toxins completely. Fasting, as a regular cleansing routine, is important and will keep you vibrant. We recommend you do your research on fasting if you are in need of rejuvenation or in ill health.

- Mental clarity is greatly sharpened and enhanced whilst brain fog is lifted.
- Rapid and safe weight loss is achieved without leaving excess flabbiness.
- The nervous system is sharpened and brought back into a state of equanimity.
- Systemic energy levels and sensory perceptions are greatly increased. The longer the fast, the more energy and vitality you have.

- Organs and cellular biochemistry are revitalised and harmonised.
- The skin becomes hydrated and silky and there is a greater sense of movement within and without.
- The entire digestive system is rejuvenated and becomes more effective, and the peristaltic action of the intestines and natural bowel movements is stronger after fasting.
- Alkalisation, detoxification and regeneration are at peak levels, normal metabolic and cellular oxygenation are restored alongside the elimination of worries, stored up emotions and past energetic blockages.
- Consciousness and spiritual growth are triggered.

'In a fast, the body tears down its defective parts and then builds anew when eating is resumed.' ~ Herbert M. Shelton[66]

The ancient healing secret of urine therapy

This is a subject that is largely dismissed by so many in the Western world. If you were to mention it to somebody, you would most probably be labelled as insane, but your own urine has natural healing powers that can control and cure all kinds of diseases and imbalances. It is very effective healing modality and a powerful natural treatment.

Urine therapy is the ancient method of treatment that has been practised from generation to generation in small global communities who understand and accept the nature of the human body's recycling and regenerating mechanism.

This ancient methodology is an entirely drugless effective system that works towards healing all kinds of chronic diseases and maintains super vibrant health. Many people have a stigma attached to urine and are heavily conditioned to perceive it as being somewhat dirty and unclean. However this is untrue as fresh urine is actually more sterile than your own blood and holds high cleansing properties as long as you're eating a balanced natural diet and you are not consuming contaminated foods laden with chemical poisons.

You should do your own in-depth research on this subject as it will allow you to develop a positive attitude and realise the natural healing powers that lie within. A person who may be suffering from chronic disease and adopts urine therapy with positive and optimistic attitude will be able to realise and observe the benefits in their mental and physical health within a short period of around 4–9 days.

'Your medicine is in you and you do not observe it. Your ailment is from yourself but you do not register it.'~ Hazrat Ali

It is a fact that millions upon millions of people worldwide are suffering due to chronic illnesses, bodily disorders and innumerable diseases, leading many feeling helpless and dejected. The numbers of those falling victim to disease are rising every single year and it is mainly due to a lack of self-knowledge and ignorance to what foods they are consuming on a daily basis.

Nature has indeed provided humans with all natural amenities such as air, water, fruits, vegetables, sunlight, which are all essential for the body to thrive and survive. Every human being has also been provided with the 'divine nectar' known as urine, which flows from the body for preservations of health and to cure various diseases, just as milk from a mother's breast has been provided for the nourishment of an infant child. Recycling urine is the same methodology of composting your soils.

Urine therapy is an effective natural remedy with has no side effects. It has been known to prevent, cure and control all kinds of chronic diseases such as cancer, blood pressure, diabetes, kidney failure, arthritis, hair loss, psoriasis, mental and emotional imbalances, cerebral palsy and more.

Consuming clean urine alongside a diet rich in minerals and enzymes can boost the immune system, improve nervous disorders and dissolve deep rooted toxins from the body. Dead tissues can also be revived and the resistance power of vital organs such as the brain, pancreas, heart, lungs, intestines etc. can be enhanced greatly.

Urine is completely drug–free, purifying the blood as it contains the necessary compounds, vitamins, minerals, salts, hormones and chemical compounds, which are essential for growth and maintenance of the human body. The taste and colour is completely dependent on what you eat and drink, consuming a balanced light diet, keeping hydrated with lots of water and juices will ensure urine is passed that will contain large saturations of multiple vitamins.

Another great use for urine is treating insect and poisonous bites. Painful, burning tired eyes and cataracts can be relieved by dropping fresh urine into them. You can gargle fresh urine to relieve tooth aches and gum problems, it should be kept in the mouth for up to 30 minutes for maximum relief.

Toothaches disappear and teeth stay healthy as the urine is antifungal, anti-viral and anti-parasitic. The human kidneys are the best filtration system in the world; they micro filter all of the nutrients and minerals to be recycled into the body and rapidly absorbed into the cells. The kidneys generate chi (life force) energy, which is what makes the urine so powerful. You are literally drinking the purest life energy available.

If you want smooth, flawless skin and a healthy appearance, then massaging fresh urine daily onto your skin with a flannel every morning and evening is recommended. This is a secret that many use in the beauty industry. Most of the skin and beauty products on the shelves are made with urea! Urine is effective as an aftershave lotion for anybody who has sensitive skin and is a wonderful aid for baldness and hair loss. There are so many benefits for urine therapy there could be whole books written on the subject – and there are.

It is important to note that when practicing the more intensive form of urine therapy, you follow a diet low in protein and salt. Avoid processed foods such as sugar, white flour, canned foods and genetically modified foods. Dairy products and meat are not recommended as they produce a great deal of mucous within the body. Reduce the intake of caffeine, alcohol, tobacco and any other acidic forming agents. Urine will alkalise the whole body and bring organs, glands and the nervous system back into equanimity.

Urine therapy is the ancient method of treatment. The powerful practice for healing 'Self-Urine Therapy' has been referred in 'Shivambu Kalpa Vidhi', part of a 5,000-year old document called Damar Tantra linking this practice to Vedas, the sacred Hindu texts.

In Tantric yoga culture, this practice is termed as 'amroli.' Amroli comes from the root word 'amar.' They termed 'shivambu' as Holy Liquid. According to them, urine is more nutritious than even milk as you are not only physically benefited by the practice, but you become spiritually advanced because it is an elixir for body, mind and spirit.

'The cosmic soul knows its need and takes to itself that which belongs to it. Auto Urine is Divine Nectar' – **Lord Shiva**

Practical steps to the practice of urine therapy

Urine consists of 95 per cent of water, 2.5 per cent of urea and the remaining 2.5 per cent is a mixture of minerals, salts, hormones and enzymes. The theory of transmutation implies that the body is capable, through energetic exchange within, to transmute certain substances or molecules into other ones.

Short-circuiting the system by ingesting one's own secreted body fluids may stimulate the trans-mutational forces within and challenge the body to transform unusable substances into usable ones without being constantly disturbed by new external input. This leads to accelerated healing at the atomic level.

Before a fast: Two days before the fast, decrease the intake of protein-rich and heavy foods, especially fried and fatty foods. Fruit and raw vegetables are easily digestible and they work towards ensuring that the intestines clean themselves so the actual fast can easily begin. In this period, start drinking greater amounts of urine to get warmed up, collecting the midstream in a glass each time. At first, it may taste and seem very strange, but it is a powerful path towards self-acceptance and love.

Actual fast: Wake at 7am and be sure to drink filtered/distilled water throughout the entire fasting period. It is best if you do not work during the fast. Although some exertion is possible, rest and relaxation are important in order for the purifying process to take place undisturbed. Every time you need to pass urine, be sure to drink it around a pint each time alternating between that and the distilled water. Once the fast has been in progress for some time, all the urine can be drunk. In this period, you will urinate quite easily (urinating every fifteen minutes is not unusual).

A complete body massage every day with old, heated urine is highly recommended. Urine massage is good for blood circulation, and massaging with old urine also ensures that you do not experience heart palpitations during the fast. Furthermore, it serves as a way of feeding the body through the skin, immediately into the muscle and lymph tissue. If you are new to fasting, start with 24–36 hours, a three day fast is highly beneficial and anything after three days is excellent, especially if you are suffering from illness. A few days into the fast, you will feel very peaceful and a strong senses of well-being. It is advised during these times to take regular breaks and do some meditation.

After a fast: This period is necessary in order to slowly and carefully return to a normal and natural eating pattern. You should take at least one week to gradually and carefully readjust eating habits. The best way to end a fast is to stop drinking urine and water at the end of the afternoon. After one hour, drink a glass of orange juice, lemon juice with water, grape juice or apple juice. The next day, drink another glass of fruit juice during lunch. From this point on, start eating juicy fruits. The following day, consume vegetable broth, steamed vegetables and rice. This is a good way to return to your old pattern of eating, excluding the unhealthy habits.

For more information on urine therapy and its healing wonders it is recommended you check out a book named: ***The Water of Life*** by J.W Armstrong[67].

'In this revolutionary treatise, J.W. Armstrong puts the compelling case that all diseases (except those caused by traumatism or structural disorders) can be cured by one simple means. The therapy is an entirely drugless system of healing that treats the body as a whole. Moreover, the only ingredient needed is a substance manufactured in the body itself, rich in mineral salts, hormones and other vital substances, namely human urine. It may seem strange to take back into the body something that the body is apparently discarding. Yet the theory is similar to the natural practice of organic composting. Fallen leaves,

when dug back into the soil, provide valuable mineral salts to nourish new plant life. The same principle holds true for the human body.'

Vegan & Vegetarianism Lifestyle for Optimum Well-Being

There are many misconceptions surrounding the topics of a vegetarian diet/lifestyle. Many people are conditioned into believing that protein can only be obtained from the consumption of meat and animal produce. Again, this is false information. Vegetarians do not get the excess second-hand animal protein that leads to liver toxicity, kidney overload and mineral deficiency diseases.

You can reap many benefits from switching to a vegetarian diet and there are a rapidly growing number of people worldwide that are becoming aware of the health benefits alongside rising consciousness levels within those that acknowledge the planetary needs and understand the animal rights issues.

It is another common misconception that a vegetarian, natural diet cannot be balanced. As previously mentioned, it is the plants that hold the highest density of minerals and micronutrients that are completely and easily absorbable by the human body. Any diet in this modern age needs supplementation either way due to the low quality soils and poisons present in the atmosphere. A vegetarian diet has a proportion of three macro nutrients, which are complex carbohydrates, proteins and fats.

'The fat in our diets should come from avocados, nuts and seeds, not cows' ~ Joel Fuhrman, MD[68]

Fruits and vegetables are high in nutrients, the very elements the body needs to live a long, disease-free and pain-free life. However, the same cannot be said about meat, as the alkaline based digestive system of humans has great difficulty in breaking down substantial acidic meat substances. This book is not aimed towards judging or undermining anybody who chooses to eat animal produce; it aims to share experience from both sides of the fence, ultimately striving towards helping anybody in need and advocating for vegetarianism/veganism (when done properly) as it is the complete answer to health, vitality and wellness.

Another myth that needs to be clarified is the so-called lack of calcium amongst a plant based diet. Many vegetables, especially leafy green ones, hold great supplies. You are what you eat at the end of the day, every 35 days your skin replaces itself and your liver regenerates in about a month. These new cells are constructed from the foods you eat daily. What you eat literally becomes you.

The spiritually aspiring person is one who attempts to consciously work on him or herself. The overall purpose of spiritual growth is to move away from the animalistic nature into the more aware, human nature that was intended by the universal creator. The same science that attempts to ignore the existence of a force higher than man also proved that aggression levels are much higher in meat eaters than non-meat eaters. The animal instincts become more powerful upon the consumption of meat.

Another spiritual aspect of being a meat eater is when one must question the necessity and killing methods of animals. Everyone has their own views, beliefs and morals that they must determine for themselves. Many spiritual people believe in auras; Kirlian photography shows that a force field remains around dead, amputated flesh and is adopted into your own aura when eaten. Living food saturation brings out the canvas of life in which all the colours of the eternal rainbow become available. By consuming colourful foods, your life becomes more colourful.

When animals are slaughtered with the modern day methods, fear and aggression enzymes are shot into the muscle tissue. They remain in the meat until they are consumed. Fruits and vegetables do not release any emotional cells when they are picked or upon digestion and vegetarians claim that they are more satisfied after they eat. The reason for this is that there are fewer ketones (protein-digestive substances) formed when vegetable protein is digested; the food is not processed, so the stomachs nerve senses recognise that the food is real and holds adequate nutrition, therefore sending signals to the brain that you are full and do not need any more food.

Living foods supplied by nature hold Qi/Chi life force energy— the same type of energy that your kidneys produce, and one which is greatly energising and healing. The ancient Chinese believed that the life force in the body is depleted upon the consumption of meats, as did the Indians, who live by ancient yogic principles.

Below are the eight different dietary states/groups available to humans:

Omnivore – Eat pretty much everything including meat, dairy, wheat, sugar, gluten, junk foods, fizzy drinks; vegetables are usually consumed only in small quantities.

Vegetarian – Eat a plant based diet (with or without eggs and dairy, but with no meat). Many eat tofu and processed foods still; these should be eradicated for optimum results.

Vegan – More conscious of what they eat, they don't eat eggs, meat, dairy, consume or use anything to do with animals. Organic and non-GMO foods are key to this kind of diet and education is necessary alongside checking food labels for hidden ingredients.

Raw Vegan – Eat 75–100 per cent raw, living foods (not cooked above 42 degrees Celsius). They do not eat any animal produce, sugar, wheat or gluten. They eat all kinds of vegetables, fruits, nuts, grains and sprouted seeds and beans. High-energy, high-detox diet.

Fruitarian– Involves the practice of following a diet that consists of only fruits (some may eat nuts and seeds). They do not eat animal products, vegetables or grains.

Mono-fruitarian– Will only eat a certain fruit for a length of time, e.g., bananas only for a whole day/week/month, which detoxes the body even further.

Liquidarian – This is the final detoxification stage where they have trained the body and mind to live on liquids only. Fruit juices, coconut water, plain water or vegetable juices.

Breatharian – A Breatharian does not consume any physical food whatsoever. They live off the purest energy of the world known as prana/qi/chi life force that is all around you in the atmosphere alongside harnessing sunlight minerals and energy through Sungazing. This is not starving and should only be attempted with proper guidance. Many highly spiritually trained yogis are at this level.

'There was no evidence of a threshold beyond which further benefits did not accrue with increasing proportions of plant based foods in the diet' – **The China Study**[69]

Building Muscle as a Vegan/Vegetarian

There are many vegan and vegetarian athletes who manage to compete and perform at top levels without having to rely on any animal products for protein, although the conditioning from the meat and dairy industries has programmed many into believing it is impossible to do so. These industries have done such a good job of marketing their products that they have fully convinced most of the world that there's no way to get the calcium, protein and adequate nutrition needed without their assistance.

It is believed that many people are getting 50 per cent more protein than they can possibly use or need. Too much protein intake puts excessive strain on the liver and kidneys as the body tries to flush out the remaining amounts which are not being incorporated into enzymes, cellular membranes, muscles and connective tissues. This is the same as you consuming more calories than your body can use. The body then stores the excess as fat resulting in toxicity build-up.

The only major difference between a beautiful, youthful, fit, athletic physique and an old, frail, weak physique is the amount of human growth hormone available to that person. When you exercise, HGH is released and, for this reason, it is extremely important to exercise regularly. HGH is also released during certain brainwave states of sleep. Muscle is needed to remain youthful and there is no age limit whatsoever where you cannot gain muscle with the right dietary practices and application of knowledge.

In the modern age, many people eat like they are major athletes, and athletes require more protein than non-athletes. A major problem is that, although many are eating like athletes, they tend to spend most of their time at a desk, computer, travelling to work or watching television on a sofa. Those who do not work out regularly should not be consuming too much animal protein and should cut down on refined sugar, cholesterol, saturated fat and general calories. The bodily instincts of modern man are still centred on the times when humanity had to get up and gather food in an active manner such as fishing, hunting, farming, cultivating fields, lifting, bending and so forth, and moving more in one day than many do in a week!

At first, when eating in a vegetarian, vegan or raw vegan way, you will lose some muscle and weight as the body starts to detoxify large amounts of waste from a diet rich in animal products. Your body fat index may drop but will eventually settle, and once it does, your foundation for clean muscle growth is ready as your absorbability rate of the gastrointestinal tract is increased. You will, however, have to work hard to achieve the results desired, but the muscle you will pack on will be very lean and strong.

Athletes also need more calories as a body that is regularly active tends to burn fuel in a more effective and rapid manner. It is possible to get the adequate amount of protein and calories on a vegetarian or vegan diet as all plant food contains protein and amino acids in some amount. This is not including supplementation and superfood smoothies, which provide powerful, absorbable amounts of vitamins, proteins, nutrients and enzymes.

If protein was the complete answer and magic formula for building muscle, it would be so simple and with the overall large protein intake everyone would be muscular and have a ripped physique. You may be aware that this is not the case; the body needs complex carbohydrates in order to fuel workouts, boost stamina and supply the power force behind repairing muscle tissue. Good healthy fats are vital in order to supply energy, aid cellular repair and control inflammation.

Remember that muscle is composed of 70 per cent water, 22 per cent protein and 7 per cent lipids or fats. You must train with sufficient intensity to stimulate new muscle growth by drawing in the amino acids from the bloodstream; this is done by trained muscles more easily than untrained muscles.

It is important that the body has the right conditions to tear muscle before it can rebuild it. Intense exercise is needed around 1–3 times per week which includes cardio workouts for lean muscle and strength training to build larger muscles. It is also important to mention cholesterol. Healthy cholesterol is needed to promote anabolic reactions within the body. Cholesterol affects the production of pregnenolone which, in turn, generates progesterone. Progesterone generates DHEA (dehydroepiandrosterone a hormone produced by your body's adrenal glands) and androstenedion, which is responsible for the production of testosterone, which, in turn, stimulates muscle growth. All major steroids descend from cholesterol.

Men can become feminised without these dietary essentials and women can become very skinny. Many people over the age of 40 become weak, fragile and have half the sex drive of a younger man or woman because of the depletion of vital hormonal messengers. This can be counteracted with a balanced vegetarian/vegan diet. Foods such as hemp seeds, kale, flax seeds, avocados, walnuts and rapeseed oil (non-GMO) have high healthy cholesterol and essential fatty acid content.

When eating a vegetarian, vegan or raw vegan diet and wanting to build muscle, you will have to increase the amount of protein in each meal or supplement with superfood smoothies (preferably the one given in the juicing section). However you will only need to assimilate a small amount per meal as any excess proteins that the body cannot absorb at one time will be stored as body fat. This is where many go wrong when wanting to build a lean figure; they eat huge meals two to three times per day, expecting the body to absorb it all in one sitting! This is just crazy and it is important to begin to eat smaller meals per day.

Growth hormone, sleep & nitrogen

If you were to believe the ads for protein supplements, there would be no way to build muscle and increase healthy body weight as a vegetarian or raw foodist. Bodybuilding magazines and websites usually recommend one to two whole grams of protein per pound of bodyweight. They have advocated such a high protein intake firstly to sell protein supplements and, secondly, due to the clogging of the cellular basement membrane for those people who stuff themselves with animal products and junk foods (which actually creates a protein deficiency) a higher protein intake is needed.

 The clogging of cell membranes and lower absorption rate is the actual reason for some people needing more protein in order to build muscle; this is not the case for those who eat clean. Raw protein from plants and superfood supplements has double the strength and effectiveness of cooked protein. A raw food eater requires half the protein that a cooked food eater needs to build quality muscle.

> *'Man is born without frying pan or stew pot. The purest natural food for humans would therefore be fresh, uncooked food and nuts'* – **George Hackenschmidt** (old time strongman)

Medical science made the discovery that growth hormone helps drastically in increasing muscle mass and strength. This finding included people who did not exercise and whose muscles were atrophied. Human growth hormone was administered to the elderly and frail as a method of regeneration as growth hormone is said to drop by 14 per cent for each decade of adult life, muscle wasting conditions also accelerate in a person who is bedridden. However, if you can stimulate human growth hormone, you can prevent nitrogen loss. This allows you to maintain muscle mass even if you are unable to work out.

For you to maintain muscle mass, you must first replace the muscle cells faster than you lose them. The word anabolic means your body is in muscle building whilst catabolic means you are losing muscle and anabolic states can only be achieved when your body can properly assimilate the amino acids obtained from food. If you cannot assimilate amino acids or have a lack of amino acids in your diet, then nitrogen will be lost. Stress hormones such as cortisol also speed up the loss of nitrogen.

These stress hormones increase blood sugar levels, impacting the fight or flight response mechanism in your body and once you enter that wired state of being you can forget about trying to gain muscle. You must have peace of mind, adequate rest and sleep to enter the anabolic state and regular exercise increases the amounts of oxygen and glucose that the brain receives, thereby clearing away mental cobwebs and dead brain cells. Exercise increases the pleasure chemicals known as endorphins and decreases high-density lipoproteins, which clog the brain circulation that helps in combating depression.

When your brain is in a delta brainwave state, you will have strong spikes of growth hormone released into the bloodstream from the pituitary gland. You may know how good you feel after a deep and dreamless sleep; this is because of the deep delta brain wave frequencies. For maximum muscle recovery, growth and repair, it is recommended that you go to sleep listening to a delta brainwave audio track, which can be found on the YUSA YouTube channel. Do this for a month every night alongside your dietary and physical exercise routine to reap tremendous benefits and have HGH soak your muscles for improved strength, size and sexual libido. You can also listen to the Delta track for 15 minutes just before a workout for optimum results.

Amino acids such arginine, ornithine and alpha-ketoglutarate are very effective when taken around one hour before a workout and before sleep. These amino's are so effective in releasing growth hormone that they have been used successfully to improve pituitary function in the brains of undersized children. These amino's can be found in the superfood supplements listed in this chapter.

Nitrogen must be consumed in equal amounts to the amounts of nitrogen excreted through urine, faeces and perspiration. If you want to increase the growth rates in human cells, the same goes for the biochemistry in plants, too. If you excrete more nitrogen than you ingest, you are in negative nitrogen balance, which means your body is in a catabolic state. An unhealthy plant will have pale leaves, whereas a healthy nitrogen rich plant will have vibrant, rich, dark green foliage.

When there is a lack of nitrogen, there is a lack of electrolytes, as mentioned previously. An electrolyte is a substance that is ionised in solution enabling it to conduct electrical currents. Where there is no spark of life, you're dead; nitro is needed to go! Nitrogen is equally important as protein when muscle growth is concerned, as it cannot be formed without amino acids and amino acids are dependent on nitrogen.

The highest nitrogen foods include almonds, pine nuts, walnuts, peas and black beans. A small nitrogen-rich, pre-workout dish: 1 handful sea lettuce, 1 handful of dulse, ¼ cup pine nuts, ¼ cup walnuts, Four TSB extra virgin olive oil, ¼ cup organic tomato sauce, steamed broccoli, dash of Himalayan salt.

A key mineral to take note of is phosphorous. Muscles cannot grow without cell division and cells cannot divide without phosphorous. It is also what regulates blood PH and is found mainly in sea vegetables, black olives, walnuts, almonds and sunflower seed sprouts. These essential minerals are delivered by fruits, vegetables, nuts and seeds that have been grown in mineral rich soil. Remember, a plant cannot give you what the soil can't furnish! To grow quality muscle, the foods must come from quality soils.

In order to build muscle, you must bring oxygen to the cells. It is a matter of having a sufficient supply of nitrogen and minerals found in leafy green plants and superfood supplements as protein stores. You will need more calories and more grams of protein than someone who doesn't work out, but half the protein intake of a cooked food eater. In order for muscular contraction to take place, the electrical potential of the nerve and muscle fibres must be high and in place, this is achieved with organic sources of calcium and almost every person is deficient in this mineral as drugs, soft drinks, caffeine block its absorption.

Calcium supports liver function so that gastric juices can be produced as well as enzymes. Your entire digestive system will not absorb vital elements if the food you eat is of poor quality as is the case with most food produced worldwide. Barley grass powder is an excellent source of calcium you can add to your daily super smoothies.

Quinoa, lentils, red rice and sprouted seeds are some of the most powerful muscle builders around. Keep the super smoothies and green juices flowing as they will mineralise the body and uphold maximum hydration, experiment with superfoods and create a program that suits you and you only. Remember to add fatty acids into your training regime as they are needed for the health of your eyes, ears, brain, adrenal glands and sex organs. These beneficial fats help create muscle building hormones and boost physical energy levels.

Flaxseed oil, avocadoes and avocado oil are the best because they are unsaturated. Unsaturated simply means they have empty spaces within the molecular structure, which allow them to link up with other beneficial biologically active substances, whilst saturated fats are completely clogged with hydrogen atoms, making them inert and useless.

Final workout words

You will never grow bigger muscles through pumping movements, as they do not reach the deeper fibres that provide for massive growth. Getting larger muscles requires overload; you must use heavy weights to make the muscle do something it isn't used to doing, and you must force the cell components to grow! When you are doing repetitions, focus your mind on the muscle you are working; really feel the squeeze and breathe slowly in and out through the nose to enhance the storage of QI/CHI life force energy. This is known as the mind-muscle connection.

Your "fast twitch' muscle fibres have a very thick nerve supply and, when properly stimulated, can give you huge muscles that deliver great power. The 'slow twitch' muscle fibres hold the ability to endure long, enduring workouts. People with a larger proportion of slow twitch fibres make great long distance runners or swimmers. The myofibrils amount to 30 per cent of a muscles cells size and to activate cellular growth, the muscle mused be taxed enough to fail in the range of 6 to 12 repetitions, with the weight at the level of 60–80 per cent of your best single.

By increasing resistance, you increase overload. Increase overload and you will increase muscle size. However, you must be overloading the largest number of muscles possible at the same time. Squatting is brilliant as it forces the body to release muscle building anabolic hormones alongside parallel bar dips. When doing dips, attach a dipping belt so you can add more weight. Do five sets of five with a weight you can handle with perfect form and you will soon be on the way to muscle growth. **You can find vegan supplements and bodybuilding products over at: www.sunwarrior.com**

The sun is the bringer of life to Mother Earth and all of her inhabitants. Every aspect of your being thrives in the sunlight, from the physical body to the metaphysical energetic body. Vitamin D absorbed directly from the sun is an excellent healing agent. Sunlight is nature's gift to mankind. You need sunlight to survive and be healthy in both body and mind. Sunlight's positive energies at sunrise help balance and promote physical, emotional and spiritual healing. Sun is perceived as co-creator and sustained of life on Earth. Scientists throughout the world cannot invent or make any other man-made alternative power equivalent to the sun.

You are more than just the atoms and molecules that make up the physical body; you a being of light as well. Bio photons are emitted by the human body and can be released by mental intention, which modulate fundamental processes within cell to cell communication and DNA.

From light, air, water and other basic mineral within the crust of the Earth alongside more than three billion years of information contained within the nucleus of one diploid zygote cell, the human body is formed. Within that body is a soul capable of at least trying to comprehend its bodily and spiritual origins. Your earthly existence is partially formed from sunlight and requires continual consumption of condensed sunlight as a form of food.

Many doctors and deceptiveness broadcasts are always trying to warn the population on how dangerous the sun is and how it can be harmful to your health. They always recommend that you wear sun screens, shades and limit exposure. Many complain about skin cancer, sun damage and sun blindness, but all of these have little to do with the sun.

The reason that many people become unwell when exposed to too much sunlight is due to what they consume on a dietary basis. The skin is the largest eliminatory organ, whereby unprocessed toxins and acidic waste are released. The skin is, most often, plugged. The sun will burn up any acidic toxicity and, as so much is stored within the skin pores of those eating a standard poisonous diet, problems are going to occur.

Interactions between these toxins and the sun's rays bring about what is known as skin cancer. Instead of adopting a balanced diet that encourages alkalinity within the cellular makeup of the body, which leads to healthy skin, social conditioning has led everybody into thinking that they need to put poisonous sun creams on their body and that the sun is an enemy.

Skin damage, such as leathering of the skin, is caused by lack of EFAs (essential fatty acids) in the diet. Sun blindness or damage to the eyes is caused by the use of corrective lenses. Glasses and contact lenses both, cause an unnatural glare on the eyes, when exposed to the sun. This can cause serious damage to the eyes over time.

Sun gazing is simply that: gazing at the sun. This is a process that actually aids in the activation of your pineal gland. There have been documented cases of people in India doing this, never getting sick and even no longer needing to eat such as Hira Ratan Manek – **www.solarhealing.com**

Hira Ratan Manek coined the sun gazing technique now known as HRM. He has been living off of the suns energy for the past 12 years. He has been studied by many researchers, including some at the University of Pennsylvania and Thomas Jefferson University. Their research concluded that his claim was completely true and he is healthier than any normal person his age. Doctors found his neurons were active and not dying. His pineal gland is actually growing, not shrinking, which is very unusual in someone over the age of fifty. The greatest average in someone over fifty is a pineal size of 6×6 mm, HRM's is 8×11 mm.

> *'Shut up the strongest man in a dark dungeon, and he becomes pale like a corpse, his blood loses its vitality, and he is liable to scrofulous disease. He loses the power of resisting disease influences,'* – **Dr. Thomas Low Nichols.**

The Sungazing Process by HRM

The Sungazing process consists of learning to stare into the Sun for longer periods of time. Every day, at either the hour after sunrise or the hour before sunset (when it is scientifically proven beyond a reasonable doubt that one is free from UV and IR rays' exposure, which is harmful to your eyes), stand barefoot on the bare earth and stare at the sun for 10 seconds until you reach 44 consecutive minutes (which could take 9–12 months to achieve). By this time, you will be solar activated, meaning not only will you be cured of mental and physical ailments, but you will now be without the desire or need to eat food.

On the first day, either at morning or night you will stare directly into the sun for 10 seconds. On day two, you will add another 5–10 seconds, on day three you will add another 5–10 seconds and so on. It is important you stay consistent with the gazing process and if you miss a day you must minus the five seconds for that day and go back one step.

By the seventh day you will be staring at the sun for 40–70 seconds. The sun gazing process is always to be practised whilst standing barefooted on bare earth to ensure you are grounded, meaning there is an electrical discharge between the energy being harnessed from the sun, back into mother earth forming a continuous looping current that delivers tremendous benefits.

The key in sun gazing is to be relaxed and let go of all thoughts, just like meditation letting go of all thoughts immersed in the moment. As the sun rises or sets over the horizon, simply gaze at the glowing ball of light for 10 seconds only with no stress or strains on the face, facial muscles or eyes. Stand at peace and let go.

During the practise, the attitude of 'surrender' to the natural divine cosmic sun energy must be there, as also an 'auto-suggestion' and implicit belief that this is going to help/heal/nourish you. Try to become aware of what your body is feeling. How is your mental, emotional and physical state of being as the sunlight energy fills every atom, every electron and every cell in your body.

For the first few moments you look into the sun, it may be very bright. After about 3–7 seconds of continuous gazing, all the brightness generally goes away and you are left staring into a soft ball of pure white light; a beautiful pulsing orb. You may notice an amazing increase in your overall energy as well as your physical stamina and positivism. Be aware of how the sunlight actually cleanses and rebuilds the whole of your being, your mind and thoughts, your feelings and your physical body; total rejuvenation. By completely surrendering to the suns greater power, and as the minutes of sun gazing increase, the awareness of your energetic being may heighten dramatically.

Once you are comfortable with the concept of sun gazing, feel free to increase gazing time at a constant rate of 10 seconds per day. You may find it helpful to get a watch or employ a friend to keep tabs on your staring time. Subtle slow increments of time are important for allowing for the rods and cones within the anatomical structure of the eye to adapt to the intense levels light.

Increase the sun gazing time by 10 seconds each day until you have reached 44 minutes, at which point you should be fully charged. At 44 minutes, you are finished with the HRM's method of sun gazing.

At this time, sun gazing has to be stopped and there is no need to continue the practise any more. According to HRM, during the first three months, the pineal gland activating and the hypothalamus or pathway to the brain from the eye is being charged. After that period, the solar energy starts reaching your brain and charging it and the solar energy starts being stored in each and every cell in your body.

Hira Ratan Manek says that humans need a lot of energy for the digestion of food and for our brain and mind, to deal with all the mental problems, depression and negative emotions. He says that since the sun gazing has removed all his mental problems, he is calm and cool so no energy is used or lost there. Since he is not eating any more, no energy for digestion is required either. So his energy needs are greatly reduced and he can easily meet them without needing food.

Grounding

Humans, plants and animals have always been in closer contact with the Earth throughout time, but unfortunately, the modern lifestyle and demands has disconnected many people from earths healing energies therefore making humans on the whole more vulnerable to stress and illness.

Today's environment is one where there is a high exposure to an ever increasing amount of electromagnetic fields (EMF's). Exposure to EMF's increases the overall amount of free radical production within the body, these are positively charged molecules that are the main culprits to inflammation.

When you come into direct contact with the Earth (walking, sitting, or laying down on the earth's surface), preferably barefooted, there is an instantaneous transfer of natural electrical energy to your physical body. Therefore, a neutralisation process takes place and the free radicals are eliminated. This induces favourable physiological changes, which promote optimum health, whilst earthing significantly reduces any oxidative stress and readily recovers the body from injuries, trauma and exhaustion.

The heart, brain, immune system and nervous system are all essentially electrical subsystems that operate within the bioelectrical body. There are many benefits to grounding; however, modern-day rubber and plastics that are used to make shoes are electrical insulators and block the beneficial flow of electrons from the Earth to your body.

'The sole (or plantar surface) of the foot is richly covered with some 1,300 nerve endings per square inch. That's more than found on any other part of the body of comparable size. Why are so many nerve endings concentrated there? To keep us 'in touch' with the Earth. The real physical world around us. It's called 'sensory response.' The foot is the vital link between the person and the Earth. The paws of all animals are equally rich in nerve endings. The Earth is covered with an electromagnetic layer. It's this that creates the sensory response in our feet and the paws of animals. Try walking barefoot on the ground for a couple of minutes. Every living thing, including human beings, draws energy from this field through its feet, paws, or roots.' – Dr. William Rossi[70]

A large percentage of illness, disease, stress and suffering is due to the disconnection between man and nature. This is a topic that holds vast importance and is applicable to 90 per cent of people in the world today.

There are many other reasons to walk barefoot on the Earth or use grounding products (mat, cable and blanket): grounding impacts your DNA immediately, an improved balance of the sympathetic and parasympathetic nervous system occurs, enhanced circulation occurs that leads to increased energy flow, sleep is improved alongside hormonal/menstrual symptoms and, lastly,

294

inflammation(which has been linked to nearly every degenerative disease such as cardiovascular, diabetes, arthritis, glaucoma, cancer and many more) is dramatically reduced.

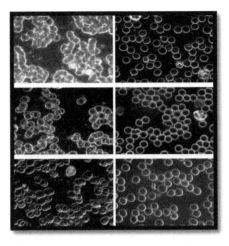

Preceding are microscope images of blood taken from three individuals just before and after forty minutes of grounding. (The before images are on the left, the after on the right.) The pictures clearly show a dramatic thinning and decoupling of the blood cells. For more information and grounding products visit: www.groundology.co.uk

'The moment your foot touches the Earth..., your physiology changes. An immediate normalisation begins and an anti-inflammatory switch is turned on. People stay inflamed because they never connect to the Earth, the source of free electrons, which can neutralise the free radicals in the body that cause disease and cellular destruction' – Dr. James Oschman, Ph.D[71].

Summary of Empowerment

Hopefully, some of the information presented within this book may be of some use to you or even somebody you may know. As you may be able to understand, a lot of this information triggers sensitive areas of thought for some people and it has been advised throughout that one must do their own research into any specified topic.

As mentioned in the introduction, the knowledge has been compiled from extensive research and experiences, a large quantity of these being painful to say the least! It was felt that a lot of the lessons and information gained throughout YUSA's journey had to be shared with others, as it is so beneficial in constructing the foundations necessary to create a better or more abundant life so to speak, a life one can experience with as little pain and suffering as possible.

If you are striving for change in your life and want to see improvements, anything is possible to achieve.

First of all, two of the most important steps are to clear the mind and also raise the cellular vibration within your physical body. This is in order for you to experience and direct more energy into your goals and desires. Dependant on how serious you are, it is advised to apply the information presented in the body section first alongside a daily routine of 45 minutes meditation. For example, cut out the poisons from your diet which are constricting your consciousness and detox the body. From experience, a fast of 3–5 days is needed in order for you to flush out past toxins and to start to feel really alive and alert. You can then start to implement new foods, as your taste buds and metabolism will have been reset.

Once your body is relatively clean your mind will follow suit. By keeping to a routine that includes eating well, drinking a superfood smoothie each day, juicing, meditation and setting your daily targets, goals, dreams and desires, you will eventually reprogram the subconscious mind with what you want to achieve, overwriting any junk that has been absorbed due to outside sources.

It is best that you experiment with foods in order to get a feel for the inner workings of your body. It is also important to exercise regularly, as this will get the lymphatic system moving, which will aid in waste elimination and tissue regeneration. It is important to note that once you detox the body and mind, they become highly sensitive as you grow closer to your own inner light. Therefore, be careful of what you listen to, watch or whom you associate with alongside what you ingest, be it drugs, alcohol or toxic foods. Remember, the body is a temple; you must keep it clean for the soul to reside in.

If you decide to delve deeper into spiritual healing, then it is again best to do so only once the body and mind have had rest and care. This will prepare you greatly (physically and energetically) for any fine frequency tunings that you may receive. For instance, if you where to go and experience Ayahuasca or Iboga plant healing with shamans, then preparation is key. If your physical body and mind is very weak and full of poisons, then the plants' consciousness will divert most of the healing to toxin elimination and the experience could be quite nasty. Healing is not about fixing anything; it is about uncovering and remembering the wholeness that has been inside all along.

Once you consciously choose to walk along the spiritual path, you may be overthrown with problems, tests, circumstances and events, which you may find difficult along the way. Sometimes the process may even feel unbearable, as the elimination and cleansing of your inner self takes place. However, the end result is worth it, especially with the help of the shamanic plants, as they can take you to inner depths that will guide you as you pursue your life's course. Remember it is all for a higher purpose; train your mind into dealing with problems, relax and breathe deeply. Difficult circumstances are the ones that make you grow overall; a problem may arise and may push you into a hole at times, but there is a purpose for it, and it is crucial that you press on and re-affirm to yourself that something wonderful will be the end result!

'Out of suffering have emerged the strongest souls; the most massive characters are seared with scars' – **Khalil Gibran**

Another useful step is the dream board construction, which was discussed at the end of chapter one. Take pride in planning goals and clearly envisioning your dreams. Ensure the dream board is placed in a position that is easily viewable as soon as you wake up, to give you that little extra push for the day ahead and make sure you rise with the sun every morning.

Finally, try not to be too hard on yourself; you're only human at the end of the day and can only do the best with what you have. Stop the voice inside the head that is always doubtful and start to shift into the heart space for intuitive answers, and never give up. You may lose some friends or family members who don't support your path, but they will, more than likely, honour your progress deep down even if they do not show it externally. They may even follow, eventually, as you lead by example. When you back away from fear, it grows and grows. Soon, it dominates your whole life and it paralyses you. But when you confront the fear, when you do the thing you fear, it gets smaller and smaller and becomes manageable.

The overall process of self-betterment and of removing the layers of conditioning may take some time; there is never an end goal or destination. It has taken you lifetimes to get to the stage you are in at this present moment. So much pain, so much suffering, have enabled you, as a creator being, to grow. You must make small steps at first and then, once you gain momentum, you can start to make plans. Think to yourself where you want to be in the next three, five or even ten years from now.

This leads us to the issues of money and material goals. It is a common misconception, especially in so called 'conscious' communities, that money and material wealth are evil and a person embracing their spiritual path cannot live in abundance or drive a nice car. This could not be further from the truth. It may be that the ones controlling the monetary system are greedy and obsessed with control, but all souls on the planet inhabiting temporary bodies are all playing their contracted roles that are, in one way or another, assisting others in their karma, growth and life lessons.

This world is set up perfectly so as to assist so many people in their spiritual journey, as there is so much diversity and suffering (which is temporarily needed for growth). The monetary system, on the other hand, is here for the purposes of mastery: one's mastery over the mind, money and the material aspects of life. As with everything else, there must be balance between having a lot of money and wanting material items. Money can corrupt, but that is the test. Do you think a powerful spiritual being, whose natural state is abundance, should really live a less than deserved life just because of society's conditioned views about money?

Money, in itself, is a form of energy, and energy magnetises energy. This ultimately means that you have to hold a sustainable amount of energy in order to attract what you want. This is the law of attraction: you get back what you give out. This is the mental, electrical and life force/chi energy you need to enhance in order to start directing it and receiving exactly what you need in order to live comfortably. Again, this process emerges from self-work, starting from within and using the information that this book contains. Insecurity is only a type of anxiety that's generated by a lack of self-trust. It is self-doubt that destroys relationships, and knowing yourself ultimately cements them.

A seeming lack is a product of a certain belief system you may have installed within your mind. A belief system is similar to one trying to drive a car with the handbrake lock on; no matter how hard you hit the pedals, not a lot is going to happen. The belief system must be overwritten and released before you can hit the gas and expect to move. If the doors of perception were cleansed, then everything would appear as it is, infinite.

Anything you can imagine is real and anything in life is possible. YUSA wishes you all the best in your journey and hopes that you achieve your dreams. Please feel free to drop us an email with any questions, comments or observations regarding our work.

'Drop the idea of becoming someone, because you are already a masterpiece, you cannot be improved. You have only to come to it, to know, to realise it' –
Osho

References.
Chapter 1, The Mind.

[1] The Ouroboros, Crystalinks.com - E. Crystal *'Crystalinks is world renowned research hub containing information about the mind, body & soul to prophecies & lost civilisations'* - *ww.crystalinks.com/Ouroboros,* Crystalinks first premiered 25/08/2011 .

[2] The Law of Attraction, Social-Consciousness.com - Dr. Neil DeGrasse Tyson - *'Acclaimed American astrophysicist, author and science communicator. 'The fundamentals of the law of attraction' www.social-consciousness.com/2012/02/law-of-attraction-fundamentals.* 12/02/2012

[3] We Are All Connected, ThroughYourBody.com - Dr Neil DeGrasse Tyson - *www.throughyourbody.com/neil-degrasse-tyson-astounding-fact. - When asked by TIME magazine "What is the most astounding fact you can share with us about the universe?"*

[4] Mid Brain Activation, Dr. Baskaran Pillai - *'International teacher, Spiritual Leader, humanitarian and scholar mystic from Southern India, The author of books such as Life Changing Sounds: Tools From The Other Side, Miracle of the Avatar and One Minute Guide to Prosperity and Enlightenment.'* This section was subject to a researching numerous teachings from this source. *www.pillaicenter.com.*

[5] How Alcohol Attacks the Brain, Image sourced from www.ijopils.com - *International Journal of Pharmacy and Integrated Life Sciences: Issue 1, 9/12/2012 There is no one Author to attribute as 'IJOPILS' are a group of enthusiastic pharmacists and doctors of all medical professions all across the world contributing to the end product.*

[6] Situations, Chögyam Trungpa 'Rinpoche' *(Tibetan honorific term meaning special one) was a Buddhist meditation master known for introducing the esoteric practise of the Vajrayana to the west and translating many ancient Tibetan teachings.* The author of many books including *Cutting through spiritual materialism, The Path OF Wisdom and Compassion, Smile at Fear: The Awakening the True Heart of Bravery* to name a few.

[7] Meditation effects on the Brain, - Yale Assistant Professor Judson A. Brewer and the lead author of *Proceedings of the National Academy. -November 2021.*

[8] Dr. Sara W Lazar, Neuroscientist, *Researches the effects of meditation on the brain documenting the progress with modern technologies.*

www.sciencedaily.com/releases/2011/01/110121144007. Massachusetts General Hospital 21/01/2011.

[9] Pain Matrix, Dr. Hedy Kober, Assistant Professor of Psychiatry and Psychology, Yale Therapeutic Neuroscience Clinic; Director, Clinical and Affective Neuroscience Lab. www.youtube.com/watch?v=mzEh5nE-tNU&feature=youtu.be.

[10] Cognitive Dissonance, Leon Festinger, *American Social Psychologist, study featured in the iconic social psychology paper Cognitive Dissonance Theorised and Demonstrated in 1954 - web.mst.edu/~psyworld/cognitive_dissonance.*

[11] DMT, Rick Strassman MD, performed extensive research into the use of psychedelic drugs in the US for over 20 years leading him to DMT *(Dimethyltryptamine)* and the connection to the pineal gland. Acclaimed author of *DMT: The Spirit Molecule. - www.rickstrassman.com* 01/12/2000

[12] Frozen Water Particles, Dr Masaru Emoto, Japanese author and researcher. Author to titles such as *The Hidden Messages in Water, The Secrete To Water & Love Thyself. Alot of his works are formulated from the hypotenuse that human consciousness has an effect on the molecular structure of water.*

[13]Earl Nightingale, *Very well-known American motivator and self help icon, highly respected to this day for works such as: The Strangest Secret (1956 selling one million copies)*

[14] Lao Tzu, Author John Heider - *The Tao of Leadership: Lao Tzu's Tao Te Ching Adapted of a New Age. 1985.*

[15] Kenneth Gabriel Cousens, *is an American physician M.D., homeopath and spiritual writer who practises holistic medicine. Published items such as: There is a Cure for Diabetes 2008, Raw Food Works 2009 & Torah as a Guide to Enlightenment*

[16] Sonia Ricotti, CEO & President of Lead Out Loud INC an author of *Unsinkable: How to Bounce Back Quickly When Life Knocks You Down.* 26/05/2011

[17] Sri Sri Ravi Shankar, *humanitarian, spiritual leader and an ambassador of peace. He is the founder of the Art of Living Foundation. srisriravishankar.org.*

[18] Paulo Coelho, *Brazilian lyricist and novelist. He has become one of the most widely read authors in the world today. Author of: The Alchemist, 1988, the Pilgrimage 1987 and Eleven Minutes 2003.*

[19] Dan Millman, *former world champion athlete, university coach, martial arts instructor, and college professor.* As an Author there are more than 10 books including: *Way of the Peaceful Warrior 1980 &The Life You Were Born To Live 2000.*

[20] Deepak Chopra, *Indian-American author, public speaker and physician. A prominent alternative-medicine advocate and author of several dozen books and videos.* www.deepakchopra.com.

[21] Shamala Tan, Confidence and Holistic Health Coach. www.shamalatan.info.

[22] Peter Ragner, *Internationally recognised author of 29 books, speaker, qi gong master and spiritual mentor. www.longevitysage.com.*

Chapter 2, The Spirit.

[23] Dr. Mohsen Paul Sarfarizi, Author and Self retired Professor of non-linear Continuum Mechanics. *multidimensional-consciousness.tripod.com*

[24] Inayat Khan, was the founder of The Sufi Order in the West in 1914 and teacher of Universal Sufism. *hazrat-inayat-khan.org.*

[25] Yasmin Mogahed, *www.yasminmogahed.com.*

[26] Sri Swami Premandanda Sarawati Maharaj, Born as *Mahabir Prasad Saxena.* Many of his teahings are available for free download from the following source. *www.dlshq.org/saints/prema.*

[27] Winfreied Otto Schumann, German Physicist. Best known for predicting the Schumann Resonances. *www.schumannresonator.com.*

[28] Sigmund Schlomo Freud. World renowned Austrian Neurologist responsible for founding psychoanalysis. Author of many manuscripts and conducted many recorded theories such as: *Beyond The Pleasure Principle, Totem & Taboo, Future of an Illusion. psychology.about.com/od/sigmundfreud.*

[29] Emanuel James 'Jim' Rohn. American Entrepreneur, Author and Motivational Speaker. DVD recordings of live seminars of his talks are available from him directly. *www.jimrohn.com.*

[30] Simone Weil, French Philosopher, Author of: *Waiting for God 1950 & Gravity And Grace 1947.*

[31] Florence Scovel Shinn, American artist and book illustrator who became a New Thought spiritual teacher and metaphysical writer publishing such pieces as: *The Game Of Life and how to Play It 1925, Your World Is Your Wand 1928 & The Power of Spoken Word.*

[32] Eckhart Tolle, German Author, *Acclaimed by Watkins List as Most Spiritually Influential person in the world,* known globally for books such as: *The Power Of Now & A New Earth 2011.*

[33] Dormant Kundalini, Spiritualresearchfoundation.org. Image sourced from, www.spiritualresearchfoundation.org/how-to-sleep-better/best-sleeping-posture-position.

[34] Judith Harris, Psychology researcher. The author of two books: *The Nurture Assumption & No Two Alike.*

[35] Yogabodynaturals.co.uk, Good Source. www.yogabodynaturals.co.uk.

[36] Dr. Konstantin Korotkov, Author and Scientific researcher. Korotkov.org. *Multiple aspects of this sources content have been used.* ww.korotkov.org/store/#!/~/category/id=5752170&offset=0&sort=normal.

[37] Grounding, Groundology.com - Reliable source to learn more on the subject. *www.groundology.com/about-grounding.*

[38] Bruce Charles, Researcher, Author, Scientist, Teacher and Biologist. *He is considered to be the 'father of permaculture',* www.networkearth.org/perma/culture.

[39] Mandukya Upanishad, Hindu Vedanta Scriptures, swamij.com. www.swamij.com/mandukya-upanishad.

[40] Panache Desai. Contemporary thought leader and author of: *Discovering Your Soul Signature: A 33-Day Path to Purpose & Passion, & Joy.*

[41] Alex Grey. American Artist specializing in Spiritual and Psychedelic Art. *www.alexgrey.com.*

[42] Sri Nisargadatta Maharaj, Spiritual Teacher regarded *'one of the great spiritual masters of the 20th century'.* A compilation of his recorded talks *I Am That* was published in 1973.

[43] Ayahuasca Retreat, YUSA experienced this journey at this retreat, we recommend thorough research before attending. *www.ayahuascaassociation.org.*

[44] Iboga Detox, YUSA experienced this journey at this retreat, we recommend thorough research before attending. *www.iboga.co.za.*

[45] Leonardo Pisa, aka Fibonnaci, Sourced from *Priya Hemenway - The Secret Code 2008.*

[46] Neil Kramer, British Philosopher and Esotericist. *www.neilkramer.com.*

[47] Scott Onstott, Fantastic research into Sacred Geometry & World Monuments. Scottonstott.com. The visual production YUSA makes reference to is, *www.youtube.com/watch?v=L777RhL_Fz4.*

[48] Dick Sutphen, Author and Spiritual Teacher. Richardsutphen.com. *Lighting the Light within 1987.*

[49] G. I. Gurdjieff. Early to Mid 20th Century Teacher. *en.wikipedia.org/wiki/George_Gurdjieff*

Chapter 3, The Body.

[50] David Takayoshi Suzuki, CC OBC. Canadian Academic, Science Broadcaster and Environmental Activist. David Suzuki Foundation. *Regularly updated blog with issues that should be recognised on a global scale. www.davidsuzuki.org.*

[51] The Organic Consumers Association (OCA). Online grassroots non-profit enterprise campaigning for the public interest. *www.organicconsumers.org.*

[52] Jose Pizarro Montoya. Chilean Farmer turned Anti GMO Activist, *Jose won a case against Monsanto in 02/2014. More information: www.ww4report.com/node/12984.*

[53]Factory Farming Facts. *www.organicconsumers.org.*

[54] *Food Inc.* Robert Kenner, Filmmaker. www.robertkennerfilms.com.

[55] Forks over Knives. Lee Fulkerson, Forksoverknives.com. Film Writer, Producer & Director, his works consist of over 170 hours of screenplay. *www.forksoverknives.com/about.*

[56] Earthlings. Nation Earth. Powerful and Informative. Multi Award winning company. *earthlings.com.*

[57] The China Study. Dr. T. Colin Campbell, Professor Emeritus Cornell University. *Fantastic study into the link between health and nutrition. www.thechinastudy.com/the-china-study/about.*

[58] Dr. Otto Warburg. Dr, Researcher and Nobel Prize Winner 1931. *www.alkalizeforhealth.net/Loxygen2.*

[59] Coconut Water. Fact sourced from *Healthyeating.sfgate.com.* Conscious Eating Blog, Written by Bryn Bellamy. healthyeating.sfgate.com/electrolyte-minerals-coconut-water-1107.7

[60] Coconut Transfusions. Fact Sourced from Bodyandsoul.com.au *www.bodyandsoul.com.au/nutrition/nutrition+tips/is+coconut+water+good+fo r+your,7301.*

[61] Green Vibrance. Raw Supplement - *www.vibranthealth.us.*

[62] Aloe Vera. Fact Sourced from Healthyeating.sfgate.com. Conscious Eating Blog, Written by Nadia Harris *healthyeating.sfgate.com/health-risks-benefits-taking-aloe-vera-juice-internally-5017.*

[63] 'Enzyme Nutrition. Fact attributed to Dr. Edward Howell. Sourced from Thelivingcentre.com. Written By Walter Kacera, Ph.D. D.N. *www.thelivingcentre.com/cms/body/enzymes-the-fountain-of-vibrant-life.*

[64] Juice Man. Norman Wardhaugh Walker, *www.vitaminb17.org/about_dr_walker.*

[65] Gerson Therapy. Max Gerson. *en.wikipedia.org/wiki/Max_Gerson. A Cancer Therapy: Results of Fifty Cases* 1958. gerson.org/gerpress/dr-max-gerson.

[66] Dr. Herbert M. Shelton. Iconic Speaker. www.youtube.com/watch?v=zm14UgVrFNo.

[67] J.W Armstrong. Author of the book *The Water of Life 1971* *www.whale.to/a/Water-of-Life-Treatise-on-Urine-Therapy-by-John-W.-Armstrong-1971.pdf.*

[68] Joel Fuhrman, MD, Author, Speaker & Media personality, Books such as; *Eat To Live* 2003 & *Super* immunity 2011.

[69] China Study, *Refer to Ref 57.*

[70] Dr. William Rossi. Podiatrist. *Nwfootankle.com nwfootankle.com/foot-health/drill/2/110.*

[71] Dr. James Oschman, Ph.D.. *Holistic & Natural Therapist & Academic* *www.ancientpurity.com/articles.asp?oid=623*

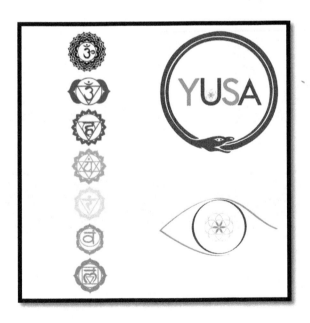

Follow Us On Twitter @YUSALIFE

Like Us on Facebook – YUSAbundance

Subscribe to Our YouTube - YUSA Abundance

Follow Us On Instagram - @YUSALIFE

www.YUSALIFE.com

Email: Connect@YUSAlife.com

Hopefully you discovered something of value.

CPSIA information can be obtained
at www.ICGtesting.com
Printed in the USA
BVOW07s1924210917
495457BV00013B/519/P